THE JOURNALISTS AND THE JULY REVOLUTION
IN FRANCE

THE JOURNALISTS
AND THE JULY REVOLUTION
IN FRANCE

THE ROLE OF THE POLITICAL PRESS IN THE
OVERTHROW OF THE BOURBON RESTORATION
1827-1830

by

DANIEL L. RADER
San Diego State University

MARTINUS NIJHOFF / THE HAGUE / 1973

ISBN 90 247 1552 0

PRINTED IN BELGIUM

TABLE OF CONTENTS

PREFACE

The "July Revolution" of 1830 in France overthrew the King, brought down the Bourbon dynasty, and ended the fifteen-year era known as the Restoration. It established the "July Monarchy" of Louis-Philippe, citizen-King of the House of Orleans, a regime also destined for extinction eighteen years later. Although the 1848 revolt is of somewhat greater domestic political importance and considerably greater in its European scope and its social implications, the July Revolution of 1830 should not be relegated to the lower levels of historical consciousness. Yet, in modern times, even in France, relatively few works have been published concerning either the Restoration or the revolution which terminated it.

New interpretations, such as the excellent works of Bertier de Sauvigny and David Pinkney have awakened the enthusiasm of scholars; but in general, the intrinsic importance of this period has been slighted for nearly a century. There are reasons for this inattention: At first glance, the era seems retrograde, born of a conservative reaction; and placid – it falls between Napoleon's giant earthquake on one side, and on the other, the dynamics of European nationalism, imperialism, and the class struggle. But the Restoration was neither archaic nor calm. It was, for all its manifest anachronisms, an age of rapid political, cultural, and social growth. France, during these years, was maturing and ripening toward nationhood – and toward the collision of many complex forces, culminating in revolution.

In all these changes, in all this political ripening, the journalists of the periodical press played a uniquely decisive role. Unique because the French press was then legally more free, for more consecutive years, under the Charter of 1814, than it had ever been. Unique, too, because there then existed a true journalism of opinion, education, and the propaganda of ideas. Newspapers were not deterred by advertising revenues or by a desire to please everyone. The dialog they provoked was real, but even more important in those years before mass communication, the dialog was effective.

In this book, the writer intends to trace the activities and influences, mainly political, of French journals and their journalists in the late Restoration years. I also propose to argue how the uniqueness of the press, at that time and place, allowed it not only to develop political attitudes, but also to guide political action, including eventually the revolution itself. Among textbook authors, the tradition has been to pause at 1830 with a paragraph or two about that "simple" and "clean" revolution, noting briefly the key role of the press in bringing it off. Here, they invariably stress two journals that were committed to the Orleanist campaign in the final six months and they overlook the long years of preparation and ordeal when the press was frequently more important than the legislative chambers as the nation's forum of opinion.

This study is concerned with the press, so that the background of political and social history is kept to what the writer considers the essential minimum, to complete a picture or to facilitate narrative. The work is also limited chronologically, except for a short introduction, to the two-and-a-half critical years that begin late in 1827 and end with the aftermath of the July Revolution in 1830. The reason for this is political: 1827 saw the fall from power of Charles X's capable reactionary minister, Villèle; a change that evoked a new stirring of activity in the political press and deepened existing schisms among the royalist newspapers.

Villèle, whose six-year ministry served two kings, came closer than any of his contemporaries to duplicating in France the kind of pragmatic reactionary control that Prince Metternich enjoyed in the German states and Austria. His pragmatism, his quasi-constitutionalism, and his sound, if politically oriented, economic policies, made him a formidable and slippery opponent. His policy in regard to the press was effective enough to force opposition editors to a defensive stance. He made it difficult for journalists to reach the small but important electorate who chose the members of the law-making Chamber of Deputies, and, through his prefectural bureaucracy, he kept a tight rein on the provinces where journalism was weak and where nine-tenths of the electors voted.

But the opposition learned the tactics of its enemy and grew in wisdom. It learned how to strike with the least risk of prison; where to aim for the most sensitive reaction; how to make use of the growing economic crisis; and above all, how to create a fanatically reactionary image of Villèle, who was neither a fanatic nor as reactionary as many of the truly "Ultra" royalists. Villèle's fall, in the closing weeks of 1827, allowed an entirely new political atmosphere to develop. Now the various ideological factions on the Left, as well as on the Right (which included some of Villèle's worst enemies) could exercise their opinions more freely than ever before. Now the opposition, conditioned to defend, could plan the attack. This attack was at first confused and diverse, but, by 1829, appeared to be consolidating into a guided political missile. At the same time, the journalism of the Right became more divided and ineffective. Profiting from its own experience, as well as the blunders of the establishment it attacked, the opposition press went on to hasten the overthrow of the old order and to shape the character of the new.

Political semantics reflect an inexact science. I have chosen mainly the terminology of contemporaries of that era. "Left" and "Right" are very general and are virtually synonyms for "opposition" and "Ultra". "Ultra" refers to ultraroyalists, of which there were at least two species, but who were all political reactionaries. "Clerical(ists)" were laymen or clergy who sought to involve the Church in politics, either formally or via the back door. Some "Ultras" were anticlerical; most were not, but all the Left was anticlerical. "Liberal" is very nineteenth century; definitely on the Left, but clearly not including the radical Left which was mostly republican. "Legitimist" refers to a doctrine of all who supported the Bourbon claim to the throne, but it became the special tag for a group of "liberal", non-"Ultra" royalists! "Defection" labels Ultras against Villèle as well as Chateaubriand's Legitimists who opposed both Villèle and Polignac.

Translations, unless otherwise indicated, are my own responsibility and I apologize for whatever gracelessness appears from my attempts to conserve meaning and intent without the courage of poetic license. I am also responsible for any errors which may have inadvertently survived the long sessions of rechecking and proofreading.

I am indebted to many friendly and helpful people: To a host of librarians in France and America; to my cherished friend, Professor Franklin Palm of Berkeley for his encouragement; to the editors of French Historical Studies for permission to use portions of an earlier article of mine; to the San Diego State University Foundation, for financial assistance in preparing the manuscript; to Mrs. Marion Leitner for her careful typing; and, not the least, to my wife and daughters for their intuition and forbearance.

San Diego State University

Daniel L. Rader

JOURNALISM IN THE REIGN OF CHARLES X: THE SOCIAL AND POLITICAL SETTING

The French have placed memorials to greatness throughout the city of Paris. From the countless names of streets to the bullet-pocked walls inscribed with the names of students who fell before Nazi firing squads, all talents and spirits have been honored. In the temple of the Panthéon, such monuments are dedicated especially to those whose courage rose from the mind and whose weapon was the pen. Beneath the great dome stands a large and prominent sculptured group – suitably in the Romantic style and labeled, "The Journalists of the Restoration".

Among the figures, a visitor may discover the aristocratic face of Chateaubriand, vain genius who died famous at eighty; or, he may recognize the more youthful portrait of Armand Carrel, reflecting a life of idealistic adventure tragically shortened by an act of romantic folly. Liberals, royalists, sceptics, militants, and conservatives are all represented here. One may wonder why such a partisan nation would enshrine, in a single statue, such a diverse group of men. The answer may be simply that most of the journalists of the Restoration shared three characteristics that bound them to their countrymen: They were critical; they were individualistic; and they loved France.

Journalism in the Restoration shaped and measured the distinctive environment in which it lived. The whole era of fifteen years was a synthesis of the turbulent past, enriched with new forces of its own making.

In 1815, Napoleon I fled his exile at Elba and reconquered France in three weeks. Everything that the conquering Allies had impressed on France in 1814 – the Bourbons, the clergy, the old aristocracy – again ran for cover when Napoleon stamped his foot. After the Hundred Days and Napoleon's final defeat at Waterloo, the Allies once again allowed the return of the royal remnants of the old regime. This "Second Restoration" was something the French were not likely to forget. Napoleon by his vainglorious return, had exposed a painful and striking contrast for all the world to see. In three weeks he had won Paris without a shot; yet Louis XVIII was escorted in and out of

Paris twice in two years by the enemies of France! The Hundred Days deepened the nationalistic stamp already on the French spirit, a spirit which rejected the *émigré* philosophy of revenge and reaction. A great number of Napoleon's haters became Napoleon's apologists. The famous author, Benjamin Constant, wrote in the *Journal de Débats* that the emperor was a "Ghengis-Khan" when he filibustered into France from Elba. Three weeks later he was singing his praises.

Such apologists were not the true Bonapartists of politics. They were often constitutional liberals like Constant, worshippers of the Bill of Rights, or conservative aristocrats, who, by instinct, opposed injustice along with radicalism. These men, writers, journalists, and politicians, were always careful to accuse Bonaparte of wasting lives, of vainglorious ambition, and of freezing public liberties, especially of the press; but they were certain to recall that he had never fought against his people and that he had given France her civil code, her public education, and above all, her lasting glory. Louis XVIII, a reasonable man, could make no similar claims.

Gouty, enormous, and partially lame, King Louis XVIII offered an obvious contrast to his recent predecessor. Although possibly the best educated ruler of his entire dynasty and a man of great personal dignity, he was not accepted as a leader by either liberals or Ultraroyalists. Opposition elements, which also included some republicans like Lafayette, and a few Bonapartists like Manuel, regarded the King with suspicion and his moderate and progressive ministers, Decazes and Richelieu, were hindered and ridiculed. Reactionary royalists, called Ultras, with increasing boldness, agitated for a return to the *ancien régime* and many considered the King a crowned Voltaire. Louis XVIII found it impossible to unite France and therein lay much of fragility of the Restoration. No large political group, no party representing all powerful interests, could be based on the compromise that the Restoration offered. The Charter of 1814, the most advanced constitution in Europe at that time, was viewed as a grudging gift by the Left and as a dangerous concession by the Right. Ultras and liberals made a battleground of the Chamber of Deputies and the press began to reflect true political opinions for the first time since Thermidor.

Then, in 1820, occurred one of those unplanned incidents which stirs all political life to the surface. The duc de Berri, younger son of the comte d'Artois and only potent heir to the throne, was stabbed to death during intermission at the old *Opéra*. The Ultras seized upon this murder, committed without accomplices by a laborer named Louvel, to demonstrate the lengths to which the "Revolution" would go.

There was fear on both sides: secret societies had been growing for several years. The Italian *Carbonari* had spread to France and attracted to their secret rituals and "cell" organization such young liberals as Paul Dubois and Victor Cousin, and such old ones as Lafayette. This society included many of the politicians, deputies, journalists, and lawyers who would emerge to prominence during the next ten years. In 1822, a "cell" was discovered within an army regiment at La Rochelle and four sergeants were executed for treason. Further suppression by police rendered the secrecy of the *Carbonari* unreliable. After 1820, the electoral reform league, *Aide-toi le Ciel t'aidera* (God helps those who help themselves), less secret than the *Carbonari*, applied itself to preventing electoral frauds by prefectural officials and to campaigning for liberal candidates. It was effective in uniting Paris with the provinces politically. Chapter meetings were occasionally public affairs in the legal guise of banquets. Some liberals were also members of Masonic lodges which were then oriented toward Enlightenment ideals. Prime Minister Decazes was a Mason and it was rumored that even the King had a degree. On the Ultra side, two politically active societies had been influential since before 1815: The *Congrégation* and the *Chevaliers de la Foi*. Founded during the Empire, the *Congrégation* was a religious society of Ultra laymen, which, though basically religious, managed to help facilitate the return of the Bourbons in 1814 and continued to exercise political power through royal ministers and voting blocs in the Chambers. The *Chevaliers de la Foi* was a secret fraternity with chivalric rituals. According to Bertier de Sauvigny, the lowest rank of members, like their Masonic counterparts, were dedicated to piety and good works, including charities for orphans, prisoners, and the poor; while the secret members of the highest echelons were involved in a political action network somewhat broader in scope. Both groups were accused by the Left of being dominated by the Jesuits, while the liberal societies were alleged to be masterminded by a secret revolutionary junta. When the King's nephew was assassinated, an atmosphere of conspiracy seemed to be everywhere.

Most of the divisive forces of the Restoration were set in motion by this event. Ultras used the Duke's murder as a pretext to change the electoral laws and the press laws. The liberals retaliated by becoming more defensive and less willing to trust the Charter of 1814. Louis XVIII, opposed to excesses of any kind, was pushed along by the ascendant power of the Ultras, and in 1822, the King named a talented reactionary, Jean-Baptiste de Villèle, as his first minister. Throughout the comte de Villèle's six-year ministry political factions grew stronger and more polarized. Villèle favored a return to the *ancien régime*, but only insofar as it was politically possible. He was shrewd enough to realize that a frontal attack on the liberties of the Charter might reap less profit to the Ultras than the more subtle patterns he chose to employ.

Because of his methods, the more reckless Ultras attempted to push Villèle farther to the right than he was willing to go and came to regard him as lukewarm. The royalist journals of the Villèle period divided sharply on their support of Villèle and started to divide the royalist camp, while the opposition press, growing more unified, began to exert great political power.

Louis XVIII died in 1824 and his brother, the comte d'Artois, former leader of the *émigrés* of 1789, and living symbol of aristocratic reaction, became King as Charles X. He retained Villèle as his minister, but the reactionary forces in the nation were at last free of that restraint which the "sceptic king" had once tried to employ.

The new monarch was kind and humane, but blindly simplistic in religion and politics, and unlike Louis XVIII, admitted that he could not read four pages of anything without tiring. His youth has been spent in gambling, enjoying mistresses, and treating his own wife abusively. Now, a lean, handsome white-haired widower in the late sixties, he was rather inclined to prudery. He once ordered to dancers at the *Opéra* to wear skirts reaching at least to their ankles and cut from opaque material.[1] The Revolution recalled to him only the insult and deprivation experienced by his own parasitical class. He was almost a stranger to the new France, bourgeois and glorious, that had risen during his long exile. He was not an inordinate Ultra, but he wanted the Ultras to succeed if they possibly could. He dutifully met his cabinet twice a week at the Tuileries Palace. His court's social life was scarcely Augustan with emphasis on table games and gossip in place of conversation. The hunt was the true pleasure of his old age and won for him his least pejorative popular nickname "Robin Hood". Charles X and his dutiful surviving son, the Dauphin Louis-Antoine, spent much of their time on horseback, pursuing captive deer in the forest of Rambouillet. Typically, the old monarch observed most of the antique forms and customs of the chase as it had been practiced by François I. Details of state bored him and, although he was not irresponsible, he left as many decisions to Villèle as he could.

Political reaction continued in every field. The power of opposition deputies was compromised by electoral frauds perpetrated by the government. Royal prefects simply removed names from the lists of eligible voters. Deputies

[1] Jean Lucas-Dubreton, *Le comte d'Artois, Charles X* (Paris, 1927), p. 153. (Hereafter cited as Lucas-Dubreton, *Charles X.)* The King's obsession for absolutism was shown in 1828 when Dom Miguel usurped the throne of Portugal and abolished civil liberties. Properly horrified by the tyrant's brutality, Charles X nevertheless remarked to his ministers: "This Dom Miguel is a wretch, but you must appreciate how adroitly he did them out of their constitution!" Quoted from Ernest Daudet, *Le ministère de M. de Martignac* (Paris, 1875), p. 220. (Hereafter cited as Daudet, *Martignac.)*

were bribed and bought. A law was passed to indemnify former *émigrés* for their revolutionary losses and the cost was to be met by reduction of the interest on government bonds. This act not only revealed the extent of Ultra ambition, but it alienated many of the powerful and wealthy who held the bonds. It must be added, however, that Villèle selected this method rather than a more offensive direct tax to raise the huge sum required and indicates his calculating talents as both an economist and a politician.

Because of widespread acts of vandalism in churches, the Ultras pushed through a law making the theft or vandalism of church objects (sacrilege) punishable by death. This stipulated that, in the case of sacrilege "with contempt for religion" as its motive, the convicted person be executed as a parricide; that is, to have his hand struck off before receiving the guillotine's final mercy.[2] Although never employed, this provision gave the liberal press lurid proof of the degree of the reactionary trend.

Other laws were introduced in the Chambers to revive the rule of primogeniture for the benefit of the nobles, and in 1827, to destroy the press as a political influence. Although these failed to pass, the King substituted a less harmful edict of his own against the press. The Ultras were trying in every way possible to re-create the old order and to crush the "Revolution".

Such, briefly, was the political atmosphere in which the journalists wrote as Villèle's ministry began to falter at the end of 1827. But laws and theories are not the real substance of societies, nor do they, of themselves, make revolutions. Then, as always, bread-and-butter issues were essential, though more shapeless, instruments of history. Recent studies of Professor David Pinkney have impressively synthesized the findings of sociologists and economists to demonstrate the social forces leading up to 1830. Aroused workers do not assist in revolutions primarily because of their political ideals and we must look in other directions to explain why inert workers and traditionalist peasants could become radicals in a few years.

Restoration France was suffering the early torments of the Industrial Revolution. Workers strikes were equated with sedition, but the employers' lockout was protected by the police. Trade unions were allowed to exist solely for the purpose of mutual aid among workers and to prevent them from becoming a drain on public charity. Small strikes and riots broke out frequently nevertheless, and police in Paris were prone to blame students for

[2] Jean Baptiste Duvergier, ed., *Collection complète des lois, décrets, ordonnances, régelements, et avis du conseil d'état* (30 vols., 1st ser.; Paris, 1824-1830), Law of 20 April, 1824, XXV, 150-54. (Hereafter cited as Duvergier, *Collection des lois*.) This law was inoperable, not only for the difficulty of proving motive, but also because title I, article 4, held the proviso that, at the moment of the offense, the sacred vessels must contain the blessed host and that the crime must be publicly witnessed!

inciting the workers. Bertier believes that the growing radicalism of Parisian workers leading up to the Revolution of 1830 stems from their migration from the more industrially sophisticated northern provinces during the 'twenties. A frequent source of unrest was the destruction of new machinery by those whom it deprived of employment. Machines, as well as a heavy influx of jobless men from the provinces, led to an unemployment crisis in Paris by 1828. Wages were declining in this employer's market and prices on staples were going up. The average price of a standard loaf rose, by 1829, to slightly over the calculated daily income of the French peasant. Hordes of beggars proliferated in Paris and a third of all births in this city were illegitimate. One must accept the fact that Hogarth's London had found its French counterpart with a vengeance.

It should be added that charity, both governmental and private, could rise to magnificent achievements on such occasions as the bad winter of 1829. But, in general, bourgeois society in the early nineteenth century could not accept a broad ideal of public welfare or hold much empathy for the urban poor.

The harvests of France were bountiful during the first half of the Restoration, but were then plagued by crop failures and severe winters. A regime of protective tariffs probably helped in a painfully slow recovery of trade after the Napoleonic Wars' long disruptions. But the overall recovery was not fast enough to prevent peasant bitterness and even violence in some regions after 1826.[3]

Unemployment in the provinces was slightly relieved by public works, the Bourbons continuing such projects as canals and highways initiated under Napoleon. All but a few roads were unpaved and the ugly *diligence*, which was replacing the coach, made passenger travel a most uncomfortable adventure, especially after rains. The Royal Post was in a rudimentary stage; mail costs were high and letters were frequently lost or opened by Villèle's prefectural police. Some newspapers were sent to subscribers by private carriers as the postal service was poorly equipped to do this task. The first commercial steam railway was started in 1827, but it posed no threat to

---

[3] Social and economic data may found in Guillaume de Bertier de Sauvigny, *The Bourbon Restoration* (Philadelphia: University of Pennsylvania Pres, 1966), pp. 201-67. (Hereafter cited as Bertier de Sauvigny, *Restoration*.) Georges Bourgin and Hubert Bourgin, *Les patrons, les ouvriers, et l'état sous la Restauration, documents inédits* (Paris, 1941); David H. Pinkney, "A New Look at the Revolution of 1830", *Review of Politics*, XXIII (South Bend, Indiana: University of Notre Dame Press, 1961), 490-501. See also Pinkney, *The French Revolution of 1830* (Princeton University Press, 1972), Ch. II.

barge or horse.[4] In the countryside, life went on very much as it had for centuries.

Public health programs were also rudimentary, but Charles X and his family submitted to vaccination and urged all citizens to follow their example. Typhus and cholera epidemics were still capable of reducing urban populations. Although Paris could produce some of the world's finest doctors, scientific research had yet to find the tools it needed to combat disease. Illness, poverty, and unemployment made a wretched slum of Paris for the poor three-quarters doomed to live there. Bourgeois lives on bourgeois streets seldom touched these *misérables*.

It is in the realm of letters and arts that the genius and glory of the Restoration may be found. The era was essentially romantic, although the titanic battle between the now conservative "classics" and the more adventurous "romantics" made it clear that there was no single dogma in arts and letters. Nearly all the important journalists of the day were men of literary talent and scholarship and, although it was still an eclectic age, each writer had his *forte*. Philosophers, historians, poets, authors, and critics were all interested in other fields. The great *salon* era was not yet dead, but its caste system had been replaced by a more democratic *élite* of merit, taste, and money. The savants, artists, and writers who met at the home of Delphine Gay, for example, were fixed stars in the intellectual universe. As journalists, these men of letters maintained their high standards, lending the better newspapers of the Restoration a quality and value impossible a generation later.

And who were some of these gifted journalists? A few names should suffice to show how closely journalism was allied with the arts in 1828. They included the philosophers Théodore Jouffroy, Victor Cousin, Charles de Rémusat, and Abel Villemain; the educators, de Sacy and Dubois; the historians, Guizot and Duvergier de Hauranne; the novelists Chateaubriand and Nodier and critics like Charles Sainte-Beuve.

Not all the intellectual life was confined to the nobility of the University, *salon*, or *Institut*. The Restoration was also the age of *La Bohème*. The Left Bank *chaumières*, places for inexpensive drinking and eating, attracted the youthful bohemians who painted, wrote poetry, joined *goguettes* (singing clubs), or attended lectures at the Sorbonne, and the "Mimis" of legend were their companions and mistresses. Impoverished young intellectuals advanced their goliardic pleasures on as few sous as possible, and long-suffering hosts of the Montparnasse cafés were only popular if their credit was liberal. Many

---

[4] Robert Burnand, *La vie quotidienne en France en 1830* (Paris, 1943), p. 192. (Hereafter cited as Burnand, *La vie quotidienne*.)

students wrote for the opposition newspapers and by 1829, some radical
journals had been established by a group of them. They loved to listen to the
idol of the Left Bank, Pierre Béranger, whose irreverent and revolutionary
songs filled them with reckless enthusiasm. The late Restoration was strong
with the spirit of the *jeunesse*. Although often of wealthy origins, these young
radicals and republicans were the only articulate journalistic champions of
the increasing masses of poor workers and other unfortunate products of
factory growth. The larger newspapers, including the royalists, occasionally
showed a sentimental compassion, but never a spirit of urgency in regard to
the poorer class.

In the midst of this political ferment, this changing economic life and varied
intellectual atmosphere, the political press of the late Restoration played its
important role.

CHAPTER I

LIBERTY OF THE PRESS IN THE RESTORATION

A remarkable paradox in this age of conservative and authoritarian politics was the rise of a relatively free press under the Charter of 1814. Although Ultra governments hounded and attacked this freedom, they failed to destroy it. The principle of press liberty, an ideal in the Old Regime, capricious in the Revolution, and a sham under Napoleon, became firmly rooted in the Restoration. A brief discussion of Restoration laws concerning periodicals is essential to understand the legal limits of journalistic expression.

Several methods for suppression or regulation of the press were available to the Bourbon government. The means of actual suppression were: Direct censorship. that is, approval or rejection of the right to publish part or all of a written work; preliminary authorization, or the necessity of publishers to submit all copy for prior approval; preventive seizure by police of copy, plates, or manuscript; interdiction of subjects, for example, detailed reports of sessions of the Peers; and finally, the principle of "tendency" or collective incrimination, by inference, from a sequence of writings. In addition, the public laws of defamation were enforced.

Regulatory measures included: The *Cautionnment*, or publisher's cash bond against fines for press offenses, usually a large sum; the tax on paper, similar to a document tax; a heavy tax on newsprint; the "preliminary declaration" by which the managing director of a newspaper had to declare himself personally responsible for his editor's words; and, of course, the common requirement that articles must be signed, unless written by the chief editor or under his responsibility. Another restriction was the requirement that all printers must license their machines. The cost of these permits resulted in the appearance of "clandestine" presses which were constantly being sought by detectives of the police whose zeal is shown by a letter in the *Constitutionnel* (21 December, 1827) reporting that two sugar refiners of Honfleur were arrested and ordered to surrender a lithographing machine used for making labels, but which they had failed to license as a printing press!

The statutes of the Restoration made use of all of these restrictive methods at various times and in different combinations.

Before 1828, six basic laws controlled the activities of newspapers in France. One was the fundamental law of Article 8 of the Charter of 1814; the other five were various legislative derivatives of that ambigous constitutional guarantee. Article 8 declared: "All Frenchmen have the right to publish and have printed their opinions, as they conform to the laws which should repress the abuse of this liberty". In the first Chamber of 1814, there had been much debate over the use of the word "repress" and controversy over the interpretation of the final clause did not cease with the promulgation of the Charter.

The second law was also ambiguous. On the twenty-eighth of February, 1817, the Chambers passed a bill to forbid the appearance of papers and periodicals "without royal authorization" which the Ministry interpreted as direct censorship. On the thirtieth of December, in the same year, another press law declared that "papers and other periodicals which treat of political news" could not (until January, 1821) appear without royal authority and was aimed at suppressing entire newspapers, not simply articles. To evade this provision, some monthly papers alternated several names so they would not appear as "periodicals". Thus, Benjamin Constant's *Mercure* of July would to be the *Minerve* of August!

Under the moderate Dessolles-Decazes government, liberty of the press was partially recovered. The laws of May and June, 1819, were definitive: Journals could now appear freely, but certain formalities were to be observed. Two managers had to declare personal responsibility for their paper and the owners had to furnish a *cautionnment* in government bonds or *rentes*. The amounts fixed varied with the types of publication, but daily newspapers posted two hundred thousand francs. Defamation of public officials was also spelled out within these laws. Although Constant denounced it, the "rich man's" bond easily fell within the limits of Article 8. The press showed a healthy growth under the short tenure of the 1819 law. In 1816, only nine new periodicals were established; in 1819, twenty-five were founded.[2]

On March 31, 1820, the Ultras turned the crime of Louvel against even this modest press liberty. When the duc de Berri was killed, liberal ideas were more easily branded as subversive and, after long and heated debates, the

---

[1] Léon Bruly, *Régime préventif des journaux et des brochures sous la Restauration* (Paris: Faculty of Law, 1907), pp. 116-17. (Hereafter cited as Bruly, *Régime préventif*.); for text of early press laws from 1819 to 1822, see Duvergier, *Collection des lois*, XXI, 114, 336-37; XXII, 212-16, 223-24.

[2] Bruly, *Régime préventif*, p. 210.

Chamber, by a vote of 136 to 109, passed a repressive law of the periodical press which would serve as a precedent for several years. The law was essentially a return to a mandatory preliminary item censorship of each issue combined with preliminary authorization to publish. In addition, a journal whose editor was indicted could be suspended during the case, and if found guilty, the periodical could be suspended for an additional six months; or, for a second offense, be permanently suppressed. It applied only to periodicals which dealt with political material. An amendment to limit the term of the law to the current year was proposed by royalist comte de La Bourdonnaye. A principal deputy of the liberals, Royer-Collard, supported this modification with the weak argument that "exceptional" legislation should never be permanent.[3] The compromise amendment passed. A panel of twelve censors, chosen by the King, were to approve all political matter before publication and only five of these censors constituted a quorum. In the departments, each prefect was to appoint a panel of three censors. Liberal clamor against this law was vehement and involved the University. Student reaction brought the suspension of one university professor who was chosen as a censor while another who had refused to serve was given a standing ovation by his class.

As this measure went into effect, the non-periodical press came to the rescue of the periodical press. A *Société des brochures* was established to publish censored articles of the journals in pamphlet form. Editors also resorted to the use of blanks to indicate suppressed words, but then the censors censored the blanks.[4]

Liberals regained some advantage by an amendment to this bill which passed on July 26, 1821 and rendered the 1820 law effective only during the sessions of the deputies. Thus, the press was to be "free" during those months when the representatives were not convoked.[5] Adoption of the amendment was a blow to the government of the duc de Richelieu as it made him appear too conciliatory.

With the new Villèle administration in 1822, came a press law more compatible with that Minister's strategy. Villèle rejected an Ultra plea to reestablish the censure for five years. In his devious way, Villèle preferred a less alarming, but equally telling assault on press freedom. On March 17, by a surprising majority, the deputies passed what was to become known as the law of "tendency". The comte de Peyronnet, a confirmed foe of all modern

---

[3] *Le Moniteur*, 26 March, 1820, session of deputies for 25 March, 1820. For the 1820 laws, see Duvergier, *Collection des lois*, XXII, 518-19.

[4] Bruly, *Régime préventif*, p. 210.

[5] Duvergier, *Collection des lois*, XXIII, 401. This provision regularized a portion of the law of 30 December, 1817 and extended it to all periodicals, whether political or not.

thought, had first proposed the law in January and it remained in force until 1828. The four main provisions were: (1) Any paper dealing with political matters must obtain royal authorization to publish; (2) A proof copy of each page must be deposited with the police prior to publication; (3) "In the case that the spirit and tendency" of an article or of several articles should be of such a nature as to "attack public peace or the respect due the state religion", the royal courts were allowed to suppress the newspaper; and (4) An optional censure was created, whereby the censorship could be invoked arbitrarily by decree, but not in permanence. This bill passed by a vote of 221 to 93, but not until an extended and well-reported parliamentary debate had advertised its implied threat to liberty under the Charter. In these debates, Royer-Collard defended the liberty of the press as a necessary institution of government, declaring that, as a form of opposition to authority, the periodical press was operating in the "moral conscience of men", and that with it, both tyranny and revolution were impossible. The resistances of the press, he declared, were "no less necessary for the stability of thrones than to the liberty of nations. Woe to governments which succeed in stifling them".[6] But, in spite of Royer-Collard's suggestion that a new revolution could burst from sealed-in pressures, the law was applied until Villèle's government resigned.

Optional censure was sufficient to hold most of the journals in check. The first major application of the "tendency" provision came late in 1825. Two liberal newspapers, with a strong bourgeois following, were indicted for "outraging the state religion". The indictments were based on an alleged anticlerical "tendency" of both papers as shown by several articles which had appeared in them during the previous May. The trial was recognized as a test case by the confident ministry. As the courts of Paris were, at that time, enjoying their annual recess, the King himself intervened to order that the editors be tried before a joint session of the peers and deputies. Although found guilty as charged by the conservative Chambers, they appealed to the regular judicial body and on December 3, 1825, the tendency law suffered a reverse at the hands of the Royal Court of Paris. Defense attorneys Charles Dupin and Joseph Mérilhou won acquittals for their clients and fame for themselves by using the defense as a smashing attack on Jesuit influence in the government and the power of clericalism in general. Charles X was furious. He wrote to Villèle, "We have a very foolish magistracy".[7]

---

[6] *Le Moniteur*, 24 January, 1822.

[7] Pierre de la Gorce, *La Restauration, Charles X* (2 vols.; Paris, 1927), II, 65-67. (Hereafter cited as la Gorce, *La Restauration*. II.)

A more reactionary press bill was introduced to the Chamber on December 26, 1826, by that vociferous Ultra, the comte de Peyronnet. It was, as the historian of the French press declared, "a masterpiece of Machiavellianism and arbitrariness whose violence argued it to absurdity and which was aimed at nothing less than the annihilation of the press in France".[8] In defending his proposal, however, Peyronnet disclaimed any intention of destroying the press and referred to his bill as a "law of justice and love". And so it was thenceforth ridiculed by the liberals. Its provisions included: Preliminary censorship of *all* printed works; subjection of all pamphlets and newspapers to a heavy new tax; and the joint responsibility of editors, managers, and *printers* for all material published. Maximum fines and prison sentences established by previous laws were to be augmented.

Even these oppressive conditions were insufficient for some of the more extreme Ultras. The marquis de la Boëssière, deputy from royalist and Catholic Morbihan, offered an amendment which was to have been the *coup-de-grâce* for the dying liberty of the press. Boëssière believed that the "license" of the press was capable of "snatching the scepter from the hands of royalty".[9] His proposal would establish a commission of five members to read all newspaper accounts of the sessions of the deputies. The journals were to report all of the debates, verbatim and with no omissions, or they would not be allowed to comment on them at all and penalties for errors were to run as high as two thousand francs! The marquis argued that the French press was getting a bad reputation all over the "civilized world", and that liberal ideas presented by the newspapers were an "odious travesty" of the true picture of France.[10] Debates over this bill in the lower Chamber lasted for a full month.

Again, Royer-Collard led the liberals, as well as some royalists of the Chamber in opposition to the project. In a brilliantly prepared speech, he stated that such legislation would so degrade society that men would, at best, only be able to achieve the "happy innocence of brutes". The press would be destroyed, he announced, and with it the key to freedom. He declared that, "with liberty strangled, intelligence, his noble mistress, must also perish".[11] Ultra opinion, which then had a majority in the Chamber, was

---

[8] Eugene Hatin, *Histoire politique et litteraire de la prese en France* (8 vols.; Paris, 1861), VIII, 423. (Hereafter cited as Hatin, *Histoire de la presse*.)

[9] La Boëssière, "Discours prononcé par M. le general marquis de la Boëssière" (Paris, February, 1827) pamphlet, Ledru-Rollin Collection, University of California, Berkeley, 175: 15, p. 3.

[10] La Boëssière, "Developmens de la proposition ..." (Paris, 15 March, 1827) pamphlet, Ledru-Rollin Collection, University of California, Berkeley, 175:17, pp. 1-5.

[11] *Le Moniteur*, 15 February, 1827.

expressed by the deputy from Haute-Loire, de Solihac. Like so many authoritarians, de Solihac wished to destroy specific liberties in the name of abstract liberty.

> But the essence of the press is the cruel enemy of liberty, this terrible weapon of revolutions and anarchy, leaving in its wake lies, defamations, outrages, breaking the most sacred ties, raising the people, declaring war on both heaven and earth, and in that fatal contest, liberty perishes amid the most agonizing convulsions.[12]

The subservient majority of Villèlist deputies passed the "Law of Justice and Love", as amended, by a vote of 233 to 134. Many moderate royalists and even a number of Ultra-royalists were shocked by the rigor of the new Peyronnet law. The august *Institut de France*, more or less above partisanship in these years, drafted a protest to the King. A learned committee chosen to present this petition consisted of the noted *savants* Lacretelle and Villemain, and the two renowned legitimist journalists Joseph Michaud of the Ultra *Quotidienne*, and René de Chateaubriand of the royalist *Journal des Débats*. Both of these representatives of the press were then ardent supporters of the Bourbons, and respected by friends and foes. Neither of them could tolerate Villèle. Charles X not only refused them audience, but peevishly retaliated in a manner which lost favor for himself and his minister even among some of the Ultraroyalists. Finding to his dismay that the petitioners' membership in the Academy was inviolable, Charles dismissed Lacretelle from his post as Royal Drama Censor, loyal Michaud from his title of Reader to the King, and Villemain from an honorary position on the Council of State.[13] Outraged, Chateaubriand struck back in a scathing denunciation of this action in his *Débats*, and a special reprint of three hundred thousand copies.[14] Royalism, henceforth, was to yield to his vanity, as the proud novelist and journalist cooled toward the Bourbons.

Charles was fully as confident that the Chamber of Peers would pass the "Law of Justice and Love" as he had been of the deputies. However, down at the Luxembourg, in the Chamber of Peers, mixed sentiments arose among the assembled nobles. Most of the peers were royalists, but few of them really approved of Villèle. Moreover, they considered themselves vaguely as the Second Estate, not as a "rubber stamp" for either the ministers or deputies, and many resented the action of the King toward the "immortals" of the *Académie Française*. The fight against the bill was, of course, led by the

---

[12] Chabrol de Solihac, "Opinion de M. Chabrol de Solihac..." (Paris, February, 1827) pamphlet, Ledru-Rollin Collection, University of California, Berkeley, 172:17, p. 1.

[13] Etienne Pasquier, *Histoire de mon temps* (8 vols.; Paris, 1895), VI, 77. (Hereafter cited as Pasquier, *Histoire*.)

[14] Daudet, *Martignac*, p. 45.

Peer Chateaubriand who called it a "vandal law".[15] Zeal found its mark here, for his ideological enemy was the censorship of ideas, while his greatest personal nemesis was Villèle. An anticlerical opposition to the law was introduced by the Jesuit-hating comte de Montlosier whose frequent pamphlets blamed Ignatius Loyola for all the evils of Europe.[16] The peers appointed a committee, composed of anti-Villèlists, to make any necessary modifications in the law.

While this committee was studying the Peyronnet Law, two incidents occurred which placed the Ministry in an even worse light. The great progressive and humanitarian, La Rochefoucauld-Liancourt, had just died. His funeral procession in Chalons attracted thousands of admirers and students of the Ecole des Arts of Chalons won the privilege of serving as his pallbearers. Since students were forbidden to participate in "political" demonstrations, the police intervened and, without hesitation, galloped directly into the procession. During the tumult, the casket fell to the pavement and the revered corpse rolled in the street. The news of this blunder quickly reached Paris and the Chamber of Peers. Soon after this, a member of the Ministry, de Corbière, was quoted as defending the adherence of a notorious Ultra, the prefect of police Delavau, to the *Congrégation*. The liberals appeared shocked by Corbière's remarks.

The Amendment Committee of the peers added so many modifications to the Peyronnet press bill as to render it useless and the Ministry at last withdrew it. Chateaubriand promptly demanded the resignation of the Villèle cabinet.[17] Paris was "illuminated" and the Chamber of Peers became the idol of the populace.

The King retaliated that June by a series of edicts against the press. Avoiding any suspicion of violating the Charter, Charles merely implemented the existing law of 1820 by establishing a complete bureaucracy of royal censors chosen from the Right. A far cry from Peyronnet's ideal, these edicts were later (November 5) modified to conform with the liberals' provision of 26 July, 1821, which nullified censure upon dissolution of the legislature.[18]

Popular opinion against Villèle was fanned by the press, especially the elegant and leonine *Débats*. Members of the bourgeois National Guard were unhappy when ordered to parade in review at the Champ de Mars. As the

[15] Alfred Germain, *Martyrologie de la presse* (Paris, 1861), p. 93. (Hereafter cited as Germain, *Martyrologie*.)

[16] Antonin Debidour, *Histoire des rapports de l'église et de l'état en France de 1789 à 1870* (Paris, 1911), p. 398. (Hereafter cited as Debidour, *Rapports*.)

[17] Pasquier, *Histoire*, pp. 80-81.

[18] Duvergier, *Collection des lois*, XXVII, 195-96, 453.

King rode past, the host of spectators cheered. But, as he returned home, a few in the ranks of the Guards called: *A bas Villèle! A bas les Jésuites!* and, as the duchesse de Berri rode past: *A bas les Jésuitesses!* Predictably the next day, Charles responded by dismissing the National Guard.[19] Here, the King had made a serious mistake. The bourgeoisie might still forgive him, but never his ministers.

Villèle's popularity soon descended to a new level as a result of another demonstration. The funeral of the great liberal deputy Manuel was attented by tens of thousands of persons. In the procession were three principals in the future drama of 1830: The young Adolphe Thiers, the banker Jacques Laffitte, and the republican emblem, Lafayette. Shortly after the funeral, François Mignet, a young Provençal on the staff of the *Courrier Français*, was prosecuted for writing a favorable description of the event. The court acquitted Mignet, however, marking another small defeat for Villèle.[20]

Liberal journals, and a few of those royalists who now opposed the Ministry, were demanding Villèle's political head. As winter approached, the atmosphere of crisis became more tangible.

---

[19] Daudet, *Martignac*, p. 49. Police had warned against holding the review three days previously, claiming the demonstrations were being carefully rehearsed. See, *Le livre noir de messieurs Delavau et Franchet ...* (4 vols.; Paris: Moutardier, 1829), IV, 40. (Hereafter cited as *Le livre noir*.)

[20] Daudet, *Martignac*, p. 53.

CHAPTER II

PARISIAN JOURNALS AND JOURNALISTS IN THE LATE RESTORATION

Paris in the 1820's was not only the cultural and political capital of France, it was also the major publishing center of Europe. Out of a metropolitan population of 816,000 in 1829, about thirty thousand persons made their living by the printing craft or by the writing, publication, or distribution of printed matter.[1] It is, therefore, not surprising that some of the Restoration newspapers were among the larger business corporations of the time.

One hundred and thirty-two periodicals were being published in Paris at the start of the year 1828. These included everything from horoscopes and ladies' fashion journals to reports of learned societies. Among them, fourteen could be classified as daily papers which dealt generally with political issues. Nine were weekly or monthly general reviews, of which only five were much concerned with political affairs.[2]

Among the nineteen "political" periodicals, no simple distinctions of "royalist" or "liberal" opinion may be made and might be designated more profitably in five groups: Liberal, "doctrinaire-liberal", liberal-monarchist (legitimist), Ultraroyalist opposed to Villèle, and Ultraroyalist favoring Villèle.

The first category, "liberal", refers to that section of opinion which evinced a strong undercurrent of antimonarchic, at least antidynastic sentiment. These newspapers were strongly anticlerical, though not quite in the spirit of 1793. The "liberal" press, while never advocating a republic, used every opportunity to undermine the prestige of the Royal Ministers. By 1828, their ideal had assumed the shape of a constitutional monarchy with a figurehead-king. They were the opposition "establishment" in 1828. The largest opposition newspapers were of this peruasion: The *Constitutionnel*, the *Courrier Français*, and the *Journal du Commerce*. The "liberal" weekly

---

[1] Alphonse de Lamartine, *The History of the Restoration of the Monarchy in France* (4 vols.; London, 1854), IV, 423. (Hereafter cited as Lamantine, *Restoration.*)

[2] *Revue de Paris* (2d ed.; Brussels, 1829), VII, 191-246.

or monthly periodicals of any significance were the *Revue Encyclopédique*, the *Album*, the *Corsaire*, the *Sylphe*, and the *Courrier des Electeurs*. The *Pandore*, a satirical revue, expired early in 1828.

The "doctrinaire-liberal" school was proud to distinguish itself from the "liberal". The term "doctrinaire" has been used to embrace all the liberals who were between Ultra and republican and, as such, it will not do. In a political sense, it is better to apply it only to men like Guizot who used it themselves. The significant distinction between the "doctrinaires" of 1825-1830, men like Guizot, Rémusat, and Dubois, and the older liberal "establishment" of Jay or Odilon Barrot was *not* in the radical-conservative equation. In their editorials we find many things as radical in the one as in the other. The real difference lay in goals. The old opposition was foe, critic, and courageous watchdog, but it was afraid of even a beneficial catastrophe, and so accepted the hope of a reformed, representative monarchy. The "doctrinaires" gave direction to opposition. If upheaval was to come, they wanted to plan ahead; hence, the Orléans compromise was their initiative. Two of Louis-Philippe's ministers, Thiers and Guizot, "doctrinaire" and militant in 1830, were regarded as enemies of democracy in 1848. A cross-section of "liberals" and "doctrinaires" would reveal a shared property emphasis and a fear of democratic society. In the period under consideration here, 1827-1830, the "doctrinaires" were distinguished by a more youthful, tolerant, and principled outlook than appeared in the old liberalism. Their philosophy is best expressed by example. While the *Courrier* and the other "liberal" papers assailed the allegedly dire influence of the Jesuits, the *Globe*, paragon of the "doctrinaires", defended the order – not from sympathy – but from the doctrine of complete religious toleration! The "doctrinaires" had three publications, none of which was primarily political in 1828: Two journals, *le Globe* and *le Figaro*, and the small monthly *Revue Française*. All three bore the stamp of the intellectual rather than the polemicist.

The "liberal-monarchists" were more than merely constitutional-monarchists. They believed in a middle-class representation in government and in significant, but limited powers for the King. They were sincerely devoted to essential civil liberties such as freedom of the press, and they were at least as sentimentally humane about such problems as Negro slavery as were their liberal colleagues. Liberal-monarchists recognized, though seldom emphasized, the infirmities of the dynasty and, though they hated Villèle, they were still committed to the principle of "legitimacy". Except for their adoration of the scepter, they were liberals. They opposed the clerical political influence and they rejected ideas which would turn back the clock of history. Liberal-monarchists were often slightly touched by the shadow of the late Napoleon

Bonaparte, as were nearly all the factions of the opposition. The great voice of this opinion was the respected and feared *Journal des Débats*, a newspaper whose opposition influence in 1828 was only approached by the liberal *Constitutionnel*.

These journals may accurately be grouped together as the press of the "opposition". In the Ultra camp, however, a deep internal rift had appeared by 1824, in opposition to the Ministry and policies of the comte de Villèle. Ultra newspapers usually opposing Villèle were the *Quotidienne* and the *Drapeau Blanc*. Those which supported him were the *Gazette de France* which he partially owned, and the *Moniteur Universel*, the official government journal which automatically reflected the views of the current Ministry in its rare editorials. Two very small Ultraclerical papers were le *Mémorial Catholique* and the *Apostolique*. Another weekly clerical periodical, *Conservateur de 1828*, appeared in April, 1828 to oppose a policy of compromise and the anti-Jesuit stand of the Ministry of Martignac.[3]

Le Constitutionnel was then the largest newspaper on the continent of Europe. In 1828, it was received daily by nearly twenty thousand subscribers,[4] over half of whom lived outside of Paris.[5] Its readership, as that of any Restoration journal, was much larger than such a figure would indicate. Several hundred copies were posted in the numerous *cabinets de lecture* or reading-salons which existed in Paris and the large towns. Many Frenchmen read their newspapers at their leisure, without buying them; the proprietor of the *cabinet de lecture* received his remuneration from the sale of coffee or brandy. The assertion that the *Constitutionnel* and other large journals were "big business" is suported by a review of their finances. Owners of the *Constitutionnel* received, from the individual rate of seventy-two francs a year per subscription and from advertising revenue, a gross income (for 1826) of 1,323,976 francs. Of this total, a huge 450,000 was spent for taxes, 102,222 for postage, and 394,000 for operating costs, leaving a net gain for the year of about 375,000 francs. Each of fifteen stockholders received an equal portion of this, or a salary of 25,000 francs.[6] The stockholders were usually wealthy men. Some of them, like the powerful politician Casimir Périer, also wrote for the paper.

The paper's editorial staff was large enough to spawn internal factions

[3] Nora E. Hudson, *Ultra Royalism and the French Restoration* (Cambridge, England, 1936), p. 147. (Hereafter cited as Hudson, *Ultra Royalism*.)

[4] Georges Weill, *Le journal, origines, évolution, et rôle de la presse périodique* (Paris, 1934), p. 168. (Hereafter cited as Weill, *Le journal*.)

[5] Comte de Salaberry, *Souvenirs politiques du comte de Salaberry sur la Restauration, 1827-1830* (2 vols.; Paris, 1900), II, 56. (Hereafter cited as Salaberry, *Souvenirs*.)

[6] Weill, *Le journal*, pp. 172-73.

which, together with wealthy patronage, tended to inhibit radical experiments. Young Adolphe Thiers of Provence was backed by several patrons when he first joined the staff. The orator Manuel and the playwright-turned-politician Charles Étienne first brought Thiers into the *Constitutionnel's* circle.[7] Jacques Laffitte, banker and shareholder in several opposition papers, had also taken an interest in this promising young man from Aix. The faction around Thiers quarreled with that of Louis-François Cauchois-Lemaire over the latter's attempts to purchase a larger interest in the shares of the newspaper. Cauchois-Lemaire, an early spokesman for the Orleanist monarchy, was himself supported financially by a wealthy deputy, Antoine Gévaudan, who owned the major stage lines serving Paris.

A more remarkable and less commercial patronage, which had a European cultural importance, was that of Thiers by the German publisher, Freiherr Cotta von Cottendorf. Baron von Cotta was scion of a journalistic and publishing dynasty which started in Tubingen in 1659. By the 1820's, the firm had presses in the chief towns of Wurtemburg and Bavaria. Baron Cotta had helped introduce to the world such luminaries as Schiller and Fichte and in 1823 he adopted Thiers as his *protégé*. He also invested money in the *Constitutionnel*. Though Thiers stoutly maintained that not any of his backers ever purchased any control over his pen, the young man deeply admired his older German patron and friend. Cotta's *Allgemeine Zeitung*, known internationally as the *Gazette d'Augsbourg*, helped Thiers' European reputation by reprinting his articles in translation. Thiers divided his time between the *Constitutionnel* and writing his history of the French Revolution for nearly nine years before he at last launched his militant *National*.[8]

Members of the *Constitutionnel's* staff also included Antoine Jay, another historian of the Revolution, André Dupin, *aîné*, a famous defense lawyer and friend of the Duke of Orleans, and Evariste Dumoulin, a Gascon republican who became chief editor after the July Revolution. Frequent contributors for this paper were Léon Thiéssé and deputies Alexandre de Lameth and the abbé Dominique Georges de Pradt, an anticlerical who later transferred his rather banal talents to the *Courrier*. A less predictable, and, therefore, more entertaining, anticlerical was the comte de Montlosier. An Ultra aristocrat in everything but religion, Montlosier's pamphlets were usually

---

[7] An interesting coincidence is the lifelong involvement with the theatre of both Étienne and the Ultra journalist Martainville. As youths, they had collaborated on a history of French drama (1802). Étienne, as a classicist, was forced by the romanticist tide to remain chiefly a critic, although he wrote several plays.

[8] Robert Marquant, *Thiers et le baron Cotta*, Travaux et mémoires des instituts français en Allemagne, No. 7 (Paris: Presses universitaires françaises, 1959), pp. 1-13, 43-50, 55, 294. (Hereafter cited as Marquant, *Thiers et Cotta*.)

quoted at length in the *Constitutionnel*. Among the more infrequent contributors to this catch-all of liberal opinion was that rising genius of criticism, Charles Sainte-Beuve, who has left us with some of the best prose portraits of the era, the young comte de Rémusat, and the subversive songwriter, Pierre Béranger, who held some of the paper's stock.

The *Constitutionnel's* political policy was well understood by Thiéssé who said that its opposition "was of those who publicize, not those who overthrow". At a meeting of the stockholders in 1819, the paper's policies were determined: To stay within the Charter; to respect the King and the Chambers; to write scandal of no individual; to reinforce the institutions of the Charter; to publicize complaints of the oppressed impartially; to give aid to all friends of liberty; and to offer no hostility to the chiefs of foreign states, while upholding the honor and glory of the French nation.[9] Quite naturally, these standards were occasionally violated. The role of the *Constitutionnel* was significant during most of the Restoration and particularly under Villèle. It is doubtful, however, if the newspaper deserves the tribute of one contemporary, who said that the *Constitutionnel* was to 1830 what Abbé Siéyès' famous pamphlet was to 1789.[10]

Le Courrier Français was more outspoken than the *Constitutionnel* and it had a circulation of approximately six thousand in 1828. Though not republican in policy, some of its editors held republican views and the masthead pictured a wreath encircling the words "La Charte".

The *Courrier's* most illustrious senior editors were the liberal statesmen the duc de Broglie and Benjamin Constant. Its staff managers were Valentin de Lapelouze and René Chatelain, both whom stood trial for their writers' offenses on several occasions. The editorial staff included four deputies who were at least not hostile to republican views: Odilon Barrot, Auguste Kératry, Joseph Mérilhou, and Albin de Berville. The last two were also prominent as liberal defense attorneys, bringing to bear on magistrates' ears the same oratorical persuasion they used in the Chamber of Deputies. Mérilhou was a principal stockholder in the *Courrier*. Augustin Thierry, historian of medieval France, was also a frequent contributor to the *Courrier*. François Guizot received much of his youthful political experience on the *Courrier's* staff and the abbé de Pradt, until 1828 with the *Constitutionnel*, was a popular editorial writer. De Pradt had been a constituent and had emigrated, only to return in 1802 as a Bonapartist. Under Napoleon he became an archbishop and received

---

[9] Hatin, *Histoire de la presse*, VIII, 454.
[10] Alexandre Baudouin, *Anecdotes historiques du temps de la Restauration* (Paris, 1853), p. 162. Baudouin was a lukewarm Bonapartist and a friend of many of the journalists of the period.

the Legion of Honor. In 1814, he turned against Bonaparte and cast his lot with the opposition of the Left. He was a pamphleteer and something of a demagogue. Chateaubriand called him a "mitred clown".[11]

Le Courrier's policy was described by de Hauranne as "Gallican, Republican, and Constitutionalist". In Restoration semantics, however, these last two terms are incompatible. The last defines the Anglophile-liberal monarchist; the second, one who rejects even the figurehead of Kingship. The position of the *Courrier* was a somewhat reluctant acceptance of monarchy as realistic coupled with a sentimental attachment to government by representatives. It was this temper that later made the *Courrier* a natural outlet for Orleans propaganda as an "ideal" compromise. Gallican it certainly was, as the antithesis to Jesuit Ultramontanism. The *Courrier's* editors occasionally went farther than protesting their Catholicism and attacking the *Congrégation*, and free-thinkers among its staff wrote articles which cast doubt upon the very foundations of Christian belief. Despite its staff, the *Courrier* was an improvident journal. Thiers said it barely made expenses, but because of that it could afford to be "bolder".[12]

The *Journal du Commerce* was, even more than the *Constitutionnel*, a businessman's newspaper. It made a specialty of market quotations and financial news. François Bert, its manager, and chief editor François Larréguy championed individual liberty, and, often displayed remarkable spirit in editorials. The tone was liberal, anticlerical, and pragmatic; its editors having once said they preferred Villèle, the scheming absolutist, to Martignac, the conciliator, because the former had employed a sounder financial policy.[13] Financier Laffitte held stock in both the *Courrier* and the *Commerce*, as well as the *Constitutionnel*. The staff and circulation of the *Journal du Commerce* were small. In 1828 it had scarcely twenty-five hundred subscribers.[14]

Another liberal-controlled daily, the *Gazette des Tribunaux* began publication in 1825 and was especially designed for lawyers, magistrates, and all who enjoyed the drama of the courtroom. Its editor, Jean-Achille Darmaing, who had been with the *Constitutionnel*, reported dialog of judicial processes. Since the accurate reporting of public hearings was perfectly legal, Darmaing, a staunch liberal, was able to advertise his political faith with no danger of prosecution. He seldom wrote editorials, but those he published were usually

---

[11] Paul Thureau-Dangin, "Les libéraux et la liberté sous la Restauration", *Le Correspondant*, LXVI (10 June, 1876), 781-82. (Hereafter cited as Thureau-Dangin, "Les libéraux").

[12] Marquant, *Thiers et Cotta*, p. 294.

[13] Prosper L. Duvergier de Hauranne, *Histoire du gouvernement parlementaire en France, 1814-1848* (10 vols.; Paris, 1857-1871), IX, 450. (Hereafter cited as de Hauranne, *Histoire*).

[14] Salaberry, *Souvenirs*, II, 56; *Gazette de France*, 27 May, 1830. These figures are approximated interpolations of 1824 statistics and a survey of 1830.

about some judicial miscarriage or an attack on an Ultra member of the legal profession. Darmaing was himself a member of the Paris bar. This newspaper, in addition to the often exciting accounts of trials, campaigned against cruel penalties in the law. The treatment of Negroes in the colonies and of the galley-convicts at home drew equally upon his anger, and along with some other Restoration liberals, he revived the Beccarian crusade for humane justice which had subsided in the Revolution. Under Napoleon's codes, still in effect, criminals were often branded; a brutality that was even more destructive socially than physically and under Charles X, parricides were to be deprived of their right hands before they were allowed to die from the blade. The *Gazette des Tribunaux* also opposed capital punishment in principle, as well as any imprisonment which was not rehabilitative. Public decapitations of criminals, which had only recently been discontinued in France, were to Darmaing, degrading festivals of perverted amusement.[15]

Although controversial political trials were his specialty, Darmaing flavored his court gazette with sufficient sex, humor, and blood so that the issues were never dull. The paper had three thousand subscribers, a remarkable number for such a specialized newspaper. The reporting was reliable and accurate, for the *Gazette des Tribunaux* was quoted by the Ultra press, as well as that of the Left. Attendance at political trials was a customary diversion for men of affairs and court chambers were usually crowded for such *cause célèbres*. The *Gazette des Tribunaux* extended this audience a hundred-fold.

Another specialized newspaper belonging to the opposition was the *Gazette Constitutionnel des Cultes*. This small newspaper, edited by one Brissaud, with over six hundred subscribers was often quoted against the "black papacy" of the Jesuits, as well as the clerical faction in France. Its policy was influenced by the writings of the famous classicist and sceptic, Paul-Louis Courier, who had been killed in 1825. The paper contained articles on Catholicism, Protestantism, Judaism, Islam, and other religious faiths. Its attacks, however, were directed at the Catholic hierarchy, the validity of sacraments, and the "conspiracy" of the Society of Jesus.

In 1828, there were several periodical reviews or magazines which did not appear daily, but which displayed liberal political views. The *Revue Ency-clopédique*, an ancient title, was a literary magazine and was edited by the Republicans Langlois, Tissot, and Alexandre de Laborde.[16] The *Album*, or *l'Ancien Album*, was a magazine of humorous satire. Jean Magallon and Louis Fontan, the editors, received in 1823 and in 1829, harsher penalties than any

---

[15] *Gazette des Tribunaux*, 20 May, 1830.
[16] Charles Marc des Granges, *La presse littéraire sous la Restauration, 1815-1830* (Paris, 1907), p. 133.

other journalists prosecuted during that decade![17] The *Corsaire* was more ribald in its satire and riduculed religious customs. The *Courrier des Electeurs* was politically liberal and was read each week by sixteen hundred subscribers. The views of Jean-Bernard Sarrans, *jeune*, its editor, were the same as those of the editors of the *Courrier* and it advertised activities of the *Aide-toi* Society. One of the most sprightly periodicals of the liberals was the *Sylphe*, the work of Louis Desnoyers, a writer of childrens' fairy tales, and his young friend Valliant. Impoverished journalists, they wished to publish the *Sylphe* daily, but the law would then require a *cautionnment*, or bond. Desnoyers was determined to pay nothing. His paper appeared, but each issue carried a new title on the masthead. Thus, the *Sylphe* was also the *Lutin*, the *Trilby*, and the *Gnome*.[18] Under each name, it was read by a small, but devoted coterie.

The "doctrinaires" found their intellectual and cultural stimulus in the famous *Globe* and the *Revue Française*, and their amusement in the arch *Figaro*. These three periodicals all displayed literary excellence and polish combined with a scholarly exposition. They were too urbane to be warmly partisan, but their liberalism was a creed of tolerance and reason and their respected names have lived on for over a century in French journalism. University professors, some of them discharged for their ideas, made up a large part of their editorial staffs.

The *Revue Française* was founded as a monthly literary, scholarly, and historical review in January, 1828, by François Guizot and the comte de Rémusat while Guizot continued to work for the *Courrier* and the *Globe* and Rémusat for the *Constitutionnel* and the *Globe*. This review was not primarily political although the very first issue contained a plea to replace Martignac's Ministry with a more liberal Cabinet.[19] In addition to Guizot and Rémusat, a number of leading intellectuals wrote for the *Revue*, giving it quality and variety. The philosophers Villemain and Vitet, the historians de Hauranne and Thierry, and the scientist Ampère all contributed articles. Guizot directed the entire enterprise and his wife proofread the manuscripts.[20] The journal had but a few hundred subscribers, and was, in some ways, a smaller edition of the *Globe*.

Figaro, the most popular of better satirical journals, was edited with taste and imagination, but it never attempted to be as ponderous or intellectual

[17] René Mazédier, *Histoire de la presse parisienne de Théophraste Renaudot a la IVe République, 1631-1945 (Paris, 1945), p. 69*. See *infra*, chapter iv, for the *Album's* later trial.

[18] Burnand, *La vie quotidienne*, p. 189.

[19] *Revue Française* (January, 1828), pp. 22-45.

[20] Charles H. Pouthas, *Guizot pendant la Restauration* (Paris, 1923), p. 295. (Hereafter cited as Pouthas, *Guizot*.)

as either the *Globe* or the *Revue Française*. *Figaro* was born in January, 1826, a tiny four-page journal and printed on the cheapest paper. Its founders were dramatist Étienne Arago, a militant republican, friend of Balzac, and a theatrical producer, and Maurice Alhoy, a young bohemian. After ten weeks of financial difficulties the embryonic *Figaro* was sold for three hundred francs to Le Poittevin, a novelist and also a friend of Balzac. Le Poittevin was one of those incorrigibles who delighted in shocking conservative tastes. When he ran for deputy from the Seine, he once printed on *Figaro's* masthead: "Candidate of the Seven Deadly Sins". Le Poittevin allowed his editors free-rein, possibly because he paid them almost nothing. A brilliant but foppish youth named Nestor Roqueplan was the most highly rewarded member of the staff at a monthly salary of fifty francs. After six months of rising popularity, Le Poittevin sold his *Figaro* to a twenty-eight-year-old millionaire named Victor Bohain for thirty thousand francs, a hundred times what he had paid for it! Bohain nurtured his investment with the talents of several contributors to other journals. Dr. Louis Véron, author of the *Diary of a Bourgeois of Paris*, was a literary and society commentator who had defected from the *Quotidienne*, when his political views changed. Others were Adolphe Blanqui, brother of Auguste, but less radical in outlook, and Auguste Romieu, a wealthy dramatist and *bon-vivant* who often treated his less provident colleagues to expensive dining.[21] *Figaro's* staff usually dined and drank in the Café Florian, at 39, rue Croix-des-Petits Champs, which adjoined their offices and which often served as their editorial conference room. Voices rose rather loudly and freely. It was almost too much for one police-*mouche* who forwarded this report to Prefect of Police Delavau:

> It would probably be difficult to find in the capital a group more disparaging of the government than that which is made up of the *habitués* of the Café Florian. The malignance of this coterie is found in the journal *Le Figaro*... Each clown at the Café Florian contributes to it, according to his abilities.[22]

The entire personality of *Figaro* was irreverent and satirical, but it was a satire nearer to Voltaire's rapier than to Swift's cudgel. Ridicule being the deadliest wound to an ambitious Frenchman in public life, *Figaro* made certain that very few inflated egos escaped from its precise thrusts.

The most important of these non-daily journals and perhaps the most widely admired periodical of Europe in the late 1820's, was the *Globe*. Its spirit was highly intellectual without pedantry, and brilliantly artistic without condes-

---

[21] Frederic Ségu, *Le premier Figaro, 1826-1833* (Paris, 1932), pp. 2-11; see also, Hatin, *Histoire de la presse*, VIII, 486. Véron also started the literary *Revue de Paris*.

[22] *Le livre noir*, II (police report, 3 February, 1826), 341-43.

cension. The *Globe* was the most universal of journals, yet it was thorough in whatever it undertook. In addition to these virtues, the *Globe* was marked by the ardor of youth. No one of its regular staff was over forty.

The first issue appeared on September 15, 1824. It was founded by a type-worker, Pierre Leroux and a professor who had been discharged for his political views from the Lycée Charlemagne. This professor-journalist was Paul-François Dubois, one of the most versatile figures in nineteenth-century French letters. Dubois' recent activity had also included a role in various *Carbonari* affiliated subversive clubs in his native Rennes. It was Dubois who gave the direction, and much of the greatness, to the *Globe*. His ideal, in establishing the paper, was to give a forum of expression to the intellectual younger generation.[23] Dubois was especially interested in religion and philosophy and he set the religious attitude of the staff. The doctrinaire "Globists" did not speak of toleration, but rather the equality of right to any belief or to no belief. Thus, the liberals were disturbed when Dubois defended the right of the Jesuits to enter France in accord with this doctrine.[24] A contemporary and friend of the "Globists" said, "They pronounced the name of God with a sort of deference, bearing more politeness than respect..."[25] Dubois' was a mind always bursting with inspiration. The critic Sainte-Beuve, who once fought a mock duel with Dubois, later wrote:

> The beautiful work I have seen him rough-sketch after a sleepless night. Such beautiful novels of Vendéeans or Chouans like Sir Walter Scott! Such beautiful plans for the history of Christianity before Rénan! And all this lost in improvising.[26]

He was a friend of the much older Chateaubriand and once threatened to "convert" that most Catholic of writers to Christianity.[27]

The editors of the *Globe* were drawn from two sources, the writers of a literary periodical, the *Tablettes Universelles*, and the academic victims of Villèle's policies. *Tablettes* had begun in 1823, as a liberal journal of high literary quality. But, in 1824, manager Jacques Coste was approached by the agents of Villèle with an offer to "amortize" or buy out the *Tablettes* for three hundred thousand francs. Coste succumbed to temptation. Thiers,

---

[23] Paul Gerbod, *Paul-François Dubois, universitaire, journaliste et homme politique* (Paris, 1967), pp. 46-48, 86-91. (Hereafter cited as Gerbod, *Dubois*.); see also, Paul Janet, "Le *Globe* de la Restauration et Paul-François Dubois", *Revue des Deux Mondes*, XXXIV (August, 1879), 484-86. (Hereafter cited as Janet, "*Globe* et Dubois".)

[24] *Ibid.*, p. 503.

[25] Comte de Carné, "Souvenirs de ma jeunesse au temps de la Restauration", *Le Correspondant*, L (10 January, 1872), 203. (Hereafter cited as Carné, "Souvenirs".)

[26] Gabriel Faure, *Chateaubriand, Dubois, et le Globe, 12 lettres inédites de Chateaubriand* (Grenoble, 1944), Introduction. (Hereafter cited as Faure, *Dubois.)*

[27] *Ibid*, (Dubois to Chateaubriand, 30 May, 1827).

Mignet, and Rémusat, rising in the literary world, first considered abandoning journalism in disgust. The *Journal des Débats* censured Coste. "The proprietor of the *Tablettes*", wrote Chateaubriand "believes his interests worth more than his opinions".[28] The jobless writers were immediately attracted by the prospect of the new journal of Leroux and Dubois. Other Professors driven into journalistic careers by the government's purge were, besides Dubois, Victor Cousin, Theodore Jouffroy, and François Guizot.[29] Jouffroy and Cousin had been together in secret *Carbonari* activities and taught private classes in revolutionary history after their dismissal from the University. Among their students were Vitet, Damiron, and Sainte-Beuve. All of these men later wrote for the *Globe*.[30]

By 1828, regular contributors to this remarkable journal were Charles Duchâtel, who wrote about economics, religion, and education; Adolphe Thiers, who wrote on a variety of topics, including Salon life; Armand Carrel, on the revolutionary past of both France and England; Duvergier de Hauranne, on English history; Vitet on aesthetics; Victor Cousin on philosophy; Augustin Thierry on medieval France; Ampère on physics; and Rémusat on politics and history. Rémusat was a cultivated nobleman of liberal convictions whose political detachment is revealed in his remark: "I have never had a very great feeling against the Restoration. I realize that it has given me, in a way, the very ideas that I employ against it".[31]

The *Globe* received occasional contributions from other men of letters. Victor Hugo's preface to *Cromwell* and works by Constant, Stendahl, and Chateaubriand were among them.

In February, 1830, the *Globe* descended into the political arena. But before this transition, as well as afterward, the high standards and ideals of Dubois and his friends were maintained and permeated every line of the journal. Defending the *Globe* when it was on trial in 1830, Dubois stated: "The idea which founded and upheld this paper is changeless. It is the idea of liberty, but liberty ruled in politics by laws, in philosophy by reason, and in letters by taste".[32]

The fame of the newspaper traveled abroad. Karl von Humboldt lavishly praised it as the "Bible of literature"[33] and Goethe was swept to raptures.

---

[28] Germain, *Martyrologie*, p. 86.

[29] Janet, "*Globe* et Dubois", p. 484.

[30] Jean Lucas-Dubreton, *La Restauration et la Monarchie de Juillet* (Paris, 1937), p. 111. (Hereafter cited as Lucas-Dubreton, *Restauration*.)

[31] Thureau-Dangin, "Les libéraux", p. 939.

[32] *Le Globe*, 4 April, 1830.

[33] Adolphe Lair, "Le *Globe*, sa fondation, sa rédaction, son influence, souvenirs inédites de M. Dubois", *La Quinzaine*, LVI (Paris, 1904), 289. (Hereafter cited as Lair, "Le *Globe*".)

He said of the *Globists*, "I am captivated by them. They give us the spectacle of a society of young, energetic men, playing an important role".[34] At another time, the sage of Weimar declared: "Such men are these gentlemen of the *Globe*!... How filled they are with the same spirit! In Germany, such a journal would be purely and simply impossible".[35] The Russian historian and archaeologist, A.I. Turgenev, referred to the courageously progressive *Literaturnaja Gazeta* as the Russian equivalent of the *Globe*.[36].

The *Globe* was indeed a force in the intellectual life of Europe, but it also became a political power during the late Restoration. Its writers were active in liberal societies and especially the electoral society, *Aide-toi le Ciel t'aidera*, which they dominated until 1828. In their dual role as journalists and electoral organizers, they assisted in the defeat of Villèle. After the July Revolution in 1830, the paper was sold to the Saint-Simonians and its brilliance came to an end.

The *Journal des Débats* was royalist and legitimist. In a sense, it was more loyal to the monarchy of the Valois-Bourbons than any of the Ultra journals. It tried to save the monarchy from its suicidal direction. But when that monarchy was beyond salvation, the *Débats* accepted the result with regret, but as historically inevitable. It must be added, however, that certain political humiliations of its senior editor hastened its conversion.

Only the *Constitutionnel* was larger than the *Débats*, which had over eleven thousand subscriptions in 1828. The three principal owners and founders of the paper were the brothers Bertin and Chateaubriand. These gentlemen were also the editors-in-chief of the *Débats*. They were assisted by many other journalists, including Guizot, Barante, Royer-Collard, and Salvandy.

Bertin de Vaux, the younger of the brothers, was extremely rich and an active participant in politics and social life. His mansion in the rue Louis-le-Grand was the setting of important society every Sunday evening. Journalists, politicians, and savants, the cream of the nation, gathered in his salon, which Bertin ruled inelegantly and where the guests often bored themselves playing whist.[37] The Bertins were liberal-monarchists, defenders of the liberty of the press and of dissent, but conservative on the issue of legitimate royalty.

Chateaubriand had not always been so favorable toward liberal ideas. He was essentially a sensitive, intelligent, and conceited blueblood. He enjoyed a

---

[34] Faure, *Dubois*, p. 22.

[35] Institut de France, *Discours de M. Charles Levêque et M. Bersot prononcé aux funerailles de M. Dubois le 17 Juin 1874* (Paris, 1874), p. 2.

[36] O. Orlik, "La révolution française de 1830 dans la presse russe", *Revue d'histoire moderne et contemporaine*, XVI (Paris, 1969), 409.

[37] Burnand, *La vie quotidienne*, p. 188.

reputation as the champion of press freedom, but he had inclined, before 1824, to a rather Metternichian view of world affairs. At the Congress of Verona in 1822, it was he who demanded the intervention of French troops in the Spanish revolution. He recognized the task of restoring a mad tyrant to the Spanish throne as a sordid one, but it was in keeping with his stubborn adherence to the principle of "legitimacy".[38] His romantic reverence for religion was also not in accord with the general liberal attitude.

Chateaubriand was rewarded for this Spanish policy by the portfolio of Foreign Affairs and his vanity was intensified as he became the official "greeter" and showhorse of Louis XVIII's government. Villèle and the others who really made the policies and decisions, resented the popularity of this famous novelist and essayist. Jealousy between the ambitious politician and the egotistical writer was further animated by pettiness. Villèle became angry when the Tsar ignored him and instead accorded Chateaubriand the order of Saint Andrew for preserving legitimacy in Madrid. Differences more basic than wounded ego also helped to alienate Chateaubriand from Villèle. These included the policy of *amortissement* – the buying-up of opposition journals, and disagreement over the conversion of government bonds to indemnify the *émigrés* of the Revolution. On June 4, 1824, Chateaubriand was discharged from the Cabinet.[39]

This date was a milestone in the history of the *Journal des Débats*. Chateaubriand swiftly became the journalistic nemesis of Villèle and all that he proposed or accomplished. Only after 1824, may the *Débats* be considered one of the leading voices of the opposition. The policy of the journal grew more bitterly antagonistic to the Ultra philosophy in both politics and religion. In 1827, Chateaubriand helped establish the "Society of Friends of Freedom of the Press", which aimed at Villèle's newspaper policy and the press lews. The schism of 1824 affected the entire group of liberal-monarchists to which Chateaubriand belonged. Nobles like de Broglie and Pasquier also became part of the growing opposition to the rise of Ultra power. Chateaubriand was frequently named to succeed the unpopular Villèle, but his pride forbade acceptance of any of the lesser portfolios which were actually offered him.[40] Reinforcement of the liberal wing by the support of the *Débats* was of great value. Villèle recognized the power of the *Débats* and in 1826, he is

---

[38] Henri Reynald, *Histoire politique et litteraire de la Restauration* (Paris, 1863), pp. 349-50. (Hereafter cited as Reynald, *Histoire.*) A scholarly account of Chateaubriand's diplomatic career may be found in Volume I of Emmanuel Beau de Loménie, *La carrière politique de Chateaubriand de 1814 à 1830* (2 vols.; Paris, 1929). (Hereafter cited as Loménie, *Chateaubriand.*)

[39] Reynald, *Histoire*, p. 381.

[40] Loménie, *Chateaubriand*, II, 259-60, 294-95; Bertier de Sauvigny, *Restoration*, p. 390.

supposed to have said to Bertin *aîné:* "You have overthrown Decazes and Richelieu in playing at royalism; to overthrow me you will have to make a revolution".[41] Bertin not only wrote against the Ministry, but furnished money and direction to the campaigns of the *Aide-toi* electoral society.[42] The *Débats*, representing constitutional monarchy, and the *Gazette de France*, representing the devious absolutist policy of Villèle, engaged in a duel of the press, which became as personal and as lethal as a duel with pistols might have been between the writer and the Prime Minister.

Neither Villèle's faction, nor his *Gazette de France*, was considered sufficiently reactionary by the extreme champions of the Right. In addition, many Ultras disliked the dishonesty which Villèle fostered. There was even a handful of men who were Ultra in politics, but who disapproved of Villèle's acceptance of clericalism. For these reasons, the royalist press in 1828 was divided on ministries and policies, but allied in its will to destroy the hydra of liberalism which the Revolution and the Empire had raised in its midst.

The *Gazette de France*, largest journal of the royalists, was received by nearly ten thousand subscribers in 1828. It was the party organ of Villèle and one of its major goals was a coalition of all the parties of the Right, under this Minister's direction. Basically it stood for Villèle, Ultramontane religion, and royalist politics. It was nearly the only reading matter of the aging King, who until 1830 agreed with Villele's policy of subtle encroachment against the Left. Charles X called the *Gazette* "an old friend, an old habit".[43]

The guiding genius of the *Gazette*, and the man who wrote most of its editorials was the marquis Antoine-Eugène de Genoude. He was a sincere worshipper of religion, monarchy, and himself; which a contemporary avowed "made an indivisible trinity of him".[44] He was, of course, a close and devoted friend to Villèle, although he was younger than the Minister. Clericalists and Jesuits had adored Genoude and expected him to enter holy orders, but to their surprise and annoyance, he shunned the celibate life and married a rich woman, a favorite of the Duchess of Condé. It was Lamartine who helped him obtain his title from the King to fit his new social position.[45] For an Ultra, Genoude was often surprisingly farsighted and reasonable. He recognized the significance of Villèle's defeat in 1827 and he feared the risk

[41] Lucas-Dubreton, *Restauration*, p. 97.

[42] *Temps*, 19 June, 1830.

[43] Daudet, *Martignac*, p. 219; Lamartine, *History*, IV, 354; M. Capefigue, *Histoire de la Restauration et des causes qui ont améné la chute de la branche ainée des Bourbons* (4 vols.; Paris, 1842), IV, 88. (Hereafter cited as Capefigue, *Histoire.*)

[44] Carné, "Souvenirs', p. 232.

[45] Lamartine, *History*, IV, 356.

of a violent *coup d'état* in 1830. His greatest error in judgment was to back the Polignac regime at the last minute before the Revolution of 1830, after a long and *politique* opposition. His Jesuit sympathies were famous and the source of much indignation on the Left. The *Globists* affected horror when he received the Order of Isabella the Catholic from the despot of Spain.[46] As an editor, Genoude proved a talented adversary to Chateaubriand of the *Débats* and others, such as the *Globists*, who engaged him in paper wars.

The *Quotidienne*, a paper with six thousand subscriptions in 1828, was the foremost Ultra journal opposed to Villèle. Although it was not a "giant", like the *Constitutionnel* or the *Débats*, it represented a large enterprise. One share of its stock was worth twenty-five thousand francs in 1830.[47]

The paper was started in 1822 by a group of devoted royalists. The chief editor was Joseph François Michaud, a respected scholar and an ardent champion of strong monarchy. Like so many of the royalist journalists, he was past middle age in 1828. As a youth during the Convention, he had defied Robespierre and refused to flee Paris as an *émigré*. The Convention sentenced him to death, but he escaped. He returned in 1799 and devoted himself to scholarly pursuits. His merits as an historian were recognized when he wrote his history of the Crusades, and later edited the great *Biographie Universelle*. He was a member of the *Institut*, but his major works were published after his death. Louis XVIII made him his reader, at which post he remained until he was fired by Charles X for courageously opposing the Peyronnet press bill. He enjoyed conversations with men of all opinions and his own speech was slightly ribald. Thureau-Dangin called him a "friendly Athenian". In matters concerning freedom of the press he could be quite broad and he attacked the "Law of Justice and Love" in his favorite aphoristic style:

How much powder is needed to charge a cannon? – Two pounds – Very well! Put in four so it will make more noise and effect. Put in four and soon the piece explodes among those who have loaded it ...[48]

The general respect which Michaud engendered was due to his moral consistency and his willingness to debate the Left. When Villèle's agent, Sosthènes tried to buy up his paper, he refused the bribe with a scorn which won praise from the liberals. He was not a friend of the Jesuits and was amused by trite accusations of his "Ultramontanism". An insight into the real Michaud

---

[46] *Globe*, 20 April, 1830.

[47] *Gazette des Tribunaux*, 10 March, 1830, reported the purchase of two and a half shares for 62,500 francs.

[48] Hatin, *Histoire de la presse*, VIII, 490-91; Paul Thureau-Dangin, *Royalistes et républicains* (Paris, 1874), p. 188. (Hereafter cited as Thureau-Dangin, *Royalistes*.)

is found in his habit, going back to his Revolution ordeals, of carrying the essays of Montaigne with him for consolation.[49]

On the early staff of the *Quotidienne* with Michaud were: Charles Nodier, the romanticist; Capefigue, the royalist historian; Dr. Louis Véron, sensualist and *raconteur*, who later moved Left and transferred his cultivated wit to *Figaro*; and Jules Janin, the literary critic. One of the later contributors to the *Quotidienne* was Pierre-Antoine Berryer, a rising, popular young lawyer and deputy who was to become a personal rival of Guizot. Berryer was devoutly royalist although he believed in the Charter and had no illusions about the recklessness of some of the Ultras.[50] The staff changed during the Ministry of Martignac in 1828-1829. When the King continued to favor Villèle and oppose his own Minister, Michaud, as a good royalist, could not actively side with the moderate faction which, though in power, had formally denounced the King's favorite. He, therefore, resigned temporarily from the *Quotidienne* and turned its editorial functions over to Pierre Laurentie, a clericalist Ultra. Laurentie brought in O'Mahony and several of the Ultras from the *Mémorial Catholique*. The paper thus became more clerical while yielding none of its distaste for Villèle.[51]

The *Mémorial Catholique* was the principal Church-directed journal of the period. It favored the Jesuits and opposed Gallicanism, but in secular matters, it could be rather liberal, due to the inluence of the great Lammenais, who wrote for it.[52] Another clerical periodical, less widely read, which defended the royalist position, was a scholarly monthly, *Le Catholique*. Its chief editor, Baron d'Eckstein, was a man of diverse background. He was born in Denmark of Jewish parents, educated in Germany at Lutheran universities, became a Catholic, and settled in Paris. A devoted royalist, he had accompanied Louis XVIII to Ghent in 1815. Although antirevolutionary, he stood by the Charter, which alienated him from most of the Ultra churchmen.[53]

For notoriety, impetuosity, and blatantly simple Ultraroyalism, no newspaper could compare with the quixotic *Drapeau Blanc*. It had retired in 1828 when Villèle stopped its subsidy for its independent stand against the Peyronnet press law, as well as for its embarrassingly revolutionary royalism. Polignac

---

[49] Hatin, *Histoire de la presse*, VIII, 487-88; Thureau-Dangin, *Royalistes*, p. 188-89.

[50] Charles de Mazade, "Un royaliste parlementaire, Berryer", *Revue des deux mondes*, XXXIV (Paris, 1879), 106-11.

[51] de Hauranne, *Histoire*, IX, 483.

[52] Félicité Robert de Lammenais was ordained in 1817. Although a leading critic of Gallicanism, he was a political radical and envisioned a stateless utopian Christian democracy with humanitarian goals. Censured for his unorthodox ideals, he became an agnostic, and, on his deathbed in 1854, he rejected the sacraments.

[53] Carné, "Souvenirs". pp. 215-17.

reinstated its support in July, 1829, but its circulation had fallen by that time from an 1824 figure of 1900 to a mere 622. During its heyday in 1819, when it had had little competition in the Ultra press, it had reached four thousand.

The little *Drapeau Blanc* was frequently the butt of ridicule by the Left and occasionally its frenzied editorials brought rebukes from the *Gazette* or even the *Quotidienne*. Despite a belligerent pose and an unrelieved extremism, this paper actually represented the views of many of the bitterest and most unforgiving Ultras. Many agreed with it, but felt more respectable reading the *Quotidienne*. Its editor regarded Villèle as both a scoundrel and a temporizer, while Martignac was no less than a revolutionary Jacobin. Only Polignac, who arranged for the paper's reinstatement, was satisfactory, and even here, the Drapeau's editor departed on the issues of clericalism, where he more resembled Michaud.

What kind of man was this mad knight-errant of Ultra journalism? Alphonse Dieudonné de Martainville, in 1828, was only fifty, but was silverhaired and aged well past his years from the exhaustion of youthful pleasures and lost crusades.[54] Under the Directory, he had edited a small Thermidorian satirical paper, the *Journal de Rieurs*[55] and had acted on the stage and written and produced plays.[56] He thus combined drama with journalism, a fusion of modest talents which remained with him to his death. During the Empire, he became disillusioned with the Revolution's results and turned to bohemian drinking clubs and a life of blissful indolence. With the Restoration of the Bourbons, Martainville reawakened to politics as an obdurate royalist. He also revived his interest in the theatre and became one of those Paris fanatics who attended controversial plays in order to partake of the lively comedies that sometimes sprang from the audience, leaving the actors to flee the stage. In 1819, after a performance of *Germanicus*, the son of a rival critic shot him in the leg. Three years later, he was pelted by other spectators for some injudicious remarks on the use of English by players at a premier performance of *Othello*![57]

The *Drapeau* was born in the political climate of reaction after Louis XVIII's moderation began to fail and it became more popular after the duc de Berri's murder. Anti-Villèle Ultras later found it reflected their views and made the

---

[54] Joseph Michaud, ed., *Biographie universelle des français* (44 vols.; Paris, 1854), under alphabetical heading.

[55] *Gazette des Tribunaux*, 5 March, 1830.

[56] Hatin, *Histoire de la presse*, VIII, 492. For circulation figures, see also, Irene Collins, *The Government and the Newspaper Press in France, 1814-1881* (London: Oxford University Press, 1959), p. 27. (Hereafter cited as Collins, *Newspaper Press*.)

[57] Pierre Jacomet, *Le Palais sous la Restauration* (Paris, 1922), pp. 278-79. (Hereafter cited as Jacomet, *Le Palais*.)

paper the first command post of the "defection" against Villèle. Some talented clericals, including O'Mahony and Saint-Victor, spoke for the *Congrégation*, while the anticlerical comte de Montlosier and the utopian Catholic Lammenais exposed quite different attitudes on Christianity.[58] But if the religious policy was somewhat eclectic, the *Drapeau's* politics were pure and simple. When it was re-created by Polignac, it became more the personal outpouring of its editor, assisted by another writer named Henrion. The paper's masthead displayed a Bourbon flag in the hands of a mustachioed hussar, and the motto: "Vive le Roi! quand même". Long live the King! No matter what happens. On the tenth anniversary of the duc de Berri's murder, the *Drapeau* carried a heavy black border.

The split in the royalist party caused by distrust of Villèle was deeply woven into the affairs of the press. The *Gazette*, as has been noted, was the only strong Villèlist newspaper and one reason for this minister's failure to achieve a "good press" was his exploitative approach toward even sympathetic newspapers.

It was customary for the government to give large subsidies to journals which supported it. These donations were not considered as bribes and were accepted by editors without scruple as long as their support was helpful. When the *Débats*, for example, turned against Villèle in 1824, it immediately lost its subsidy of twelve thousand francs a month.[59]

Villèle, seeing that his dole was failing to insure the subservience of all of the royalist press, resorted to a more naked policy which was euphemistically called *amortissement*. He offered to buy up, or "liquidate", entire newspapers. This was typical of the Minister's cynical approach to Ultra sentiments. Although Thureau-Dangin claims that Villèle disapproved of the wasteful economies of this policy, he continued to apply it. His negotiators were the Minister Corbière and the comte Sosthènes de la Rochefoucauld, a personal confidant of Charles X. Indeed, the King was more than a bijstander in this dealing, as some of the money came from the civil list. Several papers were bought outright. The original *Journal de Paris*, the *Oriflamme*, the *Foudre*, and, of course, the *Gazette* fell directly into the hands of the government. Jacques Coste, as has been noted, liquidated his literate *Tablettes* for a substantial sum and although the *Drapeau Blanc* was also bought, it persisted gracelessly to oppose its paymaster until he abandoned it to die in 1827.[60]

---

[58] Hatin, *Histoire de la presse*, VIII, 492.

[59] Alfred Nettement, *Histoire de la Restauration* (8 vols.; Paris, 1872), VIII, 5. (Hereafter cited as Nettement, *Histoire*.)

[60] Germain, *Martyrologie*, p. 86.

Chateaubriand in the *Débats* harangued against the *amortissement* and against any editors who succumbed to its allure. This was, to be sure, mild hypocrisy on the part of the aging author of *René*. He had been perfectly contented with the huge subsidies which had rewarded his royalism, but he was now outraged by the attempt of his archenemy to absorb journalism.[61]

The *Débats* found a curious ally in the *Quotidienne's* Michaud, who being above all else an intellectually honest man, defended Chateaubriand's attitude and contemptuously refused Villèle's agents when they tried to purchase control of his paper. He was said to have told the First Minister: "Monseigneur, there is only one thing for which I could be tempted to sell the *Quotidienne*: That would be a little health; if you would give me that, I would let myself be corrupted".[62]

The firing of Michaud from his position as censor in 1827 was further evidence of the growing rift among the royalist factions and their newspapers. On the eve of Villèle's fall, the Left opposition was thus unwillingly reinforced by the purely royalist opposition of a great number of the Ultras.

[61]   *Ibid.*
[62]   Hatin, *Histoire de la presse*, VIII, 491.

CHAPTER III

POLITICAL JOURNALISM IN THE FALL OF THE VILLÈLE MINISTRY, 1827-1828: A PREVIEW OF REVOLUTION

Journalism was an important element in the destruction of the comte de de Villèle's six-year reign of reaction. Animosity to this regime was not confined to the liberal press alone, but was shared by the *Quotidienne* and the *Journal des Débats*. In 1827, Villèle was served by only two major papers, the *Gazette de France* and the official *Moniteur*. Although it was the combined attack of liberal and royalist "defection" papers which helped crush the Ministry, the *Débats* probably exercised a greater influence in the victory than any other paper.

The political power of the *Journal des Débats* was at its peak in the period of Villèle's defeat. The Bertins and Chateaubriand stood in basic ideological conflict with Villèle's policies and certainly this was the primary cause of their hatred of Villèle. But it was Chateaubriand's personal pique against Villèle which provided the constant catalyst to their feud. The consuming desire of this great writer and journalist was to be renamed Foreign Minister over Villèle's objections, and so to avenge his earlier dismissal of 1824. We can but imagine what a different influence might have come from the pen of this master egotist had Villèle and the King rewarded his ambition.

The deputies, like the journalists, had formed a misalliance of anti-Villèle Ultras and liberals, which, together with the Center faction, became a strong majority against the Ministry. The force of both press and Chambers left the stubborn Charles X with few legal weapons. On November 4, 1827, he dissolved the Chamber of Deputies, and for good measure, "packed" the hereditary body by creating over seventy peers.[1]

Automatically, under the law, the edict of dissolution released the press from censorship, enabling Villèle's foes to intensify their campaign against

---

[1] *Le Moniteur*, 4 November, 1827. As a political concession, Louis XVIII had retained Napoleon's peers and had rewarded many civil servants and prominent persons with peerage, giving that Chamber a mixed political nature. By selecting a great number of new peers, Charles X was attempting to give the peerage an Ultra direction.

him.[2] New elections were scheduled for the middle of November and many of the editorials were addressed to the eighty thousand electors of France, eight thousand of whom lived in the city of Paris.

The *Débats*, the *Constitutionnel*, the *Commerce*, and the *Courrier*, engaged in spirited propaganda. Bertin, of the *Débats* gave money and influence to assist the electoral organization *Aide-toi*, already staffed by a mixture of republicans and liberal journalists.

On November 7, the *Constitutionnel* warned that the suppression of the popular will creates revolutions. "Revolutions"! cried the *Constitutionnel*, "That is what everyone wants to avoid today! Well! It is a matter of preventing them; the electors have the means if they so desire". With an anglophile allusion to the peaceful progress of English liberalism, the French editor then asked the pregnant question: "Are we as enlightened as the English under George IV, or the English under James II! We will prove this with our votes". The *Constitutionnel* was thus on record, in 1827, for posing the idea of dynastic change. But the Cabinet had grown accustomed to the *Constitutionnel's* tirades against Villèle and ministers were not shocked when Jay wrote in this paper that Villèle's press laws were "less just than in the despotisms of Spain and Turkey".[3] The Villèlists were deeply disturbed, however, by the invective of the professionally royalist *Débats*. The King of France wrote to his Minister: "The *Débats* is so atrocious, everyone is revolted. I do not believe Chateaubriand".[4] The old King hoped that the recent French-led naval victory over the Turks at Navarino (October 20, 1827) would help Villèle's cause in the coming elections.[5] In the *Gazette*, Villèle's faithful Genoude urged the electors in the rural colleges not to vote the "democratic", or city way[6] and he honored the influence of the opposition press by calling the political battle a *guerre des feuilles contre les portefeuilles*.[7] In spite of the Navarino sea fight, early voting returns showed a sweeping victory for

---

[2] This was under the Law of 26 July, 1821. In 1827, a royal edict established preliminary censorship by a crown-appointed board of royalists that included Bonald and several other intellectuals. But the earlier provision that censure be withdrawn when the session of the Chambers concluded limited the force of the edict and Charles' revenge for the defeat of Peyronnet's bill. Duvergier, *Colllection des lois*, XXVII, 195, 453.

[3] *Constitutionnel*, 5 November, 1827.

[4] Jean Baptiste Joseph, comte de Villèle, *Mémoires et correspondance du comte de Villèle*, V (5 vols.; Paris, 1890), 8 November, 1827, King to Villèle, 281. (Hereafter cited as Villèle, *Mémoires*.)

[5] *Ibid.*, 9 November, 1827, King to Villèle, p. 282. The Left was expected to applaud this victory as it helped to liberate the Greeks from Turkish oppression. The navy, but not Villèle, received the praise.

[6] *Gazette de France*, 21 November, 1827.

[7] *Ibid.*

opposition candidates. Of those Ultraroyalists who were elected, a large portion belonged to the "defection" which hated Villèle. The *feuilles* had done their work.

King Charles X, however, refused to let Villèle resign. Against all parliamentary custom, though not contrary to the vagueness of the Charter, a repudiated government ignored the voice of the electorate. The rural *grands colleges* had not reported, but even electoral frauds, in which Villèle's prefects were skilled, could not tip the balance in his favor. Villèle remained, and Paris seethed with unrest.

On the evening of the nineteenth of November, 1827, a gang of about two dozen young men, slightly drunk, gathered before the Minister Peyronnet's house and shouted *Vive la Charte!*[8] A few even cried *Vive l'empereur!*[9] Windows were smashed. As the disturbance continued, sixty mounted gendarmes with sabres drawn, rode into the neighborhood. Instead of seeking the actual source of trouble, these state military police arrested several hundred innocent persons who happened to be abroad that evening. From the Vendôme to the rue Saint-Denis, citizens were seized for questioning by the over-zealous police. In the rue Saint-Denis, because some of the crowd had resisted, the armed and mounted agents of Villèle sabred and trampled dozens of people. Shopkeepers and artisans of this region, armed with years of growing aversion to the government, rose in revolt. For the first time in the memory of most of them, barricades were erected in the streets. A spirit of panic spread across Paris as an unequal skirmish began between soldiers and citizens.

But revolt did not become revolution. The flame of rebellion was stamped out before the whole city could be kindled. Royal troops performed their task of slaughter and arrest thoroughly and a handful of martyrs died to support the arguments of the liberal press. The battle of the barricades lasted for two nights before all resistance was smashed. Paris had shown the possiblily, but not the probability, of revolution. Charles X called the recent elections "atrocities" and offered to "mount his horse" to help suppress the insurgents in the rue Saint-Denis.[10] Villèle passed off the affair as a "disorder" and refused to see a deputation of Constant, baron de Schonen, and Jacques Laffitte who urged him to reestablish the National Guard.[11] The *Gazette* blamed the "disorders" in the rue Saint-Denis on the "re-

---

[8] *Constitutionnel*, 21 November, 1827.

[9] *Journal des Débats*, 21 November, 1827.

[10] Villèle, *Mémoires*, 20 November, 1827, King to Villèle, p. 283.

[11] *Ibid.*, pp. 283-87. The National Guard had been dissolved by the King for demonstrating against the Ministry and the Royal Family. See *supra*, chapter i.

volutionary journals". Genoude pardoned the attack by the gendarmerie on the grounds that the troops were trying to protect "a peaceful citizen under attack by jailbirds". Editor Genoude used the lesson of rue Saint-Denis to show his voting readers "the blessings of radicalism". The *Gazette* went so far as to call the insurrection a celebration by the "Revolution" to honor its election triumph.[12] Genoude had an element of truth here. Mob violence did not begin until hooligans had broken some windows in houses not "illuminated" to celebrate the election results.

The opposition was clearly uneasy about the "November barricades". Editors of that party welcomed the propaganda value of the skirmish, but gave evidence that they were not prepared for full-scale revolt. The *Courrier*, often sensational, was less cautious than the others; it reported a startling rumor that Swiss regiments had been dispatched to "quell Lyon".[13] The *Constitutionnel* was filled with personal half-spurious accounts of bravery and atrocity, of bayonets and grapeshot against women and children. Jay's editorial declared that it had become a French custom to "sabre people who merely gather in the streets".[14] The electors were urged to repudiate a "murderous" Ministry which had pushed France, as Jay hinted ominously, to the "last excess of desperation".[15] The *Débats* sounded very much like the *Constitutionnel* and spared its readers none of the tearful and tragic incidents which are always part of civil strife.[16] Bertin was still editiorializing on the "massacre" three months later.[17]

The barricades had proved dramatically that Villèle's continuance would be impractical. A barrage of political intrigues exploded in Paris. For seven years, under two kings, one faction had held power; now, with the anticipated resignation of this power, all factions and politicians looked to their own ambitions. One of the most revealing intrigues played that December was, like the barricades, an omen of the July Revolution of 1830. Cauchois-Lemaire, the respected senior editor and stockholder of the *Constitutionnel*, published a pamphlet under the title: *Sur la crise actuelle, lettre a S.A.R. le duc d'Orléans...* Its sixty-nine pages were filled with an unrestrained attack against the whole Restoration and especially the Villèle administration and the massacres in the rue Saint-Denis. The entire brochure was addressed to the wealthy scion of France's second dynasty: Louis-Philippe, Duke of Orleans.

[12] *Gazette de France*, 21 November, 1827.
[13] *Courrier Français*, 20 November, 1827.
[14] *Constitutionnel*, 21 November, 1827.
[15] *Ibid.*
[16] *Journal des Débats*, 21 November, 1827.
[17] *Ibid.*, 9 March, 1828.

The concluding paragraph left no doubt of Cauchois-Lemaire's purpose:

As we grow older, the duc de Bordeaux, the duc de Chartres, and even the duc de Reichstadt are growing up. There could be the elements of a triple alliance of which one must hope its articles would not be drafted by the Jesuits. This would be admirable. I know that time brings events to pass; but it also brings forth individuals. I know that the tree finally bears its fruit; but this fruit could be more or less premature depending on the season, the soil, and the gardener. Wait, *monseigneur*, this ends with one last parable: I compare the principle, that germ of liberty living in you, developing in chains, which a happy influence will sooner or later break. I compare it to a chrysalis from which the captive will some day fly, lively and brilliant. But when will this day come? That depends on circumstances that place the chrysalis nearer or farther from the action of the sun. Thus liberty awaits the day which should let it hatch from its transient prison. And we who tire of a long wait, we call with all our voices on a favorable star to hasten it.[18]

The *Globe* and the *Débats* considered the pamphlet in bad taste, not only for its mixed metaphors, and they offered neither apology nor sympathy for Cauchois-Lemaire. General Lafayette termed the work unfortunate and tried to excuse it as a joke.[19] The *Constitutionnel*, the *Courrier*, and the Duke himself, made no comments on the incendiary writing. There is no evidence that Thiers, Laffitte, or any of the Orleanists of 1830, were direct participants in the Lemaire proposal.

Cauchois-Lemaire was arraigned and brought to trial, along with the two publishers of the brochure, on January 12, 1828. Attorneys for his defense, unable to deny the writer's intent, argued lamely that, in England, the Prince of Wales frequently led the parliamentary opposition. On January 17, the lower court rendered its decision: That Cauchois-Lemaire had attempted "to provoke the duc d'Orléans to place himself at the head of the opposition"; that the "entire work tends to provoke a change in government and the order of succession to the throne". But since the guilty provocations of the defendant were followed by no tangible effects, said the court, the maximum penalty would not be ordered. Cauchois-Lemaire was sentenced to fifteen months in La Force prison and a fine of two thousand francs.[20] The publishers, Ponthieu and Schubart, each received sentences of three months and fines of five hundred francs. The *Globe*, whose doctrinaire spirit was

---

[18] Louis-François Cauchois-Lemaire, *Sur la crise actuelle, lettre à S.A.R. le duc d'Orléans…* (Paris, December, 1827), Ledru-Rollin Collection, University of California, Berkeley, 217:10, pp. 68-69. The three names are those of the princely heirs of the Bourbon, Orleans, and Bonaparte families. See p. 161 for duc de Bordeaux (comte de Chambord).

[19] De Hauranne, *Histoire*, IX, 382-83; see also, Paul Thureau-Dangin, *Le parti libéral sous la Restauration* (Paris, 1876), p. 432. (Hereafter cited as Thureau-Dangin, *Parti libéral*.)

[20] *Gazette des Tribunaux*, 18 January, 1828.

offended by the illegal pamphlet, grimly supported the action of the court.[21] The pamphlet had failed as a political "kite"; not for the reason that it was stupidly conceived, but because it was launched into so many contrary winds.

These winds were currents of intrigue in which Ultras sought to shape the Cabinet as an all-royalist coalition and in which the Left tried to fuse with the Center. In one case, a minor official named Jean-Baptiste Flandin tried singlehandedly to form a Cabinet of liberals and constitutional monarchists under Villèle! Flandin vexed Villèle with numerous letters and unannounced visits to his home. Even the banker Laffitte became interested in this solo intrigue, but withdrew his support when he realized that Villèle was merely being polite to an eccentric.[22] Villèle still clung to the forlorn hope that he could lead an Ultraroyalist coalition and it was this idea which motivated him until his retirement in 1830.

Bertin, editor of the *Débats*, who had been so effective in defeating Villèlism in the elections, now threatened to upset any new Ministry which did not include his colleague, Chateaubriand. He demanded the Prime Minister's resignation. The Dauphin also urged him to resign and asked the constitutionalist Minister, Chabrol, to then invite Chateaubriand into the council. Vitrolles, a Villèle stalwart, hastened to tell Chabrol that Chateaubriand had "lost all influence with the royalists".[23] The King, however, had already come to fear and dislike Chateaubriand and would not listen to the pleas of the author's friends.[24] Other intrigues and ambitions promoted statesmen of the Ultra "defection", as well as of the liberal group. Each of these factions had helped to break Villèle's power and felt entitled to the spoils of political triumph.[25] The "defection" was enlarging as the refuge of dissident Ultras who had been the tools of Villèle's ruthless rise to power or those who opposed either his clericalism or his methods. This faction, strong in the Chamber, assured Villèle that he would never find its members at his council table.

Villèle next turned to the Left and the Center. In the Center he found a rising politician – ambitious, gifted, a born moderator, and a product of the Girondin-inspired legal oratory of the Bordelais bar. This was the vicomte Jean-Baptiste Gaye de Martignac, an effeminately handsome deputy from

---

[21] *Globe*, 18 January, 1828. The firm of Ponthieu was the Paris agency for Baron Cotta's German publishing empire. It seems doubtful that Thiers or his colleagues could have been unaware of the pamphlet before it appeared in the bookstalls.

Jean-Baptiste Flandin, *Revelations sur la fin du ministère de M. le cte. de Villèle* ... (Paris, 1829), p. 180

[23] Loménie, *Chateaubriand*, II, 257.

[24] Villèle, *Mémoires*, 11 January, 1828, King to Villèle, p. 315.

[25] Daudet, *Martignac*, pp. 62-63.

Bordeaux who was regarded as the most persuasive speaker of the Chamber. But Martignac refused to serve with Villèle, declaring that the old Cabinet could not endure for two more weeks.[26] Villèle at last offered to resign and even the King acquiesced and "ordered" him to disband the Cabinet. Martignac accepted the Interior Ministry and a new Cabinet was quickly formed which included men of varied political views.[27] On January 4, 1828, the roster was completed, but the King designated no president for the council. Martignac held the Interior post which gave him control of all prefects and police.

Chateaubriand was passed over for La Ferronays, the ambassador to Russia, for Foreign Affairs. An *émigré* companion of the King, he was summoned from St. Petersburg to balance the known moderation of Martignac. Actually La Ferronays proved to be a moderate himself, though devoted to the King. The comte de Chabrol was retained at the Navy post. Comte Roy was placed at the head of Finances where his influence with European bankers would be convenient. Two relative unknowns, de Caux and Saint-Cricq, accepted the portfolios of the Ministry of War and a newly created Ministry of Commerce. The comte de Portalis, a liberal monarchist, was named to the Department of Justice and a churchman, Mgr. Frayssinous, was kept at the position of Minister of Ecclesiastical Affairs.[28] Frayssinous, the titular bishop of Hermopolis, was a Gallican moderate from whom little was expected, as he naively hoped to reconcile the fanatics of the church with its liberals.

It was not a spectacular list of ministers. The mean political orientation of the new Cabinet was a trifle to the right of Center, but there were no Ultras. The former Director of Police, Franchet d'Esperey, lost his post and the unpopular Prefect of the Paris police, Guy Delavau, resigned to become an honorary member of the Council of State. Both of these policemen were extreme clerical Ultras. Delavau was replaced by Louis-Marie de Belleyme, a man more acceptable to the Left and who actually used his position energetically on behalf of the growing masses of Parisian poor and unemployed.[29]

The new Cabinet, because it represented it no special party, inherited no newspaper in which to defend its policies. The official *Moniteur*, by a long tradition, was not customarily employed for editorial purposes. Those factions which had recourse to the press, reacted variously to the advent of the

[26] *Ibid.*, p. 69.
[27] *Ibid.*, p. 76.
[28] *Le Moniteur*, 5 January, 1828.
[29] De Hauranne, *Histoire*, p. 381.

Martignac Cabinet. Of these reactions, perhaps the most significant was that of the *Journal des Débats*.[30]

From any logical judgment, one would assume that Martignac would be warmly supported by the *Débats*, his new council being the most constitutionally royalist of the entire Restoration. The *Débats* was the most constitutionally royalist of all the newspapers. But there was one discordant note to spoil this harmony: Chateaubriand had been beaten in his well-publicized attempt to lead a new Cabinet. The wounds to his great pride were visible in the pages of the *Débats*.[31] Martignac was a mere understudy; Chateaubriand the star.

Chateaubriand scorned the small favors offered by the new regime. He wanted only the post of Foreign Affairs and the dominant voice in the council. Martignac pleaded with Charles X to accept Chateaubriand, saying that his journalistic and political cooperation was essential. The King refused flatly, even stating that he would prefer Royer-Collard! When the Ministry of Public Instruction was later separated from that of cults, Bishop Frayssinous offered the position to Chateaubriand. But the writer had been so stung by the King's insults that he refused this portfolio, saying he would only accept the Ministry of Foreign Affairs.[32] In a further show of arrogance by the directors of the *Débats*, Bertin *aîné* personally threatened to the King: "The Ministry must behave well with me; if not I could easily break it like I did the other".[33]

The King offered at last to again subsidize the *Débats* if it would only back Martignac. According to Charles X, Bertin demanded full indemnification for the years under Villèle when the twelve thousand franc monthly subsidy was in abeyance! The King agreed to pay this outrageous price which amounted to a half-million francs, much of which came from the privy purse,[34] and he lamented that it was a sorry thing when journalists could drive harder bargains with kings than foreign powers. A Cabinet minister later refuted part of the King's complaint by defending Bertin's "bargain" as the just fulfillment of a contract made by Villèle himself.[35] The entire story of the *Débats* subsidy gives evidence of something more significant than the vanity, greed, and ambition of Bertin and Chateaubriand. It demonstrates the political power of newspapers during the late Restoration;

---

[30] *Journal des Débats*, 4 January, 1828.
[31] *Ibid.*, 6 January, 1828.
[32] Daudet, *Martignac*, pp. 125-78.
[33] *Ibid.*, p. 131; see also, Lamartine, *Restoration*, IV, 349.
[34] Daudet, *Martignac*, p. 131.
[35] Lamartine, *Restoration*, pp. 349-50.

power enough to bribe a king. And in the end, the King's new ministers received little support from the *Débats* in exchange for the half-million.

Eight months later, the Chateaubriand ego found an outlet in diplomacy and an escape from the humiliation of defeat. He accepted the title of Ambassador to Rome after further ministerial intrigues in his behalf had finally all failed. During this interval, the old battle between the *Débats* and the *Gazette* became even more vindictive.

The Villèlist paper also continued to quarrel with Michaud, whose Ultra *Quotidienne* was the best forum of the "defection" against Villèle. Genoude branded the *Quotidienne* as a turncoat for its 1827 alliance with the Left,[36] while welcoming the January 4 Cabinet with cordial reserve. The new Ministry, wrote the *Gazette's* editor, "can offer its hand to all friends of the throne and will find supporting it all those who fight *with the former Ministry* for the royal prerogative". But he also called on royalists of all shades to chain up the "hydra of revolution" which the "unbraked license" of the press had strengthened.[37] For a paper that stood for a united royalist Right, the *Gazette* seemed perversely determined to isolate the Villèlist party. Within a few days, the cordial tone it used toward Martignac was dropped, probably because of a late *démarche* made by some of the new ministers to the King, on behalf of Chateaubriand. On January 17, Martignac published a brave legislative prospectus in the *Moniteur* pledging respect for the crown's loyalty to the Charter. Genoude answered this in his *Gazette*, "We can only applaud the resolutions it announces and the spirit that dictates them". Then he warned: "Doubtless it is worth much more to the new Ministry to seek power in the accord of all the friends of the throne and public welfare than to weaken the King's authority by dealing with factious journals".[38] From this time forward, at every liberal move by the Cabinet and every bid for glory by Chateaubriand, the *Gazette* became more pointed in its editorials.

Throughout the month between the advent of the new Ministry and the opening of the session of deputies the *Débats* continued to attack the Villèlists and damn the Martignac Cabinet with faint praise. Bertin frequently alluded to the existence of *two* ministries, one open and rather ineffectual, and one occult – the "secret" cabinet of Villèle.[39] Rumors abounded in Paris about this shadowy government. A hidden staircase was said to lead to the King's

---

[36] *Gazette de France*, 18 January, 1828.
[37] *Ibid.*, 4, 12 January, 1828. (Italics added.)
[38] *Ibid.*, 18 January, 1828.
[39] *Journal des Débats*, 2 February, 1828.

private apartment where the secret cabinet meetings were held.[40] Villèle himself later substantiated this report.[41]

Liberal journalists, led by the *Constitutionnel* and the *Courrier* showed little confidence in Martignac. Jay wrote in the former paper: "All we can say at the moment is that the new Ministry does not seem to be composed of coherent enough elements to guarantee a long existence. We fear the cement may be poor..."[42] But if the weakness of the Cabinet should tempt Villèle, warned the *Constitutionnel*, he should realize that his "political role is finished" and that public reprobation had been "branded on his forehead in letters of fire".[43] The *Courrier* spoke of a pragmatic coalition of "defection" Ultras and moderates[44] while the *Journal du Commerce* declared that Chateaubriand would never enter a cabinet that did not include Royer-Collard and that the latter would demand the inclusion of the duc de Broglie.[45] The *Gazette* seized upon these speculations as evidence of the insatiability of the opposition. Genoude satirized the list of political dependencies, begun by the *Commerce*, to finally include Lafayette and de Pradt, each name more inimical to the King's taste as the list increased.[46]

The Ultra "defection" party, led by the ambitious comte de La Bourdonnaye, was pleased by the overthrow of Villèle, but cool to the man who replaced him. This faction's paper, the *Quotidienne*, questioned the power and authority, as well as the royalist purity of the new Ministry, but conceded that it would be "necessary to wait".[47] Politicians expected Martignac to fall soon after the debates began in the old Palais-Bourbon.

But Martignac remained, a symbol of unasked conciliation between the impatience of the liberals and the frustration of the Ultras. He was still an unknown quantity. Each of the opposing factions hoped to break the political equilibrium to which he was dedicated.

---

[40] Daudet, *Martignac*, pp. 140-41.
[41] Villèle, *Mémoires*, p. 424.
[42] *Constitutionnel*, 16 January, 1828
[43] *Ibid.*
[44] *Courrier Français*, 16 January, 1828.
[45] *Journal du Commerce*, 17 January, 1828.
[46] *Gazette de France*, 18 January, 1828.
[47] *Quotidienne*, 7 January, 1828.

CHAPTER IV

POLITICAL JOURNALISM AND THE MARTIGNAC
MINISTRY: THE FAILURE OF
CONCILIATION, 1828-1829

A frequent phenomenon of French politics has been the failure of the coalition government to achieve a successful program. Extremes of Left and Right may become so strong that they can lever the Center to the breaking point. It happened in 1948, in the infancy of the Fourth Republic; in 1934, in the senility of the Third Republic; and in 1828, near the end of the Restoration. The reason for this failure of the Center is usually found in the zeal and intransigeance of the two extremes, or in their desire to cultivate, rather than retard, the conditions leading to a confrontation.

Martignac began his Ministry with the moderate support of the established factions of Left and very little from either bloc of the Right. Increasing credibility to stories of an "occult" cabinet demonstrated how little confidence the King had in his new Minister's success. Yet Martignac held out for a year and a half. His legislative program was rammed through an opposition that branded him both "revolutionary" and "Ultra". He received no gratitude for his attempt to reconcile monarchy with liberty; to save the Charter and the Restoration. He was made the scapegoat for failings of the King, whom he patiently tried to reform into a constitutional ruler. His Ministry was able to survive two sessions of the deputies, not because it was popular, but because it served as a convenient stopgap to allow the factions to prepare for battle.

The Chambers were convoked on February 5, 1828, with the traditional speech from the throne. Charles X, in an address prepared by his ministers, recited the foreign and domestic events of the previous year. His discourse ended with a request to "work with wisdom and maturity to put our legislation in harmony with the Charter".[1] For these few minitues, at least, Charles X appeared every inch a constitutional king. Except for a reference to cordial relations between France and the King of Portugal, the opposition press

---

[1] *Le Moniteur*, 6 February, 1828.

could find little to criticize. Even the slighted directors of the *Débats* pronounced in favor of the speech and the *Constitutionnel* called it the result of a "fine movement to unite all men of good will around the ballot-box ...", and expressed the hope that what it termed *Villèlism* would never be found in the new Cabinet.[2]

The next day, the *Quotidienne* warned the King of the danger of a republic and the *Gazette* offered its warning against "concessions". Charles' speech from the throne made it quite clear that the Ministry would seek its strength on the Left, despite the lack of overwhelming encouragement from that side. The Monarch, who occasionally read something outside of the *Gazette*, wrote to the vacationing Villèle: "I see nothing but trouble so far in my ministers". He defended his nomination of Lefebvre de Vatimesnil[3] to the Ministry of Public Instruction as a good choice, "because the papers cry loudly against him". Looking back on his speech of the previous day, Charles seemed ashamed of his words. "I have just read the papers", he wrote, "and the eulogies of the *Journal des Débats* and the *Constitutionnel* make me feel I have said foolish things. I hope not, however, and I shall continue to firmly resist whatever could lead to dangerous concessions".[4] The King wrote to Villèle nearly every day during these weeks, so great was his reliance on the former Minister.

In the new Chamber, the Left opposition aided by the "defection", succeeded in electing the able liberal statesman, Royer-Collard, to the office of President. The *Gazette* and the *Quotidienne* considered the King's approval of this election as "encouragement" to the Left,[5] but the opposition viewed it as homage to public opinion. The *Débats* seemed especially pleased with the first steps of the infant Martignac regime. As the committee for the address to the King began to draft their response to the Royal speech, the *Débats* intensified its attack on Villèle. The ex-Minister must have felt these blows, for he wrote to his son:

> I do not know in truth were we will go with the deplorable direction given by the press to the opinion [Left]. The royalists are fools; the liberals profit with a skillful cunning... I suffer cruelly for all that which the King should suffer.[6]

---

[2] *Constitutionnel*, 5, 6 February, 1828.

[3] Vatimesnil accepted the portfolio which Chateaubriand had scorned. Though the Left chose to regard him as a clerical Ultra, he proved to be a moderate.

[4] Villèle, *Mémoires*, 6 February, 1828, King to Villèle, pp. 322-23.

[5] *Gazette de France*, 8 February, 1828. The balloting revealed that the "defection" Ultras and the legitimists voted with the Left to reject the Villèlist candidates.

[6] Villèle, *Mémoires*, 29 February, 1828, p. 324.

Chateaubriand's newspaper, on March 1, called on the Chamber to formally accuse Villèle for the sins of his six-year administration, but Villèle declared from the sidelines that this was simply a maneuver by the *Débats* to "frighten the King" and cause disorder in the Chambers.[7]

A change occurred in the new Cabinet as a result of the mounting attack on the former administration. The two members of Villèle's Ministry, Chabrol and Bishop Frayssinous, resigned. They had previously urged the King to "neutralize" Chateaubriand by satisfying his ministerial ambition.[8] Charles now acted upon this suggestion and offered the vacated Navy post to the illustrious journalist. Like the portfolio of Public Instruction, that of Marine was not grand enough for the troublesome Chateaubriand and he refused it.[9] The empty Ecclesiastical post was filled by the Gallican bishop of Beauvais, Mgr. François-Jean Feutrier, a member of Martignac's faction. A moderate, it was to be his misfortune to become the prosecutor of anticlerical legislation for which the Ultra clergy never forgave him. A friend of Chateaubriand, Hyde de Neuville became the new Navy Minister.[10] Having been the French ambassador to Washington and imbued with the liberal spirit, his nomination was correctly regarded by the Right as a concession to the still dangerous editor of the *Débats*.

The first important business of the new Chamber was the preparation of the traditional address in response to the King's speech of February 5. The political tone of this message, which was intrinsically a mere formality, could indicate the strength and direction of the parliamentary opposition.

The first draft, prepared by a liberal committee of the majority, was submitted for debate on the fourth of March and arguments over its text lasted five days. At issue was the last paragraph, which clearly condemned the previous Ministry: "The will of France asks of the depositories of your power only the reality of your benefits. Its complaints only accuse the *deplorable system* which renders them too often illusory".[11] In the face of a fierce royalist attack, the opposition, numerically superior since the November elections and helped by "defection" Ultras, held its ground. The address censuring Villèle was voted and formally read before the throne by a committee of deputies. Charles X, according to custom, read a short reply whose only

---

[7] Quoted from Villèle's unedited political papers in Nettement, *Histoire*, VIII, 36.

[8] Villèle, *Mémoires*, 11 January, 1828, King to Villèle, p. 315.

[9] Nettement, *Histoire*, p. 38.

[10] *Le Moniteur*, 5 March, 1828. The *Gazette*, 6 March, 1828, called this appointment an open door for Chateaubriand.

[11] *Journal des Débats*, 9 March, 1828.

force was in these words: "You will not forget, I am sure, that you are the natural guardians of the majesty of the throne ..." [12]

The mildness of the royal reply was Villèle's cue to leave the stage, at least temporarily. The "deplorable" Minister was angry with the King, as well as the 198 deputies who voted the address which he in turn called "detestable".[13] His loyal *Gazette* asserted that there was nothing astonishing in the designation of "deplorable" from men who have had "more than one occasion" to deplore a system "contrary to their faction".[14]

Chateaubriand's powerful journal was jubilant in victory. Bertin declared that the address was the triumph of constitutionalism:

> *Peuple* under the old regime, oppressors and oppressed during our horrible Revolution, slaves under the *brilliant tyranny* of Bonaparte; the Charter of Louis XVIII has made citizens of us ... It is thus that after twelve years experience, and in spite of the absurd systems and the dark tyranny of the last Ministry, France is at last represented.[15]

Liberal writers of the *Constitutionnel* and *Courrier* praised the 198 supporters of the "deplorable" address and the *Courrier* now assisted the *Débats* in promoting the cause of Chateaubriand.[16] This harmonious state of affairs in the opposition was also reflected in a letter from Chateaubriand to Dubois, of the *Globe*. The vicomte congratulated Dubois for a recent *Globe* editorial which had claimed to draw "no analogy", but which expressed admiration for English parliamentarians of 1643! The *Gazette* seized this as evidence of guilt by association and declared its archenemy was now plain "monsieur Chateaubriand", having left his nobility in the old *Conservateur*.[17] One of Genoude's favorite pastimes was to compare the Chateaubriand of the early Restoration with the Chateaubriand of the present. The *Débats-Gazette* feud was an enduring conflict, but the deputies' address intensified it. On March 24, the *Gazette* ridiculed Chateaubriand as the poet of "old monarchies and young republics"; as one who planned to crush simultaneously "monarchy and impiety ... royalism and revolution" and to bring in the "age of gold of journalism". Genoude also drew attention to Chateaubriand's authorship of both the *Génie du Christianisme* and articles for *Aide-toi*.

The "defection" group of Ultraroyalists, still hostile to Villèle, grew more

---

[12] *Ibid.*
[13] Villèle, *Mémoires*, 10 March, 1828, to his son, p. 326.
[14] *Gazette*, 9 March, 1828.
[15] *Journal des Débats*, 9 March, 1828. [Italics added.]
[16] *Courrier Français*, 9 March, 1828.
[17] *Gazette de France*, 9 March, 1828.

displeased with Martignac. The day after the address, the *Quotidienne* declared that "deplorable" was a just term for Villèle's Ministry of "fusion", which, it said, had been incompatible with the demands of the Left and the "just susceptibilities" of the Right. Here was the journal of the super-Ultras. To its editors, Villèle was guilty, not of a dark tyranny, but of compromise! The *Quotidienne* also advised the Martignac Cabinet: "Whoever would try to unite a fraction of the party of the crown with that of democracy... will assuredly enter a *deplorable* system". Forced to fight on two fronts, Michaud felt compromised, and rather than pursue the dilemma of either defending Villèle or branding the King's official choice "deplorable", he took a leave of absence. He called as his successor, Pierre Sebastien Laurentie, who also despised Villèle. Another vindication of Villèle's opposition, including that of Chateaubriand, occurred on April 2. The high court of Paris ordered all insurgents who had been captured during the November riots to be set free and exonerated. Charges of criminality, brought by liberals, were then dismissed against the policemen Franchet and Delavau for lack of "criminal intent" in attacking the barricades. Details of the evidence resulting in this decision, however, were extremely unfavorable to Villèle. The *Débats* crowed happily: "The decision absolves, but the exposure condemns".[18]

In April, the Left was itself embarrassed by an act of petulance on the part of one of its leading politicians and journalists. Abbé de Pradt, the gadfly of the *Courrier*, resigned his seat in the Chamber of Deputies, offended by his lack of political advancement in that body. In a letter to the *Courrier*,[19] he announced his dissatisfaction with the session of 1828, stating that this Chamber should be to the Restoration what the Constituent was to the old regime, and went on to assert that the four greatest epochs in history were the English Revolution, the French Revolution, the American Revolution – and the Reformation. For this, the *Gazette* denounced him as a traitor to his priesthood[20] but the *Quotidienne* only found de Pradt slightly ridiculous.[21] Antoine Jay, of the *Constitutionnel*, signed an article which treated de Pradt's resignation as a case of sour grapes and defended the Left from the Abbot's most unfortunate reference to the Constituent assembly. "We are all constitutional royalists", protested Jay.[22] The editors of the *Globe*, who considered de Pradt an insufferable demagogue, published a rare *ad hominem* attack

---

[18] *Journal des Débats*, 3 April, 1828.
[19] *Courrier Français*, 18 April, 1828.
[20] *Gazette de France*, 18 April, 1828.
[21] *Quotidienne*, 18 April, 1828.
[22] *Constitutionnel*, 18 April, 1828.

against him.[23] The opposition's loss of this doubtful combatant was soon compensated with the results of bye-elections which sent a majority of liberals to the Chamber of Deputies.

Martignac had pinned his hopes on the Left, braved the possible ire of the King, and alienated most of the Right. But the Left felt no obligation to this minister of conciliation and waited for his stand on important legislative issues.

On March 25, the Interior Minister laid before the Chamber a proposal for a new electoral law. The need for this had been glaringly obvious in the November elections, during which all manner of fraud and illegality was practiced. The Martignac bill prescribed the inviolability of the electoral lists. Only one revision per year would be allowed in order to add or subtract names on the basis of eligibility. With each elector's name was to be written his *arrondissement* and the communes in which he paid his taxes. The amount of this tax could thus be checked from public records. Most importantly, the law accorded the right of intervention to third parties in questions of eligibility.

The deputies began debate on this reform project on April 28. Martignac's brilliant oratory defended the bill from each attack by the Right. Only a few members of the extreme Left, led by Lafayette, opposed the law for its lack of penalties and they were seconded by Étienne in the *Constitutionnel*. The Right demanded the bill include provisions against the *Aide-toi le Ciel t'aidera* society, which, the Ultras declared, was a dangerously anarchic influence. Debates in the hereditary Chamber lasted throughout May; Ultra and liberal peers repeating the arguments of the lower house. The law was finally passed with only the Villèlists voting solidly against it.[24] The opposition press, from the *Courrier* to the *Débats*, wrote favorably of the new legislation. Martignac still stood on solid ground. He could perhaps succeed if he kept the Left and at least some of the dissident Ultras as the electoral bill had been directed mainly against the Villèle faction.

The next important legislation, the press law of 1828, was an attempt by Martignac to reconcile intransigent factions on a purely ideological basis and would be a more realistic trial of the new Cabinet. Liberal newspapers, which began by backing the proposal, became more hostile to it as the debates progressed. Although this bill passed the Chambers, it satisfied only part of the Left and not any on the Right and it was amended beyond recognition. With the voting of this measure, the political isolation of the compromising

---

[23] *Globe*, 18 April, 1828.
[24] *Le Moniteur*, 30, 31 May, 1828.

Bordelais Minister began. Aside from the political significance in the press bill of 1828 one may find in the parliamentary debates over this project further proof of the importance of journalism to Restoration politics. The press bill was presented to the deputies on May 19, although a prospectus of the legislation had been published in the *Moniteur* on April 17. The official organ reflected Martignac's view that there was no longer any question of whether liberty of the press belonged to representative governments. Except for the *Courrier*, which intimated that the bill was "hypocritical",[25] liberal journals welcomed the new law. The *Débats*, whose editors were self-styled champions of press liberty, called it the measure of the "happy union of King and Charter".[26] Villèle and his loyal *Gazette* regarded the bill, which would abolish censure, as a means of weakening the royal power. Villèle was spitefully pleased, however, to see Martignac struggling with the problem of journalism. Claiming that his successor was "justifying" his own administration; Villèle wrote that a new law, "a dyke against license", would be needed to combat the "oppression of the press".[27] The *Quotidienne* believed in its own version of a free press, but tightly controlled, and therefore criticized the bill as a dangerous concession. This Ultra journal, however, made it clear that it preferred the proposal to the Villèlist "Law of Justice and Love" of the previous year, saying that Martignac's bill was "nearly as moral" as the infamous Peyronnet law.[28] These responses from the Right were expected, but the *Courrier's* attitude augured darkly for the ministry. Another omen of opposition came from the roster of deputies scheduled to speak against the project. Such unlikely combinations as the baron de Schonen, editor of the revived and republican-tinged *Nouveau Journal de Paris* and the pro-Jesuit Villèlist, Montbel, were listed to argue against the Press law.[29] The factions attacked the moderate proposal from opposite poles. The Left considered it repressive and the Right felt it was anarchic.[30]

The bill, as introduced for debate on May 19, was liberal in principle and intent, but was weighted down by rigorous provisions. Previous authorization to publish, as well as the onerous facultative censure were abolished. The insidious "tendency" principle was also omitted. The proprietors of a periodical, however, were still required to furnish a *cautionnment* bond in accordance with a provision of the law of June 9, 1819. For daily

---

[25] *Courrier Français*, 18 April, 1828

[26] *Journal des Débats*, 18 April, 1828.

[27] Villèle, *Mémoires*, 16 May, 1828, to his son, pp. 331-32.

[28] *Quotidienne*, 18 April, 1828.

[29] *Le Moniteur*, 20 May, 1828.

[30] *Ibid.*

papers, this *cautionnment* was set at two hundred thousand francs, for biweekly periodicals, it was to be one hundred fifty thousand francs, and for weeklies, one hundred thousand francs. If a periodical appeared only two or three times a month, the bond was set at fifty thousand francs and there was no *cautionnment* required of monthly or quarterly periodicals.

Another feature of the bill was the requirement of responsible managers. The law would allow an unlimited number of responsible managers, but stipulated that they must be at least twenty-five years of age and must file a record of their names, addresses, and financial interest in their journal with the government. Each issue must be signed by one of these managers on pain of a five hundred franc fine. An author of an incriminating article would share responsibility with that issue's signed responsible manager. Before a new periodical could be published, a declaration of intent was demanded and was to include the names of the responsible managers, the title of the journal, and its periodicity. Any changes in title or periodicity had to be reported fifteen days in advance of the change. This provision was obviously intended to check such artful maneuvers as had been practiced in the case of the *Sylphe*, which had changed its title every day. The maximum penalty for failure to file a declaration of intent was set at one-half the total *cautionnment*. The eighteenth article of the bill abolished the special police of the press as a division of the general police.

The severity of the law was, of course, in the enormous financial responsibility demanded of journalists; its leniency was in the elimination of the hated censorship and the monopolistic preliminary authorization requirement. Thus, in the main, the Martignac proposal was progressive, while in detail it was repressive and catered to wealth.

The debates were opened by an Ultra deputy, de Conny, who, like most of his class, began by defending the token abstraction of a free press. Recalling the Revolution and the Empire, de Conny ventured that a fear of "license" was natural when liberty was granted after years of "absolute despotism". He continued: "Let us conserve the liberty of the press, gentlemen, but to conserve it, let us take care ... that, poisoned by license, it does not die victim of its subtle corruption". To assure the liberty of the press, he said, "We call for the most severe repression of its crimes".[31] The royalist speaker finished his argument with a denunciation of "popular sovereignty", and voted for the proposed law on the condition that existing judicial penalties be made more severe.

De Conny was followed by a liberal, M. Cunin-Gridaine, who voted

---

[31] *Le Moniteur*, 30 May, 1828, supplement to No. 151.

against the press law because of the *cautionnment*. "The principle upon which the *cautionnment* is based", said Gridaine "is immoral, odious, and tyrannical": Immoral, because of the temptation that large fines would instill in the hearts of royal prosecutors; odious, because it would destroy nonprofit scientific and cultural journals; tyrannical, because "only the rich would have the right to write".

Deputy Auguste Kératry, an editor of the *Courrier*, borrowed a cliché from his enemies on the Right, causing murmurs of indignation from them. Kératry opposed the invasion of privacy implicit in the requirement that responsible managers reveal their residence and financial investments. This, he stated indignantly, reminded him of "one of the most sinister periods of the Revolution".[32] Kératry's outrage over this rather moderate provision may be viewed as a change of tactics. The Left would probe Martignac's progressive reform measures to discover hidden traits of Villèlism!

Mechin, another liberal, but nearer to Martignac's Center, spoke in favor of the law. His opinion reflected that part of the opposition which had not yet decided to desert the Cabinet, as the *Courrier* staff had apparently done. He hailed the end of the censure and appealed to the Right to regard the bill, not as a concession, but as a "restitution" of freedom. He added that the *cautionnment* was justified for literary periodicals since their satire was often of a political nature. Mechin proposed, as a condition of his final approval, an amendment to the bill: The use of juries in press trials.[33]

Other members of the opposition, however, rose to reject the entire proposal. De Corcelles struck at the constitutionality of the bill since the *cautionnment* was simply a penalty for an "unspecified crime". Corcelles agreed that license was always a threat in journalism, but then asked when "oppressive laws" would cease to be a threat. If a free press means anarchy, he asked, then why is the United States not plunged into this condition?[34] Baron de Schonen, representing the Lafayette and *Aide-toi* opinion, approved of only two parts of the project: The abolition of the special police of the press and the requirement of a bond for literary gazettes. He declared that the *Globe* (which had been unfriendly to him) could well afford the assessment, but added that the cost would ruin valuable medical, scientific, and other learned reviews. Arguing that only the freedom of the press stood between the "barbarism of the middle ages" and modern civilization, he reassured the deputies that the present codes, under which the courts were free to punish journalists, were severe enough to make the Martignac proposal

---

[32] *Ibid.*

[33] *Le Moniteur*, 31 May, 1828, supplement to N. 152.

[34] *Ibid.*

unnecessary. De Schonen called attention to the editorials of Albin de Berville against the *cautionnment*, which had appeared in his own newspaper.[35] Deputies Thouvenel and Eusèbe de Salverte, both liberals, also vetoed the proposal because of the *cautionnment* and its predicted effect on such magazines as the *Clinique des Hôpitaux*. Salverte invoked the competitive principle. "The history of political journals", he said, "will always show us how they pass from prosperity to decadence, according to whether they have interpreted public opinion faithfully or unfaithfully".[36]

The cruelest blow to the Ministry's project came from a journalistic colleague of Kératry who was still one of the most powerful politicians in France: Benjamin Constant. Constant had been the first to advocate such legislation as that which he now attacked. On the first day of the 1828 session, he had called for an abolition of censure and urged the application of the jury system in press cases. But in the first words of his speech on the Martignac bill, Constant showed that his opposition was more partisan than ideological. Declaring that he was first "seduced" by the section of the law which would destroy the optional censure, Constant announced: "Since the presentation of the project, the acts of the Ministry have nearly all been contrary to my expectations and my wishes". He presented the Cabinet as the dupes of an "occult" faction and as a "hostile Ministry": A further application of the "Villèlist" stain begun by Kératry. So clearly was Constant's address a declaration of war against the moderate government, that he even received the applause of the Ultras at one point in his speech!

Constant's attempt at sabotage was answered by the Minister of Justice, comte de Portalis, *émigré*, but constitutionalist. "I will defend", Portalis bitterly remarked, "political and legal liberties against the exaggeration of those who make themselves their exclusive defenders". Another spokesman for the embattled ministerial Center, Agier, scorned the revolutionary "phantoms" raised by the Ultras in their attacks on the bill. Agier, who led a clique of the Center-Left in the Chamber, was in favor of the law but believed the *cautionnment* ought to be drastically reduced to about five hundred francs.

Final defense of the press bill was the task of the vicomte de Martignac himself. In his facile style, he revived each of his critics' arguments and then methodically destroyed them in a spirited refutation. Defending the validity of the huge *cautionnment*, Martignac asked whether a government which allows the publication of "poison, subversion, impiety and defamation"

---

[35] *Ibid.*, Berville's articles appeared in Nos. 297, 299, and 300 of the *Nouveau Journal de Paris*, 1828.

[36] *Le Moniteur*, 1 June, 1828, supplement to No. 153.

does not have the right to ask some reparations for "insulted families, outraged citizens, and a disturbed society".[37]

After the initial debates, a wave of amendments to soften the law were proposed. Martignac's supporters, seeing the need to yield for the sake of votes, agreed to these modifications. The *cautionnment*, after a suggestion by Dupin, *ainé*, was reduced from two hundred thousand francs to one hundred twenty thousand francs for daily papers with proportionate reductions for other periodicals. This began an avalanche of reductions, resulting in a maximum *cautionnment* of only six thousand francs for Parisian dailies and two thousand for the provincial journals. Thénard then gained approval to exempt from any bond those scientific or cultural periodicals appearing twice a week or less frequently. Still another amendment freed the managers from the necessity of declaring their financial interests.

An important amendment was that of Corcelles, who proposed juries for press offenses. A debate over the competence of juries ended when the Minister of Justice informed the Chamber that such a system would be impossible under the Codes, and Corcelles' amendment was shelved. It should be noted here that, while censure was abolished, existing laws for specific press crimes were still unchanged. Substantial fines and jail terms were possible for such offenses as "hatred and contempt for the government of the King".

On June 19, the nearly unrecognizable bill passed by a vote of 266 to 116. A new era of press freedom had begun under Martignac, but he was by no means gratified by the balloting: A few Ultras had been part of the majority, but the 116 who voted against the law were split almost evenly between Villèlist Ultras and crypto-republicans like Kératry.[38]

In the Luxembourg Palace, where the Chamber of Peers was convened, the press bill was treated with considerably less partisanship. The bill was a matter of "liberty" or "license", and debated on ideological grounds. Liberals stressed the unfair effect of the bond upon poor journals, the evidence that America offered of liberty without anarchy,[39] and the need for an enlightened nation to have enlightened laws. Ultras were generally uncompromising in their gloomy predictions of evil unless the law was changed or vetoed in their chamber. Some anti-Villèle peers criticized it, but voted for it.

La Bourdonnaye, the blunt reactionary championed by the *Quotidienne* for

---

[37] *Ibid.*

[38] *Ibid.*; Duvergier, *Collection des lois*, XXVIII, 249-60, 269, gives full text of laws as registered 18, 30 July, 1828.

[39] *Chambre des Pairs de France, session de 1828*, Vol. III (Paris, 1828), session of 5 July, 1928.

First Minister, voted for the law, but stipulated he would tolerate no "license", and expressed the hope that in that century of "light", mankind would not be more "indulgent of a plague infecting his soul than one which threatened his body".[40] A Villèlist peer, vicomte Dubouchage, on the other hand, would have nothing to do with the bill, declaring that the only good press law was the Peyronnet law of 1827. The press should only be free, he said, for "good", but "impotent for evil". A completely pessimistic view came from the marquis de Villefranche, who seemed to think that the flood of "pernicious doctrines" could no longer be checked. The evil had started in the Revolution and would simply go on to "corrupt the generation that will replace us".[41]

Liberal and "legitimist" peers were more friendly to the new minister's proposal than were their counterparts in the other legislative body. Even on the far Left, men like Dambray proposed such amendments as total prohibition of any *cautionnment*, without attributing false motives to Martignac.[42] One of the more amusing defenses came from the liberal comte de Saint-Roman: "The liberty of newspapers", he explained, "is a sort of exhalation from the political body of excessive intestinal fermentation, which, if stifled, would have incalculable effects".[43]

Most of the peers who spoke in favor of the bill were liberal-royalists, men who believed in the moderate doctrines of Martignac or perhaps of Chateaubriand. Baron Pasquier praised the provision which abrogated preliminary censure and "tendency" and stated that "repression must never be destructive".[44] The duc Decazes, former Prime Minister, called the law a good synthesis of two French characteristics: "Fear of anarchy and a propensity to fend off oppression".[45] The comte de Tournon attacked censorship as futile, citing the clandestine press and the wide distribution of a Bonapartist pamplet, *l'homme gris* all over France. Tournon favored the new law because it abolished "tendency".[46] Lally-Tollendal supported the proposed law, but argued that all press cases should be tried before a jury.[47]

The most moving defense of the bill came from the vicomte de Chateaubriand. With his characteristic vanity, he recalled his own fight against Peyronnet's "Law of Justice and Love" and predicted that freedom would

---

[40] *Ibid.*
[41] *Ibid.*, session of 11 July, 1828.
[42] *Ibid.*, session of 10 July, 1828.
[43] *Ibid.*, session of 5 July, 1828.
[44] *Ibid.*, session of 9 July, 1828.
[45] *Ibid.*, session of 12 July, 1828.
[46] *Ibid.*, session of 11 July, 1828.
[47] *Ibid.*, session of 12 July, 1828.

emerge victorious from their present discussions. "To overthrow the old power", he said, "it was necessary to attack with liberty; to overthrow the new power, it is necessary to attack with despotism". In a constitutional monarchy, explained Chateaubriand, the freedom of the press is essential to unite sentiments and prevent the "triple despotism of democracy, aristocracy, and crown". Chateaubriand's defense of the liberty of the press enlarged to include a brief review of the history of France since Clovis and he concluded this remarkable achievement with the startling deduction that, in fourteen centuries of Christianity, France had had but twelve years of press freedom. Scornfully, he asked: "Are we already tired of this liberty"? The author of the *Genius of Christianity* then defended the right of journals to criticize religion, because religion is "founded and defended by the free exercise of idea and word". In concluding his masterful and enlightened address, the old patrician appeared at his most generous. He asked indulgence for the youthful publishers, idealistic students, and bohemians, who could never afford a *cautionnment* for their broadsides and *feuilles*. To stop them, said the vicomte, "You would only torture yourselves. You can never stop the children of the gay *science* from making epigrams against power and teasing the stupid". Chateaubriand finished with a call to rally around the throne in a spirit of true liberty.[48] Martignac's press law passed the Chamber of Peers.

The *Constitutionnel* had backed Constant's early proposal for abolition of censure [49] and its editors had written impassioned articles on press freedom throughout the debates.[50] But now, the great newspaper turned its back on the Ministry that had authored the press law, branding it a "combination of ruses and fiscal juggling" filled with "subtle formalities".[51] The *Courrier*, which had been the first to turn against the Ministry over this legislation, dragged out the Jesuit issue, quite unreasonably, and called the law "detestable" and "monstrous". Despite the ameliorations of the bill, Constant's journal addressed Martignac: "Will you not stop yourself in this tragic career and not entirely consummate the ruin of our most precious liberties"? [52] Only the *Débats*, whose Chateaubriand had so ably defended the bill, was pleased.[53] Both the *Globe* and the *Débats*, however, credited

[48] *Ibid.*, session of 11 July, 1828. Villèle listened in horror to the speeches by the liberal peers. He wrote to his wife that he heard Chateaubriand "surpass all the evil that he has yet done by means of this instrument of ruin". Villèle, *Mémoires*, 9 July, 1828.

[49] *Constitutionnel*, 28 February, 1828.

[50] *Ibid.*, 14 March, 11 April, 1 June, 1828.

[51] *Ibid.*, 20 June, 1828.

[52] *Courrier Français*, 17, 20 June, 1828.

[53] *Journal des Débats*, 20 June, 1828.

Martignac only with the negative features of the law, not for those portions which they approved.

The *Débats* had a more compelling reason to support Martignac's laws than its twelve thousand franc monthly subsidy. The Ministry had found a diplomatic post for Chateaubriand which could somewhat appease his damaged pride: The embassy at Rome. Chateaubriand had also worked for this appointment, having connived toward the transfer of the current Vatican Ambassador to Vienna. On June 2, while the press debates were in progress, the journalist received his appointment.[54] His *Débats* expressed regret that this "noble peer" would now have no opportunity to influence politics in Paris, to which the *Gazette* answered that the "noble peer is today one of the most discredited men in all the factions". To revolutionaries, wrote Genoude, he is that "man of the *Conservateur*" and to royalists, he is a "turncoat".[55] Chateaubriand welcomed the Italian sojourn for two reasons. The Gallican bishops were exhibiting a rising sentiment in favor of the Jesuits and the Ultras and Chateaubriand hoped to influence the Pope to discipline them. Then, too, as a romanticist, the vicomte longed to live in the center of antiquity and reflect on the aesthetic values of a decayed world.[56]

In July, the Foreign Minister, La Ferronnays, suffered a paralytic stroke. From fear of a new ambitious intrigue on the part of Chateaubriand, the post was left nominally under the leadership of the stricken Minister. Martignac still considered the new Ambassador to Rome as a threat to his security and was trying desperately not to offend him. Martignac's personal newspaper, *Messager des Chambres*, expressed the kindly hope that Chateaubriand's mission would be fruitful both of literature and diplomacy.[57] Chateaubriand wrote a farewell to Paris in his *Débats* in which he boasted of his part in upsetting Villèle. Stung, the *Gazette de France* retorted that the "King of Journalism" had left orders for his newspaper to continue with the campaign to make him Foreign Minister.[58] Genoude underestimated the ambition of his opponent. Chateaubriand had also asked his friend Dubois to include his name in the editorials of the *Globe* [59] and his friends of the *Courrier Français* wrote frequently in his favor.

[54] *Ibid., 2 June, 1828.*

[54] *Ibid.,* 2 June, 1828.

[55] *Gazette de France*, 3 June, 1828.

[56] Loménie, *Chateaubriand*, II, 266.

[57] *Messager des Chambres*, 20 September, 1828. Established by Cabinet subsidy, the *Messager* had less than three thousand subscribers.

[58] *Gazette de France*, 21 september, 1828.

[59] Faure, *Dubois*, letters, 14 September, 1828 and 3 February, 1829

The *Débats-Gazette* conflict encompassed another issue in 1828. At the end of February, the *Débats* had urged the formal accusation of Villèle for malfeasance in office. Labbey de Pompières, on May 30, proposed in the Chamber an accusation of the entire conduct of the past Ministry. In a long and detailed proposal, de Pompières set forth a formal indictment of the Villèle Ministry and accused its chief, under the provisions of the Charter, of high treason.[60] Treason by a minister, explained the old deputy, exists in case he acts against the Charter, or arbitrarily assaults freedom of religion, press, or other public liberties. De Pompières then listed dozens of specific grievances, bringing up details of the treatment of Magallon, editor of the *Album*, after his conviction in 1823, as well as broader charges of electoral fraud, intolerance to protestants, and the illegality of the Peyronnet press law. A committee was voted to investigate the legal possibility of accusing Villèle before the Chambers. It appeared that the Ultra "defection" might join the Left if the ex-Minister could be brought to trial.

The accusation excited political tempers even though it was introduced during heated debates over the press law. Villèle was frightened and his letters show how dreadful the accusation seemed to him. To his wife he wrote that he would try to bear the attack "with dignity" and claimed that Martignac had called the *Débats'* joy over his accusation an "infamy". Villèle admitted some confusion over this unconfirmed report, since the *Débats* was now subsidized by the new Cabinet.[61] He feared the peers as much as the deputies. At the time when the former body was debating the press law, Villèle said, "never has the Revolution shown itself there more openly".[62] Villèle was certain the accusation would be full of "malice and poison" and added: "They would like to brand us without a trial even to excluding us forever from public affairs".[63] The *Gazette*, ever loyal to its master, announced: "The Revolution progresses. An act of accusation is directed against the Minister who first placed royal initiative on a sound basis".[64] Genoude accused the *Débats*, which on June 13, had struck cruelly at Villèle, of abandoning its "flag" and of the "most shameful defection".[65] The *Gazette* said the purpose of the accusation was to unite the liberals with the Ministry, a combination which, according to Genoude, had allowed the

---

[60] *Le Moniteur*, 1828, supplement.
[61] Villèle, *Mémoires*, 17, 30 June, 1828, pp. 334, 344.
[62] *Ibid.*, 6 July, 1828, p. 345.
[63] *Ibid.*, 11 July, 1828, to his wife, p. 352.
[64] *Gazette de France*, 15 June, 1828.
[65] *Ibid.*, 17 June, 1828.

"license of the press and the legal domination of *comité-directeur* [revolutionary junta] over elections".[66]

The journal of the Ultra "defection", though unwilling to side directly with the liberals, gave little comfort to Villèle. The *Quotidienne* asserted that, "if M. de Villèle is attacked for having done too much for monarchy, it would be almost inhuman to recall to him that he has done too much for democracy".[67] The liberal press, of course, warmly supported the accusation, not only of Villèle, but of the other members of his Cabinet. The *Courrier*, fond of anecdotes, claimed that Peyronnet had once promised the family of a condemned officer a last visit with the prisoner and then executed the soldier before the family could see him.[68] Jay, writing in the *Constitutionnel*, called Labbey de Pompières "venerable" and praised his action in accusing the past Ministry.[69] The *Journal du Commerce* charged that, if there were any softening of the accusations, it would result from sinister intrigues by the *Gazette*.[70]

On the twenty-second of July, the Committee made its report. Stating that there was insufficient evidence for a charge of treason, it nevertheless returned a scathing denunciation of the Villèle administration. Villèle was greatly relieved. To his countess, he wrote: "Not being able to find real offenders among us, we are accused of unpopularity: The royalists are too unpopular; one must side with the liberals in order to popularize the King".[71] Villèle singled out the attacks in the *Débats*, *Courrier*, and *Commerce* as "infamous" and "wicked". "It is impossible", he wrote, "to live with the liberty of the periodical press. And where to find the necessary force to repress it, when we have a democratic Chamber of Peers and a subversive election law"?[72]

The accusation at least had the effect of sending Villèle away from Paris. Realizing the liability of his disgraced Minister, the King pointedly wrote to Villèle that he regretted his inability to see him "before he left". Charles consoled his lieutenant by calling the accusation, "this dirty affair of the alleged accusation".[73] Faced by this clouded political future, Villèle left for his home in Toulouse. He did not return to Paris until March, 1830.

[66] *Ibid.*, 22 July, 1828.
[67] *Quotidienne*, 15 June, 1828.
[68] *Courrier Français*, 17 June, 1828. At his later trial, Peyronnet warmly refuted this version of the story as a distortion by the newspapers. See, *Procès des ministres*, II, 429-49.
[69] *Constitutionnel*, 16 June, 1828.
[70] *Journal du Commerce*, 16 June, 1828.
[71] Villèle, *Mémoires*, 26 July, 1828, p. 368.
[72] *Ibid.*, 28 July, 1828, p. 361.
[73] *Ibid.*, 2 August, 1828, King to Villèle, p. 364.

When the session of the deputies closed in August, Martignac appeared to have weathered the storm. His press bill, though liberal by contrast with previous legislation, had failed to satisfy the liberal Left and had alienated the strong support of the *Courrier* and the *Constitutionnel*. The *Débats* and the *Globe*, however, had continued to back the legislative program of 1828, though not always cordial to the Ministry. The moderate applause of the *Débats* had been purchased with money, high office, and a frontal assault of Villèle's faction, a party which the King favored. The *Globe*, typically, believed that any progressive legislation was beneficial and refused to undermine such an earnestly conceived program.

Several days after the session ended, the King was persuaded by Martignac to make a personal tour of Alsace-Lorraine. Playing Mirabeau to Charles' Louis XVI, Martignac wanted the King to be seen by his subjects in this strongly republican region. The journey lasted a month and thousands saw the old Monarch and his dapper Minister smiling and waving from their open carriage. In many towns, banquets and receptions drew enthusiastic crowds. Speeches by liberal deputies dutifully praised the King and extolled the dynasty. Martignac hoped that by this proof of popularity, he could gain the King's confidence. But, true to form, Charles X misunderstood the significance of the entire experience; he believed he was proving to Martignac how royalist his subjects were! [74] The *Débats*, still in cooperation with the Ministry, gave frequent reports on the royal journey and stressed the importance of constitutionalist government to maintain royal popularity. The *Gazette de France*, in a searing editorial, *Session de 1828*, branded the Ministry and its supporters who had dared accuse Villèle and his "system". The Cabinet, unable to ignore Genoude's blows, was compelled to indict the responsible editor. Judicial prosecution, a rare experience for the *Gazette*, began in November. [75]

The new press law had altered none of the machinery in the criminal code, except, of course, the law of "tendency". Before the *Gazette* stood trial, the case of the *Pucelle d'Orléans*, itself a tempest in a teapot, brought a legal ruling on the 1828 law that disappointed the Left, but a verdict which was reassuring. A bookseller named Le Clerc was arrested and charged with outraging public morality for having displayed a copy of Voltaire's irreverent *Pucelle*. The presiding magistrate ruled that the press law of 1819 had not been abrogated by that of 1822, upon which the most recent law was based. The high penalties of the earlier law were thus enforceable and periodicals

---

[74] Achille de Vaulabelle, *Histoire des deux Restaurations* (7 vols.; Paris, 1854), VII, 127-32. (Hereafter cited as Vaulabelle, *Histoire*.)

[75] *Gazette de France*, 5 August, 1828.

begun before 1822 were clearly subject to the law. In the case of the *Pucelle*, Le Clerc argued that a book fifty years old could hardly outrage the morality of the present day and that he needed the book to complete a set of Voltaire's works. Le Clerc was acquitted and allowed to retain the book. Later, in an appeal, Le Clerc received an admission by the court that the police seizure of *Pucelle* had violated the 1819 law.[76]

The most discussed political trials of that winter were the prosecution of the *Gazette de France*, for its reflections on the session of 1828, and the trial of the revolutionary songwriter, Pierre Béranger.

On november 13, the royal prosecutor accused Victor Aubry of exciting "hatred and scorn of the King's government" for his article in the *Gazette* on August 5. Aubry's editorial had been uncommonly strident for the *Gazette*. The incriminating editorial included the following passages:

The ministers of the King replaced by the ministers of the opinion, that is to say, the opinion which journalism has perverted ...

The address of the Chamber, qualifying as deplorable a system which two kings had upheld for six years ...

The monarchic principle of royal authority effaced by the law of the press, royalty deprived of the sole means it had to defend itself against journalism in times of trouble; also the license of the press consecrated by law.

The article had concluded by an extravagant prophecy of the reestablishment of the Republic, the erection of altars to the Goddess of Reason, usurpation of the throne, and the establishment of Protestantism as the state religion. The whole article tasted more of the *Drapeau* than the *Gazette*.

The prosecutor declared that the law, while it tolerated criticism, did not permit "inconsiderate, illegal, or prejudicial opinions". He argued that offenses to ministers were also attacks on the King who chose them, a point which, ironically, had been used by Villèle's prosecutors to punish critics. The defense lawyer for the *Gazette*, Antoine-Marie Hennequin, pleaded that twenty-five of the forty incriminating lines written by his client had been "solely the faithful reproduction of known facts". Although the defendant had called it "license", his defender invoked the concept of the liberty of the press, reaching back to Racine for support. This remarkable appeal for free expression, on behalf of a newspaper which often opposed it, lasted for nearly an hour. In a decision which offended the liberals, the court president, a Villèle appointee, granted full acquittal to Aubry.[77] If

[76] *Gazette des Tribunaux*, 8 November, 1828, 8 April, 1829.
[77] *Ibid.*, 13 November, 1828.

Martignac hoped to quell the Ultras by recourse to the judicial courts, he was doomed to frustration.

The same judge was not so charitable to the famous poet-composer Béranger who appeared before him a month later. This friend of youth, whose satirical songs, both Bonapartist and revolutionary, but above all, human, were chorused in the Left Bank and Montmartre cafes, was indicted under five counts for having published several guilty lyrics. The court, which convened on December 10, was filled with ticket-holders two hours before the trial was to begin. Special orders were given to the wardens to jail for a full day anyone who shouted or laughed too loudly. Béranger arrived in court with his lawyer Felix Barthe and several friends, including Jacques Laffitte, General Sebastiani, and the Prince de la Moskowa, son of marshal Ney. Béranger, the author, M. Baudouin, the editor, Fain, a printer, and three booksellers were all jointly charged for the distribution and creation of a book entitled *Chansons Inédites de Béranger*.[78]

Three song-lyrics, included in the edition, resulted in five charges against the defendants and the Crown prosecuting attorney repeated the incriminating songs for each count of the indictment. Béranger was cited for "outrage to public and religious morals" and "outrage to the state religion" because of his *l'Ange Gardien*. In this song, the author made light of the sacrament of extreme unction and suggested that a nonbeliever could to to Heaven. The second guilty poem, according to the prosecution, linked a Carolingian despot to the present King. In *Le Sacre de Charles le Simple*, Béranger recalled that in 898, Charles III was crowned at Reims, against the national will, by foreigners and bishops. Since Charles X, a millenium later had also been crowned at Reims with antique rites, including the release of birds inside the cathedral and even to anointment with ancient coronation oil, the analogy was obvious. The song describes the people at the coronation, who warn the free-flying birds to guard their liberties. The birds then become sycophants and lose their freedom; the people, it is understood, lose their freedom with the advent of Charles III. In another stanza of *Le Sacre de Charles le Simple* the prosecutor found the criminal suggestion that Charles III, who, he said, meant the present King, would violate his coronation oath. Another passage implied that the Monarch owed his crown to priests.[79] This song netted for Béranger the

---

[78] *Ibid.*, 11 December, 1828.
[79] This stanza:

> De Charlemagne en vrai luron
> Des qu'il a mis la ceinturon,
> Charles s'etend sur la poussière.
> Roi! crie un soldat, levez-vous!

charges of "offense to the King's person" and "attack on the royal dignity". The most serous accusation, brought by the prosecutor, was "hatred and contempt of the King's government". The song which supposedly provoked this sentiment was called *Les infiniment petits* or *la Gerontocratie*. In this almost Swiftian treatment of the Bourbon dynasty, Béranger described the France of a century later – 1928 – in which mediocrity, littleness, and priestcraft are supreme. Each stanza concluded: "Mais les barbons regnent toujours [But the graybeards rule forever]". There was no attempt to conceal what was intended by "Barbons", Béranger's song dealt with "choleric little Jesuits and thousands of other little priests" and "good little famines". Béranger's concluding lines, not quite amusing today, prophecied the invasion of "pygmy" France by a giant heretic who braves "little speeches and puts the kingdom in his pocket"![80]

With this mass of sedition, the royal prosecutor was well-armed for the assault. When he quoted the last lines of *Gerontocratie*, such a tumult resulted in the courtroom that the president recessed court for a quarter of an hour. The prosecutor recalled that the poet had gone to prison before, in 1821, for the excesses of his "too licentious muse", and added that, although songs were well-tolerated in France, this toleration was not without limits and that Béranger's "songs" were really published verse. He defended the King from the cruel analogy and called him the promotor of liberties and material progress.

Béranger's defender, Barthe, based his plea largely on the claim of poetic liberty, stating that no artistic imagination should be thwarted. Then, turning from the present case, he lashed out at the *Gazette de France* which had recently expressed a desire to see Béranger sent to Bicêtre, the prison depot of galley slaves. Perhaps realizing the impossibility of an acquittal, Barthe used the forum of the court to deliver an hour-long harangue, punctuated by "bravos"! on the case for liberalism versus clerical Ultra reaction. He said the *Sacre* poem was an attack on the clerical menace, not royalty. He defended Béranger for his intense patriotism, his love of liberty, and his hatred of foreign

                Non, dit l'évêque, et par Saint-Pierre
                Je te conjure, enrichis-nous;
                Ce qui vient de Dieu, vient des prêtres,
                Vive la legitimité!
[80] The last stanza of *la Gérontocratie*:
                Enfin le miroir prophetique
                Completant ce triste avenir,
                Me montre un géant hérètique
                Qu'un monde a peine a contenir.
                Du peuple pygmée il s'approche
                Et bravant de petits discours
                Met la royaume dans sa poche:
                Mais les barbons regnent toujours.

invasion, but he wisely refrained from mentioning the poet's tendency to Bonapartism.

Albin de Berville, lawyer, deputy, republican, and journalist, next addressed the court in defense of the editor Baudouin. To accuse the writer of criminal intent for writing the word "barbons", he declared, was unjust; and it was unbelievable that an editor should be held responsible for divining that "Charles the Simple" meant Charles X. "One must guess that or go to jail", said Berville, "thus the Sphinx proposes enigmas and devours the unfortunates who cannot guess them". Berville concluded that, although the French may not become physical and mental pygmies in the future, the twentieth century will surely ridicule them for making a major political trial out of a few couplets from a song.

When the defense was concluded, the president and his colleagues retired for forty-five minutes of deliberation and then rendered this decision: The printers were acquitted; but Béranger and Baudouin were guilty of deriding the state religion, outraging morality, exciting scorn of the King's government, and offending the King. Baudouin, the publisher was sentenced to a six months prison term and a fine of five hundred francs. Béranger was given a sentence of nine months in La Force and a huge fine: Ten thousand francs. The pronouncement of this penalty was received by the audience with such noisy protests that the court ordered guards to enforce silence.[81] Béranger became a martyr to the extreme Left and several of the opposition journals published every line of his guilty poems, causing a far greater circulation of the songs than the suppressed edition could ever have attained! Newspapers, it must be recalled, could print the *procès-verbal* of any public trial. If these trials included radical poems or the liberal polemic of lawyers, the law was impotent to prevent their publicity. Thus, as in nearly every judicial repression of printed opinion, the Ultras reaped a harvest of self-destroying propaganda, and in addition, created another martyr. Only the extreme liberals or republicans openly protested Béranger's conviction. The *Courrier* refused to defend him, though its editors privately praised him. The poet was not forgotten while he resided in prison. A subscription to pay his fine, organized by his "young friends in *Aide-toi*", fell short of its goal, but Bérard, the deputy, led a collection to complete the amount. In jail, Béranger formed a warm friendship with a fellow-inmate Cauchois-Lemaire. Lafayette, seventy-two years old, climbed three flights of stairs to visit him in his cell, as did Constant and the rich and powerful Laffitte.[82] Béranger's "licentious

---

[81] *Gazette des Tribunaux*, 11 December, 1828.
[82] *Ibid.*, 9 April, 1829; see also his preface to *Chansons de Béranger, 1815-1834* (Paris, n.d.), p. v.

muse" shared his confinement: He covered the walls of his cell with *graffiti* against the regime.

During the first half of 1829, most of the controversial political press trials were those concerned with attacks on the church, the clergy, or the Jesuit order and these will be discussed in a later chapter. Between February and July, however, two notorious political heretics were hailed before magistrates for offenses which did not concern religion. One of these culprits was Auguste Marseille Barthélémy, poet, arrested for his stanzas in praise of Napoleon's son, Duke of Reichstadt. The other was a small satirical periodical, *l'Ancien Album*, which was prosecuted on several occasions for the sins of its indiscretion.

The case of Barthélémy began in late July. He had narrowly escaped prison for his *Villèliade* of 1827 and was returned to the prisoner's dock in 1829 for a sentimental bit of Bonapartism called *Le fils de l'homme*. This poem glorified the captive heir of the French Empire who was then growing to manhood in Vienna.

Prosecutor for the King, Menjaud-Dammartin, called the popular poet a "corrupter of youth", but, in a generous gesture, added that he admired Barthélémy's youthful zest and poetic talents. He charged the poet with attacking the hereditary rights of the King and attempting to provoke a change in the form of government. Noting with alarm that Barthélémy had recently visited Vienna in the vain hope of seeing the Duke of Reichstadt, Dammartin chided the young man for having such an "old idolatry" as Bonapartism and quoted the following lines to back his accusations:

Petit fils d'un César et fils d'un Empereur
Légataire du Monde et paissent Roi de Rome,
Tu n'es plus aujourd'hui rien que le fils de l'homme!
Pourtant quel fils du roi contre ce nom obscur.
N'echangerait son titre et son sceptre futur? [84]

The public interest increased greatly when Barthélémy rose in his own defense. Instead of polemics, the young man recited his entire defense in verse, which he had composed. In the poem, whose wit and satire impressed the court, Barthélémy referred to a royalist, De Lille, who had penned sedition under Napoleon and had been tolerated. The poem also cleverly wove the argument that, as Bonapartism was but a memory, it could hardly be subversive. The judges and even the prosecutor sat enraptured by the novel defense plea. When the long poem was concluded, the eminent lawyer, Joseph

[83] Nettement, *Histoire*, p. 206.
[84] *Gazette des Tribunaux*, 30 July, 1829.

Mérilhou, gave a more prosaic defense of Barthélémy in which he warned against imputing of political qualities to artistic genius. It was, in all, a very Gallic trial. The publishers and booksellers were acquitted, but the young poet was given the minimum sentence of three months in jail and a thousand franc fine.[85] His defense in verse greatly enchanced his popularity and much publicity was given the trial in the periodical press. Sales of Barthélémy's works increased rapidly.

On February 17, 1829, the case of the satirical journal, l'Ancien Album, was tried in a lower correctional court. Joseph Magallon, the owner, who had been imprisoned in 1823, and one of his writers, Auguste Briffaut, were charged with "outraging public morality" and "attempting to provoke assassination"! This last charge stemmed from the content of an article in l'Album called L'ami de vertu. In this piece, Briffaut had recalled the execution of the German assassin of Kotzebue, Karl Sand, in 1819. Although the crime was a decade old, had been expiated, and had been committed, not against a French King, but against a Russian spy, the mere recollection of it was deemed subversive! The prosecutor belittled the liberal sentiments expressed and called them the "glorification of a murderer".

The defense was able to prove that a provocation to assassinate would be impossible from the writing, but was unable to save the defendants from the charge of "outrage to morality" for condoning homicide. Magallon received the severe term of one year in jail, plus a moderate fine. The author, Briffaut, was ordered to prison for two months.[86] In an unsuccessful appeal, two months later, the defense denounced the first conviction as a veiled use of the now illegal "tendency" principle in law.

In July, Magallon was taken from his prison cell to stand trial for another series of articles in his Album, for which he remained as responsible manager. With him was Louis-Marie Fontan, a twenty-eight-year-old writer on the Album staff. Magallon, as manager, was indicted with Fontan for the latter's two editorials: L'Ane Beni et Pendu, a light satire on priestly functions and Galotti et Portalis, a more serious political tirade. Galotti was a Neapolitan patriot who had sought asylum in France, but comte de Portalis, as acting Foreign Minister, had allowed his extradition to Palermo where he was immediately executed. Fontan had lashed at the Minister of Foreign Affairs:

Galotti has been hanged!

Understand, M. Portalis! Hanged by the monarchical power! You, Minister of France, you have placed the rope around his neck, the Neapolitan hangman took care of the rest. Honor to both of you![87]

[85] Ibid.
[86] Ibid., 18 February, 1829.
[87] Ibid., 11 July, 1829. See chapter ix for a further ramification of the Galotti affair.

Fontan had then threatened the Minister: "We will hold you to strict account; we have contracted a debt with you which we ardently hope to pay". The defense attorney passed lightly over the anticlerical passage as a "pleasantry" and the charge as "prudery", but admitted the difficulty of defense in the case of *Galotti et Portalis*. The lawyer declared that Galotti's extradition was indeed an outrage and an abuse of ministerial power.

The court spent two hours in deliberation and returned with a very light sentence for each defendant. Magallon, who was already a prisoner, was fined one hundred francs. Writer Fontan received only fifteen days in jail and a two hundred franc fine. The judge included the important decision that criticism of ministers was a basic right of French citizens.[88]

The next affair of the controversial *Album* was more notorious and the results of this trial immortalized Magallon's small gazette. The incorrigible Fontan had written a short satire which appeared in the *Album* while he was serving his fifteen-day prison sentence. At first reading, the story would have seemed slightly absurd, but if read with a "key" in mind, the article became a direct attack on the sacred person of Charles X. *Le Mouton Enragé* was about "Robin-the-Sheep", a pretty pet who suffered children to play with him. But Robin is jealously, insanely, afraid that someone will shear him:

Shear Robin? My God! Take care! He will defend his fleece ... because despite his air of sweetness, he is vicious when treated thus. He sometimes bites. I am told that a ewe of his flock [Duchess of Berry] nips him ... because she finds that he does not govern his flock despotically enough. And I confide to you ... that poor Robin-the-Sheep is insane.

Fontan's fable continued: Robin tries to conceal his madness, because he "fears bullets". He wishes he were a big ram with sharp horns so he could show his "prerogatives over the sheep-people who follow him", but then he sadly recalls that only sheep's blood flows in his veins. Fontan next tells Robin to take care, to live his life of indolence as his fathers have "vegetated", and warns that the "Heaven that has created you a sheep, slaughters sheep".[89]

Apparently, Fontan he had not realized that his labored metaphor would be so publicly exposed. In one sense, the story was nothing. In the sense used by the prosecutor, however, the "mad sheep" was the King. Especially damning was the fact that the King, whose livery for the chase was green, was often called "Robin Hood" by the public. Thus, the young writer was charged with one of the worst political crimes, direct offense to the King's person. His lawyer

[88] *Ibid.*, 16 July, 1829.
[89] *L'Ancien Album*, X (1829), 108-10 [B.N. Z 2284].

tried desperately to quote some English law to the effect that in writing, unless analogy be proved, it is illusory, but the court refused a full reading of these laws. Fontan, speaking in his own behalf, further injured his case by his obstinacy: "I have the right", he grandly announced, "not to explain myself on this subject. I allow no one to descend to the bottom of my conscience to hunt for an idea which I have not expressly stated".

After a short deliberation, the presiding judge decided that the "mad sheep" was intended to mean the King. Magallon in prison was fined another five hundred francs as manager on this occasion and Fontan became overnight a martyr from the unprecedented degree of his penalty: Five years in jail, five years loss of civil rights, and a fine of ten thousand francs! [90]

The period between the legislative sessions of 1828 and 1829 was gravid with political discord. Martignac had crossed the Rubicon to appease the Left and oppose the Ultra Right, especially the Villèle faction. Yet, by autumn, even the modest support he received on the Left had begun to crumble. The *Courrier* was openly hostile; its editors having led the fight against his press bill. The *Constitutionnel* had also begun to scorn the compromise Cabinet and even the *Débats* and *Globe* were only loyal to the administration on general principles. Even Martignac's fine and courageous gesture of restoring Guizot, Villemain, and Cousin to their academic privileges went virtually unnoticed.

The *Courrier* launched a new attack on the Cabinet, demanding that Martignac demonstrate his faith in constitutionalism by dismissing scores of minor officials appointed under Villèle, who were still holding office. Several Ultra employees were replaced during September, which the Ultras said was a result of this liberal pressure. The *Courrier* demanded that Martignac tell these functionaries: "You have violated the laws ... you cannot go on with us".[91] The *Quotidienne* called this government by newspapers, declaring: "The Revolution commands. The King's ministers must obey"![92] On the same day, Martignac's personal journal, *Messager des Chambers*, admitted that such dismissals would be a "reasonable" move to put the Cabinet "in harmony with itself". Villèle's *Gazette*, feeling another wound in the palpitating corpse of the former Ministry, was more caustic than the *Quotidienne*, and said, "that the holocaust demanded by liberal opinion is almost ready". The *Gazette* rightly announced that the Left was still unsatisfied with this "half-concession" and predicted with equal accuracy,

---

[90] *Gazette des Tribunaux*, 28 July, 1829. For Fontan's escape and later appeal, see chapter xi.
[91] *Courrier Français*, 22 September, 1828.
[92] *Quotidienne*, 22 September, 1828.

that Martignac would soon lose his usefulness to the "Revolution" and would become in its eyes, a "counterrevolutionary".[93]

On November 14, the official *Moniteur* published a rare "manifesto", urging a more liberal program and promising the ouster of more Ultra officials, for the "maintenance of... new institutions". This declaration was followed by deeds; several more Villèlists were soon fired and replaced by moderate liberals. It was apparent that Martignac would now perform nearly any task within reason to restore his flagging support in the opposition. The "Manifesto" won favor from the *Débats* and even seduced the critical *Constitutionnel* to congratulate the Ministry.[94] But this revival of loyalty proved ephemeral. The "party-line" of the Left had been set by the *Courrier* months before and, when the session opened, Martignac was in such an unstable position that another wave of ministerial intrigues swept over Paris.

A factor that quickened these bids for power was the report of the doctors of La Ferronays, the invalid Foreign Minister, that their patient was incapable of holding office. The ruse of having Portalis as "acting" Minister had to be dropped. The Foreign Ministry was vacant! In Rome, Chateaubriand resumed his campaign for the post, in which the *Débats* supported him.[95] Bertin, in the January 26 issue proposed a Cabinet headed by Chateaubriand and Pasquier. The *Constitutionnel* refused to put its weight behind Chateaubriand and prayed for the miraculous recovery of the paralyzed La Ferronays. The *Gazette* painted Chateaubriand as a pestilence which should be kept out of Paris.[96] Far more disturbing than the ambition of this old novelist was the impolitic zeal of the Ambassador to London, Prince de Polignac. Polignac dashed to Paris in quest of La Ferronay's position and had a private audience with his old friend, the King of France. Press speculation was suddenly concentrated on the political chances of this man, whose admission to the Cabinet would signal a shift of power to the extreme Right. Opposition papers dredged up Polignac's *émigré*, reactionary past for all to read. The *Quotidienne* alone found something savory in this symbol of emigration and counterrevolution. The *Gazette*, still hopeful for Villèle, tried to discourage the King about Polignac.

Whatever hopes existed for Villèle at this moment were shattered by the appearance of a bombshell in four volumes titled *The Black Book of Messieurs*

---

[93] *Gazette de France*, 23, 25 September, 1828.

[94] *Constitutionnel*, 15 November, 1828.

[95] Jeanne Françoise Julie de Récamier, *Souvenirs et correspondance tirés des papiers de Madame Récamier* (2 vols.; Paris, 1860), letters from Chateaubriand, 12, 17 February, 1829. (Hereafter cited as Récamier, *Souvenirs*.)

[96] *Gazette de France*, 27 January, 1829.

Delavau and Franchet or Alphabetic Tabulation of the Political Police under the Deplorable Ministry. Using actual records of Villèle's now-deposed Police Prefect, Année, of the *Constitutionnel* started on the book soon after Villèle's Cabinet resigned. The work, arranged alphabetically by names, is a collection of espionage and surveillance reports from police informers (*mouchards*) and instructions to them from the Prefect. These describe the attitudes and movements of thousands of persons from Lafayette and Manuel down to poor, but suspect students or foreign visitors. The crudity of these observations when applied to well known statesmen and the obvious nastiness of spying upon even a short business trip of a "revolutionary" suspect, made Villèle's police system seem monstrous indeed. In the lengthy introduction, Année points to the police budget for Paris alone of over six million francs, of which a million went to reward the despised informers.

Delavau's police had ruthlessly violated privacy; they had seldom distinguished between appearance and fact; they had acted as lackeys for foreign embassies in tracking down liberal nationals; and worst of all, they had repeatedly passed moral judgments on the innocent and the great. A few samples from the *Black Book*: "Young Perrin is animated by the worst political doctrines"; "His political opinions are notoriously recognized as being excessively bad"; "The rooms are decorated with portraits of Bonaparte and he always leaves home around eleven or twelve and does not return until three or four in the morning". This last suspect was at least partially absolved for his nocturnal ritual: A friend had given a permanent pass to the Opera! These reports dealt frequently with the journalists, but seemed disappointed that so much of a newspaper's business was public knowledge.[97]

But when the Chambers opened on January 27, 1829, Martignac still led the Ministry. Charles X's speech was as moderate and progressive as it had been in the previous year. He reviewed the liberal legislation of the session of 1828 as if he had been its author. The only major new proposal was to reorganize department and commune governments on a more federalist basis, a change vainly sought since the days of the Girondins. This bill was introduced on February 9. To appeal to the Left, Martignac stressed that local governments would create an entire new social and political class of responsible citizens and an outlet for the talents of men of ideas and action.[98] In the debates which followed, the bill was first prodded and pricked by delays over procedural details. Then, after the projects were introduced, they were subjected to the

---

[97] *Le Livre Noir*, I, lxxxiv; II, 115, 264, 268, 321; IV, 157. For a complimentary review of the work, see *Globe*, 7 February, 1829.

[98] *Le Moniteur*, 9 February, 1829.

wildest denunciations from the Right and annoying and destructive amendments from the Left. The Left opposed the municipal section, fearing royalist power centers would be established, while the Ultras argued that electoral right was illegal on a local or municipal level. Martignac, unfortunately, lost his equilibrium on several occasions and spoke sharply to the oddly-paired factions attacking the bill. Even when the government suppressed the section which allowed municipal councils, the chief objection of the liberals, only the dwindling Center faction voted for it! It was clear that the Ultras and the liberals were united for a specific goal: To destroy the Ministers who believed in the coexistence of two political philosophies.

On the eighth of April, Martignac dramatically left the Chamber with Portalis, briskly crossed the Pont Royal to the Tuileries, and returned a few minutes later with an edict, signed by the King, retiring the only important legislation of 1829! [99] Martignac had been driven to political suicide, but he had at least denied the opposing factions the privilege of striking the mortal blow. His Cabinet was now alienated from the Left press and only the *Débats* gave him the slightest encouragement. The *Courrier*, in an editorial filled with scorn for both the Center of Martignac and the Ultra Right of Villèle and Polignac, alluded to the "real" or secret government and asked:

Should the government handle the affairs of the nation or a faction which envisions *coups d'état* and absolute power? There is the question. It is necessary to choose between the nation and Coblentz [headquarters of *émigrés* like Polignac in the Revolution].

The *Courrier* later declared that the Left "disavowed and disdained" Martignac.[100] The *Globe* remarked with scorn that the Chamber had "at least saved its honor by hiding its responsibility".[101] Villèle's paper was as cruelly vindictive as the *Courrier*, stating "The anarchic law presented by the *pitiable* Ministry has been crushed before the noble fidelity of the Right".[102] The *Quotidienne* made the same decision in kinder words, asking the Cabinet to resign. Pierre Laurentie truly observed that Martignac and his "pernicious system" had compromised too long, but had at last learned they could not satisfy the liberals.[103]

---

[99] Daudet, *Martignac*, pp. 254-75.
[100] *Courrier Français*, 29 May, 9 April, 1829.
[101] *Globe*, 9 April, 1829.
[102] *Gazette de France*, 9 April, 1829.
[103] *Quotidienne*, 9 April, 1829.

CHAPTER V

THE POLITICAL PRESS AND THE *PARTI-PRÊTRE:*
THE ANTICLERICAL CAMPAIGN OF 1828-1829

... Charles X is not a Christian if he wishes to uphold the Charter which is an act against religion. We should not pray for him any more than for Louis XVIII, who was the founder of that Charter. They are both damned.

These seditious words were in a letter, written in 1825, by a village curé to a fellow priest.[1] They define the political outer limits of clericalism and the extravagant hatred felt by some members of the clergy for liberal thought. The period after 1815 was one of ascendant political involvement by the Catholic clergy; an inevitable reaction to twenty-six years of secular domination which either had suppressed or neutralized its influence. After the duc de Berri's murder in 1820, neither liberals nor the good intentions of the King could stay their hand as the Gallican high clergy and the counter-revolutionary priests of the "little Church", grew more impatient and demanding. The Society of Jesus, still formally an outlaw in France, had regained Papal recognition in 1814 and its members were allowed to return in increasing numbers.[2] Their novitiate in the suburb of Montrouge was regarded as a nest of sinister plots by the Left, as were the two lay organizations, the *Congrégation* and the more covert *Chevaliers de la Foi.* The latter had disbanded politically by 1826 because of its resentment of Villèle's attempts to manipulate it,[3] but the former society continued to be politically effective and had a membership estimated at over two thousand.[4] A religious revival was also expanding in the rural areas, partly as a result

---

[1] Adrien Dansette, *Histoire réligieuse de la France contemporaine de la Révolution à la IIIe République* (Paris, 1948), p. 241. (Hereafter cited as Dansette, *Histoire réligieuse.*) This passage is also cited as a part of a sermon by a priest who asked for, and received, a hearty endorsement from his congregation; and, for the latter action, was brought to trial. See, Stanley Mellon, *The Political Uses of History* (Stanford University Press, 1958), p. 188.

[2] Dansette, *Histoire réligieuse,* p. 247. The term "little church" refers to clergy who were not licensed under Imperial law, i.e., royalist.

[3] Bertier de Sauvigny, *Restoration,* pp. 383, 390.

[4] Dansette, *Histoire réligieuse,* pp. 254-55.

of "missions". These included outdoor sermons by friars who evoked fervid emotions in their rustic audiences with the aid of such props as jack-o-lanterns. The anticlerical press made much of this and also reported that these harangues often resulted in bonfires of "wicked" books.[5] Shades of the *auto da fé*! For all these incidents, real or imagined, the liberals usually managed to blame the Jesuits.

With the succession of Charles X to the throne, the clericalist movement was encouraged. In 1825, the anachronistic Sacrilege Law, discussed earlier, was passed. The press laws already in force specified the crime of "contempt for religion", which was often interpreted as contempt for a member of the clergy. The government also made an effort to cater to provincial France as Catholic and royalist, as opposed to the hopelessly irreverent city of Paris. Indeed, a report of 1828 showed that over half of all books printed in the provinces were religious while religious books comprised but one-eighth of those published in Paris.[6]

The chief periodicals of the Church have been discussed in an earlier chapter, but it is useful to recall that they by no means presented a united front. The best edited, the *Mémorial Catholique*, was pro-Papal but, under Lammenais' influence, was intellectual enough to refute the obscurantist charges hurled by the liberals. Public education was another area where clericalism was tempered by a sense of social responsibility, due to the leadership of Bishop Frayssinous.[7] The existence of some moderation or even progressiveness in the Church, however, was virtually ignored by the Left newspapers as they grew more militantly anticlerical in emphasis.

Anticlerical opinion even produced a specialty periodical, the *Gazette Constitutionnel des Cultes*, to oppose the *Mémorial*. The *Débats*, partly because of Chateaubriand's hatred of Villèle, joined the liberal papers' anticlericalism rather wholeheartedly. This was an important alliance as the Bertins' and Chateaubriand's credentials in both legitimism and Catholicism were immaculate. In Paris, the sale of sceptical, deistic, and simply irreligious books and pamphlets rose steadily. In one instance, fifty thousand copies of *Tartuffe* were printed on scrap paper and sold for three sous apiece, while the play (with emphasis Molière had not intended!) enjoyed a new popularity on the stage. Collected works of Voltaire ran to twelve editions even before 1824, those of Rousseau to thirteen.[8]

---

[5] *Ibid.*, p. 270. For another viewpoint on these missions by a Catholic royalist, see, Thureau-Dangin, *Parti libéral*, pp. 364-65.

[6] *Revue de Paris*, VII (2d ed.; Brussels, 1829), pp. 202-4.

[7] Adrien Garnier, *Frayssinous, son rôle dans la université sous la Restauration (1822-1828)* (Paris, 1925), pp. 133, 148. (Hereafter cited as Garnier, *Frayssinous*.)

[8] *Ibid.*, p. 138.

The leading gadfly against the Church, Paul-Louis Courier, had been mysteriously murdered in 1825 and his place was taken by the old politically conservative peer, comte de Montlosier. Instead of playing the eighteenth century materialist, as Courier had done, Montlosier aimed his attack against the more immediate Jesuits, *Congrégationists*, and their rumored conspiracies. In liberal papers, clerical references became almost as common as political commentary, and these allusions were woven into articles dealing with the most secular events. Only the King, for legal reasons, was spared from attack, but as the campaign mounted, even Charles himself lost some of this immunity to repeated innuendoes.

The King was, of course, known to be in sympathy with many Ultras and clericalists and his personal religious views were speculated upon quite freely, if only by inference. In fact, however, the old King had few friends among the most powerful bishops and his personal chaplain was a simple man who had no role in politics at court. As far as is known, Charles X's narrow piety had never led him to a hostile gesture toward the French Protestants or Jews, of whom he was the honorary patron.[9] A comparison between Charles and de Quélen, Archbishop of Paris, for example, on the subject of Protestants would illustrate the King's relative lenience. In spite of all this, and because of his medieval coronation ritual and his costumed appearance in a large religious procession, he came to be characterized in one clandestinely printed cartoon, as a Jesuit with fangs![10] Such direct offense to the King was always criminal, however, and the regular press left such risky affronts to garret printers and the coffeehouse rumor networks.

The journalists' anticlerical campaign was a mixture of facts, slogans, intentional distortions, and atrocity stories. The words *Parti-Prêtre* (Priest Party), even more than *Montrouge* or *Congrégation*, were used to mean the whole idea of clerical political intrigue, especially of the Villèle, and later the Polignac, faction. Another catchword of useful currency was *camarilla*, to refer to the secret cabinet; this had a Spanish and therefore un-French and "Jesuit" connotation. Journalists would include the phrase "Spain and Portugal", often rather irrelevantly, in an article. This implied the association of the Bourbons with the Inquisition and the religious traditions of such unpopular despots as Dom Miguel and Ferdinand VII.

In the opposition press, only the *Globe*, and occasionally the *Débats*, showed any restraint in these anticlergy indulgences. The *Globe's* lofty ethic of toleration extended even to those who would deny it, while Chateau-

---

[9] Vaulabelle, *Histoire*, VII, 300.

[10] Lucas-Dubreton, *Restauration*, pp. 100-01; see also, *Globe*, 26 June, 1830, for a reference to Charles X's religious outlook, also Vincent Beach, *Charles X*, Boulder, 1971, pp. 218-19.

briand's devotion to the romantic and mystic splendors of the Church still broke through the polemic in an infrequent passage. Nevertheless, even these journals did not hesitate to speak of a *Parti-Prêtre*, or to show alarm over a "clerical" victory in the courts, such as the Senancour case in 1828. Despite a brilliant defense by Berville, a fifty-eight year old publisher, Étienne de Senancour, was imprisoned for nine months for merely reprinting an edition of the sceptical work, *Résumé des Traditions Réligieuses*.

For accounts of atrocities attributed to men of the cassock, the *Courrier* and *Constitutionnel* led the field. Some of these stories were vaguely phrased to avoid libel and usually involved guilt by association, pointing in a Jesuit direction. The evil curé was the only newsworthy one and the thousands of simple pastors who served their flocks and set a Christian example on their beggarly government salaries were hardly noticed by the editors of the Left.

A priestly crime, perfect grist for papers like the *Courrier*, came to light in 1827 and made an execration of the name of its perpetrator: Contrefatto. He was a twenty-eight year old Italian priest employed in Paris as almoner and instructor in Mlle. Sauvan's Institute for Young Girls in the rue de Clichy. Except for an informal manner and a habit of giving candy to the little ones, there was nothing exceptional about him. In 1826, he started to offer Italian lessons in his home and one of his pupils, six-year-old Hortense Le Bon, complained to her mother of frightening and improper behavior. Madame Le Bon brought charges in police court, but the case was dismissed when other children would not give confirming testimony. But the mother persisted indignantly and the tutor was finally brought to trial. Contrefatto's misdeeds were clearly a matter of sexual assault on several children and he received the maximum penalty: Branding, exposure in the courtyard of the *Palais*, and a life sentence at hard labor in shackles! "Attacks on chastity", as these crimes were then called, were cruelly punished in an era when an offender's psychological compulsions were of no interest to a magistrate. The Church made no effort to defend him, but in the outraged liberal press, the priesthood had spawned a monster.

The political-clerical union was "exposed", much to the delight of the liberals, when a strict press censorship was imposed on the case and its trial. In addition, Contrefatto had pleaded for leniency after this terrible crime on the grounds that he was a man of God and a rumor circulated that France refused the extradition plea of his native Italian state. Another cleric, abbé Molitor, committed a sex crime in Versailles, which was covered by the same censorship. Molitor and Contrefatto were chained together when they were led off to prison. Another such assault was committed by a priest named Mingrat, whose name was also protected. The *Constitutionnel*, when at last freed of censorship by the parliamentary dissolution of 1827, gave a detailed account of the Contrefatto case, stressing the censorship imposed by Villèle's government. Étienne wrote of the "solicitude of the censor for that abominable Contrefatto" and the "mask of religion" worn by the government to protect "false piety and Ultramontanism". The editor revealed that the judge's remarks on the piety and goodness of the victim's family were censored for the press, as if to prevent favorable sentiments.[11] On December 21, another long editorial against Contrefatto and his offical "protectors" appeared in the *Constitutionnel*. A year later, at the Béranger trial, the lawyer Felix Barthe recalled that the *Gazette* had expressed a wish to see Béranger in a chain of galley convicts. Barthe was applauded when he said:

> Infamous connection... the horrible wish to see Béranger shackled to rowers! To see his face in the chain of convicts, doubtless replacing this Contrefatto, of whom the exclusive defenders of public and religious morality have so well proved the innocence... in protecting him from the immorality of the century.[12]

Contrefatto's case remained politically viable for a decade. An exemplary convict, steadfastly proclaiming his innocence, his sentence was amended to simple incarceration in 1838 and, in 1847, Louis-Philippe approved his parole. At each of these events, the press revived the case for its polemical value.

Although anticlericalism, to be effective, did not require a parliamentary airing as a point of reference, its propagandists were pleased when a national issue was handed them by the Jesuits.

Bishop-Minister Frayssinous had let slip, in a speech defending the clergy's role in education, that a very small number of high schools were run by Jesuits. In 1828, the opposition demanded a program to expose and suppress these illegal schools, long protected by the Villèle administration. Martignac's Cabinet yielded to pressure and, on January 22, appointed a commission to study the problem of the "little seminaries" and report on their legality. Appointments to this nine-member commission showed that the Ministry was halfhearted in regard to such a politically dangerous program. Five of the appointees were expected to be sympathetic to the Jesuits, including the comte de La Bourdonnaye, the Archbishop d'Alby, and the Archbishop of Paris, de Quélen.[13]

It was immediately apparent that Martignac had failed to please both extremes as a result of the nominations, and had walked into a snare, perhaps consciously planted by the liberals. The *Gazette* was horrified because four

---

[11] *Constitutionnel*, 7 November, 1827. This case is reviewed in Jacomet, *Le Palais*, pp. 176-78.
[12] *Gazette des Tribunaux*, 11 December, 1828.
[13] *Le Moniteur*, 22 January, 1828.

of the members were poisoned with the heresy of liberal Gallicanism. Urging his readers to reject the description of the Jesuits given by the liberal press, Genoude blamed the whole anticlerical spirit on the "unbraked license of journals". The *Gazette's* editor woefully predicted the proscription of individuals "suspected of following a Catholic rule" and the trials of Jesuit leaders.[14] The *Courrier* opposed the commission because it would not go far enough. Jacques Sarrans, writing in this newspaper, declared that mere enforcement of anti-Jesuit laws was insufficient. The problem, he stated, was to expose the creation of the subseminaries and added that the very commission was *de facto* recognition of their illegal existence. Sarrans even urged the expulsion of all seminarians from the university system, asserting: "Professors of seminaries who are Ultramontane are the enemies of representative government and the Gallican church".[15]

While the Chamber awaited the report of the commision, the Jesuit question was raised frequently during parliamentary debates over other matters. Since the seminaries had been shielded by Villèle, the vindictive *Débats* found another club with which to belabor the ex-Minister and censured the religious order:

All our readers will remain convinced that the morality of Jesuits is that which is most perfect to form a nation of hypocrites, and to insure the feeble conscience of prostitutes, thieves, and murderers.[16]

The *Constitutionnel* combined its defense of press freedom with its attacks on the Jesuit *camarilla*. Antoine Jay predicted a revival of the onerous law of "tendency", calling it "a method of destruction which Villèle's party and the *Congrégation* believed would destroy the periodical press". Jay quoted from an alleged prison interview with the notorious Contrefatto in which the latter had praised Peyronnet, author of the censorship, as his defender.[17] On another occasion, he prophecied that the King was planning to openly recognize the *Congrégation* and solemnly announced that a medallion had been struck with the words *Carolus X* on one side and the initials *I.H.S.* on the reverse.[18] Jay neglected to mention that this emblem was used in many church devices besides that of the Jesuits, or that the medal had probably been a production of the Left!

On May 28, the commission which had been designated in January pu-

---

[14] *Gazette de France*, 22, 23 January, 1828.
[15] *Courrier Français*, 22, 23 January, 1828.
[16] *Journal des Débats*, 9 March, 1828.
[17] *Constitutionnel*, 17 April, 1828.
[18] *Ibid.*, 2 June, 1828.

blicized its findings.[19] As was expected, the Ultra majority brought the most favorable verdict possible for the Jesuits. According to the majority report, there were 126 secondary schools under religious control which were authorized because they met the requirements of the University of France. There were, however, fifty-three unauthorized schools, mostly seminaries, which were to be brought into "conformity with the laws". Thus, the commission had recognized the *de facto* establishment of fifty-three illegal schools, of which eight prepared students for the Jesuit discipline. With this recognition, however, the commission members had been forced to call for regulatory legislation, else they would have seemed to favor illegality.

Bishop Feutrier, Gallican Minister of Ecclesiastical affairs, prepared the articles and the King reluctantly signed them, complaining that it pained him to thus be at odds with his "most faithful servants!"[20] These edicts appeared in the *Moniteur* on June 16, 1828, and, in essence, ordained the following: On October 1, the eight Jesuit "subseminaries" were to enter the jurisdiction of the University of France; all seminaries were to affirm they were independent of any unauthorized brotherhoods; the number of students in training for holy orders in all seminaries was to be limited to twenty thousand; no student older than fourteen could enroll as a seminarian and, after two years of schooling, all seminarians were to wear cassocks.

A journalistic storm broke a few hours after the edicts were published. The bishops of France, expecting trouble, had prepared their defenses two days earlier. De Quélen sent a circular letter to his forty-odd episcopal colleagues in which he resolved to uphold the rights of bishops in clerical education and to check "encroachments that menace spiritual authority". This letter started a flurry of circular and pastoral letters by the bishops to lesser members of the hierarchy.

The *Gazette* and the *Quotidienne* both cried "concession to the Revolution", the Villèlist journal declaring: "Today, if the laws against Protestants were enforced, one would have exactly what has just been undertaken against those who wish... to live under a Catholic rule under the freedom of cults". Such edicts, said the marquis de Genoude, were a "confiscation" and a sign of "revolutionary atheism".[21] The editor of the *Gazette* wished the protesting bishops success and warned Martignac that such anticlericalism could again

---

[19] *Le Moniteur*, 28 May, 1828. The report stated: "Even though these priests follow the rule of Saint Ignatius for their internal rule, it is not contrary to the laws of the Kingdom".

[20] Daudet, *Martignac*, p. 198.

[21] *Gazette de France*, 15, 20 June, 1828.

lead to "a prostitute on the altar of Notre Dame, a King on the scaffold".[22]
The *Quotidienne*, now edited by nearly the whole staff of the Ultra *Mémorial*,
concentrated on the religious, rather than the partisan aspect of the new
laws. Its new coeditor O'Mahony announced that this "concession" spelled
the ruin of religion and monarchy as he threatened the Ministry with the
Ultramontane loyalty of "forty-five sovereign pontiffs" and "forty thousand
priests of the Lord".

The opposition attacked the Jesuits, the Ultra protests against the decrees,
and the decrees themselves. Pastoral letters of bishops and curés which
defended Jesuits[23] were denounced by the *Journal des Débats*. "Jesuitism
is no more religion in 1828", stated the *Débats*, "than Jacobinism was
liberty in 1793".[24] Liberal editors found in the solution as much am-
munation to use against Martignac as had their opposite numbers on
the staff of the *Gazette*. The day before the edicts appeared, the *Constitutionnel* announced that Martignac was hedging before the power of
Montrouge and Kératry wrote in the *Courrier* that Bishop Feutrier was too
torn between his secular oath and his religious orders to countersign the
decrees. While the Left chided Feutrier's "weakness", the Right called him
"swelled-head" and "tyrant".[25] The bishop of Beauvais was learning, to his
sorrow, the price of serving moderation in the midst of conflict.

The bishops' protest to the edicts was at last drawn up in one document
and presented to the King by the cardinal of Toulouse, Clermont-Tonnerre.
The net effect of the polite but cool defiance was a *non possumus*, a refusal to
cooperate with the seminary laws. For the first time in many years, clergy
and crown were at odds. The Dauphin advised his father: "Sire, if I were
King, the archbishop would sleep tonight at Vincennes"![26] But prison was
not the discipline for such a powerful and haughty priest. Charles hoped that
there was still one authority that these rebellious prelates would heed – Rome.

The episcopal protest played directly into the trap set by the Left as
opposition journalists piously exploited the open defiance toward the King.
The *Courrier* called it an "invasion" of secular government and proof of
the liason between episcopate and Jesuits. With a passing thrust at Martignac
for being "too generous" to the Jesuits, the paper of Benjamin Constant
announced that the clerical tyranny of Villèle's reign would attempt a

---

[22] *Ibid.*
[23] Letter from curés of Amiens to the Archbishop of Amiens, which termed Jesuits "models
of the clergy". See *Gazette de France*, 20 June, 1828.
[24] *Journal des Débats*, 17 June, 1828.
[25] *Gazette de France*, 21 July, 21 September, 1828.
[26] Daudet, *Martignac*, p. 204.

comeback.[27] The *Constitutionnel* held that the factious bishops could only weaken the real spirit of religion which it declared, "their ambition perverts and their intrigues dishonor".[28] The paper praised the four bishops who refused to sign the *non possumus* as the "*elite* of the episcopacy"; since Feutrier was one of this *elite*, the *Constitutionnel* had paid him one of the few compliments he was ever to receive from the Left.[29] The *Journal du Commerce* called the *non possumus* "disobedient and insubordinate".[30] This was all very hypocritical; the *Commerce* was delighted.

The arguments lasted for months in the press. The Right defended the bishop's action, and in doing so, "exposed" its clericalism. The Minister of Education, Vatimesnil had said hopefully that University control of little seminaries would allow members of all faiths a chance to learn the truths of their own religion. But to this ecumenical ideal, the *Gazette's* Genoude replied hotly that there was only one true church, hence there were no "truths" in other sects.[31] Genoude lamented that the edict, in forbidding special auditor-students from attending Jesuit seminaries, was violating Christ's appeal to suffer the little children to come unto him,[32] and reached still further to complain that the liberals were acting illiberally by placing the seminaries under the "tyranny" of the University![33] Pierre Laurentie, in the *Quotidienne*, attacked the transfer of the seminaries to University control as an invasion of academic freedom,[34] to which the *Constitutionnel* replied by citing the *Quotidienne* of November 13, which had opposed a course at the Sorbonne by Professor Charles Comte as "dangerous for youth". Lost amid these broadsides was the best argument of the Right: That Jesuits had a right to follow their professions as individual priests, not as members of an illegal order. Opposition journalists used the "little seminaries" issue to attack clericalism and royalist papers. They also found here a convenient means to discredit the Ministry. The *Constitutionnel* predicted "ridicule" for Martignac and warned him he could not appease Villèle unless he were "fanatically loyal, unscrupulous, and apostolic".[35] The Jesuit edicts, even more than the press law, had exposed the Center Cabinet to the combined assaults of the partisans. But Martignac still survived between the musketry of the two armies: In Irene

[27] *Courrier Français*, 17 June, 1828.
[28] *Constitutionnel*, 7 August, 1828.
[29] *Ibid.* These prelates were the Bishops of Bordeaux, Saint-Flour, Strasbourg, and Beauvais.
[30] *Journal du Commerce*, 21 July, 1828.
[31] *Gazette de France*, 21 September, 1828.
[32] *Ibid.*, 19 August, 1828.
[33] *Ibid.*, 21 July, 1828.
[34] *Quotidienne*, 24 September, 1828.
[35] *Constitutionnel*, 16 November, 25 September, 1828.

Collins' words, "Charles X chose a moderate ministry under Martignac because its defeat seemed least inevitable".[36]

Through all of this partisan strife, religious bigotry, and indignation, the young pundits of the *Globe* had retained their intellectual urbanity. At the peak of the Jesuit crisis, Paul François Dubois wrote that the clergy was then the "greatest obstacle" to peace and progress in France. With ruthless objectivity, he then inquired: "What is the principle and base of its opposition?" And answered: "Liberty of conscience, which it does not wish to submit to a 'Test Act'". Dubois could show both sides of the coin. By his definition, a liberal was one who extended liberty even to those who would destroy liberalism. He recognized the political and cultural threat of the Ultramontane forces, but he would defend their right to threaten. The Jesuits, stated Dubois, in establishing private institutions, were practicing individual liberty. Any nationalization of individuality, added this young editor, was a step toward conformity and mediocrity.[37] This editorial helps to explain the qualities which set the little *Globe* apart from the other journals of it generation. The conflict over the seminaries was finally stilled. It was only a truce, however, because it did not heal the partisan and ideological wounds suffered by the combatants.

The negotiations which brought this truce were carried on with officials in Rome, who included the French ambassador, Chateaubriand and the Pope, Leo XII. Lassaigny, a special representative, was sent to Rome to present Chauteaubriand with a picture of the recent events in Paris, and to persuade the Pope to intervene on behalf of the government. The *Quotidienne* attempted to establish some liberal heresy in the past of Lassaigny, who had been a lawyer in the Court of Cassation. The editors prematurely declared that the "wise pontiff" had already rejected the Lassaigny appeals.[38] Fortunately for Martignac's Cabinet, the aged Pope welcomed a chance to deflate some episcopal egos, though he had to rely on Gallicanism to accomplish this purpose. The Pope discussed the issue with Chateaubriand who criticized the lack of understanding of liberty among the French clergy. Leo XII agreed that this was unfortunate, stating that republican democracies in the new world allowed Catholicism to flourish.[39] Chateaubriand, still coveting the Portfolio of Foreign Affairs, proclaimed his authorship of the entire negotiation to Mme. Récamier and to his fellow-journalists in Paris.[40]

[36] Collins, *Newspaper Press*, p. 53.
[37] *Globe*, 21 September, 1828.
[38] *Quotidienne*, 24, 25 September, 1828.
[39] Chateaubriand, *Mémoires*, III, Chateaubriand to La Ferronays, 12 January, 1829, 471.
[40] Récamier, *Souvenirs*, II, Chateaubriand to Mme. Récamier, 14 October, 1828, 237.

Officially, the Pope issued no encyclical, bull, or mandate, but through his Secretary of State, sent a message to the French bishops: That they all should take confidence in the wisdom of the King in the execution of the edicts and go in "accord with the throne". What a blow to those who had felt themselves more royalist than the King and more Catholic than the Pope! Most of the bishops obeyed the command, but their leader, Clermont-Tonnerre, penned a high-handed refusal to Charles X, for which he was permanently barred from court.[41]

With the death of the old Pope in 1829, the Ultras hoped for a new pontiff who would rescind the recent letter commanding their obedience. Chateaubriand, busy around the conclave, supported Cardinal Castiglioni, who was reputed to be pro-Gallican, anti-Austrian, and anti-Jesuit. When Castiglioni was elected as Pope Pius VIII, Chateaubriand claimed another personal triumph. He felt the Ministry should reward him for having preserved the Gallican liberties,[42] and referred to Pius VIII as "my Pope", urging Mme. Récamier to see that Kératry of the *Courrier* publicized his triumph.[43] Kératry duly satisfied Mme. Récamier's request and wrote in the *Courrier*: "M. de Chateaubriand wants a Pope who understands the needs of the present and the future ... [He] wants Christianity to travel with the times".[44] The vicomte's own *Débats* quite naturally called him the savior of Gallicanism. The *Gazette*, in no position, as a clerical champion, to speak against a Pope, glumly announced that its hated enemy had worked for the election of *losing* papal candidates.[45] Chateaubriand did not enjoy the sweet revenge of the Foreign Office, but he had severly pinked his antagonist, Villèle, in their continuing duel.

Although the seminary problem was resolved with no reward for the Ministry, the war of words continued between the *parte-prêtre* and the "atheist revolution". Ultra journalists held to the theme that equated liberal opinions with "atheism", while constitutionalists and liberals argued against theological concepts or described the sins of transgressors among the clergy. In reporting the rape of a sexton's daughter by a provincial priest, the *Constitutionnel* happily announced: "The Departement of Vaucluse also has a Contrefatto"![46]

Typical of the less sordid type of anticlerical news reported by the

[41] Daudet, *Martignac*, pp. 204-5.
[42] Loménie, *Chateaubriand*, II, 306.
[43] Récamier, *Souvenirs*, II, letters, 31 March, 11 April, 1829, pp. 351-52.
[44] *Courrier Français*, 8 April, 1829.
[45] *Gazette de France*, 5 April, 1829.
[46] *Constitutionnel*, 25 January, 1829.

Constitutionnel was an account of a bearded cleric in Chambéry. This man, abbé Desmazures, was said to frequently denounce the liberty of the press from his pulpit. The *Constitutionnel* injected the rumor, without substantiation, that Desmazures was transported from his home in Jerusalem by the Navy and had been salaried as the almoner to the French envoy at Constantinople! "It is very edifying", scorned the *Constitutionnel*, "to know that our ministers take five or six thousand francs each year from our pockets to gratify a bearded monk who is vowed to poverty, and who preaches against the Charter".[47]

In due course, certain anticlerical comments of the opposition press brought their writers before magistrates, giving enlarged and unpunishable publicity to liberal views.

A harassed, but undaunted provincial newspaper, the *Aviso de la Mediterranée* of Toulon received one of the first clerical indictments of the Martignac regime. Its editor, Rousseau Marquézy, twenty-six, was a frequent defendant in the Toulon courts. On January 21, 1829, Marquézy was charged with "outraging a minister of the state religion" in one of his articles wherein he had ridiculed the Ultra views of the rector of the village of la Crau. Marquézy's lawyer concentrated his defense on a plea for freedom of the press, urging the motto *Laissez-dire; Laissez écrire*. The prosecution speech demonstrated the Ultra fear of the increasing influence of the small provincial newspapers. The prosecutor referred to them as "faithful auxiliaries of the revolutionary journals of Paris... seeking to implant their exaggerated opinions in our provinces", and asserted the provincial journals hoped to weaken religion among the French. The judges, however, found no outrage in young Marquézy's criticism of the rector and acquitted him of the charge, and liberal papers in Paris published the magistrate's decision as a victory.[48]

Three curious political trials, on anticlerical charges, were held in Paris during the summer of 1829. No defendant in these cases received the mercy that had been shown to Marquézy in Toulon.

On June 26, René Chatelain of the *Courrier Français* was charged, as responsible manager, with outraging the state religion, other Christian cults, and public and religious morals.[49] These indictments centered on a discussion of Renaissance art in a recent number of the *Courrier*; a discussion which had strayed from esthetics to religion. The tone of the incriminating article seemed to cast doubt upon the durability of Christianity. The editor had written in the *Courrier* that he had always been "more or less" impressed

[47] *Ibid.*, 25 May, 1829.
[48] *Gazette des Tribunaux*, 26 January, 1829.
[49] *Ibid.*, 27 June, 1829.

by a great religious idea, particularly if it were explained by arts which "deal strongly with the imagination". The crime was found in this passage:

Again we prostrate ourselves, but for a moment and when it is the painting which asks it, before the pious images which have subjugated our fathers. The virgins of Raphael have not ceased to be divine, though their altars be half-destroyed. The immortal spectacles of the Last Supper, the Transfiguration, and the Communion of Saint Jerome will still be masterpieces, even when Christian beliefs will be completely vanished, if the durability of their fragile materials could last until then.[50]

Menjaud-Dammartin, the royal attorney, declared these words to be an affront not only to Catholicism, but to Protestant sects as well, and that the outrage was especially great in the supposition that Christian beliefs might not survive. Chatelain's defense lawyer, Joseph Mérilhou then took the stand. Mérilhou denounced the indictment as an attempt to revive the now illegal Villèlist principle of the law of "tendency", and launched into a long and frequently inspired oration on the liberty of religious beliefs. His summation involved an anecdote which gained a chorus of *bravos*! for Mérilhou and perhaps also for the name he invoked. Bonaparte himself, said the lawyer, avowed that freedom of conscience should prevail. The defense explained that Protestant ministers had asked Napoleon, in 1804, for the protection of their cult and the Emperor had answered that should be ever fail to respect freedom of conscience, he would deserve the name of "Nero". The magistrates, however, held that, since the perpetuity of faith is a dogma, the guilty article negated a dogma and hence outraged several Christian cults. Chatelain was ordered to spend three months in prison and pay a fine of six hundred francs.[51] Many critics saw this condemnation as a revival of the law of "tendency" trial of Villèle's days. The angry *Constitutionnel* on the following day, demanded that the government clarify the limits within which a journal might safely refer to religion.

Le Corsaire, a small satirical journal, next felt the judicial wrath of the Ultras for a witticism on the results of the *Courrier* trial. Viennot, the editor, had published the following comments, titled *Sottise des deux parts*, on June 30:

By decree of the National Convention, on the order of Maximilian Robespierre, the French people recognize the existence of the Supreme Being and the immortality of the soul. (7 May, year of disgrace, 1794.)

By order of the correctional Tribunal, composed of MM. Philippe de la Marinère, Colette de Baudicourt, Mathias and Huart, on the conclusion of M. Menjaud-

---

[50] *Courrier Français*, 29 May, 1829.

[51] *Gazette des Tribunaux*, 27 June, 1829. For Chatelain's famous acquittal on appeal, see chapter ix.

Dammartin, the French people cannot doubt the permanence of Christian beliefs. (26 June, year of Grace, 1829.)

Albin de Berville, Viennot's defender, attempted to disprove any insult to the court which had convicted Chatelain. He tried to draw a fine distinction between words which were "injurious" and those which were "irreverent". Lawyer Berville admitted *sottise* to be an unseemly term, but protested that the judges were not being compared, but *contrasted*, to Robespierre. Unable to believe this, the judges gave Viennot fifteen days in jail and a fine of three hundred francs.[52]

Another satirical journal, *Le Grondeur*, was prosecuted in July for outraging religion, public morals, and priests of the Church. The defendants included the *Grondeur's* manager, Chabot, two writers, Binet and Pollet, and the printer, Plassan. The three anticlerical satires in the little *Grondeur*,[53] which had resulted in prosecution, would have remained in obscurity had the court overlooked the offense. But, due to legal publication of trials, thousands of Parisians who never saw *Le Grondeur* now read every piquant word.

The first offending passage was *Le Foi et le Pape Alexandre VI*, an ancient story, repeated by Voltaire: A prince meets Pope Alexander at the house of a prostitute. The Pope's daughter-in-law is known to be pregnant, but no one knows whether the Pope's son Cesare, or the Pope himself, is the father. Alexander asks the prince for his opinion and the latter declares that the Pope's son is the father. "How can you believe such foolishness"? asks the Pope. "I believe it by *faith*", answers the prince. The defense denied any guilt for the defendant for this writing, declaring that Voltaire himself was on trial.[54]

A second article was called *Le Gendarme Orthodoxe*. In this story, a Protestant refuses to doff his cap at a religious procession, claiming refuge in the Charter. A passing gendarme scorns the Charter and knocks off the man's cap. *Le Grondeur* had added, in reference to the *Courrier* affair, that the defense of Christian beliefs "has been confided to the brutality of the gendarmes".[55]

The most gulty article, *Les Caricatures*, dealt with more personal innuendoes. The narrative opens in a bookstore. A priest and his companion are asking the bookseller to interpret a book of caricatures. A man with an owl's face and a woman who resembles a screech-owl are identified as the

---

[52] *Ibid.*, 5 July, 1829.

[53] A fourth article was directed against capital punishment and appealed for sympathy for a recently executed murderer. This had brought the charge of "troubling the public peace", of which the editors were acquitted.

[54] *Gazette des Tribunaux*, 15 July, 1829.

[55] *Ibid.*

"Cardinal of C. [Clermont-Tonnerre]" and "Mme. de C. [Cayla, a friend of Louis XVIII]", who have "worked for the return of the Jesuits" to France. A number of other caricatures are then explained by the bookseller. A horned beetle becomes the "Archbishop of P. [Paris]". "His jagged horns and scales represent avarice and durability"! A Satan-headed figure is defined as "Hermopolis [Frayssinous]"; a crayfish becomes the "Archbishop of Tours". "This worthy man", says the bookseller, "wishes to return us to the old regime".

After these irreverent citations had been read before the crowded courtroom, the defense was heard. The attorney called for religious toleration, even quoting Fénélon on that subject, and modestly declared that the free press only "reflected" opinions. The prosecutor congratulated the defense on its reasoned arguments, but called for the penalty of the law. The court was lenient. The printer and writers were acquitted, but the manager of *Le Grondeur*, Chabot, received a three-month sentence.[56]

In the closing days of the Martignac administration, occurred an event, which, in the theatre world, was a *cause célèbre*, and a classic demonstration of the government's sensitivity to the anticlerical attacks.

Young Victor Hugo had recently written a play, *Marion Delorme*, which centered about the intrigues of a royal courtesan in the seventeenth century; The company of the Salle Richelieu was scheduled to open the drama when, on August 6, a ministerial order suddenly forbade its presentation. When Hugo demanded an explanation from Martignac. the Minister informed him that the character of Louis XIII in the play would be identified with the present Monarch. In *Marion Delorme*, Louis XIII is treated as a priest-ridden weakling. Victor Hugo was indignant. When, under the succeeding Polignac Ministry, he was offered a large compensation for canceling his play, he grandly and publicly refused it.[57]

The *Globe's* Sainte-Beuve, in an article entitled "First Literary *Coup d'état"*, wrote: "Victor Hugo has had the honor to receive the first political stroke in this war to the death which begins against ideas".[58]

Fear of seeing a priest-ridden king on the stage had resulted in an unpopular censorship and in publicity for the dramatist. By the time of Martignac's fall, anticlerical pressure was capable of driving the government to such blunders. The *Parti-prêtre* had been examined, dissected, and greatly exaggerated by the press. When it fought back in self-defense, it had only made its public position worse.

---

[56] *Ibid.*

[57] Jules Garson, "L'évolution Napoléonienne de Victor Hugo", *Le Carnet*, II (1900), p. 43.

[58] *Globe*, 15 August, 1829. The *Constitutionnel*, August 8, 1829, remarked: "Marion left the censor's office even less a virgin than when she had entered".

CHAPTER VI

THE PRESS IN THE CRISIS OF AUGUST 8, 1829

Martignac's moderate Cabinet had been isolated from the crown, but it might still have survived if it had held the support of a majority of the deputies. The Left, however, ignored the sincere constitutionalism of the Bordelais orator, and continually blamed him for yielding to the far Right. At the same time, the Ultras demanded his head for yielding to the "opinion". His own support in the Center-Right was neither stable nor numerically large.

As neither main wing of politics felt the necessity for a Ministry of compromise, they had joined in an unholy alliance, frankly determined to topple Martignac and attempt a showdown. They were finally successful and the test of strength was clearly presented to both Ultras and liberals, when, on August 8, 1829, the last of the Bourbons announced a new list of ministers. The very names of these men were at once a war-cry for the Ultras and an open challenge to the "Revolution". Although the change had been long anticipated, the journals reacted violently to the crisis, each according to its political faith.

The first time Prince Jules de Polignac's arrival had disturbed Paris was during January of 1829.[1] Ostensibly, his reason for leaving the embassy in London had been to confer with the Ambassador to Russia. The opposition press claimed loudly that this was a mere pretext. When a rumor spread that Polignac had really been recalled to form an Ultra Cabinet, the Prince made use of his rank to address the Chamber of Peers in a denial. "By what right." he asked, "do they impute to me the intention of sacrificing liberties legitimately acquired?"[2] He also offered that, were the editors of these "calumnious inculpations" to but visit his home, they would see him surrounded by his labors which were solely directed toward "consolidation

---

[1] Nettement, *Histoire*, VIII, 209.
[2] Lamartine, *Restoration*, IV, 362.

of our present institutions". Polignac left for England a few days later, but his assurances had failed to quell the speculation.[3]

At the end of July, as the deputies of 1829 debated the budget proposals for the next year, the vicomte de Martignac offered a brilliant defense of his own administration. The marquis of Villefranche, one of the old Ultras, had accused him of "proscribing" the clergy by his rulings, in 1828, against Jesuit establishments. The First Minister replied hotly that if such laws were proscription, then every Christian king had been guilty of them. Charles X later admonished him for this, saying cryptically, "They will never forgive you for that". Who were "they"? The King could only have meant the clerical Ultras who would soon have their representatives in the Council of State.[4]

On July 26, Polignac again appeared in Paris. He had left London so eagerly that he had failed to request leave from the Minister of Foreign Affairs.[5] Rumors flew again; this time more heavily charged. A palace intimate politely warned the King that a Ministry under Polignac might have serious effects on public opinion. Charles scoffed at the suggestion: "You can't believe that! Poor Jules, he is so incapable"![6]

The press of the Ultras was confident of having a Ministry to its taste and urged the King to take immediate action. The *Gazette* announced the resignation of the Martignac Council as imminent and presented ill-disguised pleas for the recall of Villèle.[7] The *Quotidienne* was enthusiastic about the potentialities of Polignac. The *Drapeau Blanc*, now legally reborn with Polignac's assistance, proved its ardor had not slackened while the paper was suppressed. Before Polignac even returned, Martainville sounded the impatience of the men of "1815": "No more intermediate shades! There can no longer exist more than two enemy banners ... Republicans, attack if you dare! Royalists, let us attack if they do not dare to engage in battle"! This challenge also warned that anyone cowardly enough not to join one side or the other, might soon find himself crushed under the hooves of combat.[8] Such a daredevil was Alphonse Dieudonné de Martainville of the *Drapeau*, and such was the eagerness with which the most extreme Ultras awaited a Cabinet of their own persuasion. The *Débats* seemed unimpressed by the importance attached to Polignac's arrival, adopting a wait-and-see

[3] Nettement, *Histoire*, VIII, 212-13.
[4] Daudet, *Martignac*, p. 298.
[5] Viel-Castel, *Histoire*, XIX, 577.
[6] Daudet, *Martignac*, p. 300.
[7] *Gazette de France*, 2 August, 1829.
[8] *Drapeau Blanc*, 22 July, 1829.

attitude. Among the papers of the Left, only the *Courrier Français* and the usually nonpolitical *Globe* admitted the probability of an extreme Ultra Ministry. In the former, the abbé de Pradt [9] wrote such a Cabinet would be the deserved punishment of the Left for having temporized instead of having destroyed the Ultras in the Chamber.[10] The *Globe*, in a brief descent into politics, declared that Polignac alone would have to bear the responsibility for any resolution to create an extreme Right Cabinet. Not wishing to portray Martignac as a martyr, the *Constitutionnel* predicted a shift, but not a clean sweep, in the Council of State. Its editors felt that Polignac would be given the honorary portfolio of *Maison du Roi*, where he would wield great influence, but that Martignac would be kept as a useful figurehead.[11] The *Constitutionnel* had no faith in the assurances of Martignac's own paper, the *Messager des Chambres*,[12] which stated that the present ministers would remain. In any case, the prelate-baiting *Constitutionnel* chose to consider even the defeated ministers as "devoted to the *Congrégation*". It was this paper which offered the first clear suggestion of a new tactic for the opposition:

> It would be dangerous to choose ministers who, by their opinions, by their antecedents, by their positions, would not completely reassure 30 million citizens devoted to representative government and who know that there is no legal and possible taxation except that which has been voted by the legislative power, as is instituted in the Constitutional Charter, ...solemnly sworn to by Charles X.[13]

Here we see a reference to that enemy of representative liberty, arbitrary taxation. Was there not also in this passage a veiled threat of resistance to power, by a legal budget veto by the Chamber? Liberal historians had popularized the story of Sir John Hampden's refusal to pay "ship money" to Charles I of England. The *Constitutionnel* was probing toward this end, but carefully skirting the laws of sedition. The idea of legal resistance by refusal to pay taxes had not long to wait for light. Soon the liberal press was to lead in a nationwide propaganda campaign recalling the English parliamentary methods of 1640; although the more radical precedent of 1688, the change of dynasty, would later replace, in the press, the "legal

---

[9] "His pamphlets made him one of the heroes of liberal opinion. His fame seemed to be great, especially among the masses. His entire ambition was to be a deputy". Barante, *Souvenirs*, III, 455.

[10] *Courrier Français*, 2 August, 1829.

[11] *Constitutionnel*, 29 July, 1829.

[12] Martignac still employed this journal to defend his policies, although its readership was now very small.

[13] *Constitutionnel*, 29 July, 1829.

resistance" theme. In another passage, the *Constitutionnel's* editors offered this caution:

> If the enemies of public liberty, of national independence, rejoice in the hope of seeing M. de Polignac change the direction of our affairs, the friends of France and of constitutional monarchy are anxious over it.[14]

During the first week of August, several of the leading Ultras were seen entering and leaving the Tuileries. On August 2, comte Guy de Montbel, a dear friend of Villèle, and the Prince de Polignac conferred together with the King. Montbel had received word from a friend, the violently Ultra comte de La Bourdonnaye, that the latter would accept a portfolio Charles had offered him.[15] This presented a problem to Charles X. The King wanted La Bourdonnaye because he had been a leader of the Ultra bloc in the Chamber, not because he had also been a notorious advocate of the "White Terror" in 1815. Montbel asked the King to agree, however, not to name anyone as "president" of the Council, as the condition of La Bourdonnaye's acceptance. In other words, one of the two Ultra rivals to lead the Ministry was an experienced politician, the other a crony of the King. The prospect of a compromising struggle for supremacy between these two gentlemen caused the other ministers to consider the former Prime Minister, Villèle. Villèle's closest friend on the new Ministry, Montbel, was asked to propose to the shrewd ex-Minister that he head the new Cabinet. Villèle refused the honor, doubtless recognizing the great political risk involved in such an adventure.[16] The *Gazette*, loyal to Villèle, hailed the prospect of a Villèle Cabinet, but the independent *Quotidienne* warned against it. The *Quotidienne-Gazette* feud was now growing rapidly as it polarized the Ultra royalist camps, and the liberals rejoiced in such evidence of disunity, which was the only real effect of the Villèle *démarche*.

Polignac himself had earlier visited the retired moderate duc Decazes, who had been First Minister during a more liberal era under Louis XVIII, and offered him a chance to create a constitutional fusion. Decazes felt no assurance in the verbal guarantees of the Prince and demanded as his condition of acceptance, the appointment to the Ministry of two moderates, the

---

[14] *Ibid.*

[15] Nettement, *Histoire*, VIII, 301.

[16] Montbel wrote to Villèle: What the journals are saying, of quarrels, of discord is false, but it is based on a knowledge of characters. La Bourdonnaye is ardent and loves vigorous measures, without hesitating too much on the Possibilities. The prince [Polignac] has a great loyalty. Chabrol and the prince are actively preoccupied with the idea of you... The prince declares he would be happy to see you at the head of affairs... We cannot exist with the license of the press, there is one of our most violent diseases". Villèle, *Mémoires*, V, 378.

duc de Pasquier and comte Roy.[17] Thus, rebuffed by leaders of the Center, Polignac faced the open rivalry of the powerful La Bourdonnaye. The comte de Chabrol accepted the Navy Portfolio with reluctance only after the personal insistence of the King. He was a Martignac moderate whom the King wished to preserve as a *politique* measure. The Dauphin Louis, who was a military pedant, selected the unpopular traitor of Waterloo, Marshal Bourmont, for the Portfolio of War. The latter had, in exchange, consented to give *Monseigneur* the war office's customary function of awarding promotions in the army.[18] On August 5, Chabrol, thoroughly disgusted, resigned his Navy post, creating an embarrassing stir in the press. In desperation, Martignac's name was suggested by Roy, but Charles flatly rejected it.[19] Forming an Ultra Cabinet was proving to be more difficult than conceiving it.

On the next day, August 6, the old ministers resigned and the signatures of a new Ministry were recorded; all but one. To fill the vacuum left by Chabrol's sudden change of heart, the King appointed, without his consent, Admiral de Rigny to the Navy post. This officer was a popular hero because of his recent victory over the Turks at Navarino in the Greek War of Independence. He was also a nephew of the powerful liberal banker, baron Louis. Almost as quickly as he arrived in Paris, de Rigny informed the King that he would not serve with a deserter, and referred specifically to General Bourmont. The King answered to the effect that de Rigny was the traitor for thus criticizing the choice of the Crown. The Dauphin, now gleefully in charge of promotions, rudely added that de Rigny might forget about any chance for promotion in the future. This ugly conversation became the property of the press and caused de Rigny's popularity with the liberals to soar even higher.[20] It also illustrates the distorted view Charles had concerning loyalty to the Crown.

The press was able to turn to its advantage another embarrassment of the Court. The Dauphine, who was also the surviving daughter of Louis XVI and a symbol of the *ancien régime*, visited Le Havre on August 6 while the duchesse de Berri visited Dieppe.[21] The cool public reception given these princesses by the Normans [22] contrasted glaringly with the almost triumphal tour which old Lafayette and his son George Washington, were making for *Aide-toi* in the South at the same time. They were acclaimed in such cities as

---

[17] Daudet, *Martignac*, p. 301.
[18] *Ibid.*
[19] *Ibid.*
[20] Nettement, *Histoire*, VIII, 323-24.
[21] *Le Moniteur*, 6, 9 August, 1829.
[22] Viel-Castel, *Histoire*, XX, 52-55.

Grenoble and Lyons by speeches, banquets, toasts, and wildly cheering crowds.[23]

On the morning of the ninth of August, 1829, number 221 of the *Moniteur* appeared with three royal decrees which created the last Ministry of the Restoration. The first decree appointed the Prince de Polignac to the Ministry of Foreign Affairs. He was not designated as President of the Council. The second decree named General Bourmont for War, La Bourdonnaye for the Interior, Courvoisier, a moderate, for Seals and Justice, Montbel, the Villèle partisan, for Ecclesiastical Affairs and Public Education, leaving the right of ecclesiastical appointment to holdover Frayssinous, a minor concession to the Center. This decree also included the name of Admiral de Rigny, though it was common knowledge that he had refused. The third decree placed Chabrol, another Martignac moderate, at Finances, though he was not expected to remain there any more willingly than he had at Navy. The former ministers were given the customary pensions, decorations, and honors, although significantly, none who were not peers were raised to the peerage. The Gallican Bishop Feutrier, who had prosecuted the anti-Jesuit edicts of 1828, received nothing.

The public and the liberal press could not have been greatly suprised, since the secrecy of the recent palace negotiations had completely broken down. The Ultra preponderance made it clear that there was no serious intention to appease any moderate, not to mention liberal, opinion.

Three of the names in the *Moniteur* appeared as a triple nightmare and propaganda slogan to the Left: Polignac, Bourmont, and La Bourdonnaye. Nearly all its attacks were aimed at this triumvirate whom the duc de Broglie termed the "Ultra-Ultras". The journalist Saint-Marc Girardin identified them in the *Débats* with three sorrowful memories of France: "Coblentz, Waterloo, 1815".[24]

"Coblentz" had been the *émigré* capital of the exiled Bourbons. It was there that young Jules de Polignac extended the friendship with Artois which endured for a lifetime. Jules was the son of Yolande de Polastron, a favorite lady of Marie-Antoinette. He was also a nephew of Louise de Polastron, a mistress of the future Charles X. The ties that bound the comte d'Artois to the Prince de Polignac went back to another age. Jules had served in Russia, then emigrated to England in 1800 to join *Monsieur*. With his brother, Armand, he later entered France with the Cadoual

---

[23] Vaulabelle, *Histoire*, VII, 186-88. An idea of the republican spirit that greeted Lafayette's tour may be found in the description of a banquet in his honor, published in the *Tribune des Départmens*, 9 August, 1829, expressing delight in the "American" sentiments of the gathering.

[24] *Journal des Débats*, 15 August, 1829.

plot to kill Napoleon and overthrow the Empire, and was among those arrested in that affair. Napoleon commuted the brothers' death sentences to prison terms, but, due to legal carelessness or imperial cruelty, Jules was kept in prison long after his term had expired; bitter years which did nothing to soften his *émigré* prejudices. After being set free during the decline of France in 1813 he received his title of Prince from the Pope. At the Restoration, he became *Aide de Camp* to *Monsieur* and part of Artois' "green cabinet" at the Louvre. His religious zeal was more visionary than fanatical and he was a charter member of the *Chevaliers de la Foi*. Named ambassador to England, Polignac came to appreciate the idea of an aristocratic parliamentary regime as reflected in the Wellington-Castlereagh wing of the Tories, although he failed to become an Anglophile in any "liberal" sense.[25] His long patrician features were often set in a preoccupied expression; interpreted by some of his colleagues as "daydreaming". His reputation for seeing holy visions, however, appears to be overstressed and could best apply only to his rather erratic behavior during the July Days.

"Waterloo" referred to the desertion of Marshal Bourmont three days before that battle. He also had a record as a counterrevolutionary leader and plotting against the Empire. The last, and most familar to contemporaries, of this menacing trio was the comte François-Augustin de La Bourdonnaye. As a deputy in 1815, he had made a speech demanding the proscription of Bonapartists according to "categories" and the spilling of "some blood". Even more, he asked for "death" and "torture" for the worst of those he denounced. A royalist version of the *enragés*, he would make a beautifully exposed target for liberal propagandists. Chateaubriand once said that La Bourdonnaye, a small man always furious over something, reminded him of a "male shrew" or an "irritated bat".[26]

The opposition press found in this roster of ministers an unprovoked attack upon an obedient, loyal people, a defiance of the parliamentary majority, and a program that was pregnant with the most serious dangers. In the "pure" Ultra journals, the announcement was a royalist triumph over the "Revolution" and a cause for rejoicing.

The *Quotidienne* could feel doubly rewarded. Two of its favorite Ultras had been named and Villèle, whom it despised, was not included. Perhaps Villèle realized that the faction represented by La Bourdonnaye would never

---

[25] Vincent Beach, "The Polignac Ministry: A Re-Evaluation", *University of Colorado Studies*, No. 3 (Jan., 1964), 87-146, offers the most detailed account of the relations between "Jules" and the King as well as the inner workings of the royal mind during the creation of the cabinet.

[26] Bertier de Sauvigny, *Restoration*, pp. 15, 132, 143; Vaulabelle, *Histoire*, VII, 144-45; Thureau-Dangin, *Royalistes*, p. 179.

give him its cooperation. It is true, that on the morning of that fateful August 8, the King received, in private audience, none other than Joseph Michaud, editor of the *Quotidienne*,[27] whose August 9 issue was full of praises for the adventure. The next day's paper presented a strong defense of the Royal prerogative in these words:

> ... if it were admitted that the King should, in all circumstances, yield to the voice of the majority in the elective Chamber, for the choice or the dismissal of his ministers, that majority would reign, the crown would be stripped of initiative, of sanction, and of administration; the King would be no more than a powerless idol, without freedom, without opinion, without action.[28]

Martainville echoed similar views in his *Drapeau Blanc*. He revived the old argument for an alliance between the Crown and the masses against the pretensions of the bourgeoisie and he called on Polignac for an unrelenting war against the liberals. He praised the vigorous measure of the King: "It is ... the King himself whom they [the liberals] have called to their bar. No intermediary between outrage and the sacred person ... of the monarch. The King alone has willed; the King alone has acted".[29]

Intoxicated with their victory of royal prerogative, the Ultras were demanding a decisive and immediate action against the opposition. They urged the King to use his emergency powers under Article 14 of the Charter; an ambiguous section which authorized the King to rule by decree, if required for the "security of the state". Liberal journalists predicted that such an attempt would be made, but, unlike their opponents, they referred to it as an impending *coup d'état*, a term Ultras scrupulously avoided. The press of the Ultra faction also argued that, since the King's prerogative was sacred, it was criminal of the opposition journals to attack either his choice of ministers or the ministers themselves. For the following eleven months, until those final acts of Ultra stupidity which led to open revolt, the polemic of the press was based largely on this phantom of a *coup d'état*. The Ultra's journals implored the ministers to perform this feat and thus crush the liberals, while the opposition press bent all of its energies toward warning and educating its readers to the growing menace of the *coup*. Neither faction made any attempt to wish the phantom away.

The *Gazette de France*, its dream of a new Villèle Ministry shattered, pleaded for a union of royalists of all shades, and attacked Martignac for having made an "incalculable blunder in allowing notions of order and

---

[27] *Le Moniteur*, 9 August, 1829.

[28] *Quotidienne*, 10 August, 1829.

[29] *Drapeau Blanc*, 10 August, 1829.

disorder, principles of revolution and monarchy, to be confused". In an editorial entitled, *Paris, 8 Août*, Genoude branded the so-called government of *comité directeur* a "plague" and added that "whatever will deliver France from it will be favorably received".[30] The Ultraroyalists, and especially Villèlists like Genoude, had for two years described the various *réunions* of liberal electors as such revolutionary juntas. These gatherings of deputies and electors had never been clandestine; indeed, they were often held in some large public restaurant or at the mansion of a Laffitte or a Baron Louis. But the Ultras knew that the driving force behind such meetings had been the electors' association *Aide-toi, le Ciel t'aidera*.[31] Its activities had unearthed electoral frauds under Villèle and had helped to unseat him. *Aide-toi* had, except for the *Globe*, the solid backing of the opposition press, and was able, in that way, to speak to all of the eighty thousand electors in France. The royalist charge of *comité directeur*! was an answer to the liberal cry of *Congrégation*! and these words were frequently exchanged during debate in the Chamber.

Villèle's idea was to make the Right to strong that it could rule in peace and the *Gazette* preached his doctrine. "May the royalists be united and the revolutionary faction vanquished", intoned the *Gazette*, and recalling perhaps the "unbelievably" royalist Chamber of the Restoration's early years, stated that this faction never could do anything against united royalists, and "its progress was born of our divisions".[32] It was now impossible for the *Gazette* to back Villèle openly for the Cabinet. Genoude was Villèle's friend, but he was also a supporter of the King.[33]

The Ultra "defection's" victory helped to heal the recent schism of the Right, but it had opened an older wound. Chateaubriand's legitimist "defection", though pleased with Villèle's disappointment, could not be loyal to the King's latest choice, and the royalist *Journal des Débats* now openly agreed with the liberals. In a strongly-worded editorial it announced that once again "the bond of love and confidence which had united the people with the monarch"

---

[30] *Gazette de France*, 9 August, 1829. Although Professor Artz, *Journal of Modern History*, I (June, 1929), p. 211, relates this Ultra label, *comité directeur*, to the leadership of the loosely controlled electoral society that preceded *Aide-toi*, and which included Laffitte, Manuel, and Constant, the term also appears in police jargon at the time of the *Carbonari* prosecutions of 1822. This latter usage relates to an alleged junta of a more revolutionary nature, supposedly headed by Duval, Laffitte, Talleyrand, Labbey de Pompières, and several others. Reports by detectives indicate they were unable to verify allegations ranging from dealings with Spanish rebels to counterfeiting – to ruin the Bank of France! See, *Le livre noir*, II, 115.

[31] Guizot, *Memors*, I, 313; Weill, *Parti républicain*, p 21: Pouthas, *Guizot*, pp. 423-24.

[32] *Gazette de France*, 9 August, 1829.

[33] Lamartine, *Restoration*, IV, 364.

had been broken, that what France had "gained in forty years of labors and sorrows, has been stripped from her". The *Débats* asked why such discord had to be sewn and why with such a threat: "Were ever people more submissive to laws", it asked, and recalled how warmly the people had greeted the King on his last visit to the provinces: "Today he will again find most of his subjects faithful, but all afflicted by an unmerited defiance". Of the new men chosen for the Ministry, the *Débats* said, "The hatreds that their names awake in all hearts are too deep not to be considered. Dreaded by France, they would like to be dreadful to it". The ministers, the editors wrote, will at first make pretensions of liberalism, but that "Their unfamiliarity with these words will betray them. One will only be able to see there the language of fear and hypocrisy".

Étienne Béquet, in the same issue, posed the question of the Ministry's intentions: "What will they do? Will they seek to apply the force of bayonets"? Béquet warned, "Bayonets of today are intelligent, they know and respect the law". The writer went even farther, stating that the ministers could not last three weeks with a free press, yet to remove that freedom, they would have to violate the laws. The strongest and most challenging part of this famous editorial was reserved for the end, restating the idea of legal resistance and borrowing ominously from English history:

Are they going to defame the Charter that gave immortality to Louis XVIII and power to his successor? They must think well of it! The Charter maintains an authority against which may be broken all efforts of despotism. The people will pay a billion to the law. They will not pay two million to the decrees of a minister. With illegal taxes, a Hampden would be born to break them. Hampden! Is it again necessary that we should recall that time of trouble and of war? Unlucky France! Unlucky King![34]

The regular press of the liberals, while indicating horror and repugnance over the new appointments, seemed also to show some feeling of relief. These journalists had fought compromise as represented by Martignac and had called for a showdown. The *Courrier Français*, while terming the composition of the Ministry "a subject of alarm for the nation", admitted its belief that under Martignac's "regime of hopes and meticulous care", both public opinion and the Chamber of Deputies would have grown "soft".[35] Thus did Benjamin Constant and his colleagues excuse their intentional sabotage of France's only experiment in liberal "legitimacy".

---

[34] *Journal des Débats*, 10 August, 1829.
[35] *Courrier Français*, 10 August, 1829.

The *Constitutionnel* showed a similar satisfaction over the death of conciliation. "As long as we were destined to submit to a Ministry of the
extreme Right", it stated, "it is better that this should be sooner than later".[36]
These newspapers had asked what circumstances warranted the confidence
of power to men who, in themselves, represented the counterrevolution and
the "saddest memories of 1815", men who even considered M. de Villèle
"as a revolutionary".[37] The *Constitutionnel* and *Courrier* agreed with the
Débats in denouncing Polignac as the willing instrument of Lord Wellington
and his Tory policies. This association, scarcely justified, made the anti-French
and antinational connotation of Polignac's name even more odious to the
opposition. Polignac was indeed favored by Wellington and was an admirer
of Tory domestic politics, but his foreign policy was later to prove that there
had been no British influence in his administration. The *Courrier* searched
far afield for guilty foreign connections and even linked Polignac's name with
that of the new tyrant of Portugal. On November 18, it stated that, though
Dom Miguel had outraged humanity, law, and religion, he still had the
Jesuits; "a recommendation which should find favor with M. de Polignac".

The charge of clericalism was easy to apply to the August eighth Ministry
and the press never missed an opportunity, however remote. One must read
this violence to discover in what sensational forms these attacks were made.
The *Constitutionnel* of August 9 published two lurid stories concerning the
behavior of certain priests. One concerned a local case in which a woman was
alleged to have been rudely handled by a priest because she had appeared
in church with her hair in curlers. The other story, perhaps even less
relevant, described the shocking career of one Rembauer, a priest in Bavaria
(and somewhat beyond Polignac's jurisdiction). This cleric was reported to
have fathered children by his domestics, to have slit a servant's throat, to
have fathered another child by a farmer's daughter and then killed both
mother and child, and then, nothing if not thorough – to have performed
two abortions. As if these crimes were not wicked enough, the *Constitutionnel*
also reported that he had forged a deposit slip for fourteen francs! Of course,
the symbolic name of Contrefatto was again brought before the public.

The next day's issue turned its hatred of the *parti-prêtre* on events at
hand and declared: "The *Congrégation* has triumphed"! The editors also
warned readers to verify the next electoral lists and refer any irregularities
to the courts. "What", they asked, "can the *Congrégation* do against an
honest National Representation"?

---

[36] *Constitutionnel*, 10 August, 1829.
[37] *Ibid.*, 9 August, 1829.

From the vengeful cries of the Ultra press to the sombre and disturbing statements of the opposition, the organs of public opinion had described, on August 9, the preliminaries of violent conflict.

Pamphleteers assisted the periodical press of the Left in its war on the Ministry. The more radical ones dealt with bloody revelations about Polignac and his associates, while others were simply reprints of newspaper editorials. The titles of two of these brochures were: *la Polignacide* and *Le Cri d'Alarme*.[38]

But what was the reaction of those "little journals" so dear to the Parisian heart, those which delighted with humor, satire, and scandal? The most respected and erudite was the *Figaro*; founded in 1826 by Balzac's republican friends, it rapidly became famous and popular.[39] Before the police seized its plates on August 9, *Figaro*, in ten thousand copies, had escaped to the streets. By evening, single issues were bringing ten francs (two dollars).[40] Dr. Louis Véron, literary critic of *Figaro*, left an account of the origins of this famed edition. On the evening of August 8, Véron, with some other young writers, dined at a restaurant called Chez Véry. At his table were Victor Bohain, *Figaro's* editor-in-chief, Nestor Roqueplan, and Auguste Romieu, *Figaro's* political editor. Also present was Étienne Béquet, author of the famous *Débats* editorial which was soon to appear. The young journalists were in good spirits and their lively discussion of the new Ministry caused the gentleman at the next table, a general officer and a peer, to smile broadly. Bohain suggested to his friends the idea of publishing the next day's *Figaro* with a black border and of filling it with little prophecies of a Polignac-dominated future. The waiter furnished pens and paper and each man fell to composing his share of the next edition.[41] Their final product was one of the most audacious tracts of the Restoration. It succeeded in not only making the Ministry seem a ridiculous anachronism, but also in making itself immortal.

As planned, the issue appeared with a quarter-inch black mourning band around each page.[42] A bold-type statement of defiance to the Ministry, signed by Bohain, was in the center of the first page. In this manifesto, Bohain promised his subscribers that they would continue to receive their *Figaro*, if the police made an illegal seizure of his press, even, he added,

---

[38] A collection of these pamphlets may be found in the classification (Lc 49) in the *Bibliothèque Nationale*.

[39] Fréderic Ségu, *Le Premier Figaro, 1826-1833* (Paris, 1932), p. 2; see *supra*, chapter ii.

[40] Louis Véron, *Mémoires d'un bourgeois de Paris* (5 vols.; Paris, 1853), II, 382.

[41] *Ibid.*, p. 381.

[42] *Figaro*, 9 August, 1829.

if he had to publish the paper in Holland! This was followed by a long list of sharp and scandalizing little announcements. Their general theme was the prophecy of life under the new *ancien régime*, or perhaps under thirteenth century feudalism, re-created by Polignac. Many of these *quolibets* dealt with minor personalities and private scandals, making them pointless today. Although both humor and seasoning may be obscured in translation, the more political of these railleries were:

In place of illuminations at the next festivity,[43] all the houses in France should be draped in black.

M. de Hermopolis (Frayssinous) has been given the portfolio of benefices.

It is by the solicitation of Lord Wellington, *duc de Waterloo* that M. Bourmont has been named Minister of War.

M. Debelleyme [44] had in view the extinction of mendicity; M. de Renneville will work for the extinction of publicity.

A band of false salters have harassed the populace of Orléans for several days. The agents of the *gabelle* have shown the greatest ruthlessness in punishing this audacity.

The Polytechnical School will assume the title of School of Cadets.

A Huguenot, they write from Foix, was hanged last week for the crime of his religion.

The French government has demanded the extradition of MM. Mingrat and Contrefatto, called to direct the primary education of both sexes ...[45]

The Court architect has been commissioned to present a plan for the reconstruction of the Bastille. The prisoners of state were temporarily lodged this morning at la Force.

M. Franchet is going to present tomorrow a report on the reestablishment of *lettres de cachet*.

The members of the Center Right having been handed over to Dom Miguel, this prince has ordered that they must suffer a billion leeches. The Jacobins, says the *Gazette*, are at last going to be punished.[46]

---

[43] The *fête du roi* (King's "official" birthday) was the next major holiday.

[44] Debelleyme had been Martignac's popular and innovative Prefect of Police, who was now retired as a magistrate of the Paris Court of Commerce. Contrary to *Figaro's* assumption, he was not replaced by Renneville, but by a notorious clericalist and Ultra from Poitiers, J. H. Mangin. See, John P. Stead, *The Police of Paris* (London: Staples, 1957), pp. 99-101.

[45] The crimes of these two clerics are discussed in chapter v, *supra*.

[46] Dom Miguel was the brother of Emperor Pedro of Brazil and Regent of Portugal for Pedro's daughter, Maria da Gloria. In 1828, he usurped the throne and ruled despotically for five years. French liberals denounced the Bourbon's recognition and toleration of this most reactionary regime.

The farming of salt and coal has been given to M. de Villèle. (Economics were Villèle's *forte*.)

Father Rootham, General of the Jesuits, has been named Marshal of France, replacing the Prince of Hohenlohe.

M. Bohain[47] must be broken on the wheel next Thursday; no testimony has been extracted from him up to now; he has refused to hear the Almoner of Prisons.

M. Véron,[47] director of the *Revue de Paris*, literary magazine burned this morning at the foot of the Great Staircase, has gone to seek asylum in Holland.

M. Auguste Romieu,[47] curator of antiquities in Morbihan, has received a threat of dismissal if he does not reassemble in eight days all of the bones of the royal and Catholic army deceased at Auray and Quiberon.

The quarrels between the Armagnacs and the Burgundians will, they say, soon be appeased.

M. Roux, surgeon in chief of the hospital of Charité, should operate immediately on the cataract of an august personage.

Figaro appeared the following day more in its usual style, but with another column of sallies directed at the August 8 Cabinet. The front page contained another bold editorial, titled: *Les Voila!*[48] dealing with the ministers and the probability of a *coup*. The issue included a few more *bigarrures*, notably one which announced that Bishop Frayssinous had jilted his mistress in the *Opéra* and that the other dancers were in a frenzied rivalry over him.

The polemic of the press was soon repeated in the courtroom. As usual, these public press trials were well attended, and widely circulated verbatim accounts of judicial activities legally extended the incriminating editorials. The Ministry did not wish to strike at the press immediately. Indeed, the King and his ministers were not agreed on the nature of such an attack. The total defection of the once loyal *Débats* and the tart sauce of the *Figaro*, however, could not be ignored by a government under the goad of its most zealous supporters.

Louis Bertin as responsible editor-in-chief of the *Débats*, had assumed full responsibility for Béquet's famous article, and appeared before the

---

[47] Bohain, Véron, and Romieu were the editors who collaborated in creating this memorable issue. References to refuge in Holland relate to the anticipated suppression of the press. The King of the Netherlands, William, and his Minister, Van Maanen, had more reactionary press laws than did France; and editors who offended the government, especially those who advocated independence for Belgium, could receive up to ten years in jail. The Holland references are also satirical in recalling that French critics once fled to that country to escape the censure of the Sun King.

[48] *Figaro*, 10 August, 1829.

sixth chamber of the Correctional Police of the Seine on August 26, 1829. In the packed courtroom were, among others, the Duke of Chartres, son of Louis-Philippe, François Guizot, and the philosophers, Villemain and Victor Cousin. The royal prosecutor, Levavasseur, began with a reference to the "loyalty and devotion" of the new ministers, a remark which caused a stir in the court. Levavasseur attacked as incriminating, the *Débats'* line, "Once again is broken the bond of love and confidence which unites the people with the Monarch". The prosecutor called this an offense to the King, and asked if the people had not seen their Monarch in public and unprotected since August 8. He asked the court, "Was his brow less calm, his expression less serene, his guards less numerous"? At this unfortunate slip, the audience broke into general laughter and some shouted, "No, *more* numerous"!

André Dupin *aîné*, dean of the advocates of Paris, now rose to defend Bertin. The defense held first that the Ministry was trying to coerce the *Débats* into selling out in the old Villèle manner. On another track, Dupin claimed that Bertin was such a lover of constitutional monarchy that he had gained, under Convention, Directory, and Empire, a close acquaintance with several prisons, and that he had followed Louis XVIII to exile in Ghent in 1815. Dupin shouted:

This is the man that, from the beginning, the Ministry attacks as one of the suspects in a conspiracy called *Jacobin and Imperialist!* A royalist, whose hair has turned white in the service of the Monarchy, is the first victim designated by the right arm of the extreme Right".[49]

Dupin then defended the paper itself, saying:

The *Journal des Débats* is religious, but it is not Ultramontane: It wants religion within the state, not above the state… It is enough to say that it is in dissidence with these men, so zealous and devoted, who would like to govern France like Spain and Portugal.[50]

Dupin then praised the *Débats'* royalism and even admitted that this paper was "aristocratic" – but it was, he noted, a nobility "of good taste" and talent, and not one created by a few magic words. He claimed the *Débats* was singled out because it "served liberty too well" and might persuade independent royalist readers in their opinions, something a liberal paper could hardly do. To be accused of an attack on the King, argued Dupin, was "absurd". Since Charles X was inviolable, it would be impossible to attack him. He added that people were not required to *love* their king, only

---

[49] *Gazette des Tribunaux*, 27 August, 1829. Bertin also published his own account of the trial, titled, *Liberté de la presse, procès de M. Bertin* (Paris, 1829), B.N. (Le 49 1145).

[50] *Gazette des Tribunaux*, 29 August, 1829.

to obey and respect him, and he ridiculed the idea that such love could be commanded.

Each incriminating passage that Dupin defended gave him a new opportunity to praise his client's love of liberty, to expound his own political views, and to strike at the Polignac group. While explaining the guilty phrase, "The court with its old rancors", Dupin drew a murmur of surprise when he quoted Cardinal Richelieu, "The throne is a chair where the King alone should be seated, and not a bench where other powers take their place beside him". In regard to the incriminating phrase "the emigration with its prejudices", lawyer Dupin attacked the ease with which titles of nobility were obtained from the Crown and reminded the court that Napoleon's marshals had been given only nominal titles and that they had fought battles for France. Of the line Béquet had written, "the priestcraft with its hatred of liberty", the lawyer remarked, "It is not evident that it is the enemy of liberty of the press, and above all, free inquiry, of the two conditions vital to representative government"?

In a fervent peroration, Dupin then assailed the character and past record of each of the three most unpopular ministers and rested his case. The court spent well over an hour in its deliberations before handing down a decision. Béquet, the author of the incriminating article, was acquitted, but Bertin the responsible editor, was found guilty of offense to the person of the King and was sentenced to six months in prison and a fine of five hundred francs.[51] The case was appealed and, on Christmas Eve, 1829, the *Cour Royale* of Paris acquitted Bertin in one of the famous decisions of the era: A judicial blow to the Ultra's view of the "royal prerogative" – a legal precedent to criticize the ministerial choice of a King.

Two days after Bertin was sentenced, the same court heard the case of *Figaro*. Bohain, as responsible editor, was charged with outrage to the person of the King because of two of the witticisms which had appeared on August 9. These were the first and the last of the jests in that issue. One had suggested that houses be decked with mourning at the next *fête du Roi*. The other passage had urged that a surgeon should operate on the cataract of an "august personage".

Dupin, *jeune*, the brother of the *Débats'* lawyer, defended Victor Bohain. He lashed out at La Bourdonnaye and claimed that only a national sorrow had provoked *Figaro's* black borders. The defense argued that the court must interpret the couplets by their letter, not by their spirit As for the "cataract" reference, Dupin stated that the duc de Bourbon had recently

---

[51] Guizot, *Mémoirs*, I, 327.

contracted an eye disease and that the Prince of Hesse was in Paris expressly for such an operation as described. But, he added, what if the passage *had* referred to the King? Still there would be no offense, he argued, because the King's blindness was only caused by courtiers and that sight could be restored to him by a free press. The defense ended with a phrase which caused a sensation in the court, "There is but one thing that is not pardoned in France, that is dishonor! Even power cannot offer a refuge from public scorn"! This defense won a minimum sentence for the rich young Bohain who was convicted on a double charge of offense to the King's person. He was ordered to six months in prison and to pay a fine of one thousand francs.[52] Not as fortunate as Bertin, Bohain's later appeal to the higher court resulted in the same sentence.

Such were the opinions, impressions, and activities of the political press of Paris in response to the advent of a Ministry of the extreme Right. This event marked a point of departure in the political journalism of the opposition. Henceforth, the idea of legal resistance was both organized and proclaimed in the press, Great new militant journals would soon spring into being. Their goals would be the destruction of the Ultras and, if required, of the dynasty. The vast publicity given to the prosecution of press offenses served only to strengthen the opposition. One of these journalists, Guizot, who later became a Prime Minister, said of that eighth of August, "Charles X had raised the flag of counterrevolution upon the Tuileries".

[52] *Gazette des Tribunaux*, 26, 28 December, 1829.

CHAPTER VII

THE NEW MILITANT PRESS

In the summer of 1829, the opposition press began transforming its character from that of a critic to an active and calculating antagonist. The first stirrings of this shift were provoked by the appointment of Polignac's Cabinet and its first clear manifestation was seen in the widely disseminated propaganda for the Breton Association which advocated legal resistance by taxpayers, a program which will be described in the following chapter. The initial tirades of the liberal journals against the nomination of the Polignac Ministry, however, were merely an intensification of their old editorial role of critical opposition, a policy mainly of holding the line, maintaining the fervor of the liberal camp, and feeding its flames of partisan indignation. These had been the polices of that middle-class giant, the *Constitutionnel*, of the *Courrier Français*, and since Villèle's rise to power, of the royalist *Débats*. The old journalism had included heavy doses of anticlerical propaganda and exaggerated warnings of a threat from the Jesuits. The older policy had attempted to educate the eighty thousand electors of France in their political rights and responsibilities, through publicity of the electoral society *Aide-toi*, but it had not attempted to mold political philosophies or direct strategies.

Indignation came more readily than indoctrination to the established liberal editors. Their collective readership and their sponsors included republicans, Bonapartists, moderate legitimists, Orleanists, and a great number of readers, including a large proportion of deputies, who feared a drastic shift in political thought and merely hoped to reform and rationalize the existing order. This last category encompassed most of Martignac's "Center" and its supporters, many of the Chateaubriand-type legitimists, and a number of men like Casimir Périer, new industrial millionaires who posed as liberals in the legislature, but who were always deeply afraid of any political change that might alter the social and economic order in which they thrived. So, for most of the liberal press, the crisis of the August eighth Ministry was sufficient "cause" for the moment. Polignac's Cabinet appeared to the Left as something more than an outrage; it was viewed as an immediate threat to constitutional liberty. Why, asked the liberals, would men whose very names recalled the "White Terror" be placed in authority, unless it were to hatch some monstrous conspiracy against the law-abiding people, so content with their Charter?

Certain young creative journalists, convinced that a *coup d'état* was brewing in Paris, determined to create opinion of their own. The *Constitutionnel*, the *Journal du Commerce*, and the *Débats*, were excellent, they admitted, to maintain opposition; but to give this opposition a goal and a course, and to map its strategy, demanded a new kind of journalism in France.

The movement was initiated by some young radicals who called themselves republicans and some older men who backed them. As early as January, 1829, a group of these republicans had begun a paper called *La Jeune France*, but financial troubles caused it to be "stillborn"[1] The era had arrived whem journalism was a business, even a major business, and it was exceedingly difficult, by 1829, to create a newspaper with mere zeal.[2] In June, when rumors of a Polignac Cabinet were beginning to circulate, *Jeune France*, supported by Armand Marrast, made a successful reappearance with a clear statement of its youthful idealism.[3] Its office in the Palais-Royal became a center of radical political gossip and agitation. One of the editors, Léon Gozlan, attempted to define the rather vague region of "republicanism" in the late Restoration:

> By republicanism, I mean to speak of that thirst for equality and justice, of that universally proved disdain for distinctions which do not arise from personal merit, of that necessity for control of all acts of power, and finally that consciousness of the dignity of man and the citizen which makes him resist arbitrariness and scorn the idea of despotism.

If ideologically imprecise, these young radicals were outspokenly clear on issues and immediately predicted an inevitable revolution, declaring that the best intentions of the Chambers could not prevent it.

The spirit of *Jeune France* was further expounded in an editorial in the August 9 issue, written by a student, Hippolyte Mansion. Attacking the irritating cliché that age alone brings experience, he countered that youth alone was the dynamic force of a society; and was in itself, a revolution. At last the idealistic and alienated generation was finding its voice in the press. *Jeune France*, appearing every five days, was edited with a rather skillful

---

[1] Alphonse d'Herbelot, *Lettres d'Alphonse d'Herbelot a Charles de Montalembert et Léon Cornudet* (Paris, 1908), d'Herbelot to Montalembert, 24 January, 1829, p. 18. (Hereafter cited as d'Herbelot, *Lettres*.)

[2] *Ibid.*

[3] *Jeune France*, 15 June, 1829.

caution, avoiding prosecution through metaphor, innuendo, and abstraction. On that fateful August 9 it shrieked: "Another Blood-Bath!" then asserted that the nation which had been bled for fifteen years was now about to be bled white. The "final" blood-bath was at hand, its editors wrote, but avoided an explanation of what form it would take or why it was to be the last.

The *Tribune des Départemens*, a more important, but less strident republican organ, was also established during June of 1829. Although this paper became famous for its later role in opposition to the Monarchy of Louis-Philippe, it was to play a significant and somehow tragic part in the Revolution which converted that prince to a King. Its first editors were the brothers Auguste and Victorin Fabre, who had previously edited a small literary periodical, and had experienced political action as leaders, with Godefroy Cavaignac, in the *Aide-toi* society.[4] When the doctrinaire liberal journalists of the *Globe* deserted the society in 1828, these young republicans had quickly filled the vacuum.[5] The *Tribune* was abstractly republican and its editors preferred the term "patriotic" rather than "liberal" or "republican" to describe their policy. The first issue, June 8, 1829, exposed the comparatively utopian views of its writers. The paper stood for a decentralized federated republic and even suggested that the electors and deputies of France consider themselves as representatives of *all* the people.[6] Republican journalists were, in fact, the only serious spokesmen for the working class poor.

The *Tribune's* writers, or "Fabrists," scorned the conservative view that the small electorate need not represent the populations of the departments in which it voted. Typical of more recent *Aide-toi* members, the *Tribune* editors favored the provinces and provincial reports preceded the news of Paris. The *Tribune*, along with other republican papers, was very pro-American, as shown by its choice of Lafayette as a patron saint. To love America was to praise "democracy". The liberals of France, on the other hand, were politically Anglophile. That each group had its model of government only partly explains the gulf between the republican and the liberal factions; a gulf that widened after 1830 and was always more the result of economic class conflict than of abstract ideals. The first issue of the *Tribune* accused the liberals of narrow partisanship and playing politics in coteries. "France is through with coteries", wrote Auguste Fabre, "their role has lasted too long: It is time for that of the patriots to begin".

---

[4] Weill, *Parti républicain*, p. 17.

[5] Pouthas, *Guizot*, p. 398.

[6] *Tribune des Departemens*, 8 June, 1829. The masthead spelling of the title omitted the final "t".

The August 9 issue, which struck hard at Polignac, also contained a contemptuous reference to he materialism of the upper bourgeoisie. Remarking that the 3 percents had fallen nearly one franc during the night, the *Tribune* wondered: Was it from the danger of a war with England? With Switzerland? With the Dey of Algiers? No, declared Victorin Fabre, the "terror of our rentiers" comes from enemies a hundred times more dangerous than the Algerians or the English; enemies who live in the heart of the nation, "ever conspiring against her prosperity, her liberty, and her glory, and wishing ... to put her back under the yoke of ultramontane fanaticism and absolute power".

In October, the shareholders, led by Ascension Montgolfier, wealthy son of the aeronaut, withdrew their support, despite the editors' disclaimers about being "revolutionary", and the *Tribune* disappeared. However, in the growing political tumult of the following year, it was reborn with the help of a young medical student named Morhéry and other student members of the University-based republican society, "Friends of Truth". For its second appearance, it also had the prestige of Lafayette's support.[7]

The pejorated "liberals", for their part, had little relish for the contamination of those radicals who wrote for the *Tribune* or *Jeune France*.[8] They would have been even more offended had they known that the staff of the *Tribune* had a cache of weapons and a secret organization, similar in structure to that of the *Carbonari*, under the nominal command of General Lafayette.[9] Auguste Fabre gravely plotted to convoke primary assemblies which were to elect judges and deputies for a constituent assembly.[10] The Fabrists made good use of their muskets and paving stones during the July Revolution, though they failed, with words or force, to create the Second Republic. Unlike the legitimists or the Orleanists, republicans were unable to advertise either their program or their potential "candidate", Lafayette. Their clandestine plans, had they appeared, would have scattered all the bourgeois support they had and would have been viewed as a manifesto. As for their undeclared presidential candidate, it must be recalled that this professing republican, who had already helped to midwife two constitutional monarchies, was never comfortable in a lost cause. At least Lafayette lent his prestige to these young disciples and did not later turn his back on them, as many did.

In 1832, Doctor Morhéry denounced the "betrayers" of the only radical and popular cause in 1830 and published the supposedly "dangerous" mani-

---

[7] Weill, *Parti républicain*, pp. 19-23. The Deputy Marrast was also a backer.

[8] Hatin, *Histoire de la presse*, VIII, 523.

[9] Weill, *Parti républicain*, pp. 22-23.

[10] *Ibid.*

festo of the Fabrists' political cult; among their constitutional proposals were:

1. A free press, "even for the *Drapeau Blanc*".
2. No property qualification for franchise.
3. A unicameral legislature with separation of the executive to prevent a "Convention".
4. Election of all prefectural and local officials.
5. Primary elections and secret ballots.
6. "One" National Guard, open to everyone, as in 1791.
7. Industrial legislation in behalf of *all* classes.
8. Election of all army ranks below general.
9. Jury trials for all offenses.

When one contrasts such generous humane sentiments with the disillusioning reality of the Monarchy that was created, the bitterness of these young patriots is more appreciated.[11]

A trio of small republican journals appeared in the winter of 1829-30: The *Révolution, journal des intérêts populaires*, the *Patriote*, and the *Nouveau Journal de Paris*. The *Patriote* was edited by a lawyer named Franque, who also wrote for *Jeune France*. Franque claimed that the name of his paper signified his abhorrence of the more moderate terms "constitutional" and "liberal", which he said were "hollow words... created for times of timidity, lying, and corruption". The *Journal de Paris* was an old title, revived in 1828 by the deputy of the Seine, baron Auguste de Schonen and a former judge, Jacques-François Bavoux. It is important to note that not one of the five journals of the republicans had a large circulation before June, 1830. Staffed largely by unpaid students, their readership was mainly on the Left Bank. Although these newspapers represented a prelude to a new militant journalism, they had to wait for a major political crisis before they would be widely read. They had begun before the advent of the Polignac Ministry and seemed then as much a rebellion of youth against corrupt age as they were the expressions of a radical political doctrine. By the time they were being taken more seriously, the Orleanist propaganda was well known as a possible antidote to their democracy, as well as to the Bourbons. But, as will be seen, during the July Revolution, these radicals threw consternation into the liberal Left as they demonstrated their political skill and military courage. The young republicans failed in their crucial hour and then again in 1850, but they were the vanguard of the ideals of the Third Republic, as well as the only voice of the masses in 1830.

---

[11] Morhéry, D.M., "Réponse aux outrages" (Paris, 1832), in Auguste Fabre, *La Révolution de 1830 et le véritable parti républicain* (2 vols. in one; Paris, 1833), pp. lxix-lxxvii. (Hereafter cited as Fabre, *Revolution*.) Morhéry became a controversial pioneer in the field of gynecology.

A far more influential militant force in political journalism went into action soon after the King formed his Cabinet of Ultras. Like the republicans, its spirit was somewhat youthful, and it too would focus its energy to exploit the revolutionary potential posed by the existence of the new Ministry. But this new force, rejecting the remoteness of the republican ideal, would urge a more "practical" goal: A change of dynasty. Leading this well-plotted campaign were *Le Temps* and *Le National*.

The *Temps* first appeared on October 15, 1829. Its godfather was the great "doctrinaire", François Guizot,[12] a rising power on the Left. Already esteemed as an historian, the young southerner had also achieved fame in journalism as an editor of the *Globe* and as chief editor of his own magazine, the *Revue Française*. With his creation of the *Temps*, Guizot was launched directly into militant politics. Supported by Lafayette, the duc de Broglie, and Dupont de l'Eure, as well as the editorials of the provincial newspaper *Pilote de Calvados*, Guizot was elected deputy from Lisieux in Normandy. Although he had never lived in Normandy, he received two-thirds of the total vote cast. His campaign was based simply on the national issue of opposition to Polignac.[13]

The *Temps* directorship, as well as some of its financial backing was supplied by Jacques Coste, who had previously directed the literary *Tablettes Univer- selles*, founded in 1823. It may be recalled that it was the collaboration of the young writers of the *Tablettes* with a group of sacked University lecturers that had created the greatest of all Restoration literary periodicals, the *Globe*.[14] The stock company formed to incorporate the *Temps* was unique. Though many newspapers had shareholders among the deputies, the *Temps* was almost completely owned by a group of seventy-four opposition deputies. These stockholders included such men as the capitalist Casimir Périer and General Émile Oberkampf, heir to an Alsatian industrial empire.[15]

The new *Temps* was highly literate, strongly anticlerical, and bold. It attacked the Polignac regime for its "complete inaction", daring it, baiting it, to strike at the Charter. It was part of *Temps* policy to point up alleged dissensions within the Ministry,[16] and Guizot also used it as a medium to propagandize the Breton Association.[17] Vehement about encroachments by

---

[12] Hatin, *Histoire de la presse*, p. 510.

[13] Pouthas, *Guizot*, pp. 407-16. Residence for eligibility depended upon property rather than domicile. Friends of candidates often purchased land in a likely constituency to promote an election, as in Guizot's case.

[14] Hatin, *Histoire de la presse*, p. 498.

[15] *Temps*, 15 October, 1829.

[16] *Ibid.*

[17] *Ibid.*, 3 January, 1830.

the government on freedom of the press, it prophesied that Polignac's first blow would fall there. The *Temps* predicted a ministerial *coup d'état* from the beginning of its existence and urged an organized but "legal" resistance to it. Rightly forecasting that the *coup* would be directed against the electoral law, as well as the press, the editors sought to train electors in their rights and duties under the Charter. These ideas were given force in pointed editorials, under such captions as "Sinister Plot" or "How a Ministry Risks its Head". More outspoken than the liberal establishment represented by the *Constitutionnel, Le Temps* was still bourgeois in its view of society.[18]

The leader of the new militants, indeed one of the most effective newspapers in French history, was the *National*. The brilliant success of this journal may be credited to the three young men who served as its chief editors: Adolphe Thiers, François Mignet, and Armand Carrel.

Adolphe Thiers, whose career influenced French history during two monarchies, an empire, and two republics, was born in Aix-en-Provence during the time of the Directory. As a law student in Aix, he formed a lifelong friendship with François Mignet, another Provençal. Thiers and Mignet practiced law in Aix and in their early careers, they were much alike. In 1821, both moved to Paris where they were rewarded with the patronage of Étienne, Cotta, and Laffitte.[19] Mignet had already received, at twenty-five, the highest cultural honor, membership in the *Institut de France*.[20] Both men, while too young for elective office, immediately engaged in journalistic activities. Mignet joined the *Courrier*, while Thiers wrote especially for the *Constitutionnel*, but also for the *Globe* and both made important friendships with great men in and out of government. Thiers also continued to write his famous *History of the French Revolution*, which appeared in ten volumes in 1827 and was more approved for its bias than its considerable scholarship. Mignet's book on the same subject had been printed in 1824, but failed to measure up to his superior romantic histories on medieval themes. Both young men had assumed, as an obligation of their post-Revolutionary generation, the task of placing the Great Revolution in a respectable historical setting. Thiers first political fame resulted from his historical and economic research. In 1825 he wrote a brochure for Jacques Laffitte, the banker, in which he supported a sound program of the Villèle Ministry for conversion of government bonds. Recognizing Thier's authorship, Villèle began to consider him

[18] *Temps*, 27 November, 1829.

[19] See *supra*, chapter ii.

[20] Edouard Petit, *François Mignet* (Paris, 1889), p. 24. (Hereafter cited as Petit, *Mignet*.) Mignet's treatise on monarchy provoked a critic to render fully the homage of the romantic era: "He has the look and stamp of the historian; he does not recite, he paints".

for the Portfolio of Finances,[21] and sent him encouraging, but anonymous letters. Thiers, although attracted by the proposals, insisted on direct negotiations with Villèle. The First Minister, however, was a careful man and refused to risk Ultra support by dealing openly with the young liberal writer and the whole matter was dropped.[22] His friend, Mignet had, during this period, become a protegé of the prince de Talleyrand and was a frequent guest of the old diplomat in his great house in the rue Saint-Florentin. Mignet, along with Thiers, frequently attended *soirées* at the home of Lafayette, of de Tocqueville and at the palatial suburban residence of Laffitte.[23] Mignet was also privileged to attend one of the high courts of romanticism – the literary salon of Delphine Gay, where he met Victor Hugo, Charles Nodier, and Alfred de Musset.[24] For lighter diversions, the younger staffers of the *Courrier*, the *Globe*, and the *Constitutionnel* would often meet at the cabaret of Mme. Saguet, in the Montmartre, there to sing treason with Pierre Béranger, the culture-hero of Parisian students.

Through a mutual friend, Mignet met another historian, young Armand Carrel, and introduced him in turn to Thiers. Though he hailed from Rouen, the adventurous Carrel was soon inseparable from his southern comrades and the trio of the *National* was complete.

Carrel, whose death in a duel at thirty-six ended one of the most tempestuous lives in French letters, had lived many careers. As a soldier he had been devoted to the military glory of France. As a *Carbonaro* expatriate, when that organization was being hounded by the police, he had gone to fight for the Spanish insurgents before the disgraceful French intervention of 1823. As a scholar, he had achieved fame for his essays on the English Revolution and his justifications of the French Revolution. In a review of Thier's forthcoming work on the French Revolution, appearing in the *Constitutionnel* for January 14, 1826, Carrel showed that motivation was the basis of his historical method. Always a frank partisan, his psychological insights helped to compensate for his lack of detachment.

Carrel's most important historical essay was also his most controversial and provocative. In 1827, the publisher Sautelet (later manager of the *National*) issued his suggestively pointed *History of the Counter-Revolution in England under Charles II and James II*. Popular for its style, as well as its message, the work was translated into English by Hazlitt in 1846. Carrel's message

---

[21] John M.S. Allison, *Thiers and the French Monarchy* (Boston and New York, 1926), p. 77. (Hereafter cited as Allison, *Thiers.*)

[22] *Ibid.*

[23] Petit, *Mignet*, pp. 30, 36.

[24] *Ibid.*, p. 37.

is not wholly new, even in 1827, but it is startlingly clear: Two restored monarchs trifled with the liberties of a free people and, in the case of the later one, associated with ultramontane clericalists; for this subversion of a hard-won revolution, James was replaced by rulers chosen from a related dynasty. It was not an Orleanist statement, except, of course, by popular inference. The book did not state the unspeakable, as Cauchois-Lemaire was to do a few months later. Nevertheless, the introduction to the first edition had to be altered for revealing too boldly the analogy between 1688 and contemporary political events.[25]

A romantic man of honor, the handsome young Carrel threw away his life in a foolish duel.[26] But the greatest merit of Armand Carrel was in his genius as a political journalist. He cared little for discretion or the laws of the press. Once, to a friend, he desribed this attitude, and in doing so wrote his own prophetic epitaph:

> To write, that is to be always in the breach, especially for him who, of good faith and without a sidelong glance at personal interest, means to drive ahead the high ideal he follows... It is not one man, nor even a thousand men that he effects, but the very spirit of liberty which must spread itself. The waves which beat the coast are broken there one by one, but the ocean advances slowly, it wears, it swallows the rock... Life is not in the number, but in the employment of days.[27]

Carrel was not a radical in the Fabrist sense when the *National* was created and was even a trifle contemptuous of the "masses". It was his appreciation of the Parisian's courage during the July Days, that later caused him to adjust his opinions toward democracy.[28]

The *National* founded by the inspiration of Thiers, Mignet, and Carrel, was a stepchild of the *Globe*, the *Courrier*, and the *Constitutionnel*. Both of the latter papers were controlled by wealthy men of moderately conservative tendencies and much of their readership was among the substantial bourgeoisie who worshipped the cult of stability. Many of the younger, more radical editors of these papers felt that their share of influence in journalism was being thwarted. Thiers, one of the frustrated, had worked ceaselessly to make the well-rooted *Constitutionnel* accept a more forceful direction. In

---

[25] Colin Forbes Brown, Jr., *Armand Carrel: His Historical and Political Ideas Relating to the Revolution of 1830 in France* (Washington: Catholic University of America, 1949), pp. 42-51, *passim*; see also, Thureau-Dangin, *Parti libéral*, p. 462.

[26] His antagonist was Delphine Gay's husband, Émile de Girardin; who, under Louis-Philippe, pioneered cheap journalism in France. See Louis Fiaux, *Armand Carrel et Émile de Girardin: cause et but d'un duel* (Paris, 1912).

[27] René Gustave Nobecourt, *Armand Carrel journaliste* ((Rouen, 1935), pp. 25-26.

[28] Weill, *Histoire*, pp. 45-48.

this attempt, his efforts were unsuccessful, although he had the support of the chief editor, Charles Étienne, and Evariste Dumoulin.[29] Some of the more conservative directors, however, merely regarded the stocky, outspoken little Provençal as the paper's "pet" radical.

Plans for the creation of the new journal were probably begun in November of 1829. Considerable time was required for planning conferences, engaging young writers, and raising money. The principal financiers of the *National* were the two liberal bankers, baron Louis, erstwhile Finance Minister to the Emperor, and the millionaire adviser to the Duke of Orleans, Jacques Laffitte. Baron Cotta von Cottendorf, the German publisher and patron, also supported this new venture of his young friend Thiers, but not with such substantial funds as he had once invested in the *Constitutionnel*. Thanks to Cotta's *Gazette de Augsbourg*, the *National's* reprinted polemic could be read widely in the Confederation, and Thiers, in turn, received exclusive European reports from his German associate – analogous to a modern wire service.[30] An important, but shadowy backer in the foundation of the *National* was Prince Talleyrand, with Lafayette, the last of the old kingmakers. At seventy-five, he still possessed a nose able to detect changes in the wind's direction. He had once toyed with the possibility of an Orleanist movement during the political crises of 1814-1815.[31] In 1829, in a conversation with Thiers, he again suggested that he might favor a crown for Louis-Philippe.[32] Talleyrand had influenced many of Thiers' articles in the *Constitutionnel* and the young journalist was always deferential to the old statesman. There is no evidence of Talleyrand pulling Thiers' editorial strings, but he unquestionably encouraged his Orleanist policy. The duc Decazes, former First Minister, believed the Polignac government would attempt a *coup d'état* and that Talleyrand was its original Cassandra. Decazes accepted the rumor that Talleyrand issued daily bulletins to the liberal journals, warning them of ministerial plots.[33] De Rémusat, of the *Globe*, however, as an intimate of the Prince, doubted this report.[34]

The problem of Talleyrand's influence in the creation of the *National* is qualitative. Most of his contemporaries agreed that the old intriguer gave

[29] Allison, *Thiers*, p. 87.

[30] *Ibid.*, p. 88.

[31] Louis Madelin, *Talleyrand* (Paris:Flammarion, 1944), pp. 268, 392; comte de Sainte-Aulaire, *Talleyrand* (New York: Macmillan, 1937), pp. 195-96.

[32] Louis de Viel-Castel, *Histoire de la Restauration* (20 vols.; Paris, 1878), XX, 185. (Hereafter cited as Viel-Castel, *Histoire*.)

[33] Guillaume Prosper de Barante, *Souvenirs* (4 vols.; Paris, 1890-99), 2 December, 1829, III, 528. (Hereafter cited as Barante, *Souvenirs*.)

[34] *Ibid.*, 28 November, 1829, Rémusat to Barante, III, 528.

Thiers counsel and backed the *National's* Orleanist policy. They disagree on whether he gave financial assistance. A modern royalist historian asserts that Talleyrand gave money to the enterprise.[35] The vicomte de Chateaubriand, who despised Talleyrand, referred, to him as the "boss" of the *National*, but declared: "Prince Talleyrand did not add a sou to the till, he only soiled the spirit of the journal by throwing into the common fund his share of treason and corruption".[36] Chateaubriand had good reason to resent the *National's* dramatic debut. For so many years his own *Journal des Débats* had been the Warwick among newspapers. Now all attention was being focused on a *parvenu* whose staff seemed to have little respect for that "legitimacy" which the author held so precious. His disgust for Talleyrand was due to his appraisal of the man as a turncoat and opportunist. Chateaubriand, who considered himself the world's greatest diplomat, refused to recognize Talleyrand as the savior of France of 1814. Vaulabelle has said that neither Talleyrand nor the Duke of Orleans contributed money to the *National* and that even Laffitte owned but one share of the paper's stock.[37] From such diverse testimony, one may venture that Thiers, Mignet, and Carrel were not the sole creators of the *National*, but that they were not the mere agents of great bankers and politicians.

The three editors issued the *National's* prospectus on New Year's Day, 1830. This and the first regular issue of January 3, revealed it to be no ordinary opposition newspaper. In the prospectus, Thiers described a new generation which had risen during the fifteen years of the Restoration, a generation that would fight its battle on new terrain, the terrain of the Charter, which allowed liberty under the law. It was no longer necessary to fight for liberty in France, it was merely necessary to guard the Charter from usurpation. Thiers warned that the "counter-revolutionary" party would be obliged to profess loyalty to the text of the Charter, while seeking to violate its spirit. The prospectus further defined the newspaper's underlying policy:

> The authors of the *National*, in trying to rally the will of France around the Charter, also deem it necessary to insure to it all the power which has been given it. They wish to prove that the Charter is the fruit of the Revolution and that the Monarchy, in reappearing in France, has reaped this harvest.[38]

[35] Marquis de Roux, *La Restauration* (Paris, 1930), p. 313. (Hereafter cited as Roux, *Restauration*.)

[36] Chateaubriand, *Mémoires*, V, 257.

[37] Vaulabelle, *Histoire*, VII, 283. Laffitte first seriously proposed a "national" monarchy under Orleans in a conversation with Jay, soon after Waterloo. See, Laffitte, *Mémoires*, p. 123.

[38] *National*, prospectus, 1 January, 1830.

The emphasis on the Charter was clear. Henceforth that document of French liberties, sworn by the Crown, was to be the buckler of the liberals. Legal resistance would be constructed on a solid foundation. If the sacred (and "revolutionary"!) Charter was to be ravished, it would *not* be the crime of the liberals, but of usurping Ultras; and usurpers, according to the tradition of 1688, simply forfeit their claims to sovereignty.

The first regular number of the *National* continued to develop this pattern. Thiers pointed out the various "perfidious restrictions" which, he wrote, Villèle had placed in the path of constitutionalism during his recent Ministry,[39] specifically citing harsh press censorship and the law of "tendency" as examples of the manner in which the Charter had been abused. Thiers then described ideal monarchy under the Charter, piously denying that French liberals desired any sort of republic or "democracy leading to revolution". The *National's* ideal of government was:

A representative monarchy with its necessary, inevitable forms, that will be well-heeded. An aristocratic nation, like England, where equality, as in France, may serve to vary the picture, but which would not change the essential conditions.

And farther along, in a direct reference to Charles X:

Such a King is not impotent as they say. When he names his ministers, he has the power to show his sentiments, to achieve his will, to check and even oppose the public will, but not for long or forever, but long enough to give him an effect and a part in government. Doubtless he is influenced by someone. When are kings true masters? Instead of submitting to the influences of courtiers, women, and confessors... [he] experiences the influences of public opinion affecting him gently and regularly. If that is true monarchy, it is also a true republic, but a republic without dangers.

Thiers also exposed that opportunistic trace of Bonapartism which occasionally escaped in the pages of the *National*. Referring to Waterloo, he wrote, "In making France respectable, even when she had ceased to be strong, this glorious blood imposed on the conqueror a certain moderation".[40] The *National* frequently decried the blood sacrifice Napoleon had exacted, yet it refused to denounce him in violent terms and kept a vague aura of respect around his name. Armand Carrel once showed himself such an apologist by writing in the journal:

Perhaps he would not have been abandoned as an emperor, unless he had succumbed as a general. ... It was only after Waterloo that he condemned himself to be nothing more for France than a magnificent and immortal memory.[41]

[39] *Ibid.*, 3 January, 1830.
[40] *Ibid.*
[41] *Ibid.*, 24 March, 1830.

Adolphe Thiers was prepared from the start for a deathwatch on the Bourbons; an integral step in his advocacy of dynastic change. In later life, Thiers summarized his Orleanist policy of 1830 with its repeated analogies to British history and recalled:

My friends and I, we were like Louis XVI who always had open before him the history of England. After Charles I, we had seen Cromwell, after Cromwell our sceptic and moderate Charles II; we then seemed to find ourselves in the presence of a James II, and we predicted some William of Orange who would finish up the revolution.[42]

Thiers denied trying to precipitate the July Revolution. He stated that his plan had been to await the course of events and he explained his plan of action succinctly. It had been, he said, "To shut the Bourbons up in the Charter, to close the doors tightly", and force them to escape by "jumping out the window".[43] Even before Polignac's appointment, Thiers had predicted an "Ultra wind", which "will drive us to a last storm, but a final one".[44] It was to Thiers' credit as a political prophet that he adhered to the effective but moderate course he outlined: To use the obvious example of James II and the pattern of "1688". With a reactionary government and a liberal Chamber, it was to be simply a matter of trapping the offender in his own laws. The concept of legal resistance, without resort to any force but that of the Charter, and the historic example of Britain became the ground of the *National's* polemic.

During the first month of the paper's life, its chief editor was greatly concerned over the public's response. Like a dutiful nephew to his stern old uncle, Thiers respectfully appealed to Chateaubriand:

All my collaborators join with me, to beg you to consider yourself, not as a subscriber, but as our benevolent critic. If, in the first article, an object of great concern to me, I have succeeded in expressing opinions which you approve, I would be reassured and certain of finding myself on the right track.[45]

Chateaubriand, legitimist to the death, was a man for whom the world was either saved or damned and he could only regard the *National* as something akin to the republican *Tribune*. Of the three leading editors of the

---

[42] Bernard de Lacombe, "Conversations avec M. Thiers", *Le Correspondant*, CCLXXXVII (Paris, 10 October, 1929), 20-21. (Hereafter cited as Làcombe, "Conversations".

[43] *Ibid.*

[44] Fernand Bemoit, "Monsieur Thiers a la conquête de Paris", *Le Correspondant* (Paris, 10 June, 1922), Letter to Severin Benoit, July, 1829, CCLXXXIX (10 June, 1922), 812. (Hereafter cited as Benoit, "Monsieur Thiers".)

[45] Chateaubriand, *Mémoires*, V, 257-58.

National, Chateaubriand preferred young Carrel for having "upheld with his sword the opinions which these writers unsheathed".[46]

To our age, the venerable President Thiers of 1871 seems the very embodiment of French bourgeois republicanism; but how "republican" was the upstart political climber of thirty-two who founded the *National?* In a revealing letter to Ampère, written that January, he sums up the paper's objectives as twofold: The primary task, of course, was to "teach the nation how it can rid itself of a dynasty"; but then he adds, as an equally essential goal, to prevent the possibilty that the nation "should accidentally find itself hurled into innovations for which the times were not yet ripe".[47] Certainly, his calculating appraisal of his own era left no room for uncertain innovations like republics, but we find him to be free of that outright horror of popular government felt by some of the wealthy liberals. Its was good politics for the Orleanist militants not to offend the more radical Left. We find Thiers, Laffitte, and other Orleanists frequently praising such abstractions as the "republican spirit", if not the real thing, while always stressing the stability they believed only a constitutional monarchy could provide. Thiers wrote in the *National*:

France wants to govern itself because it can. Will they call that a republican spirit? So much the worse for those who like to frighten with words. This republican spirit, one might say, is manifested everywhere, and becomes impossible to compromise.[48]

Most of the opposition was more receptive than Chateaubriand to the militant stance of the journal. Barante, more typical of the moderate aristocratic Left, wrote to Guizot:

They are beginning to talk a great deal about the *National*. This will not be of the same tone [as the *Globe*]. In all, the press is on the right path, provided that all the activity of the Nation is not concentrated there.[49]

A week after the *National* was launched, Talleyrand made a suggestive observation:"We are going to see what issues from the French ardors for liberty and French inclinations for servitude. Will some treaty be made between these two dispositions? We shall see."[50]

---

[46] *Ibid.*, p. 258. Chateaubriand was alluding to Carrel's activity in Spain in 1823. Sainte-Beuve was sceptical, believing Chateaubriand's motive was to promote his reputation among the younger romantics. See, Charles Sainte-Beuve, *Causeries de lundi* (15 vols., 4th ed.; Paris, 1890), II, 303.

[47] Quoted in, Thureau-Dangin, *Parti libéral*, pp. 475-76.

[48] *National*, 18 February, 1830.

[49] Barante, *Souvenirs*, III, 540.

[50] *Ibid.*, 11 January, 1830, Talleyrand to Barante, p. 537.

Thiers himself was overjoyed at the initial public reception to the *National*, and wrote to an old friend in Aix-en-Provence:

Up to now everything makes us hope for success. The subscriptions come in great numbers and the effect in Paris is tremendous. From all sides we are told that a newspaper has never been done like ours. This is from people of the highest rank.[51]

Not many issues of the *National* had appeared before the public learned that all of its urgings to legal resistance, all of its references to the English precedent, all of its denunciations of the regime, had one common end: A change in the ruling dynasty of France. Without yet mentioning his name, the *National* was nominating Louis-Philippe de Bourbon-Montpensier, Duke of Orleans, prince of the blood, for the throne of the French nation. Candidly, but without the seditious use of proper names, the *National* began to fill in its analogies to "1688". The identity of "William of Orange" was soon known and repeated in cafés, salons, and reading rooms.

On February 18, Carrel wrote an article minimizing the importance of the Monarchy and the aristocracy, while suggesting an Orleanist revolution:

[The People] could, if this were agreeable to its repose, improvise a Monarchy and an aristocracy which would prolong indefinitely the exile of the Monarchy. It must then, be free; it has in it the power, even more than the right.[52]

A few days before the *National* had appeared, François Mignet was asked by a friend about a current rumor, that the new journal was to exist "for the purpose of overthrowing the dynasty". The friend asked what new government Mignet hoped to substitute for the old and the journalist had replied: "Isn't there someone at the Palais-Royal"?[53]

In one of the early editorials of the *National*, Mignet steered closer to the rock of sedition:

It required but a simple modification of persons in 1688, to complete a revolution of principles begun in 1640, and it neatly placed on the throne a family which had a new faith. England was so far from revolutionary at this period, that, respecting, insofar as it could, the old law, it chose the closest parental family of the disgraced prince.[54]

For these remarks, the *National* was accused by the royalist paper, Q*uotidienne*, of attempting to revive the Revolution.[55] On the following day,

[51] Benoit, "Monsieur Thiers", p. 812.
[52] *National*, 18 February, 1830.
[53] Petit, *Mignet*, p. 64.
[54] *National*, 14 February, 1830.
[55] *Quotidienne*, 13 February, 1830. Polignac began subsidy of his own paper, *L'Universel*,

Thiers refuted the charge in the *National*, asserting that there was "no more Bastille to take, no longer three estates to confuse, no more Night of August Fourth", nothing more, he added, except "a Charter to be freely executed and ministers to be overthrown by virtue of this Charter"[56]

While the royalist papers, the *Quotidienne* and *Gazette de France* declared war on the *National*, the *Gazette* once paid it an oblique tribute. In his paper for January 7, Genoude characterized the *National* as the "secret of the *Constitutionnel* that escaped", a reference to Thiers' leadership. And, although the Villèlist paper dismissed François Mignet as a "political metaphysician", it praised the style and courage of Armand Carrel. Such rare compliments between sworn enemies of the press were probably less in a political spirit than in the ancient camaraderie of journalism.

In February, Thiers and Carrel each wrote articles for which they were indicted on demand of the Royal Prosecutor. In his most acutely Orleanist statement to that moment, Adolphe Thiers had written:

> France ought to be quite disenchanted about persons: She has loved genius and she has seen what this love has cost her. The simple, modest, solid virtues, which a good education can always assure the heir to the throne and that a limited power could not corrupt, that is what France needs!

And, if this were not clear enough:

> The question is thus uniquely one of things. It could be someday one of persons, but for the mistakes of the latter, the system is indifferent to persons; but if they were not indifferent to the system, if they should hate it, attack it, then the question would become one of both things and persons. But it would be the persons who would themselves have posed it.[57]

A question of persons! And no trace of doubt as to what the *National* meant by "solid virtues" or a good education for the heir to the throne! Louis-Philippe would one day be despised for his cultivation of such an image, but in 1830, the Paris bourgeoisie loved to watch him swinging his black umbrella as he walked down the rue de Rivoli, so different from the remote, erect majesty of their ruling King. It was also widely known that the Duke sent his sons to the University of Paris. The Duke himself had made certain to advertise it.

---

in November, 1829. He considered the *Quotidienne* too rash, the *Gazette* too unfriendly, and the *Drapeau* too foolish. *L'Universel* tried to allay rumors of a *coup*, but in February it began to advocate use of Article 14, thus "confirming" such rumors through its own naive candor.

[56] *National*, 14 February, 1830.

[57] *Ibid.*, 19 February, 1830.

Thus, within seven weeks of its birth, the *National* had professed a clear Orleanist position for all to read. The relentless application of this policy to all matters of political importance continued to the very days of the July Revolution. It was also becoming evident that the *National* was dragging other opposition journals in its wake.

The *Globe*, periodical of the academy and *salon*, soon found itself swept into a position nearly as militant as that of the *National*. In February, 1830, the *Globe* became a political journal and began to appear daily. Where before on might find an occasional political essay in company with articles on the drama, the novel, Chinese art, or electricity, there was now a wholly partisan message. A fair prophecy of the *Globe's* new role had appeared a month after Polignac's nomination in an editorial that succinctly suggested the Bourbons might be faced with a prospect of having to lie down "beside the Stuarts in the dust of forgotten dynasties". Apropos of the *Globe's* transition, so significant to the intellectuals, the young comte de Rémusat wrote to a friend, "It is a great enterprise but very uncertain. The general state of the press and our internal affairs make our undertaking it a necessity".[58] Augustin Thierry, the romantic historian, voiced the concern of many intellectuals when he inquired of Guizot:

What do you think of the *Globe* since it has changed its character? I don't know why I am vexed to find all these trifling points of news and daily discussion in it. Formerly we concentrated our thoughts to read it, but now that is no longer possible, the attention is distracted and divided.[59]

The "new" *Globe* maintained a merciless assault on the Polignac Ministry and it delighted in posing, in a dozen different forms, two questions: For what purpose were the eighth of August ministers appointed? What will result from the certain clash of this Cabinet with the liberal Chamber? For both questions, the same answer was provided by the *Globe*: Coup d'état. Before the 1830 session of the Chambers was convoked, the *Globe* reflected: "It is a strange situation... A Ministry certain to be beaten and trying to get itself beaten and a Chamber gravely convoked by a system which it has denounced and is sure to denounce again".[60]

One of the more important political trials of the Restoration was that of the *Globe's* editor, Paul-François Dubois, for having written an article titled "France and the Bourbons". Dubois' own impressive defense at his trial, which will be discussed in a later chapter, was a triumph for the Left. The

---

[58] Barante, *Souvenirs*, 5 February, 1830, Rémusat to Barante, III, 541.
[59] Guizot, *Memoirs*, Thierry to Guizot, I, 312.
[60] *Globe*, 6 February, 1830.

article which provoked the Ministry to prosecute the *Globe* dealt with the
"legitimacy" of the Bourbon Restoration. Dubois had written, "Whoever
has spent thirty years in France recalls the atmosphere and circumstances
under which the Bourbons had returned; they were forgotten or hardly
known by their contemporaries". Referring to the coalition armies of 1814,
the *Globe* stated that the Bourbons were accepted because "another danger,
more pressing, forced the national will ... There was no longer a head to our
empire, the son of Napoleon was still in his cradle and this cradle had the
Emperor of Austria for its protector". Later on, Dubois called the Restoration the "demi-conversion" of France, its "somewhat compromised legitimacy" having been accepted as an "innocent pretension". With the same
taunting token of Bonapartism one found in the *National*, the *Globe* added
that the Bourbons, upon the return of Napoleon from Elba, were "broken
like glass" because they had "menaced the rights aquired by the revolution"
and had "wounded the people and the army".[61]

By such journalistic virility, the *Globe*, a new fighter in the arena of politics,
was to prove a welcome comrade to the *National*. Soon, even the old *Constitutionnel*, the *Courrier*, and the *Journal du Commerce* began to sharpen their
blades. Their attacks grew bolder and more gravid with suggestion, while the
Débats, still claiming "legitimacy", increased its fury against Polignac's
Council. Only the *National*, *Globe*, and *Temps* developed a strong Orleanist
line, but the old liberal papers, perhaps through their inspiration and the
boldness of their campaign, stayed with them against a common enemy, and
frightened of the republican alternative, soon found themselves playing
follow-the-leader.

---

[61] *Ibid.*, 15 February, 1830. For the *Globe's* transition, see also Gerbod, *Dubois*, p. 92.

CHAPTER VIII

LEGAL RESISTANCE: THE "BRETON ASSOCIATION" AND THE PRESS

The liberal opposition carefully avoided the "revolutionary" innuendoes of the militants and began instead to speak in terms of "legal resistance". Communication with the provinces was possible through the well-organized *Aide-toi* electoral societies and also by the press, preponderantly critical of the Bourbon regime. Since the Chamber of Deputies was in recess, the first response to the August 8 challenge had to be in the press.

Revolutionary history gave the Left several examples of "legal resistance". One of these was the public refusal to pay "illegal" taxes as in the Hampden ship money case of the English Civil War era. Backers of the Duke of Orleans, who were soon to declare themselves, had, in their newspapers, often innocuously referred to "1688" and the change of dynasty and the republicans could find some identity in the Puritan rebellion of the 1640's.

The opposition was certain that Charles X would also dissolve the hostile Chamber and attempt to raise necessary revenues without its consent. When and if these acts should occur, liberals planned to arm themselves with the Charter of 1814 and, using their dominant press, start a "legal resistance" to the Crown.

The inevitable stalemate between ministers and elected representatives was expected with the first session of the deputies. In preparation for that day, opposition propagandists kept the public alert to the threat of a reactionary *coup* and the danger of illegal taxation.

On July 29, 1829, the bourgeois *Constitutionnel* had noted Polignac's arrival in Paris and pointedly reminded its readers that there was no "legal or possible taxation except that voted by the legislative power".

Étienne Béquet, in his now famous editorial in the Journal des *Débats* on August 10, recalled the English ship money precedent and announced: "With illegal taxes, a Hampden would arise to break them".

The Ministry could not win cases based merely on historical implications. Prosecution of the press required a more overt act. On September 11, 1829, the small *Journal du Commerce*, warned its 2500 subscribers and their friends that any attempt by the government to order "illegal" taxation would be dangerous and published what it called the prospectus of a group of citizens in royal and Catholic Brittany. This declaration of the so-named Breton Association accused a "handful of political troublemakers" of attempting to overthrow the Charter and called for contributions to defray the cost incurred by a member who might be sued for payment of an "illegal" tax. The text of this prospectus appears below.[1]

François Bert, of the *Journal du Commerce*, had added a few favorable remarks about the manifesto and for this he was brought before a judge. Liberal papers, as well as the very royalist *Gazette de France*, quickly reprinted the article; some reflected editorially, some did not. The liberal provincial press, meanwhile, was suffering an ordeal by prosecution. Polignac's government feared the opposition of the provincial press as much as it did the *Aide-toi* organizations in the provinces.[2] Nine-tenths of the voters lived outside the capital. Later, Thiers wrote in his Orleanist *National* that royal prosecutors had been most zealous in attacking small provincial papers, and he commended the wealthy Parisian dailies for having given financial aid to their less affluent fellow-journalists.[3]

[1] Act of the Breton Association (*Association bretonne pour le réfus de l'impôt*).

"We, the undersigned, inhabitants of both sexes in the five departments of the old province of Brittany, under the security and protection of the Royal Court of Rennes, bound by our own oaths and by those of our family heads to owe loyalty to the King and attachment to the Charter, considering that a handful of political troublemakers threaten to try audacious plan of destroying the bases of the constitutional guarantees consecrated by the Charter; considering that if Brittany has been able to find in these guarantees the compensation for those which assure to it its contract of union to France, it is in its duty and interest and preserve the remainder of its liberties and freedoms, it is in its character and of its honor to imitate the sacrificial resistance of its ancestors to enroachments, caprices, and to the abuse of authority by ministerial power; considering that resistance by force would be a frightful calamity, that it would be without motive as long as means remain open for legal resistance; that the surest means of preferring recourse to judicial authority is to assure to the oppressed a fraternal solidarity; we do declare, in the bonds of honor and law;..."

This Act then stipulated that: Members individually subscribe 10 francs to a common fund to be used to defray costs incurred by any Breton who refused to pay illegal taxes made "without free, regular, and constitutional concourse of the King and the two Chambers". Other articles stated that in the case of an official proposal for an unconstitutional change in electoral laws, or even the establishment of an illegal tax, two delegates from each *arrondissement* should meet at Pontivy. With a quorum of 20, they must name, from those who subscribed to the fund, three general procurators and one sub-procurator for each of the five departments. The mission of the general procurators was to collect subscriptions; to satisfy indemnities as prescribed; on resquest of a subscriber injured by illegal taxation, to use any legal means to defend him from his creditors; to lodge civil complaints against any originators or accomplices of illegal taxation. (*Journal du Commerce*, 11 September, 1829).

[2] De Hauranne, *Histoire*, X, 342-46. Lafayette was touring the South in behalf of *Aide-toi* when the prospectus was published. His speeches included references to "legal combat".

[3] *National*, 5 June, 1830.

The government demanded prosecution of the six Paris newspapers which had published the Act of the Breton Association.[4] These were the *Journal du Commerce*, the insignificant *Echo Français*, which printed the prospectus on September 11, the liberal *Courrier Français* and *Constitutionnel* which issued reprints of the act on the following day, the *Débats*, legitimist enemy of Polignac, and *pro forma*, the royalist *Gazette de France*. Cases against all of the editors except Bert of the *Journal du Commerce* and Valentin de Lapelouze of the *Courrier* were dismissed on grounds that they had merely reprinted an item of interest. The Ultra *Gazette* was thereby freed without apparent favoritism. The *Journal du Commerce* was accused of having fomented the Breton affair by giving it its first publicity. The *Courrier* had sinned in commenting favorably upon the prospectus. Each editor was charged with three specific violations of the press laws: Excitation of hatred and contempt for the King's government, provocation to disobedience of the laws, and attack on the constitutional rights of the King and the Chambers. Similar accusations were also leveled at several provincial journals which had been so indiscreet as to advocate the views of the prospectus.[5] Press trials in the provinces started some time before those in Paris. The official reason given for the delay in the prosecution of Bert and Lapelouze was that the regular magistrates of the Paris court were currently out of the city, enjoying the summer vacation.[6] This may have been a pretext. Polignac's Council was not yet well established and was unprepared for such a major battle. The Ministry decided not to rush the affair into the courts and so hoped to avoid sudden provocative action against the tax-refusal agitators, which might be interpreted as an ill-timed *coup d'état* against the strong Paris press.[7]

The *Moniteur*, official organ of the government, was not editorially partisan, but on the subject of the Breton Association its editor, François Sauvo, departed from custom and replied to this new threat. Sauvo used the argument that was soon to be brought out in the trials of the *Courrier* and other offending newspapers. He stated that "the Breton Association had no existence before September 11 except in these journals".[8]

To demonstrate the prior existence of the society, the opposition had but one piece of documentary evidence, and this was far from conclusive. As was later explained at the trial of the *Journal du Commerce*, a letter had

    [4] *Gazette des Tribunaux*, 26 September, 1829.
    [5] *Ibid.*
    [6] *Le Moniteur*, 25 September, 1829.
    [7] Vaulabelle, *Histoire*, VII, 193.
    [8] *Le Moniteur*, 25 September, 1829.

reached the editor's desk from Dinant on September 1. Enclosed with it was a copy of the Breton Association's prospectus, dated August 30, and signed by a Charles Beslay.[9] Beslay was a deputy from Côtes-du-Nord. First elected during the "Hundred Days", he was returned to the Chamber in every election between 1815 and 1853. Republican sentiments had once led him to reject a title of nobility from Louis XVIII.[10] Although the Beslay letter alone cannot establish the authenticity of the alleged petition in Brittany, its existence is confirmed in a report of he Prefect of Côtes-du-Nord, dated October 25.[11]

Guizot leaves the impression in his memoirs that the Breton Association, which he zealously promoted, originated before September 11.[12] His biographer, however, believes that the whole idea of tax-refusal associations emanated from the newspapers of the capital. An organization for the *refus de l'impôt* was actually established in Rennes, Brittany, on September 14. The *Association parisienne*, for the same purpose, was not created until mid-October. It was followed by similar organizations in Lorraine, Normandy, and Burgundy in the same month. In November, eight more departments were represented. By the July Revolution, *refus* associations were effectively established in fifteen departments.[13]

Baron Pasquier, a liberal peer, whose account is both opinionated and authoritative, wrote of the Breton Association:

> This pretended association was no more than a plan edited, I believe, by a former deputy of Brittany. The journal had presented it as being in full course of operation before it was even documented by a single signature. There was in this a criminal act.[14]

The first newspapers in France to go on trial for publishing the Breton Act of Association were in the provinces. If the Ultra government, not yet sure of itself, was hesitant to assault the Parisian press, it had declared war on the opposition papers of smaller French cities.[15] To Polignac's Cabinet, "revolutionary" ideas were evil enough when confined to Paris; but how much greater a threat when spread by journalism to every corner of France

---

[9] *Gazette des Tribunaux*, 28 November, 1829.

[10] Maurice Beslay, "Souvenirs d'un vieux républican", *La nouvelle Revue*, Ser. 4, VI (15 April, 1963), 395.

[11] Pouthas, *Guizot*, p. 427.

[12] François Guizot, *Memoirs to Illustrate the History of My Time* (3 vols.; London, 1858), I, 333.

[13] Pouthas, *Guizot*, pp. 428-29.

[14] Pasquier, *Histoire*, VI, 196.

[15] *National*, 5 June, 1830.

and to the provincial electors! Between the coming of Polignac and the July Revolution the government brought nineteen cases against eleven important liberal papers in the provinces, and many appeals were tried in the higher courts.

The battle opened in Metz on October 22. Harmand, editor, and Lamort, printer, of the *Courrier de la Moselle* were charged with provocation of hatred and scorn of the royal government, provocation to disobey laws, and attack on the legal authority of King and Chambers. They had published the Breton Act on October 6 and proposed that since four of the six papers indicted for the same deed in Paris had been dismissed, their journal would also be safe. Harmand had, in addition, permitted himself the personal observation that the Breton Association would become the "code of the peaceful and constitutional association of all friends of order and liberty in France". For this the Royal Prosecutor demanded a jail sentence of six months and fines of one thousand francs for both Harmand and his luckless printer.[16]

The defense attorney argued that opposition was necessary for thrones and nations and that "bad luck" would befall any government which tried to "stifle" it. He then turned from the Breton question to a long recitation of the evils threatened by Polignac's Cabinet and he reminded his audience of the new Minister La Bourdonnaye's cry for blood in the reaction of 1815. He accused the monarchist papers of being anarchic because it was they, not the liberal press, who rejected the fundamental law. The lawyer denied that anyone wanted a revolution in France, not even, he added, "those who would like to recall the reign of *bon-plaisir*".

The printer's lawyer spoke next, and made such a direct statement of "legal resistance" that he was reprimanded. He countered the necessity of "blind and passive obedience" to royal acts and asserted that the present legal order of France was "menaced". At this point, the president of the court interrupted him to deny the accusation, saying "you are creating phantoms for yourself to fight". With this rebuke the printer's attorney rested his case. At the end of one and a half hours of deliberation, the president gave the following judgment: Lamort, the printer, was acquitted without cost; Harmand, the editor, was found not guilty of "provocation to disobedience to the laws" or of "attacking royal authority". The court also ruled that the reprint of the Breton Act itself was permissable since the Charter *forbade* illegal taxation. By adding his personal wish to expand the Breton idea nationally, however, Harmand had contravened a law of March 25,

---

[16] *Gazette des Tribunaux*, 26 October, 1829.

1822. The judge found him guilty of the government's charge of "hatred
and contempt", but fixed the minimum penalty because he believed Harmand
had misunderstood the facts about the indictments of the Paris journals.
His sentence was only one month in prison and a fine of 150 francs.[17]
Although this light punishment was not far from vindication, in January
of the next year Harmand appealed the case in the high court of Metz.
Despite angry denunciations by the Royal Prosecutor, the court acquitted
the *Courrier de la Moselle* of all charges. Its well-advertised case was a triumph
for the provincial opposition.[18]

The editor of the *Nouveau phocéen* of Marseille was brought to trial on
November 9 upon charges of outrage to the state religion and outrage to
the royalist mayor of Marseille. The Prosecutor also charged the editor with
criminal action for reporting the support of an eminent lawyer and deputy
of Paris, François Mauguin, for the newly-formed *Association parisienne*,
counterpart of the Breton league. Although the accused publisher received
a heavy sentence for defaming the mayor, he was acquitted of the Breton
Association charge.[19]

The propagandists of the Association were next attacked in Bordeaux and
Rouen. Coudert, *fils*, of the *Indicateur de Bordeaux* was indicted on November 20 for publishing a desription of the new association. The court acquitted
Coudert of all charges but that of "hatred and contempt of the King's
government". The judge ruled that this phrase might indicate the Ministry,
as well as the sacred person of the Monarch. The light punishment of one
month in prison and the lenient decision by the court were not unfavorable
to the liberal cause. The editor's later appeal to the *Cour Royale* of Bordeaux,
resulted in a sustained sentence.[20]

Undaunted, the little journal took its case before the court of cassation
in Paris the following March. Coudert was this time represented by the
rising Parisian politician, Odilon Barrot, who called the earlier proceeding
a mistrial. He based his claim on the court's failure to distinguish between
"government of the King" and "ministers of the King". The court of cassation ruled in favor of the lower court, but at least the liberals had augmented
their propaganda for "legal resistance".[21]

The trial of the *Journal de Rouen* on November 19 and 20, brought the
first unqualified victory in a lower court for the proponents of the Breton

---

[17] *Ibid.*
[18] *Ibid.*, 20 January, 1830.
[19] *Ibid.*, 27 November, 1829.
[20] *Ibid.*, 16 December, 1829.
[21] *Ibid.*, 23 March, 1830.

plan. The paper's manager, Baudry, and its editor, Visinet, were charged with the usual series of crimes attributed to others in similar recent court actions. The defendants retained three skilled lawyers. Each of this trio, in his turn, used the freedom of the bar to expound the liberal sentiments of the era with great enthusiasm.[22]

The first defense advocate called the court's attention to witticisms which the *Journal de Rouen* had reprinted from the satirical Paris *Figaro* of August 9. He argued that if the government failed to prosecute his client for such impudence, certainly it was then unjust to prosecute for a mere transcript of the Breton Act. The defense termed the *Figaro* reprint a matter of the King's person and the Breton Association article as a criticism of the King's Ministry. The lawyer added that the King of England once saw a man in the pillory, guilty of having written tracts against the ministers. "The idiot"! said the King, "why didn't he write against me"?

The other lawyers for the *Journal de Rouen*, in considerable digression from the question of the Breton Association, attacked the dogma of the inviolability of the ministers. They invoked the writings of Boulainvilliers, the acts of the old parlement of Paris, and even the oath taken by the leaderless deputies after the news of defeat had come from Waterloo. They asked if there had been an inseparable bond between King and ministers when Louis XVIII allowed the regicide Fouché into his Council.

The President, Letourneur, gave an unqualified acquittal to the *Journal de Rouen*, and, in an additional service to the liberal cause and the Breton Association, gave his motives for rejecting the Royal Prosecutor's demands:

> Be it known that one cannot construe as a crime the simple enunciation of their journal for September 13, 1829, of an act of association which appears to have been made in the said province of Brittany, concerning an event which has not even taken place, and which, according to our constitutional guarantees, certainly ought not to take place.[23]

The most decisive battle in the campaign of the Breton Association occurred in Paris a week after the acquittal of the *Journal de Rouen*. Bert, manager of the *Journal du Commerce* and Lapelouze of the *Courrier Français*, at last went on trial before the correctional tribunal. The Crown Prosecutor was the famous Levavasseur, who had won convictions against many opposition journals. Levavasseur cited the words of the Breton Act itself to support the accusation of "hatred and contempt" of the King's government. The incriminating phrase was as follows: "Considering that a handful of political

[22] *Ibid.*, 23 September, 22 November, 1829.
[23] *Ibid.*

troublemakers are threatening to try the audacious project of destroying the bases of the constitutional guarantees consecrated by the Charter ..." The Royal Prosecutor then proceeded to build up a strong and reasoned argument for the government's complaint. Avoiding the usual bog of royalist generalities about the "revolution" and the press, Levavasseur trod the safer ground of the wording of the act itself. He asked why anyone with honest motives would agitate for the Chambers to reject a budget or the people to refuse a tax, when the budget for 1830 had already been approved. He predicted that if the Chambers would pass the 1831 budget bill, the journals would then cry that deputies had been coerced by "violence and terror" and that the people might then react by refusing a legal taxation. "The article", he concluded, "is obviously anarchical".[24] The Crown also attacked the assumption that Charles X was capable of proposing an unconstitutional tax. And, asserted Levavasseur, if any of the ministers should attempt this deed, a "single word from the royal mouth" would prevent them! Further, he argued, the editors had implied either that Charles did not have the strength to keep his word or that he would deliberately perjure his coronation oath of allegiance to the Charter. Either interpretation, according to the lawyer, was an insult to the Crown.

Bert spoke in his own defense and remarked that the trial was a "travesty", that the government was making "a peaceful association, convened to resist the encroachment of an illegal tax" into a "dark conspiracy against the throne and the state". Bert accused the *Moniteur* of having falsely reported the origin of the Breton league. His own version was that, on September 1, he had received a copy of the letter written by Beslay, describing an organization in Rennes to resist illegal taxation. Bert praised the integrity of Beslay and assured the court that a deputy who had opposed "Imperial despotism" in 1814 would not now deceive his fellow-citizens with an enormous lie. The Breton subscription, he concluded, was organized well before the *Journal du Commerce* published it. Louis Bernard, known as "Bernard de Rennes", Bert's defense lawyer, then spoke. With good humor, the advocate apologized to the court for his own lack of eloquence as compared with that of the orator Barthe, the lawyer whom Bert had first sought to retain. To the crowded courtroom he declared:

This is not the Association which is on trial: These are not the members of the subscription who were summoned. Their pact circulates freely; it is everywhere adopted or imitated, it is covered with thousands of signatures. It is the publicity

[24] *Ibid.*, 28 November, 1829.

which it has been given that they attack, apparently because it seems simpler to condemn a newspaper than an entire population.[25]

One of the signers of the act, the historian Duvergier de Hauranne, asserted that the ministers dared not prosecute the actual subscribers because so many of them were political moderates or powerful financiers.[26] Nevertheless Polignac had not hesitated to prosecute the rich, moderate, and powerful Bertin of the *Journal des Débats* for his editorial of August 10.

Bert's lawyer did not contest the details of the accusation, but promised to prove the legality of both the Breton Association itself and the subsequent publicity. He declared that the first duty of a citizen was to obey the law, hence, the refusal of an unlawful tax was not merely a right; it was a duty. He also sought to establish the right of citizens to attack the actions of ministers. He quoted from the royalist *Gazette*, which had once said that the moderate Martignac was leading the way toward the "erection of a republic", and asked the court: "Will that which is a right for the *Gazette de France* become a crime for the *Journal du Commerce*"? and he added: "Let it be advertised that defiance is the protectress of liberty. Sleep on the pretty words of the ministers and courtiers and you will see what will become of the Charter and the throne itself". Bernard punctuated his concluding remarks with an extremely bitter denunciation of the new Ministry. Asserting that the apprehension felt by the members of the Breton subscription was justified, he recited recollections of the royalist terror: "Does it believe, this faction, that we have forgotten 1815? It speaks of moderation! Who armed the assassins of the Midi? Who supported these bands, whose passage through twenty frightened towns was marked by blood"? The impassioned speech ended as Bernard cried that the "dread reactions" of the Ultras in 1815 had served to "rock the cradle of the Restoration in blood"! These words produced considerable excitement.[27]

Joseph Mérilhou, the prominent lawyer who, with Barthe, was one of the leading orators of the Chamber, now rose to offer the defense of Valentin Lapelouze, manager of the *Courrier Français*. Mérilhou said he was pleased that "Breton Associations" were all over France, that these groups were not only legal but desirable, and that he considered his own subscription to the *Association parisienne* one of the "most meritorious" acts of his life. The lawyer remarked that probably the very magistrates he was then addressing would not hesitate to sign the subscription. He then made the

---

[25] *Ibid.*
[26] De Hauranne, *Histoire*, X, 365.
[27] *Gazette des Tribunaux*, 28 November, 1829.

telling point that in 1788, when the princes of the blood opposed any reforms in the laws of revenue, they were led by the comte d'Artois, "today King of France"! Mérilhou created an even greater stir a moment later when he demanded that the ministers reassure the nation that they planned no *coup d'état.* He hinted that France was threatened with armed intervention of the powers and with a blunt reference to the new Minister of War, Marshal Bourmont, he added that the foreign powers were "well aware that the man of treason would not fail to open our fortresses to them". The President of the court intervened at this point to admonish Mérilhou: "You go too far... The ministers of the King are not to be insulted at the bar of this court: Stay in your case". After this reprimand, Mérilhou's defense cooled considerably, and he concluded with a general accusation of the Ultras as the only revolutionaries of 1829.[28]

After two hours of deliberation, the President announced the decision of the court. Bert and Lapelouze were acquitted of the first two charges, "attack on the constitutional authority of the King" and "provocation to disobey laws". Turning to the third charge, "excitation to hatred and contempt for the King's government", the judge found the editors guilty. He declared that, inasmuch as the papers had inserted editorial reflections supporting the Breton Association's forecast of danger, the directors Bert and Lapelouze had violated the law. He sentenced each of them to a month in jail and a fine of five hundred francs, nearly the minimum penalty.[29] In March, 1830, the case of Bert and Lapelouze was appealed to the Royal Court of Paris. The prosecutor read his accusation, but the defendants failed to appear, giving the excuse that their case was not prepared. The President, Baron Séguier, accordingly upheld the original decision in view of the default of the appellants.[30] Soon after, the directors of the *Journal du Commerce* and the *Courrier* requested a second appeal. This time they both appeared in the courtroom, where a distinguished and partisan audience was crowding the aisles and doorways.

Bernard, who posed as the "country" lawyer of Rennes, and whose dramatic speech had helped win his clients' partial acquittal in their first trial, was again the apostle of the Breton Association. Bernard's defense was, by turns, impassioned and didactic. At one point he evoked loud applause from the audience when he praised the presiding magistrate, Baron Jean-Antoine Mathieu Séguier. All were aware that Séguier had braved the displeasure of the Crown by his recent decisions. They were also aware of this judge's

[28] *Ibid.*, 29 November, 1829.
[29] *Ibid.*
[30] *Ibid.*, 11 March, 1830.

Fouché-like career of apostasy and sycophancy: A fawning Bonapartist until 1815, but by 1820 so Ultra he urged the King to restore torture because of his alleged distress over the Louvel crime! Again, by 1828, clearly disenchanted with Villèle and Charles X, he became more accomodating to the Left. Séguier's latest switch was sustained by constant flattery in the courtroom, as well as in the liberal papers and the opposition regarded it as a singular stroke of good luck.[31]

Mérilhou spoke next in defense of Bert of the *Journal du Commerce*. At one point, when Mérilhou predicted that the Chambers would be dissolved five months before the next session, Baron Séguier lifted his hand. "M. le President", asked Mérilhou, "do you think I go too far"? "I think so", said Séguier. "If you think so, M. le President", answered the lawyer, "then I should think so too". The Crown Prosecutor then announced that in his dossier there was no record of the names of any alleged signers of the Breton subscription. Defender Bernard rose to defend the authenticity of the Association and digressed to report that a recent Ultra brochure had referred to the august High Court of Paris as a "small-scale Convention". The trial was recessed until the following week when, on April 2, President Séguier read the majority decision which acquitted Bert and Lapelouze of all charges and nullified the sentence of the lower court. News of this acquittal created a jubilant outburst in the crowded court chamber.[32]

Even before the acquittal of these large Parisian papers, two more provincial journals had scored victories for the *Association pour le refus de l'impôt*. These were both monthly newspapers, the *Revue mensuelle du Cher* of Bourges and the *Sentinelle des Deux-Sèvres* of Niort.

Both the editor and manager of the small newspaper of Bourges were acquitted at their first trial on all charges connected with publicizing the Breton Association. The court decided that, although it was "tactless" to suppose that the King could disregard the Chambers, the expression of legal resistance was more "inert" than active, and therefore not criminal. The court also ruled that the words government of the King" in the charge could not refer to the Ministry or the individual ministers.[33] This interpretation by the court of Bourges was not, however, binding on other courts of France.

Niort's *Sentinelle des Deux-Sèvres* was almost constantly under indictment or trial during the tenure of the Polignac Ministry. On January 22, 1830,

---

[31] *Ibid.*, 26 March, 1830. See also, Jacomet, *Le Palais*, pp. 16-17, 284-85, for Séguier's political views.

[32] *Gazette des Tribunaux*, 26 March, 3 April, 1830.

[33] *Temps*, 3 January, 1830.

its editor, Clerc-Lasalle, and some local citizens who wrote for it, were brought before the tribunal of Niort. One writer, Proust, was accused of exciting hatred of the King's government for composing a verse which had appeared in the November issue of the monthly *Sentinelle*. In these lines, Proust had referred to an "anti-French Ministry". Editor Clerc-Lasalle was cited for provoking disobedience to the laws. He had inserted, in the same issue, an account of a recent *Aide-toi* electoral banquet held in Niort in honor of several liberal deputies of the region. The paper also published part of a speech given at this banquet by the deputy François Mauguin, and a letter by him in which the Breton Association program was defended. Deputy Mauguin was also the defense counsel in Clerc-Lasalle's case.

The prosecution was compromised from the start by the fact that the entire November first issue of the paper had been confiscated by the police on the eve of publication. Thus, the incriminating number had not been made public. The prosecutor's defense of this point, that he had "no idea how the copies had arrived at his desk", served only to provoke laughter in the courtroom. He defended the seizure as a matter of expediency to impede the "progress of evil". The defense immediately claimed a mistrial on the grounds that what was not actually publicized could not be guilty of provoking anything. Seizure, under the law, could only occur after an issue had been indicted and the incriminated issues could be seized.

The prosecutor, nevertheless, called for the full penalty of the law and struck hard at the idea of "legal resistence" by refusing taxes as expressed in the Breton Act. He proclaimed that to print the act was to provoke disobedience, not only to the law, but to the Charter of 1814 as well. The prosecutor noted that the Charter specifically required the civil list, amortization of the public debt, and pensions to be permanent budgetary items; hence, if no revenue were returned, these provisions would be violated. He admitted the right of a Chamber to reject parts, but not the whole of a budget bill.

Mauguin then took the floor to plead for his client, as well as for himself.[34] He set the stage by quoting a choice piece from a recent issue of the small Jesuit-Ultra journal, *L'Apostolique*. This weekly paper had asked what remedies were needed to save France. Its own concise answer was: "Public and general penitence, the destruction of Gallicanism, the elimination of all impious, atheistic, and absurd laws and institutions, the exemplary punishment of the brigands... known under the name of liberals".

---

[34] *Gazette des Tribunaux*, 27 January, 1830.

All this, declared Mauguin, was in the threat presented by the Polignac Ministry.[35]

The prosecutor answered by again attacking the "Breton" idea of refusal of taxes. "Do you give each citizen", he asked, "the right to say: 'Government, you have not carried out your engagements, I refuse the tax that I have agreed to pay you'?" Such liberty would encourage rebellion and constitute a frightful "heresy", continued the Crown's advocate. He then belittled the actual strength of the *refus de l'impôt* societies, stating that only eight thousand signatures had been obtained in a nation of thirty-two million people. Mauguin countered these attacks with a dissertation on sovereignty, summarizing grandly:

> Caligula and Nero terrorized the world, and here both Charles IX and Louis XI bathed in blood. Out of this, for all thinking minds, came the need to discover if, in any case, obedience is due a prince who abuses his rights; it was asked if a people, however miserable, must submit to a Caligula, for example, if he should come to reign over them, with his excesses and his furies.

The Crown Prosecutor also concluded his arguments in a lofty vein. He recalled that when the Judeans asked of Christ whether they should pay tribute to a usurper, he had pointed to the portrait of Tiberius on a coin and enjoined them to "render unto Caesar that which is Caesar's". All of the oratory of this trial, despite its value as propaganda, was unnecessary to the defendants. The President of the court ruled as follows:

> Be it known that as a result of a combination of different laws of the police of the periodical press, there exists a principle as clear as it is incontestable, that to have been criminal matter, it was necessary to have been published. Seizure relaxed and defendants acquitted.[36]

In the press cases the liberal opposition had won a substantial victory. Of six provincial and two Parisian journals prosecuted in this matter, three were acquitted by lower courts, three were acquitted on appeal, and two were convicted but received only minimum penalties. Each of the trials with its unhampered political oratory was given wide publicity and, by prosecuting, the government had multiplied the propaganda value of the Association.

In its beginnings the *refus de l'impôt* scheme had the support of most of the opposition, from constitutional monarchists and doctrinaire liberals to young republicans. In 1830 as the suicidal career of the Polignac Ministry grew more bold, however, the idea of strictly legal resistance, characterized by the Breton Act of Association, was to lose the support of the more active

[35] *Ibid.*
[36] *Ibid.*

liberals and republicans. Adolphe Thiers, writing in his militant *National*, disagreed with Benjamin Constant's proposals which appeared in the *Courrier*. Item rejection of the budget by the Chamber was opposed by Thiers as contrary to principle. He demanded that the Chambers reject all of a budget or nothing. Thiers noted that a tax could be refused only by the people, and then only if the levy were illegal. Constant's view lost favor, and he later closed ranks with the more radical Thiers on this issue.[37]

The most ardent champions of legal resistance by tax refusal were to be found among moderate legitimists such as the duc de Broglie. Even during the July Days, when the popular victory seemed assured, this gentleman bitterly denounced the use of force to oppose tyranny.[38] It was also safer to sue the tax collector than to pile furniture across a street or hurl it from rooftops onto files of soldiers. Later, Armand Carrel was to recall that France had been full of would-be Hampdens, each anxious for the "least dangerous honor of constitutional resistance".[39]

The July Revolution would be an accomplished fact before anyone had an opportunity to play the Hampden role. Propaganda for legal resistance, however, continued into the July Days. Aside from the great publicity offered by the press trials, the personal activities of François Guizot were of great importance. Already a leader in *Aide-toi le Ciel t'aidera*, Guizot helped to put the influence of this efficient machine behind the Breton idea. In the electoral circulars published by the leading opposition papers, *Aide-toi* urged citizens to support the idea of legal resistance by refusing to pay taxes.[40] Guizot, writing in the recently founded *Temps*, as well as in his own literary periodical, *Revue Française*, campaigned vigorously for the Breton Association. In the latter organ, he encouraged liberals in the provinces to accept the *refus* idea. He urged the deputies to reject the budget when the Chambers convened. If the Chambers were then dissolved, the taxable citizens should refuse to pay taxes.[41] One of the *Temps'* wealthy stockholders, de Richemont, wrote a brochure entitled *Du gouvernment constitutionnel et du refus de l'impôt*. The author stated that public rejection of a budget based on illegal taxes was the "only legitimate defense against the pretensions or aggressions of power, favoritism, and armed force".[42] Guizot wrote an editorial in the

[37] Viel-Castel, *Histoire*, XX, 167-69.

[38] Charles Victor de Broglie, *Personal Recollections of the Late Duke de Broglie* (2 vols.; London, 1887), II, 328.

[39] *National*, 28 November, 1831.

[40] *Temps*, 3 January, 1830.

[41] *Revue Française*, XIV, March, 1830, 225-34.

[42] *Temps*, 3 January, 1830.

Temps in which he explained the principle of legal resistance in the light of Article 48 of the Charter, which forbade any tax not approved in the budget by both Chambers. Here Guizot made the point that the Breton Association should never arrogate to itself the decision whether a given tax was legal, but that such questions should immediately be taken to court. Since the Association was legal and and did not claim the right of judicial interpretation, Guizot asked, why did the government prosecute its propagandists?[43]

Perhaps this question had already been answered in the words of one of the Ultras, the comte de Guernon-Ranville. He was soon to join the Polignac Cabinet as Minister of Ecclesiastical Affairs and Public Instruction. In a speech to the counsellors of the Royal Court of Lyon, Guernon-Ranville indicated that propagandists were more dangerous to the Monarchy than either deputies or outraged taxpayers:

A plague on these craftsmen of sedition and scandal, who, finding a weapon of destruction in the most precious of our prerogatives, have made the press into the instrument of their shameful speculations or of their criminal hatreds, trying to fan the fires of revolt in a people which is peaceful, but easy to deceive ... Public indignation will not be the only punishment reserved for their perversity; using the powerful authority which the Ministry has confided to our loyal hands, nothing can stay them from the just vengeance of the laws, of which you must show yourselves the worthy interpreters.[44]

[43] *Ibid.*, 27 March, 1830.
[44] *Gazette des Tribunaux*, 21 November, 1829.

CHAPTER IX

WINTER QUARTERS: NOVEMBER, 1829
FEBRUARY, 1830

The winter of 1829-1830 was one of the worst in the history of western Europe. Some wealthy Parisians learned the novelty of ice-skating on the Seine, but for the poor of Paris, this cruelty of nature meant a challenge to their miserable quest for survival. Private philanthropists responded with a record number of soup kitchens and the press asked for charitable contributions. For literary citizens and playgoers, the cold season was warmed by a great clash of "classics" and "romantics" – its centerpiece a play called *Hernani*, written by the rising dramatist, Victor Hugo. For the opposition journalists, infused with a new and aggressive spirit, winter was a time for mounting forces and digging editorial trenches. And, at the Tuileries during these months, an Ultra, but divided, Ministry found an opportunity to consolidate and plan its offensive against the Left.

On November 15, 1829, a growing rivalry between the Minister of the Interior, La Bourdonnaye, and the Foreign Minister, the prince de Polignac, reached a crisis. The *Courrier*, with the other opposition papers, saw nothing hopeful in the schism. On November 18, it declared that Polignac and La Bourdonnaye were too jealous of each other to remain as colleagues, but warned:

> Whether the Cabinet calls its leader La Bourdonnaye or Polignac, it is an administration always animated by the same intentions, odious to the nation and which, sooner or later, must fall before its justice.

La Bourdonnaye had entered the Cabinet under the guarantee that no presiding minister would be named, but several of the other members were urging the appointment of a president to facilitate action.[1] When the King consented to these .demands, the bombastic La Bourdonnaye resigned, apparently mollified by promises of a peerage and a modest pension. This

---

[1] Viel-Castel, *Histoire*, XX, 78.

Minister, though an Ultra of Ultras, was not sympathetic to the strongly clerical tendencies of Polignac and he was personally disliked by his colleagues. His resignation, however, was more based on simple political sense than principle. In his words, "It was a matter of gambling my head; I wanted to keep my cards".[2]

Genoude wrote to his friend, the comte de Villèle, that La Bourdonnaye had "preferred a republic to what he had just left".[3] The *Quotidienne* which had supported La Bourdonnaye's Ultra "defection" party, regretted the resignation of this irascible man of action, but praised the subsequent reinforcement which a presidency would give the Cabinet.[4] Genoude's *Gazette* welcomed the resignation as another chance for its idol, the ex-First Minister Villèle to return to power. Genoude urged his return to the Council of State, assuring him that no one liked Polignac and that even the King preferred Villèle.[5] These pleas failed to move the former Cabinet head, who regarded politics as the art of the possible. On the seventeenth of November, a royal edict filled the vacant Interior post by transferring to it the Villèlist Minister of Public Instruction, Guy de Montbel; but this promotion was the only concession made to that important segment of the Right. Prince de Polignac, as expected, was named President of the Council, and a new Ultra minister was found to hold the portfolio of Public Instruction.[6]

The new member was Martial Magloire, comte de Guernon-Ranville, whose recent speech against the press to the Royal Court of Lyons had demonstrated his political views. He proved, however, to be the most independent and the most principled officer on the Polignac Cabinet. The new *Temps* fired broadsides at Guernon-Ranville, emphasizing his recent boast, "I am a counterrevolutionary", a remark convenient for the militants' policy of using the term "revolutionary" unashamedly. The paper also deplored the power he would wield, in his new position, over the faculty of the University.[7] To this, the *Drapeau Blanc*, never mincing, responded that "counterrevolutio-

---

[2] Bertier de Sauvigny, *Restoration*, p. 425; see also, Vaulabelle, *Histoire*, VII, 201. Bertier indicates that La Bourdonnaye was actually dropped as a troublemaker.

[3] Villèle, *Mémoires*, Genoude to Villèle, 29 November, 1829, V, 396.

[4] *Quotidienne*, 17 November, 1829. The *Drapeau Blanc* had pinned all its hopes on La Bour-donnaye. In the October 22 issue, the editor stated that Villèle was the leader of the "secret junta of the *Congrégation* and allowed no one to enter the Polignac council without being "duly confessed and communicated"! Martainville proved once again to be as toxic to his own side as he was to the Left.

[5] Villèle, *Mémoires*, Genoude to Villèle, V, 388-97.

[6] *Le Moniteur*, 17 November, 1829.

[7] *Temps*, 19 November, 1829.

nary" was the most honorable title a man could bear.[8] However menacing, the new Ministry appeared rather artless, and therefore delightfully quotable to its enemies.

To the editors of the Left, the Cabinet change was one more omen of the approaching *coup d'état*. As had been evidenced by their reactions to Polignac's arrival in August, these journalists welcomed more than they feared the predicted *coup*. They taunted the Ministry for its "inaction" and "disunity" and then, whenever the Ministry acted, as in the elevation of Polignac to the presidency, they denounced it as perpetrating a counterrevolution. In an editorial entitled "Sinister Plot", the *Temps* predicted a *coup* and spoke of "widespread" rumors that Polignac was plotting to change the electoral law by decree.[9]

Most embarrassing to the government was the support given to the liberals' prophecy by the *Drapeau Blanc*. Editor Martainville, ever the *enfant terrible* of the Ultras, fairly screamed for a ministerial deathblow.

The official *Moniteur*, apparently vexed by this agreement between Right and Left, announced that "despite seditious clamors", the ministers "will not deviate from the line traced for them by honor and duty; they will be shown worthy of the Prince who chose them; they known his unbending will to consolidate the institutions handed down by his august brother".[10] Such assurances from Polignac failed to assuage the liberals, who preferred to see, in the silence and secrecy of the Ultra Cabinet, only conspiracy. Any action of the ministers caused suspicion; any silence had the same effect.

Early in December, the King made a short visit to Compiègne with some of his ministers and a minor courtier had blurted that the reason for the trip was to "reinforce" the Ministry. This report nourished a month of speculation in the press. The Ultra papers expressed the hope that the journey would result in vigorous measures, while the Left predicted that it would lead to a further crystallization of the Ministry. The *Temps* ventured that three new Ultras, all extremists, would be named. According to its prophets, Peyronnet, archfoe of the press during Villèle's government, would succeed to the Seals and Justice portfolio held by Courvoisier; Ferdinand de Bertier, a founder of the *Congrégation* and an occasional editor of the *Quotidienne*, would replace Montbel at the Interior; and baron Jean-François Dudon, a fiery Ultra would succeed the moderate Chabrol at Finances. These predictions later proved valid in spirit, but wide of the mark in detail. The *Temps*

---

[8] *Drapeau Blanc*, 20 November, 1829.

[9] *Temps*, 27 November, 1829.

[10] *Le Moniteur*, 3 December, 1829.

attacked the "complacent" royalist press as foolish to expect anything reasonable from Polignac. This was aimed largely at the *Débats*, whose Chateaubriand still held the vain hope that he might be called to liberalize the regime.

Temps' writers unearthed another report of schism in the Cabinet, declaring that War Minister Bourmont had voted against elevating La Bourdonnaye to the presidency, and that the latter had therefore called him a "traitor".[11] As the royal trip to Compiègne had yet failed to produce Peyronnet and the other Ultra "reinforcements"; and thus bear out the *Temps'* eager prophecy, the editors sought to discredit those moderates who still sat in the Council of State. Courvoisier, the Minister of Justice who had been retained from the Martignac Ministry, was damned with faint praise:

> Everyone has his *dada* [idiosyncrasy]... Thus M. de Polignac believes himself a Pitt charged to defend the royal prerogative, which everyone respects... Well, the *dada* of M. de Courvoisier is to believe himself a member of the center Left, and destined to represent that shade in the Council. A man of the center Left in the same Council where sit M. de Guernon-Ranville and M. de Montbel! What an insult to common sense![12]

The *Drapeau Blanc*, meanwhile, continued to press for a *coup* against parliamentary rule in its own disconcerting way:

> The question of majority no more concerns the Ministry than any of these petty themes left to the prattle of idlers in *cafés* and the morons of the *salon*. If the ministers have the majority, they will save the throne with it; if they do not have it, they will save it without it. *The Majority, that is the King.*[13]

Athough not as factional as the opposition press had charged, the Cabinet was still far from unanimous in its program. As early as October, a clear plan for a *coup* had been presented by baron d'Haussez, Minister of the Navy; this was to pack the Chamber of Peers by Ultra appointments; then, if the Chambers still refused the budget, to dissolve them and levy taxation under the emergency power of Article 14 of the Charter. Haussez also urged that the press be muzzled by edict, that prefects discharge liberal employees, and that the National Guard, reactivated under Martignac, be disbanded after regular troops were brought to Paris.[14] In a New Year's Day résumé of the previous year, (1829), the *Constitutionnel* lashed the August eighth Ministry as representing "a few people, who for their stupid vengeance, beaten

---

[11] *Temps*, 14 January, 1830.
[12] *Ibid.*
[13] *Drapeau Blanc*, 10 December, 1829.
[14] Viel-Castel, *Histoire*, XX, 71-72.

back again and again in the past forty years, are still willing to set France on fire".[15]

As liberal journalists continued to forecast a *coup d'état* and scourge the ministers, they also furthered the analogy of the English Revolution of 1688, a comparison which the new *National* and *Temps* used more frequently to serve their veiled Orleanism. The deputy-controlled *Temps*, probing the limits of outright sedition, stated:

> Indeed, the house of Stuart would yet reign in England, if... the rights and powers [of Charles I] had been as clearly recognized, as well defined and regulated with as much precision, as they are in France by the Charter.[16]

By the end of January, all opposition papers were relating events to England either in the Civil War or in the "Glorious Revolution". The *National*, as has been noted, was in the process of extending these analogies toward substituting the name of Louis-Philippe for William III, but it remained circumspect in its allusions, never using proper names in seditious parallels, and always including some false-sounding reassurances about the inviolable nature of the Charter or the absence of a revolutionary crisis.

To counterattack the first tide of this reborn and militant journalism, the government had to rely on the courts of law, as it had in regard to the Breton Association. Martignac's press law still reigned. The Cabinet was not yet prepared to revive censorship, since that could be achieved only by edict, the legislative majority being more opposed to censure than ever. During the winter months of 1829 and 1830, political trials of newspapermen created the usual public excitement and publicity for the opposition. Now that the *coup* and "1688" had been predicted, no one was certain how the Ministry would respond in court. Trials were held for a variety of causes. Some writers were prosecuted for "defamation" of Ultra officials; two cases concerned foreign envoys to France who had brought suit against Parisian journalists; one important affair was the appeal of the *Journal des Débats* from its conviction for the famous August 10 editorial by Béquet. Another trial, of less significance, was that of the editor of the *Courrier Français* for questioning religious doctrines. Two cases involving the widespread heresy of Napoleon Bonaparte were also in the courts.

Two frequently indicted provincial newspapers again underwent judicial ordeals in November. Clerc-Lasalle was charged with defamation of the Prefect of Deux-Sèvres, the Sub-Prefect of Parthenay, and the Sub-Prefect

---

[15] *Constitutionnel*, 1 January, 1830.
[16] *Temps*, 14 January, 1830.

of Melle.[17] The alleged outrage had been discovered in an article in one of Clerc-Lasalle's publications, the *Tribune des Départments*. This small news-paper was printed in Niort and was no kin of the Parisian republican journal of nearly the same name. Clerc-Lasalle also edited the monthly *Sentinelle* at Niort, one of the most persecuted voices of the provincial press. According to the prosecutor, Clerc-Lasalle had outrageously attacked the Sub-Prefect of Parthenay for the latter's defense of a local priest. The priest in question had caused public indignation, when in his zeal to baptize an unborn fetus, he opened its dying mother's belly with a knife. Thus, again, a political trial was enlivened by sensational anticlericalism. Clerc-Lasalle received a light sentence of fifteen days in prison and a fine. In February, the high Court of Poitiers rejected his appeal and upheld the sentence.

In the south of France, the liberal *Aviso* of Toulon was having a similar trial.[18] Its young editor, Rousseau Marquézy, was accused of defaming the Prefect of Basses-Alpes, who had discharged one of his assistants, the mayor of Digne. *Aviso* had declared that the firing occurred when the honest mayor refused to act as an *agent provocateur*, and, in anger, had written to the Minister of the Interior, exposing the Prefect's activity. It was this letter that Marquézy had published. Although the editor was acquitted by the lower court, the offended Prefect appealed as plaintiff to the Royal Court of Aix. The government could not suffer the dignity of a royal prefect to be compromised. It was also insufferable that the provincial magistracy had begun to assert its independence in the same way as the courts of Paris. On the contention that Marquézy's paper had operated a long-range policy of "slander" against the Prefect, the court gave the editor a minimum penalty of one month in prison and a fine of two hundred francs. Marquézy was thus convicted under the outlawed "tendency" principle. He had previously been sentenced to a three month term for an article "outraging" religion in a July issue of the *Aviso*.[19]

Two other defamation trials involved the foreign affairs of the Bourbon government. Both dealt with states which were despotically ruled by clerical absolutists, and with which France maintained cordial relations; facts the liberals seized upon with considerable relish.

In November, one Aguado, a fiscal agent of Spain in Paris, brought suit for defamation against Laurentie of the Ultra *Quotidienne*, Bert of the *Journal*

[17] *Gazette des Tribunaux*, 10 February, 1830.
[18] *Ibid.*, 1 December, 1829.
[19] *Ibid.*, 7 March, 1830.

du Commerce, and Bailleul of the *Courrier*. All three newspapers had accused the Spaniard of fraudulently misrepresenting the worth of some Spanish securities he had sold on the Paris market. The dubious stock, according to the one royalist and two liberal editors, had been concealed by its inclusion with some bona fide *rentes*, which were backed by the gold of French bankers. As the honor of the Madrid Bourbons, as well as the business sense of the Paris Bourbons was under fire, this case, which was merely a minor civil process, became a diplomatic event. The trial was unusual, not only because the Ultraroyalist *Quotidienne* was charged, but also because François Mauguin, a great defender of liberal causes, acted as attorney for the Spaniard! The honor of the unpopular King Ferdinand was upheld by the judges at a cost of five hundred francs to each of the defendants, to say nothing of the thousands which Aguado's swindle had cost French speculators.[20]

Another case of foreign diplomat versus French journalists occurred in December, but is related to grimmer issues and appealed to greater partisanship. The Ambassador of the King of Naples, who called himself the prince de Castelcicala, sued the editors of the *Constitutionnel*, *Courrier*, and *Journal du Commerce* for defamation of character. They had charged the envoy with the use of false allegations to obtain the extradition, to Sicily, of a Neapolitan refugee in France during the previous summer. The patriot, Galotti, had been hanged upon arrival in his native land and French liberals had immediately launched a journalistic campaign to denounce this violation of the French "tradition" of asylum.[21] It will be recalled that one of these editors, Fontan of the often persecuted *Album*, had been indicted for printing an unbridled letter to the Minister of Justice, objecting to Galotti's extradition.[22] Now, several months after the potentialities of Galotti's "murder" had been exploited, the Neapolitan Monarch's own Ambassador chose to reopen the case and, unwittingly, to embarrass Polignac. The most serious accusation leveled at Ambassador Castelcicala was that he was an imposter, whom they exposed as a notorious intriguer whose real name was Fabrizio Ruffo, a villain once associated with the despotic junta of Lord Acton in Naples.[23] In a trial which clearly revealed the truth of these charges, the three defendants were acquitted. The martyr's crown of poor Galotti thus received a new lustre and the Bourbons of Naples, like their cousins in Spain, had stupidly allowed their *pecadillos* to be advertised. More significantly,

---

[20] *Gazette des Tribunaux*, 19 November, 1829; Viel-Castel, *Histoire*, XX, 112-15.

[21] *Ibid.*, pp. 115-16.

[22] *Gazette des Tribunaux*, 11 July, 1829. See *supra*, chapter iv for the Galotti case.

[23] *Gazette des Tribunaux*, 3 December, 1829; *Constitutionnel*, 8 August, 1829.

guilt by association had tarnished the crown of Charles X, whose Minister had accredited the false envoy.

Bonapartism, under a slight but constant pressure, rose no higher under the Ultra Polignac than under his predecessor, but it was always just below the surface and furnished an antiestablishment vehicle. Evidence of this appears frequently in the judicial accounts of the period. Pure Bonapartism, as distinguished from the qualified admiration for Napoleon, invidious to the government, of such organs as the *Temps* or the *Courrier*, did not have a newspaper of its own. Indeed, such a newspaper would have been illegal. Bonapartists had, however, their poet: Auguste Marseille Barthélémy. In July, Barthélémy had been sentenced to three months in prison and a heavy fine for publishing a poem about Napoleon's son, *Le fils de l'homme*. His appeal had now come before the high Court of Paris under the presidency of baron Séguier, who admonished the demonstrative audience to behave quietly, and to utter not even "so French a cry as *Vive le roi*"! and recalled that his court had been chagrined by the outcries during the *Débats'* recent appeal trial. The lawyer Mérilhou, defending the poet, disclaimed seditious intent by his client and compared the toleration which Napoleon had shown to legitimist poets with the repressive measures of the Bourbons. The court, however, upheld Barthélémy's original sentence,[24] while liberal papers exploited their right to again publish the long poem, since it was part of the evidence used in court.

A similar case occurred in Corsica at this time. A poet named Bindocci was brought before the magistrate for printing a verse called the "Meeting of Caesar and Napoleon on the Champs-Elysées", and was charged with the extreme offense of provoking civil war! Bindocci's defense was his declaration of love for Corsica and his opinion of Napoleon as simply a regional hero who embodied his insular patriotism! The originality of this appeal was heightened because Bindocci, like Barthélémy, gave his entire defense in verse. Quite unable to guillotine or imprison such an entertaining and harmless young man, the Corsican court restored his full liberty. [25] Soon after this, a publicist of Lille, one Chivore, was sent to prison for placarding a more prosaic notice all over the walls of the city hall:

I drink the health of the son of the first Emperor of the French, Napoleon the Great. His virtues will one day come to the support of the unfortunate youth and be the most handsome cortege to the throne which awaits him... Long live the R. de R.. and his father N....... the Great.[26]

---

[24] *Gazette des Tribunaux*, 8 January, 1830. See *supra*, chapter iv for Barthélémy's earlier trial.
[25] *Ibid.*, 23 December, 1829.
[26] *Ibid.*

Much of the outspoken Bonapartism of the late Restoration was of this sporadic type, and apparently from testimony, was as frequently induced by the fermented grape as by sudden conspiratorial impulses.

A great victory for anticlerical liberals was won in court when Rousseau Marquézy, convicted two days before on a charge of defamation, won a partial acquittal from a graver conviction of "outrage to religion". In July, editor Marquézy had reprinted in his *Aviso* of Toulon an article of the *Courrier Français* of Paris. In this article, he copied the *Courrier's* suggestion that Christian beliefs might eventually disappear from the world, but that the beauty of a religious painting by Raphael would live forever. In December, both the *Aviso*, before the Royal Court of Aix-en-Provence and the *Courrier*, before the Royal Court of Paris, were given chances to appeal, as both had been convicted by the lesser courts for publishing the anticlerical article. Marquézy was acquitted of the crime of "outrage to religion", but held guilty of "derision of the state religion" for having added the relatively mild comment that the Church was the "friend of worldly pomp".[27] His old sentence was upheld, but the acquittal decision which noted that the negation of a religious dogma was not a crime, augured well for the appeal arguments of the *Courrier Français* to be heard two weeks later, on December 17.

This appeal was held before the Royal Court of Paris, under the presidency of baron Séguier. The editor-in-chief of the *Courrier*, René Chatelain, was defended by the deputy and orator, Joseph Mérilhou, as well as himself. Chatelain called the court's attention to the fact that, as a Catholic, he was being prosecuted for enjoying his rightful liberty of conscience; whereas, if he were a Jew or a Protestant, he could have criticized his own faith with impunity. He also asserted that both St. Augustine and St. Irenius had cast doubt upon the perpetual survival of Christian doctrines. The lawyer Mérilhou avoided theology, and, as had been expected, entered a plea for dismissal of the precedent of the recent acquittal of the little *Aviso*.

The court's decision, although holding the Toulon case irrelevant, completely acquitted Chatelain on all charges, and was hailed as a blow to the regime. The President announced: "Chatelain, in predicting an event, however impossible, did not use expressions... outrageous to the Christian religion".[28]

Of all the judicial decisions that winter, however, the one most encouraging to opposition forces was the appeal of the elder Bertin, managing editor of the *Journal des Débats*. This appeal, from the previous conviction for the August 10 editorial against the new Ministry, was held the day before

---

[27] *Gazette des Tribunaux*, 12 December, 1829. For the *Courrier's* first trial, see *supra*, chapter v.
[28] *Gazette des Tribunaux*, 18 December, 1829.

Christmas in Séguier's court.[29] The eagerly spectacle was attended by a crowd of famous partisans, including the comte de Montlosier, scourge of the Jesuits, General Sebastiani, and the Duke of Montebello. André Dupin, *aîné*, again retained to defend Bertin, first repeated his earlier protest that the Bertins and their paper were stoutly legitimist, monarchical, and religious. One of the incriminating phrases which had aided in Bertin's conviction was: "Once again the bond of love which had connected the people with their Monarch is broken". Dupin leveled his assault on this line and, referring to similar remarks by certain Ultras, ridiculed the charge to absurdity. The lawyer revealed that Polignac, upon the removal of the comte d'Artois from command of the National Guard in 1818, had written in the *Conservateur* that Louis XVIII had "untied the knots which attached the National Guard so honorably to the throne". This telling point, so indicative of the personal ties between Charles X and his chief Minister, caused laughter in the court.

Later in his defense, Dupin asserted that recent prosecutions of the press were the objective of the *parti*, which can never come to power without censorship and exceptional laws, and which "even today, demands in its journals that harshness be used against writers". This speech emasculated the plea of the Royal Prosecutor which followed, when the Crown's advocate assailed the "license of the press" and asked that repressive action be taken. Bertin *aîné*, speaking then in his own behalf, reminded the court that it was he who, with Chateaubriand, had edited the *Journal de Gand* for Louis XVIII during the King's exile of the Hundred Days. At that moment, the anti-Jesuit comte de Montlosier walked down the aisle, shook Bertin's hand, and announced that they had met when they were both captives of the Revolution in the Temple!

With such testimonials of his royalism, the hearings were finished and baron Séguier, with his colleagues, retired for deliberation. The announcement he gave a short time later sent the audience into waves of enthusiasm, through which was heard even the cry, *Vive le roi!* Séguier stated that although the wording of the *Débats* article may have been "unseemly", there was no guilt in it.[30] The next day, the Christmas number of the *Gazette de France* took some comfort in the fact that the court's decision had been by a mere majority of one vote. But the joyful spirit of the opposition had spread throughout the city.

The recent decisions of the Royal Court of Paris, particularly the acquittals of the *Courrier* and the *Débats*, had begun to nettle not only the members

---

[29] *Gazette des Tribunaux*, 25 December, 1829. For Bertin's first trial, see *supra*, chapter vi.
[30] *Ibid.*

of the Polignac Cabinet, but even the Monarch himself. As was customary, a royal reception for officials was held on New Year's Day, 1830, at the Tuileries. This year, the magistrates of the *Cour Royale* were greeted with a curt lecture from the King: "Never forget the important duties you have to fill. Prove, for the welfare of my subjects, that you seek to make yourselves worthy of the signs of confidence you have received from your King".[31] Baron Séguier was next presented to the Dauphine, but before he had even completed his bow, she waved him and his colleagues along with an irritated "passez"![32] The magistrates next visit was over at the Palais Royal, where they were received with every courtesy by the Duke of Orleans and his family.[33] The obvious contrast was not lost on the journalists who heard of it.

Exploiting the New Year's incident thoroughly, the *Temps* noted that the King had been especially cordial to the lesser magistrates of the sixth Correctional Tribunal, the inferior court which had first *convicted* the *Débats* and the *Courrier*, and added that opposition by the courts was a necessary "counterpoise" to "men in authority who are always inclined to throw reason aside".[34] The largest representative of the Ultraroyalists, the *Gazette de France*, openly attacked the Royal Court in these words:

It would be dangerous for public order that anyone would suspect the least opposition on the part of the magistracy to the government, and that partisan spirit should have the slightest influence on its decisions. Nothing would be more capable of exciting popular passions and bringing them to more serious excesses.[35]

Whether the rebuff from the Crown influenced subsequent decisions of the malleable Séguier and of his colleagues, one cannot say. But, within a short time after the reception, the Royal Court *upheld* three convictions by lower tribunals; that of Barthélémy for his Bonapartist poem, that of Bohain for his famous black-bordered edition of *Figaro*, and that of Chatelain of the *Courrier* on a minor conviction of defaming the magistracy. Ironically, Chatelain in his journal, had ungratefully accused the judiciary of partisanship! Séguier's court confirmed Chatelain's sentence of fifteen days at Sainte-Pélagie and a fine of three hundred francs. Whether Séguier was intimidated to any degree is not as important a factor as the new encouragement which his moderation had kindled in the Left. Coincident with the creation of the

---

[31] Guizot, *Memoirs*, I, 335-36
[32] *Ibid.*
[33] Vaulabelle, *Histoire*, VII, 203.
[34] *Temps*, 20 January, 1830.
[35] *Temps*, 3 January, 1830.

militant press, this stimulus gave to liberals a hope that "legal resistance" might be upheld by the courts.

While the liberals promoted legal opposition, they protested their innocence of revolutionary designs. The *Globe* for December 17 asked what would befall any "malcontents", who conspired in a "dark corner" to overthrow the dynasty. It is clear, said the *Globe*, that they would suffer the same fate as the four sergeants of La Rochelle! – A reference to the four soldiers who plotted a *Carbonari* mutiny in the garrison of La Rochelle in 1822 and became martyrs after they were executed.

The opposition continued its challenge to the Ministry, goading it to rid itself of the moderate Cabrol and Courvoisier, whom it labeled as "obstructionists", and the editors continued to forecast the nomination of the Ultras Bertier, Peyronnet, and Dudon to the Council of State. This nomination, according to the Left, would be the "reinforcement" necessary to produce the *coup d'état*.[36]

For the expected disease of the *coup*, the *Temps*, the *National*, the *Courrier*, and the *Débats* offered specific medicines. Brochures and books, such as the "Life of Hampden", were offered for sale, and the necessity to refuse "illegal taxation" was widely preached. Editors spoke rather differently of their British cousins, however, when they accused Polignac of being the willing tool of the Duke of Wellington:

> England was in danger, it is in her interest, when she is troubled, to trouble her neighbor, so she made use of a visionary diplomat. She sent M. Polignac to save a Monarchy that was in no danger and which was never more compromised than in its own fatal rise to power.[37]

It was easy to brand Polignac as the pawn of a hostile, reactionary Europe. But during the Algerian War, six months later, these writers could not bring themselves to admit that, whatever the merits of that war, it was contrary to the wishes of all foreign powers and was a remarkable intrinsic success for France.

Another criticism of the alleged foreign "control" by the *Temps* stated that both Metternich and Wellington had written to the court, urging it to "show more firmness before the Chambers, which do not express the opinion of the nation". The *Temps* even alluded to Charles X in reporting: "It is said that one [the King] wishes ardently to mount his horse, and that, as a result, Dudon and Peyronnet are going to join"[38]

---

[36] *Ibid.*

[37] *Constitutionnel*, 1 January, 1830.

[38] *Temps*, 27 January, 1830. The phrase *monter à cheval* meant to take drastic action.

It was no coincidence that the journals continued to predict the replacement of one of the moderates in the Ministry by baron Dudon. Three important bye-elections were scheduled for the last week of January. Dudon was a candidate for the Loire-Inférieur in one of these contests. Another Ultra, the lawyer Berryer, was also a candidate for the department of Haute-Loire. The third contest was in Calvados and resulted in the election of François Guizot to his first elective office. Although the victory of Guizot was praised by his own paper[39] and several others as a liberal victory, it must be remembered that he had the backing of all the Parisian classes of opposition, from Chateaubriand to Lafayette.[40] Berryer won his seat by a large majority and, in Nantes, Dudon barely won his election with the slight margin of 133 to 109 votes. The press of the opposition promptly accused the electoral college of Nantes of having prevented an even smaller margin by invalidating the ballots of several constitutionalist electors. A few weeks later, evidence of government interference in behalf of Dudon was proven.[41]

Ethical or fraudulent, the election of baron Dudon from a constituency recently subjected to such liberal influences as the Breton Association, infused the Ministry with confidence. Berryer's election had been no surprise, his college being thoroughly royalist; but Dudon's narrow victory may have been Polignac's signal to knead the Ministry into its final shape, the form it would need for unanimous and bold action.[42] As winter passed into a freezing February, the Ministry began to resemble, in some degree, the scheming *camarilla* which the opposition had described.

[39] *Temps*, 27 January, 1830. See p. 111.

[40] Pouthas, *Guizot*, pp. 404-16.

[41] Viel-Castel, *Histoire*, XX, 242; see also, *Temps*, 10 February, 1830.

[42] The Left seemed concerned over Dudon's success. The *National* (4 March, 1830) called his election a "national disgrace" because he had been a slaver after the ratification of the Vienna convention against the slave trade. The Ultras were caught by surprise on March 3, when liberal papers announced that the comte Donatien de Sesmaisons was cashiered as a colonel of the Royal Guard because he had opposed Dudon at Nantes! The "safe" royalist constituency in Ain, for which baron Dudon also stood, elected him by a clear majority.

CHAPTER X

THE PRESS AND THE "221"

The Chambers were to be convoked on the second of March and both Ultras and constitutionalists faced the day with anxiety. It was customary in France, as in England, for the King to open the legislative session with an address. This *Discours du roi* reflected ministerial sentiment and sketched the legislative program of the Royal Council. It usually included a review of the past year's events, and was understood, although spoken by the Monarch, to be written and inspired by the ministers. Thus, the King's speech had become an important political weather vane. It was also customary for the Chambers to appoint a committee to edit a response to the King, acknowledging his speech point by point and pledging their cooperation. The response was subject to debate since its drafting committee consisted of deputies elected by the majority. Both addresses were eagerly awaited by journalists of both camps.

In 1830, all factions were agreed that the address from the throne would at least contain some reference to "royal prerogative" and a forceful attack on the opposition. There was less agreement on the type of response the liberal majority would write after the speech on March 2. The *Gazette* predicted, and doubtless hoped, that the Chamber's answer would be "insolent".[1] Defiance by the Left would, according to the *Gazette*, facilitate the use of the emergency powers of the Crown under Article 14 – the article which, to the Left, was now synonymous with *coup d'état*. Guizot claimed the Chamber would not be so foolish as this and assured its enemies that the address from the deputies would be "respectful, but strong", declaring it would "unmask" them.[2] Ultraroyalists and the far Left hoped that both speeches would be so bellicose as to insure a *coup d'état*, since they saw in them the opportunity for the anticipated showdown.

A widely discussed concern of the government, certain to be noted in the

[1] *Gazette de France*, 3 February, 1830.
[2] *Temps*, 3 February, 1830.

royal speech, was the proposed military and naval campaign against the Dey of Algiers. Polignac had long nourished a "grand design" of diplomacy which included partition of the Ottoman Empire and even the annexation of Belgium by France. A political dreamer, he had hoped his plan would satisfy the nation's lust for glory, an urge that had been growing in the peaceful France of the Restoration and was stimulated by the cult of Napoleon. Polignac's imperial reverie, rejected by St. Petersburg, London, and Vienna, was at last given substance by an event which occurred a few weeks before he became chief adviser to the King. The guns of the fortress of Algiers had fired upon the flagship of a blockading French fleet.

A blockade of Algiers had begun in 1827 as a result of deteriorating relations. Maritime powers of the world had long opposed the high cost of trading concessions on the African shore and they considered their tribute to the Barbary pirates to be an indirect source of revenue for the Dey Hussein of Algiers. For these reasons, the French withheld payment for concessions and attempted to negotiate a new agreement. The Dey responded angrily; summoned the French consul, Deval, accused him of influencing the stoppage of payment, called him a "scoundrel" and an "infidel" and cut him across the face with his jewelled fly swatter: A perfect casus-belli![3] Yet, there was England's Mediterranean policy to consider and Polignac, then Ambassador to England, and aware of the relative positions of the two nations, was content with a naval blockade. Two years later, however, the Algerian shore batteries not only opened hostilities, but exploded into the schemes of Polignac's domestic politics.

Here was the chance that would never return. By a decisive campaign across the Mediterranean, the August 8 Cabinet could divert French energy from its homeland to Africa and could demonstrate French independence from "foreign" control. By training and equipping a small army, which would, if victorious, also become popular, the Ministry would develop a truly national royal army to discourage any future "uprising". In addition, by assigning command of the expedition to the new Minister of War, General Bourmont, the traitor of Waterloo, a bad reputation would be expiated and covered with glory. By the end of February, regiments from every garrison in France were flooding into the new cantonments near Toulon. The more militant journalists quickly penetrated the motivation of the Algiers affair and denounced it.

In opposing the campaign, the liberals found they had to brave the Ultra's accusation that they were "anti-French". The Temps assured its readers that Marshal Bourmont would keep his Cabinet portfolio, as well as his "floating

---

[3] Lucas-Dubreton, Restauration, pp. 139-40.

baton" and that the decision to attack Algiers was contrary to the expressed wishes of Wellington and Lord Stuart, the Tory-Minister to France. Although the liberal press, aware that the campaign, against British interests, might also clear Polignac of his "Wellington" stigma, avoided that particular piece of logic and blithely continued to denounce Polignac as a tool of the British! Under the caption, "Polignac's Dream", *Temps'* editors wrote that the address from the Chamber would be termed "insolent" and would be rejected by a proroguement of the Chambers until October 1. Then, according to the *Temps*, over 30,000 French troops, fresh from heroic exploits overseas, would parade through Paris and the newly convoked Chamber would be forced into timid acquiescence before a show of force.[4] The *Globe* said the campaign would be "uncertain and bloody", that it would give no patriotic aura to the Ministry and that it was an "English policy in nearly every point"![5] Here, the *Globe's* logic had faltered badly. The newspapers of the Ultras, of course, were on this point unanimous in their passionate praise of the glory that was to be added to their tarnished *fleur-de-lys*. They stressed the "insult to our flag" and denounced anyone who would not be indignant over it. A new factor, advantageous to the Right, had emerged, but since war preparations required nearly three months, the opposition skillfully capitalized on other issues.

The *National*, when predicting a *coup*, had suggested that a "change of persons" might be necessary. The *Temps* and the *Globe* hinted their support of Thier's Orleanist program, but kept up an unctuous fiction of loyalty to the person of the King, the *Temps* asserting that the King was being "deceived" by his ministers when they assured him they would have a parliamentary majority. The editor termed Polignac's view of royal prerogative as "monstrous, illegal, and unlimited", and as a desire to return to the days of *bon plaisir* when government was by the privileged class.[6] The opposition was sure that the more moderate ministers, sub-ministers, and prefects would soon be replaced by extreme Ultras, a mass sacking that would be one more step towards the expected *coup* and they continued to defend Ministers Courvoisier and Chabrol whom, they claimed, would soon resign. Several of these newspapers were apparently deceived by the Villèlist Montbel, Minister of Interior since La Bourdonnaye's resignation. They considered Montbel as reactionary, but incapable of participating in a *Coup*. He would say to his colleagues, stated the *Temps*, "Our task is to combat a revolution, not to create one"![7] It was inconceivable to them that a follower of the pragmatic Villèle would

    [4] *Temps*, 10 February, 1830.
    [5] *Globe*, 3 March, 1830.
    [6] *Temps*, 4 February, 1830.
    [7] *Ibid.*, 27 January, 1830.

court the risk of a *coup*. They did not realize it was Montbel who had first suggested that, if the address was hostile, the Chambers be prorogued.[8] The liberals also predicted the employment of Franchet d'Espérey, former Director of the Police and an Ultraclerical, and Delavau, who was accused of responsibility for the rue Saint-Denis "massacre" of 1827.[9] Together with J.-H. Mangin, already Prefect of Police, this pair would be able to enforce the "order" so eagerly demanded by the Right.

In this atmosphere of speculation over the forthcoming opening of the Chambers and the symptoms of a *coup d'état*, the militant Left redoubled its propaganda. Newspapers were in conflict over more fundamental questions than whether certain Ultras would be added to the government. The very structure of the French Constitutional system was examined. Alphonse de Martainville wrote candidly the legal government of France was a "republic" and that if the King wished to rule he must begin by destroying that system.[10] The most radical opinion of the new militant Left was written by Adolphe Thiers in the *National*, in an editorial which became famous for its later prosecution, as well as for its intrinsic boldness.[11] As has been described in an earlier chapter, Thiers had declared that it was then a question of things, but that it could become a question of persons,[12] and had posed the theory that "the King reigns but does not rule": A view intended as a direct challenge to the Ultra philosophy of monarchy.

In this article, Thiers had asserted that the degree of representation of the people in their government depended upon conditions; no one blamed Russia for autocracy, because her people were backward. He had praise for the American form of government, but declared it unsuitable for France because of "Latin" temperament and the attitudes of France's monarchical neighbors, a remark intended for the republican militants. The English system, he concluded, was the best, where a king reigns but does not rule.[13] French monarchy, stated Thiers, was but *one* of the many guarantees of the Charter of 1814 – "Monarchy is but a single man, but one family at the most, against an entire nation; we know this". Quickly he tried to soften his strong phrase by adding: "If we overthrew him, we would alarm all crowned heads like his... and bring all kingdoms to arm against us for defense. This is what

---

[8] Villèle, *Mémoires*, 13 January, 1830, V, 409. It seems possible that Villèle was using Montbel as a wedge in the door. As the Left assumed, it is inconceivable that Villèle, had he been First Minister in 1830, would have had so incautious a policy.

[9] *Temps*, 10 February, 1830.

[10] *Drapeau Blanc*, 28 February, 1830.

[11] *National*, 19 February, 1830.

[12] *Ibid*.

[13] *Ibid.*, 19 February, 1830.

the revolution has taught us about monarchy".[14] Thiers' disclaimers did not prevent the Royal Council from demanding judicial action, and the *National's* director soon found himself before the magistrates.

A few days before this provocative editorial appeared, the *Globe* had published its article "France and the Bourbons".[15] This has been described in an earlier chapter to show the virility of the *Globe* after that journal became wholly political. Editor Paul-François Dubois, was cited to appear before a lower court of correctional police to answer for "France and the Bourbons" and on the very day he was indicted, his *Globe* announced that the dynasty itself was in question! It posed the question "with sorrow, but with resolution".[16] The trials of the *Globe* and the *National* were held in March and were of major interest to all political factions because they centered on Orleanism.

The young dissenters who had begun to forge this new political weapon in journalism, Thiers, Carrel, Dubois, Guizot, and the rest, became a source of anxiety to their more moderate colleagues in the opposton press. The *Constitutionnel*, well-established and not given to adventures, feared that these newcomers might ignore its own cherished ideal of "legal resistance". They agreed, however, that as long as the Ultra Press could demand a *coup* by the Ministry and go unpunished, the journals of the Left had every right to attack that threat.

The *Journal des Débats* was again in a unique position. Polignac and his absolutist faction had no more bitter foe than the *Débats*, and the vicomte de Chateaubriand made a spectacle of his resignation as Ambassador to Rome by verbally flaying the First Minister. Yet the *Débats* was still reverently loyal to the descendants of Henry of Navarre. To its staff of writers, a kingdom, unless of the Bourbons, would be merely a sham republic. They had no more taste for Orleanism than for a Convention and assumed the role of anxious parents toward their "young friends" of the *Globe*. The *Débats*, like the *Constitutionnel*, however, tolerated this lack of "prudence" in the light of the unpunished violence of the Ultra papers. Irritated a trifle more, the *Débat's* editors would not even try to restrain their more adventurous friends.

In the meantime, the government was attacking on all fronts: Courts were kept busy with press prosecutions; propagandists were flooding the stalls with new brochures; and at the Tuileries, the last of the French Bourbons

[14] *Ibid.*
[15] *Globe*, 15 February, 1830.
[16] *Globe*, 19 February, 1830.

and his ministers were weighing the risks of that final scheme which was to be doomed to failure.

The ministers knew that the opening speech must indicate to the Chambers neither fanatical rashness nor frail moderation. Polignac and the King considered amendments to the Charter which would alter the electoral laws and wished to suggest this legislation in the royal speech.[17] But the other ministers discouraged this proposal as too weak a start. It was then agreed that the speech should be a strong assertion of the royal prerogative, with enough allusions to the personal authority of the King as to render it unmistakably defiant. The speech was written between February 13 and 20. The only objections to the inclusion of the threat of royal power were voiced by the new Minister of Public Instruction, the comte de Guernon-Ranville,[18] a Norman respected for his frankness even by his enemies.[19] He was to prove his independence and his sense of legality several times before his dissent was at last drowned in the clamor of his colleagues.

Individual Ultras, pressing for action, initiated a pamphlet war whose purpose was certainly not to dissuade the Left of its belief in a *coup d'état*. Charles Cottu authored two brochures that appeared at the end of February. Cottu, who had been a liberal pamphleteer under Villèle, had suddenly become an Ultra in 1828. He was a counsellor to the Royal Court of Paris, the body recently reprimanded by the King. Cottu remained, however, anti-clerical and thus was allied more closely with La Bourdonnaye and the *Drapeau Blanc* persuasion than with the Polignac or Villèle followings. One of these pamphlets was bluntly titled: *On the Necessity of a Dictatorship*, and contained these provocations:

> Who is there today who doubts that if, on last August 8, instead of creating a Ministry whose composition alone came to excite the fury of the revolutionaries, the Monarchy, as I advised it in Council, had thrown itself on the Revolution, the Monarchy would have crushed it in the first encounter?[20]

Cottu enlarged on this theme, suggesting a very secretly planned *coup*, to be launched thoroughly and suddenly, by a declaration of the state in danger and proclamation of a new electoral law under the provision of Article 14. In a second pamphlet, issued a few days later, entitled: *The Necessity of an endowment*, Cottu urged the increase of the peerage, to enable the King to so "pack" the upper Chamber with Ultras that it could veto any acts of

---

[17] Viel-Castel, *Histoire*, XX, 223.
[18] *Ibid.*, p. 226.
[19] Chateaubriand, *Mémoires*, V, 226.
[20] Viel-Castel, *Histoire*, XX, 188.

the deputies. Cottu also offered an angry reproach to baron Séguier, his superior.

Another Ultra pamphlet, regarded by the Left as more menacing than that of Cottu, was published on March 1, immediately before the Chambers convened. It was the work of the comte de Madrolle and several other "Drapeau Blanc"-style Ultras and bore the obvious title: *Memoir to the King's Council, on the True Situation of France and on the Urgency of a Government Contrary to the Revolution.*[21] Clearly, here was a companion for the Cottu brochures, a demand for a *coup d'état*, but it ventured farther than the others had dared and called upon the government to subvert its own laws. The authors urged the Ministry to cast timidity aside and to change the electoral law and the press laws by edict. These writers also took a passing thrust at the magistracy, and particularly Séguier's court for its recent impartiality. In regard to the Christmas Eve acquittal of Bertin of the *Débats*, the pamphlet stated injudiciously, "The tribunal which absolves such a criminal subject, who listens graciously to its apologist, thinks basically like them. It probably also behaves like them. It is a scaled-down Convention"!

The provincial courts were also flogged without mercy for their "revolutionary boldness" and even for forcing royalist plaintiffs to pay court costs when their cases were lost. As for the acquittal of the *Courrier* on charges of outraging religion, merely setting the editor free was the maximum possible outrage to religion, sputtered the Ultra pamphlet! The strident little manifesto then concluded in a wrath of personal denunciations. The rich Laffitte and General Oberkampf it labeled "presumptuous bankers, who, having only money, wish at any cost, to have titles too". The voice of the embittered old aristocrat of 1789 was evident in this tract.

Listing prominent opposition journalists from Bertin to Thiers, the pamphleteers charged: "These journalists, with no other motive but pride, are scheming to achieve by the domination of thought, a tyranny of peoples and even governments". The candid booklet also scorned the bourgeoisie for their "veneer of refinement" and cried, "They torment their priests in the little parishes; they torment the noble families with their pretensions. They read republican [!] newspapers like the *Constitutionnel*, *Débats*, and *Courrier*".[22] The pamphlet's attack was also extended to the Lafayettes as "apostates of monarchism", and to such ex-Imperial officers as Baron Louis and General Sebastiani. It was signed by the comte de Madrolle, comte Achille de Jouffroy, Benaben, Ducancel, and Henrion. A short notice praising the work was added

[21] Comte de Madrolle, *et al.*, *Mémoire au Conseil du roi* (Paris, March, 1830).
[22] *Ibid.*, pp. 5, 13, 21, *passim*.

at the end was signed by the Ultra peers Vaublanc, Salaberry, and Frenilly.
It was all dedicated to Polignac as the "man to save France". Coauthor
Henrion was the fanatical monarchist who now helped Martainville edit the
Drapeau Blanc.

It is doubtful that the government directed any of these indiscreet publications. The ministers were laying their snares carefully and were depending
on several factors, such as the Algiers war or the effect of the *Discours du
roi*, to guide their hands. Such pamphlets could only impair their long-term
planning by giving credence to the prophecy of the Left.

The Left immediately exploited the pamphlet campaign to the discomfort
of the Ministry. The *Constitutionnel* began by praising the tolerance of
Séguier for not formally censuring his underling, Cottu.[23] Earlier, the *Constitutionnel* had done some investigating, and revealed that, in the early morning
of February 21, a gendarme had been seen entering Cottu's home. Alleging
that this officer had been sent by Bourmont and Polignac the paper warned,
"The Ministry is thinking of some great folly".[24] The next day the *Quotidienne*
replied that the mere presence of a *gendarme d'ordonnances* before
Cottu's door was no occasion for creating "phantoms" or "mystifying"
readers. When the pamphlet appeared in print, the *Constitutionnel* crowed
that its suspicions had been justified. "The mystery is solved", it announced,
"The *Camarilla* dreams of dictatorship; that means the overthrow of the
Chambers, the courts, and all legal authorities; it needed a man to edit its
manifesto, and it was assigned to M. Cottu".[25]

A group of the counsellors of the *Cour Royale* published a signed protest
against Cottu for an "indecent outrage" to their "respectable chief".[26] The
Globe, in its March 3 issue, allowed the pamphlet calling for a dictatorship
to speak for itself and turned one of Cottu's phrases upon its author: "Those
who wish the unlimited liberty of the press shall perish by the press". The
National (March 4) insisted that Cottu and Madrolle had both violated several
press laws and joked that all the royalists were "trying to save France". All
the press of the Left, as well as the *Débats*, agreed that the brochures had
called for illegal acts by the Ministry. The *Temps*, on March 8, published a
counterattack on Cottu's pamphlet entitled "Revolutionary Spirit of the
Absolutists". This article sought to show that dictatorship was in no way
suitable for "modern Europe"; that all supragovernmental institutions were
invariably the results of "usurpation".

[23] *Constitutionnel*, 8 March, 1830.
[24] *Ibid.*, 22 February, 1830
[25] *Ibid.*, 3 March, 1830.
[26] *Gazette des Tribunaux*, 9 March, 1830.

Ultra Journals divided in their response to the pamphlets. The *Gazette* sharply criticized Cottu, leaving the deflated *Temps* to label the criticism an insidious part of their plan. When the pamphlets appeared, the *Drapeau Blanc*, of course, shouted its jubilation. The Cabinet, compromised and embarrassed by all this premature frenzy of Ultra reaction, and goaded by the liberals, was forced to prosecute. The court formally indicted Martainville of the *Drapeau* and the comte de Madrolle for attacking the prerogatives of the Chamber. The two Ultra publicists were brought before the lower court of the correctional tribunal and quickly declared "not guilty" because they had merely "exercised their right to publish their opinions"! The contrast between this judgment and others of the same court regarding liberal papers was not overlooked by the opposition. Cottu himself was never indicted and his tenure as a member of the most important trial court in France shielded him well.

To further display the partisan inconsistency of this lower court, a case involving a liberal tract was treated much differently. A lawyer named Alcibiade Wilbert had written a piece, *Qu'est ce que c'est le côte droit?* (What is the Right Wing?) soon after the arrival of Polignac, and the *Gazette de France* had branded it "revolutionary". Wilbert then wrote a rebuttal to Genoude of the *Gazette*, and demanded he print it, in compliance with press laws, concerning defamation. Genoude refused this request. Later, in March, Wilbert sued for his right. The *Gazette's* lawyer held that Genoude was *correct* in his appraisal of the pamphlet and hence need not have inserted the rebuttal. The judge agreed and Wilbert had to pay the court costs![27]

As the opening of the legislature drew near, opposition newspapers tried to stiffen the backs of the deputies to prepare them for the expected shock of the royal speech. There was apprehension among the militants of the press because most of the moderate deputies were hoping that a simple Cabinet change would save the Monarchy from peril.[28] The *National*, *Globe*, and *Temps* denounced any "deals" between deputies and ministers. And, now that Chateaubriand's last hope had vanished, the legitimist *Débats* also joined in this warning. In the *Temps*, Guizot regretted that some deputies still relied on courteous moderation, warning that the Ministry felt differently and "would rather engage the battle". Guizot then recalled that, if the Chambers had stood firm in 1829, there would have been no Polignac. If the Chambers are victorious tomorrow, he added, they will cause royal displeasure, but they will "save the nation".[29] He then predicted a prorogation of the

---

[27] *Gazette de France*, 5 March, 1830.
[28] Viel-Castel, *Histoire*, XX, 225.
[29] *Temps*, 1 March, 1830. He was presumably referring to the center-Left.

Chambers soon after the address. Guizot wrote portentously that in England, prorogations under the Stuarts had the object of bypassing Parliament: "We all known what happened".[30]

The *Globe* had printed, in its now famous February 15 editorial, "France and the Bourbons":

Parliament is about to open and the Monarchy finds itself face to face with the nation ... There is nothing so dismal or humiliating for a great people as to be forced, each morning, to foresee or to frustrate the follies of an authority both menacing and despicable.

Editor-in-chief Dubois was soon to pay dearly for these daring words. On the eve of the convocation, the *Globe* declared that the "unity and resolution of the Chamber will test the prudence of the Ministry", and foresaw a new check each day for the ministers until they must at last decide whether to retreat and fail or to strike and violate the Charter.[31] The *Drapeau Blanc* had already stated the case for its coterie of fanatics when it termed the Restoration government a "republic" and urged the King to "destroy" it. Martainville now went even farther to declare that the Chambers had reduced the King to a "political supernumerary, an old *rentier*", predicting that, if he attacked the opposition in this weakened condition, he would be "expelled like a Stuart"![32] We could expect that Martainville would one day remind the King of his resemblance to James II.

The pageantry of England and of France were combined in the ceremonies which opened the Chambers on March 2, 1830. The King and his family[33] left the Tuileries in a gilded coach to the echoes of twenty-one guns at the Invalides. The ministers, the deputies, the peers of the realm, the marshals of France, the archbishops, the diplomatic corps, and even Talleyrand, the Grand Chamberlain, stood in their finery when the Royal family entered the Louvre, where opening joint-sessions were held. As the King sat on his throne, a minor accident occurred. His coronet slipped and tumbled to the floor, but the Duke of Orleans deftly helped to replace it on the old Monarch's

---

[30] *Ibid.*

[31] *Globe*, 2 March, 1830.

[32] *Drapeau Blanc*, 28 February, 1830.

[33] The royal family consisted at this time of the King; his childless older son, Louis, the Dauphin (duc d'Angoulême); Marie-Therèse, his wife and first cousin, and the daughter of Louis XVI; Caroline of Naples, the controversial duchesse de Berri and Henri, her son, the comte de Chambord, "miracle child" of 1820. The duc de Berri, Charles's other son, was murdered in 1820 when his wife was already pregnant. The wife of Charles X, Maria Teresa of Savoy, died at Gratz in 1805, abandoned by the comte d'Artois. The comte de Chambord, who died in 1883, was the last male descendant of Henry of Navarre. A good Ultra, he insisted on being called Henri V as his grandfather had taught him.

head. In the hushed splendor of the assembly, few witnesses could have ignored the symbolism of that moment.[34]

When the invocation ended, the King rose grandly, bade the peers be seated, gave the deputies "permission to sit", then began the address. He delivered the first part of the speech in a softly refined voice, reviewing the financial improvement of the nation, the agricultural bounty of the preceding year, the rise in manufactures, industrial patents, and other economic aspects of the kingdom. The King then turned to foreign policy: The recent war against the Turks which had delivered Greece and the stable relations with the King of Portugal, Dom Miguel. He also spoke proudly of the vengeance France would soon enjoy for the "outrage to the flag" at Algiers.

When Charles had finished the discussion of foreign affairs, he stopped for a moment and his face seemed to grow tense. From the silence, his voice was heard again, now more sharply intoned, more animated, almost angry.[35] He concluded the address in this voice in the words he had been impatient to say, words which everyone had been waiting to hear:

> Peers of France, Deputies of the Departments, I do not doubt your accord in effecting the good I wish to do; you must reject with scorn the perfidious insinuations that wickedness seeks to propagate. If guilty maneuvers raise obstacles to my government that I cannot, that I wish not, to foresee, I shall find the strength to surmount them in my resolution to keep the public peace, in the just confidence of the French people and in the love which they have always shown their kings.[36]

Here was an unmistakable challenge; The battle so long expected had formally begun. Much depended on the way in which the opposition would respond.

As the Chambers considered the problem of answering the King, Right wing newspapers exulted. The *Drapeau Blanc*, obviously considered the speech as step one of a *coup d'état*. Martainville gaily announced that Charles had resolved all the problems created by "faithless orators and seditious journalists". A few days later, Henrion, who had coauthored the recent Madrolle pamphlet, added an editorial titled: "The Inevitable Dissolution of the Chambers and of an Election Edict".[37] Certain that the Chamber's response would be "hostile to the Crown", Henrion noted that one of the framers of the deputies' response was Benjamin Constant, whose writings, he said, the King had urged everyone to "scorn". Although Constant was not the sole editor of the response, this old-style liberal served to personify the Revolution to Henrion, an old-style reactionary. The *Drapeau* assumed, and correctly

---

[34] Lucas-Dubreton, *Restauration*, p. 136.

[35] Chateaubriand, *Mémoires*, V, 263.

[36] *Le Moniteur*, 2 March, 1830.

[37] *Drapeau Blanc*, 6 March, 1830.

so, that the "wickedness" which Charles X had mentioned was the liberal press. The paper predicted dissolution of the Chamber since the deputies were clearly the "obstacles" of which the King had spoken!

Henrion also forecast the event which the Left would call a *coup*, a new electoral law by edict. Acknowledging the grim possibility that this could turn the King over "to his executioners", he argued in this issue that a new electoral law should be a part of the dissolution order, to thus operate in normal, constitutional processes and return deputies to Paris who would "represent all the monarchical opinion of the country". Henrion's ideas were then extreme enough to vex the ministers, yet a short time later, most of them would decide upon a similar program. But Henrion had actually been more sensible than they would be, for he had recognized the real danger of a revolution.

The *Gazette* was less blatant, but more thorough, than the *Drapeau*. It defended the King's closing words as "well-intentioned",[38] praised the spirit of the final paragraph, and turned its attack on the leaders of the opposition. Again it charged the Left with falsely accusing the government of plotting a *coup*. It was the liberals themselves, argued the *Gazette*, who had violated legality, and the paper recalled Lafayette's revolutionary career as one of "throat-cutting" and "leading an armed mob". All of the liberals, the *Gazette* then declared perceptively, were insincere in their liberalism as they were really hoping for a dictatorship.[39] The *Quotidienne* was pleased by the speech and urged the administration to follow through on the lines set down by the King's final statement.[40] Here again, the practical absolutism of the *Gazette* may be contrasted with the braying emotionalism of the *Drapeau* and the dogmatically authoritarian conviction of the *Quotidienne*.

The reaction of the opposition press was by contrast, united and strong. On the address, there was little to distinguish between the moderate, established journals and the new militants, and all treated the *Discours du Roi* as the gauntlet thrown down. They attacked not only the final threatening lines, but many other portions of the speech as well. They delighted in accusing the *Gazette* of having changed the text of the speech in its earliest edition. The *Temps* announced that the *Gazette*, in its first printing for March 3, omitted the phrases "with scorn" and "that I cannot" from the royal address. The *Temps* also charged that the *Gazette* substituted "in my own right" for the

---

[38] *Gazette de France*, 15 March, 1830.

[39] *Ibid.*, 3 March, 1830. Villèle had earlier advised the King *not* to make too provocative an address; see, Thureau-Dangin, *Parti libéral*, p. 482.

[40] *Quotidienne*, 3 March, 1830.

stronger "in my resolution".[41] The section of the speech concerned with Algeria was also criticized, the *Temps* maintaining that the real cause of the coming war was not the "vain pretext" given by the Cabinet, but rather a "dispute with the Vatican" which would make 30,000 French troops into "crusaders". Behind this odd remark was the meagre fact that two Papal vessels had been seized by pirates to enforce tribute.[42] Guizot agreed with his opposite, Martainville, in identifying the "obstacle" mentioned by the King as the elective Chamber.[43] In the *Temps* of March 15, he argued almost hopefully for the probability of a *coup*, reasoning that if the "King is at war with the Revolution", then his ministers are foolish to advise him to delay his assault. "To delay a moment would be to admit defeat", he taunted in the *Temps*. This friendly advice followed a reminder of the price Louis XVI had paid for hesitation! Concluding this article with a totally insincere protestation of royalism, Guizot said: "But of course the King would never *think* of this. ... He is the sworn guardian of liberties". The *Globe*, too, translated the word "obstacles" as the Chamber of Deputies. Dubois noted that if the King wished to conquer this particular obstacle there was but one legal method: Dissolution, and prayed: "May all our good citizens arm themselves with courage and increase in wisdom". The *Globe's* article continued, "A dark future is perhaps approaching; but all hope is not yet lost: The Chamber has said nothing".[44]

Liberals appeared anxious over the address the deputies were preparing. Though the Left majority would edit this address, the Ultra and center-Right deputies would be certain to challenge it on the floor. Adolphe Thiers argued for a strong reply from the pages of the *National*. To this paper, the King's speech was a composition of "servility abroad" and "mistaken and politically threatening administration at home". Thiers called the last paragraph, "a repetition in four lines, of all the Ministry has been saying for eight months... a résumé of all its threats... Article 14, in its entirety, understood as certain men have habitually interpreted it".[45]

The next day, Thiers again attacked the *Discours du Roi* in three categories: "Servility of our foreign policies", "Algiers expedition", and "Theory of a *coup d'état*".[46] Under the first title he reached far to criticize French support of the English-backed Monarch of Greece, Leopold of Coburg, as well as

[41] *Temps*, 3 March, 1830.
[42] Roux, *La Restauration*, p. 296. The Roman Navy was then under French protection.
[43] *Temps*, 4 March, 1830.
[44] *Globe*, 4 March, 1830.
[45] *National*, 3 March, 1830.
[46] *Ibid.*, 4 March, 1830.

France's "Machiavellian conduct in regard to the tyrant of Portugal". On the second head, "Algiers expedition", Thiers struck at every aspect of the approaching invasion. It was an abuse of royal power, he wrote, to request unrestricted budgets for unnecessary wars, and hinted that the deputies should refuse the appropriations. Previously, he had scorned religious motives for the campaign which were implied in the King's speech. "In a word", he wrote, "God is invoked to make the enterprise profitable".[47] The third editorial, "Theory of a *coup d'état*", gave Thiers another chance to warn his readers of the dangers ahead, that Polignac, in drafting the royal address, had revealed too much and had proved conclusively that a *coup* was afoot.[48]

The largest journal, the *Constitutionnel*, assumed a melancholy air of injured virtue. Concerning the last words of the *Discours*, Étienne wrote, "The majority was struck through with the meaning and the gravity of the duties they had to perform. They complained especially of the Crown offering defiances which nothing justified". The *Constitutionnel* asserted that stronger language had been added to the draft of the speech only after the election of the Ultra Dudon. Étienne warned his fellow deputies that their assembly would inevitably be dissolved, whether they were "docile or strong, complacent or severe". He then described an event which would become more common, a "réunion" or caucus of many deputies in the rue de Richelieu (the *Temps'* office) immediately after the opening speech and his editorial concluded in a pessimistic tone: "If all resistance is nothing but a 'guilty maneuver', then there is no more Charter, no more institutions, no more laws; France is nothing more than a Spain or a Portugal".[49]

The *Débats* was still protesting its devotion to royalism, but without much enthusiasm. Bertin wrote (March 3), "Tomorrow, all France will share our deep emotion, emotions of sorrow and very royalist anxieties", and pointedly warned that the Charter provided for trial of ministers before the peers.

One tangible result of the royal address was the increased prestige of the militant wing of the press. The King's words would now remind the complacent that a *coup d'état* was not only possible, but probable, and liberal writers accelerated their campaign to alarm readers. The Orleanists led by Thiers and his friends, made more frequent allusions to Louis-Philippe and promised an end to *coup d'état*, to Polignac, to the *Congrégation*, and to nearly forty years of "Revolution".

For the moment, however, the reactions of the deputies themselves absorbed the journalists' attention, balloting for the presidency of the new

[47] *Ibid.*, 3 March, 1830.
[48] *Ibid.*, 4 March, 1830.
[49] *Constitutionnel*, 3 March, 1830.

Chamber being the first order of business. One deputy, Martignac, declined the nomination, as he did not wish to be a symbol of defiance to the Crown. The vote brought Pierre-Paul Royer-Collard, philosopher and orator, to the presidency of the Chamber, a position he had held in the previous session.[50] Royer-Collard was the nominal leader of those "doctrinaires" of the liberal faction, the group which dominated the *Globe*. Although Charles X, with sensible grace, sanctioned Royer-Collard's election, the *Gazette* could not resist reminding its readers that the "man of the hour" was "chief and founder of the doctrinaire school which gave us M. Guizot".[51] Guilt by association: Guizot, because of the *Temps* and *Aide-toi*, was currently a primary target for Ultra guns.

François Guizot, as deputy from Calvados, was one of the seven opposition members, including one republican, Dupont de l'Eure, selected to draft the reply. He and Étienne led the liberals to overcome the commission's Ultra minority and wrote their draft. Retracing the Monarch's speech article by article, the response courteously supported all sections until it arrived at the King's final paragraph. The deputies' response then concluded:

> Sire, the Charter consecrates as law, the intervention of the nation in the deliberation of public interests. This intervention makes the views of your government, in permanent accord with the wishes of the people, the indispensable condition for the normal progress of public affairs. Sire, our loyalty, our devotion, orders us to tell you that this accord does not exist.[52]

"Respectful but strong", as had been predicted earlier in the *Temps*, the draft caused a triangular debate in the Chamber. The Right, a minority, was outraged and, of course, protested violently. The Left, led by Guizot, Sebastiani, and others, formed a solid bloc in favor. Reasoned objections, however, rose from the Center, that dwindling fraction which still hoped to compromise the crisis by the weight of its vote. The oratory of Martignac, its nominal leader, urged that the address be softened, for which the *Globe* derided the ex-Minister was "one who can always find a way to evade decisions".[53] Another Center deputy, the comte de Lorgeril, presented an amended version, which, in sugary phrases, merely notified the King of his prerogative to "assure constitutional harmony". The Ultras, led by the intelligent and conscientious Berryer, attacked this feeble protest as still far too insulting to the King's prerogative, while Guizot and the Left rejected it as being far

---

[50]   Viel-Castel, *Histoire*, XX, 234-35.
[51]   *Gazette*, 3 March, 1830.
[52]   Chateaubriand, *Mémoires*, V, 263.
[53]   *Globe*, 18 March, 1830.

too weak. As in the 1829 session, the Martignac faction was again left isolated with its dream of conciliation. Profiting from Martignac's loss were two legislative newcomers. Guizot and Berryer, in attacking from opposite sides to prevent compromise, were launching political careers which would cast them as leading opponents in the July Monarchy.[54] The *Globe* (March 17) predicted that the Chamber would "strike a blow for representative government". The original draft of the response passed with 221 for, 181 against. Only twenty-eight votes had been cast for the Lorgeril amendment.[55]

The blow fell on the next day, when Royer-Collard led his deputation before the throne of Charles X to read the response. When the address had been read, the King, with an unregal gesture, took a scrap of paper from the seat of his throne and read his terse answer. His resolution, he said, was "immovable", and he would let the deputies know his will through his ministers. Now, the formalities of the duel were ended; the challenges had been given and accepted.

The Guizot-Étienne response to the King, immediately termed the "Address of the 221", was described by the *Globe*, with rare exaggeration, as, next to the Charter, the "most memorable act of French liberty".[56]

The Ultras saw it as a signal for revolution. The *Quotidienne* stated that the "221" had "sanctioned the first manifesto of the Revolution of 1830".[57] Michaud's talent for prophecy was still acute; This is the first use of such a phrase. In his *Drapeau*, Martainville asked, "What should be done about this address, so insolently respectful, so politely factious"?[58] The most offended royalist journal was little *l'Universel*, which Polignac had recently purchased as his own propaganda medium. Said the *Universel*: "It is these ["221"] who, under a mask of submission and respect, have insulted the majesty of the throne, struck at the royal prerogative, and imposed violently their hatred... on the Prince".[59] Clearly, if the deputies had used vile epithets to the King in their response, their censure by the Ultras could not have been more complete. This game, however, required the players on both sides to perform in a certain way.

On the following day, March 19, the *Moniteur* published the expected edict which prorogued (suspended) the Chamber of Deputies until September 1. The prorogation was no surprise to anyone, least of all to the 221

---

[54] Thureau-Dangin, *Parti libéral*, p. 490.
[55] *Globe*, 18 March, 1830.
[56] *Ibid.*
[57] *Quotidienne*, 19 March, 1830. Michaud was again writing, but not as editor.
[58] *Drapeau Blanc*, 18 March, 1830.
[59] *l'Universel*, 18 March, 1830.

deputies who voted the hostile address. The press now stood very much alone as the opposition's voice.[60]

The *National* blamed the Ministry for breaking the "accord" in government, as prorogation was illegal, a view that had little support among lawyers, and was based on the idea that the Chambers were now unable to exercise any fiscal control, while the Cabinet was reserving credits from previous budgets to finance the Algiers campaign. Like all opposition papers, the *National* predicted the dissolution of the Chamber as the next step toward a *coup*. The *Temps*, recognizing the press's responsibility in the absence of the deliberative body, spoke of the possibility of a new law of censorship. Under the law of 1828, censorship had been abolished and the *Temps* now warned that, if a *coup d'état* should reestablish it, the journals would disobey the edict.[61] This too, was good prophecy, as when the edicts finally came, it was the *Temps* which first resisted force by disobedience.

The *Globe* did a satirical turn. It scolded the liberals for causing the prorogation, announcing that the Ministry had planned to introduce a bill for veteran's pensions, as well as a proposal to reduce the wine duty for five years. "And you have sacrificed all that – you imprudent liberals!... to your deep and empty dogma of popular sovereignty. Oh how popular you will be with the army and the vinters now"![62] Two days later it vowed that the press would be able to preserve liberty and "frighten away" the dictatorship.[63]

The *Gazette's* editor, who admired Villèle's skill, but not Polignac's blindness, stoutly attempted to defend the Ultra Cabinet. Genoude cautiously denied rumors of an edict of censure: "Censorship is not necessary", he wrote, "against papers which have fallen by their own lies... into the bottom rank of discredit".[64] The little *Drapeau* asserted on the day before the prorogation, that "unless the Monarchy dissolved the Chamber, the Chamber would dissolve the Monarchy". On the day following the prorogation, this attitude was modified. Perhaps it was wiser than a dissolution, Martainville reflected, "Like God, royalty is never more severe than necessary".[65]

As the spring came, the reactionary government appeared everywhere on the offensive. All the machinery for provoking or for operating a *coup d'état* was being set in motion. The opposition press had prepared its defenses. It had the support of the moderate royalists of the *Débats* and the larger newspapers of the Left had begun to whirl in orbits at varying distances from the

---

[60] *National*, 20 March, 1830.
[61] *Temps*, 20 March, 1830.
[62] *Globe*, 20 March, 1830.
[63] *Ibid.*, 22 March, 1830.
[64] *Gazette*, 20 March, 1830.
[65] *Drapeau Blanc*, 18, 20 March, 1830.

Orleanist sun, while the republican press continued on an independent, but lively course. The Chamber had done its constitutional duty, paid its constitutional penalty, and left the printing press as the only spokesman against royal absolutism. The government had moved swiftly against the Chamber, but the newspapers posed a different sort of question. To suppress them prematurely by an edict of censorship at the moment, might leave their counterrevolution stillborn. There was, however, the authority of courts of justice and the laws. With these tools, the Ministry tried to blunt the edge of the best weapon of the Left.

CHAPTER XI

JUDICIAL ORDEALS, FEBRUARY-MARCH 1830

While the ministers impatiently awaited a horoscope favorable to their *coup*, they accelerated their campaign against journalists in the courts. In Paris and in the provinces, February and March were marked by a great variety of political press trials. Nearly all the possible applications of the press codes were employed: Outrages to individuals, attacks on the "government of the King" (a phrase conveniently indefinite), attacks on the King's prerogatives, and with the appeals of two Breton Association cases, the charge of "hatred and contempt of the government of the King". Other cases involved the alleged intimidation of printers and their right to refuse service to liberal journalists. The small weekly or monthly opposition papers of smaller cities, were rallying points of provincial opposition. They were now being constantly harassed by royal prosecutors and prefects in an effort to reverse a rural electoral shift to the Left which had been growing since Villèle's fall.

In Normandy, the *Pilote de Calvados* of Caen was indicted. The editor, Lepelletier, who had recently helped to elect Guizot from that constituency, was charged with slandering the new Minister, Guernon-Ranville. Lepelletier had accused Guernon, a fellow-Norman, of fraud when he was inspector for the electoral college of Bayeux in 1821 and 1822. He was sentenced for a "criminal abuse of the freedom of the press", to fifteen days in jail and a fine of five hundred francs.[1] Several weeks later, on March 24, the editor was allowed to appeal this judgment before the Royal Court of Caen. His defense attorney admitted that the paper had alleged an electoral fraud in Bayeux because the ballot box had contained eleven more ballots than there were electors! He denied, however, that Guernon-Ranville's name was directly linked with this indiscretion. The "outrageous" part of the article had asserted that citizens of Caen, who had "severely censured" the new Minister, were now "astonished" to see him rewarded by a Cabinet office. The defender

---

[1] *Gazette des Tribunaux*, 10, 11 February, 1830.

referred to the acquittal of Madrolle for his "incendiary" royalist pamphlet and said he was grateful that he had the "honor" to represent the *Pilote* instead of the "sinister pages" of Madrolle's Ultra brochure, which called for dictatorship. The defense lawyer claimed the *Pilote de Calvados* had been "chosen among all the other journals to be immolated on the altar of today's divinity". All this rhetoric failed to acquit Lepelletier and he was ordered to serve his original sentence.[2]

In the Royal Court of Poitiers, the case of the *Tribune* of Niort was appealed. Editor Clerc-Lasalle was a frequent visitor to this court, since he published the only two opposition papers in the entire region, the *Sentinelle des Deux-Sèvres* and the *Tribune des Départements*. In November, he had been sentenced to fifteen days for "outrage" to the local prefect and a sub-prefect. The high court of Poitiers, in rejecting his appeals, upheld the prosecutor's view that the phrase "government of the King" meant the *ministers* of the King. This was a significant legal point as the law forbade editors to "outrage" the government of the King. Such loose construction could be used to incriminate critics of the Cabinet and could nullify the principle of ministerial responsibility. The defense lost its case and Clerc-Lasalle was ordered to prison for fifteen days. The Charter's most glaring flaw was still constitutionally moot.

Five days later the same editor appealed another conviction for an offense published in the *Sentinelle*, his second newspaper. He had been given a sentence of one month in prison and a three hundred franc fine on December 11 for a *Sentinelle* article in which he had characterized War Minister Bourmont as a "traitor", Polignac as a "conspirator", and Interior Minister La Bourdonnaye as a "classifier of categories under the sword of foreign troops".[3] The actual authors had been a Dr. Bodeau of Niort and a man named Proust, but Clerc-Lasalle, as manager, was also held accountable. In the defense, the criticism of Polignac as Wellington's servant was again made. The editor's previous sentence was upheld, increasing his days in prison to forty-five, and, in an unusual procedure, earlier acquittals of Bodeau and Proust were reversed and they too, each received a month in jail!

Proust was also convicted on the charge of "provoking the army to disobey" for his suggestion that old soldiers might not obey the "traitor" Marshal Bourmont, for fear of having to sabre a compatriot. The monthly *Sentinelle* had ceased to publish after the December 11 indictment. The law still allowed temporary suspension of newspapers which were on trial and this small monthly journal was almost perpetually in the dock. In March, Clerc-

---

[2] *Ibid.*, 28 March, 1830.
[3] *Ibid.*, 28, 29 February, 1830; 7 March, 1830.

Lasalle launched a "new" journal called the *Nouvelle Sentinelle des Deux-Sèvres*. By this now obvious and transparent ploy, he was able to continue as a journalist while serving his sentence.[4]

The Breton Association also obtained more publicity in the provinces. Although the *Indicateur* of Bordeaux's final appeal from its Breton Association verdict was rejected by the Court of Cassation that March, Odilon Barrot's defense of the little paper was broadly quoted as the propaganda for legal resistence reached into all corners of the kingdom.[5]

Reproduction of the *Globe's* article "France and the Bourbons" by a Toulouse newspaper, *La France Meridionale*, created an interesting legal case. The trial opened on March 27. The editor of the Toulouse journal, Armand Dupin, was arraigned differently than Dubois had been for the original *Globe* editorial, as some of the *Globe's* indictments were not regarded as seriously by the prosecution in Toulouse. The printer was also accused. The Royal Prosecutor, de Moly, called the *Globe* and the *France Meridionale* "shameless" and "execrable". Vaquié, the defense lawyer, noted that his client's journal regularly reproduced, without comment, Paris editorials drawn from diverse political sorces, and then quoted some Ultras who had honored the *Globe*. The *Drapeau Blanc*, he stated, had once praised the "steadfast character" of the *Globe's* writers. The lawyer told how Lamennais had spoken well of the Globists and said that, until recently, when it became political, the *Globe* had been the most exclusive highbrow periodical in France. The attorney who spoke for the printer attacked the whole indictment as invalid since the precedent of the Paris court was not being followed.[6] When the court convened again, three days later, editor Dupin received a jail sentence of six months and a devastating fine of six thousand francs.[7] Fortunately, a flood of donations from Paris paid not only this huge cost, but enough more to support editor Dupin's family while he was confined. The *Globe*, "responsible" for Dupin's sorrow, was a heavy contributor.

Printers were placed in a difficult position everywhere. The legal question was whether a printer had a right to refuse his service to a publisher for fear of incrimination. The printer was, even under the 1828 law, legally liable for the content of publication, even though he might be the only printer available. In Moulins, the editor of the *Gazette Constitutionnel d'Allier* sued his printer for refusal to print an article on March 17. The hearing was secret, but the announced decision of the court held that there must be a reasonable distinction

[4] *Ibid.*, 22, 23 March, 1830; 11 April, 1830; 6 May, 1830.
[5] *Ibid.*, 22, 23 March, 1830.
[6] *Ibid.*, 7 April, 1830.
[7] *Ibid.*, 10 April, 1830.

between the "capricious" refusal of a printer and a justifiable refusal, from fear of incrimination. In the case of the Moulins paper, the court ruled that the refusal was valid.[8] In a similar case before the *Cour Royale* of Paris, the editor of a Chartres paper, the *Glaneur*, sued a printer, for the use of his withheld press. President baron Séguier ruled that the law of 17 May, 1819, which imposed responsibility on printers, presupposed their right to refuse their presses, and the editor thus lost his case.[9] This interpretation meant, of course, that the government, by intimidating printers, could continue to deny the freedom to publish, especially to small provincial journals too poor to buy their own machines. Printers paid dearly for their coveted licenses and intimidation of them became an efficient weapon against journalism.

Another printer, named Albin, had agreed to print a new liberal newspaper in Limoges, to be called the *Contribuable (Taxpayer)*. In publishing the prospectus, however, he failed to deposit a copy with his declaration of intent, as required by law, on the desk of the Prefect. The Royal Prosecutor asked that Albin be fined one thousand francs for not depositing a copy of the prospectus and another one thousand for not declaring his intent to publish. Albin's defense attorney offered an anecdote to illustrate his argument against the charge. He told of an unruly, lazy prince who had vexed his tutor. The latter, unable to physically punish the royal charge, ordered a peasant lad brought in to be flogged for the misdeeds of the prince. The lawyer compared the prosecutor to this tutor, who would whip the printer to hurt the *Contribuable*. "The pretended infraction of Albin is but a pretext", he stated, "The real purpose is to crush the first free press to be set up in our town".[10] The printer was fined, but not nearly such a sum as had been demanded by the Crown.

Judicial cases involving newspapers in Paris during February and March were, like those of the provinces, generally unfavorable to the opposition. Chatelain, manager of the *Courrier Français*, was charged on February 10, with the crime of defamation.[11] The slander was against the new Ultra and clericalist Prefect of Police Mangin, and was in an article describing a workhouse for beggars, recently established as a philanthropic enterprise. The paper accused Mangin of having sent only sixteen paupers to the house, despite the fact that it had feeding accommodations for 1500 and that the

---

[8] *Ibid.*, 28 March, 1830.
[9] *Ibid.*
[10] *Ibid.*, 11 April, 1830.
[11] *Ibid.*, 11 February, 1830.

price of bread had risen sharply during that terrible winter. The alleged
defamation was contained in these lines:

> Instead of sending beggars to the house of refuge, M. Mangin finds it simpler to
> let them go to prison and there let them expire from want and misery...
> M. Mangin above all should not allow *beggars* to die from hunger and misery,
> because they are not guilty of political crimes.

Joseph Mérilhou defended Chatelain again and refused to retract the accusations made by his client, and instead, affirmed that Mangin had sought every
means to hinder the operation of the house of refuge. But Chatelain was
sentenced nonetheless to fifteen days and a five hundred franc fine. The next
day, the *Courrier* committed the indiscretion of criticizing its manager's
conviction, calling the charge "absurd and ridiculous".[12] For this, two weeks
later, Chatelain appeared before another lower court, charged with defamation of the magistrates who had convicted him of defamation! The Crown
claimed the *Courrier* had insinuated the court was partial and not interested
in evidence of defense and the court added fifteen days to Chatelain's term and
three hundred francs to his fine.[13]

There were several important cases which had begun soon after Polignac's
arrival and which were now being heard on appeal. Perhaps the most
discussed of the appeal trials was that of Victor Bohain of *Figaro*, on
February 25 before the *Cour Royale*. In August, he had been sentenced to
six months in jail and a fine of one thousand francs for the saucy raillery
about Polignac's Cabinet in his August 9 edition. Again Bohain was defended
by Dupin, *jeune*, who had served him in his first trial and who denied any
possibility of guilt in the two cited passages of *Figaro*, since no actual names
had been used. He blamed the ministers for not heeding "hisses from the
galleries, as well as the applause". "That which is, for the vulgar, a matter
of opposition", said Dupin, becomes for the ministers, "sedition, revolt, crime,
and a matter for the courts: They need condemnations to cure the wounds
to their ego". Dupin asked why the indignation of *Figaro* and other papers
was more criminal than the jubilation of the *Drapeau Blanc* on August 9.
Despite these pleas, the court upheld Bohain's original condemnation.[14]

Another controversial case was appealed under strange circumstances on
March 4 before the *Cour Royale*. This was the appeal of saucy Louis-Marie
Fontan of the *Album*. In his first trial, he had been handed the unprecedented
sentence of five years in jail, five years loss of civil rights, and a fine of ten

---

[12] *Courrier Français*, 11 February, 1830.
[13] *Gazette des Tribunaux*, 26 February, 1830.
[14] *Ibid.*

thousand francs.[15] The cause of this severity had been an article by Fontan in which, by clear innuendo, Charles X had been compared to a maddened ram. Fontan had escaped to Dutch-ruled Belgium, immediately following the conviction, but there he ran into another reactionary government. Van Maanen, the Polignac of the Netherlands, was busy persecuting his own opposition journalists and had little welcome for a foreign one. Fontan was hounded by special residence and naturalization obstacles until at last he chose to return to France, where he was finally located by detectives. When his first appeal came up, he was still in hiding and lost his case by default. At his second appeal in March, the court denied a hearing and sent Fontan back to his cell at the prison of Poissy. The extremity of his sentence made a martyr of this young firebrand, even to moderates who thought his writing tasteless and irresponsible. Opposition newspapers made frequent references to his sentence and the fact that he had been marched to prison shackled to a "common criminal". Two months later, a fellow journalist visited Fontan at Poissy and reported that the young man's hair had turned white! Unlike debtors, political prisoners during the Restoration were usually segregated, however, and treated humanely by their jailers.[16] Fontan was probably no exception to this practice.

A diverting press trial occurred in March, and revealed another skirmish in the belligerent past of Martainville, the Quixote of the *Drapeau Blanc*. He had brought suit for defamation against another journalist, Viennot, director of the literary periodical, *Le Corsaire*.[17] Viennot had offended Martainville in a January 31 article, which had commented on a *Drapeau Blanc* story. In this story, Martainville had described a recent flood that had washed away two arches of the bridge at his native suburb of Le Pecq. The *Corsaire's* article remarked that the storm had done what Martainville had refused to do in 1815, "when he opened the passage to the enemy to gain his spurs as an absolutist champion". Thus the man of loyalty above all else, stood accused of bowing to the Allies during the second Restoration. This cruel canard, which Michaud, in the *Biographie Universelle*, correctly describes as a "calumny", had haunted Martainville for fifteen years. When Napoleon returned from Elba, the dramatist-editor and his wife retreated to his suburban home at Le Pecq. Three months later, as Allied soldiers swarmed around Paris, some of Blucher's foragers pillaged several homes in Le Pecq, including that of the Martainvilles. But as he was already known as a partisan of

---

[15] *Ibid.*, 25 July 1829.

[16] *Ibid.*, 5 March, 1830; see also, *Globe*, 25, 26 May, 1830. For the treatment of convicted journalists, see Burnand, *La Vie Quotidienne*, p. 192.

[17] *Gazette des Tribunaux*, 5 March, 1830.

Louis XVIII and the town's most important zealot, he was blamed by later gossip for helping the Prussians in their unopposed crossing of the bridge over the Seine at Pecq.

Martainville demanded ten thousand francs as damages. Henrion, his lawyer, and colleague on the staff of the tiny *Drapeau*,[18] spent several minutes haranguing about the press and its "license" and "revolutionary spirit", and then produced a document, signed by the former mayor and several leading citizens of Pecq, which denied that Martainville had collaborated in 1815. So heated was Henrion in denouncing his client's accusers that Albin de Berville, the *Corsaire's* lawyer, interrupted: "They would make believe that it was the *Corsaire* who destroyed the two arches of the Pont du Pec [Le Pecq]"! When Berville had the floor, he demonstrated that the feud between the *Corsaire* and the *Drapeau* had two sides. He quoted from the *Drapeau* of October 13, 1829, in which Martainville had called Viennot a "huge bulldog" who was destined to go mad in his journalistic "kennel".

Berville also quoted from a more ancient document, No. 8 of the *Journal des Rieurs* for the year III of the Republic. The text of this paper showed that its editor, then a seventeen-year-old youth named Alphonse de Martainville, had in fact, been a republican! The Ultra of 1830 had written, in 1795, about the "tree of liberty reddened with the sweat [sic!] and blood of patriots" and had denounced the "stupid" hope of royalists that Thermidor would be the counterrevolution. Although it did not suit his case, Berville might have noted that Martainville, while still a boy, had defied Robespierre and become one of those "gilded youth" of the Thermidorian reaction. This case offers another illustration of the vast liberties and irrelevancies allowed to the defense in Restoration courtrooms – irrelevancies which made trials entertaining, as well as propagandistic.

The exposure of his salad days in court made Martainville even more angry when his turn came to speak and he hotly defended his conduct at Pecq in 1815. The octogenarian mayor, it appears, had suffered an epileptic seizure just as the Prussians drew near the town, and the situation was rendered hopeless because there were no more cartridges and the villagers were starving. Martainville boasted that he supplied these people with "munitions of the mouth" and that, were he ever called to account, he doubted that he could be accused of graft. The ten thousand francs he sought in damages would be given to the poor, he said, and he "would be enchanted to distribute the money of the *Corsaire*". But the judge ordered Viennot to give Martainville

---

[18] By April, 1830, the *Drapeau Blanc's* circulation had fallen to 666, but it still received attention disproportionate to its size, because of its colorful style of extremism. The paper was deeply in debt.

only two hundred francs as an apology. A few days later the *Drapeau's* crusty editor wrote an open letter in his own newspaper, in which he included the court's decision to clear his name and referred to Viennot as a "cowardly defamer".[19] Viennot allowed him to have the last word.

Among the most discussed political events of that March, were the trials of the *National* and the *Globe*. The *Globe* was indicted for seven criminal actions for its articles of February 15 and 19, entitled "France and the Bourbons" and the *National* was finally held to account for its contention that the "King reigns but does not rule" as expressed in its numbers for February 18 and 19. Since the arraignments, the entire opposition had been preparing the defense of the two journals, with the aid of the finest legal orators in France, and much publicity was given to the forthcoming judicial event. Obviously, the Left hoped to make use of these trials as great political debates, a sounding board for all the notes of opinion that had been struck since August 8. Although the two cases were heard in the same court during the same weeks and were closely associated in the public mind, they deserve individual consideration.

The trial of the *National* began on March 10, 1830, before the sixth court of correctional police.[20] In the audience were such illustrious figures as Victor Cousin and Abel Villemain of the Sorbonne, Charles de Rémusat of the *Globe*, Theodore Jouffroy, the philosopher, and, again a free man, Pierre-Jean Béranger. Augustin-Charles Renouard, the attorney chosen by the *Globe*, requested that his client's case be heard first, since that paper was the first to be indicted, and accused the prosecution of planning to use the *National's* trial to influence the later-scheduled case against the *Globe*. Renouard's plea was turned down, however, and Sautelet, manager of the *National* and left-wing book publisher, assumed full responsibility for his paper's incriminating article when the indictment was read.

Levavasseur, the prosecutor, a man now experienced in press cases, began with the usual philippics against the excesses of certain writers, who "publicize dangerous discussions" and accused Sautelet of "attacking the rights the King holds from his birth" because of this passage in the *National* (February 18):

We have recalled the acts of the two bodies which had the right to set conditions for France, when France, having to capitulate, on one side to an armed Europe that did not want a continuance of Bonaparte, and on the other side to the old reigning house, who, seeing the throne vacant, naturally utilized its rights to remount it. We have established that worthy and advantageous conditions had been made, accepted at first, and since partially retracted.

[19] *Drapeau Blanc*, 6 March, 1830.
[20] *Gazette des Tribunaux*, 11 March, 1830.

The second charge against the *National*, "attack on the constitutional authority of the King", was based on the section beginning: "The King reigns but does not rule". This, of course, aimed at the core of the *National's* philosophy and program. The third charge, "attack on the rights by which the King granted the Charter", was founded on passages of the *National* which referred to the Charter as the "pretended concession of Louis XVIII", and had called Louis XIV "the old husband of Mme. de Maintenon". The prosecutor concluded his demands for punishment with the rare, and politically explosive, charge that the *National* was guilty of "provocation to change the dynasty".[21] Not since Cauchois-Lemaire's Orleanist proposal of 1827 had such an accusation been brought – "1688" was about to receive its first great public exposure.

The second session of the *National's* trial was held on March 24, after the *Globe* had also begun its trial. The two journals, though of different orientations, became close comrades during their ordeals. Thiers had termed the seven point accusation against the *Globe's* Dubois as "so serious it appears ridiculous", lamenting "a strange accusation that hangs over one of the most distinguished and sincere writers of our age".[22]

On the *National's* second day,[23] the defense attorney, François Mauguin, took the floor and his first words indicated that the trial was to be broadly political and not always relevant to the immediate cause of Sautelet. Mauguin divided the French nation into three classes: First, the Ultra party, "left alone by a regime forever vanquished, but fortified by the priest party, tries to rebuild, at our expense, a past it cannot defend"; the second class, liberal France, was responsible for the world's "greatest spectacle… ardent but generous, great in its virtues, I almost dare to say in its crimes". Mauguin praised the youth of France as those "to whom France owes its liberty". And the third class he castigated as the militarists, with selfishly contrived motives. And where, he asked, has the sifting of all these divergent segments of French life occurred? Why, in the courts and the press, the only civilized substitute for armed battle when ideas are in conflict.

Mauguin had spoken in this vein for about half an hour, when he began the actual defense of his client. Announcing the *National's* aims to be "the thoughtful development of our institutions, a reasoned respect for the existing ones, and the demonstration of their necessity", he admitted that the paper's words were often sharp when it "cut down the vanities" of the old Monarchy. As for the whole affair, Mauguin declared to the judges:

[21] *Ibid.*
[22] *National*, 18 February, 1830.
[23] *Gazette des Tribunaux*, 25 March, 1830.

Except for a few theories that are not your place to judge, the present trial is concerned more with things than with words, less with suspected intentions than with formulas which are unpleasant and above all, with accumulated incriminations!

Here, Mauguin was apparently branding the trial illegal, as under the repealed law of "tendency" provision.

In defending the *National's* contention that the "King reigns but does not rule", the famous liberal advocate caused a stir in the crowd by asking: "Will we always forget the tragic death of two kings and the tomb of Saint Helena"? "Two kings" – who but Louis XVI of France and Charles I of England? Mauguin then refuted each of the charges against Sautelet separately. He denied that the phrase about the "throne being vacant" was an attack on the King's birthright, and claimed the reference was to Louis XVIII, a dead King, and that the *National* plainly did not contest, but rather recognized, the former sovereign's rights. For the accusation that the King's right to grant the Charter had been criticized, by calling it a "pretended concession", Mauguin's defense was again that the passage referred to a former King, and that the present King "gave nothing" except an oath of fealty to the Charter. When Mauguin returned again to the most serious of all the charges: "Attack on the Constitutional authority of the King", he sailed into the heart of the argument as advocated by Thiers and his militant colleagues:

If the King reigns and governs at the same time, if he has the simultaneous right and exercise of power, then I ask, in what way does constitutional monarchy differ from absolute monarchy? Is it that in the latter he governs according to his will and in the former according to the laws? But this law, is it anything else than the rule, the will, the idea? The executive power – is it something besides the arms which obey the idea, the will? Say that the King exercises the executive power directly, say that he governs, and you thereby destroy the will of the Chambers. Thus, you degrade royalty and when you think you are raising it, you are lowering it.[24]

On March 31, the *National's* hearings were concluded. Prosecutor Levavasseur launched his final squibs against public opinion, treating that ancient force as if it were some recently unchained monster. He addressed the court itself with the admonition not to be "seduced" by public opinion. "Public opinion!" he exclaimed, "It is always to the glory of legislators and magistrates to fight its prepossessions". The court's decision was postponed until the completion of the *Globe's* trial.

On March 19, it was the *Globe's* turn to stand formally charged with grave political crimes before the same panel which tried the *National*. Once

[24] *National*, 25 March, 1830; *Gazette des Tribunaux*, 1 April, 1830.

again, the courtroom was packed with curious and excited partisans. The various intellectuals who staffed the *Globe* were there, of course, as well as Guizot, Victor Hugo, Destutt de Tracy, "last of the *philosophes*", and the duc de Broglie.[25] The appearance of so many brilliant friends and well-wishers testifies to the reputation of Dubois, the chief editor, who now stood indicted on seven counts because of his paper's editorials on February 15 and 19. The Royal Prosecutor, again Levavasseur, read the charges: Attack on the rights of the King held by birth, attack on the constitutional authority of the King, hatred and contempt of the government of the King, *provocation to change the order of succession to the throne*, and attack on the person of the King and princes of the blood. The prosecutor then formally withdrew this last charge and failed to even mention two others for which Dubois had originally been indicted:Exciting citizens to arm against royal authority and attack on the rights of the King held by virtue of the Charter. Thus, the editor of the *Globe* was cited for only four of the original seven charges.[26] To support the first accusation, that Dubois had attacked the King's hereditary right, Levavasseur quoted passages from that February 15 *Globe* beginning with: "They [the Bourbons] were forgotten, unknown by their contemporaries", and later, as if these words were a mere overture, he read a more candid paragraph to the bench:

> The declaration of Saint-Ouen, the promulgation of the Charter, although seeming offensive to purist theory, achieved the demi-conversion of France. Louis XVIII began with some favor a reign which he back-dated 25 years in memory of legitimacy. But soon, around this somewhat compromised legitimacy, accepted as an innocent pretense, were raised all this swarm of grotesque and insolent legitimacies whose remembrance is only a comedy.[27]

Levavasseur also called attention to the *Globe's* remarks that the Bourbons had, in the first Restoration, "menaced the rights acquired by the revolution" and "wounded the people and the army", for which they had been "broken like glass", a reference to Napoleon's triumphant return from exile. The prosecutor appeared very indignant upon reading these words and from the *Globe* of February 19, he quoted in shocked tones: "We have never affected the false love for princes to whom we are attached by no other bond but that of law". The royal advocate, now in high dudgeon, asked the court: "Attachment for a prince is no longer of our age? Must that be left to the Gothics and the time of barbarism"? The lawyer's blunder led to peals of

[25] *Globe*, 27 March, 1830.
[26] *National*, 20 March, 1830.
[27] *Globe*, 15 March, 1830; *National*, 20 March, 1830.

laughter and affirmative remarks from an audience preponderantly of the Left!

To support the charge of attacking the King's constitutional authority, Levavasseur, having recovered his dignity, recalled the *Globe's* dictum that the true mission of the Crown was to "reign and not to govern, thus stripping the prince of storms of public intimacy and battles of majorities and minorities in Parliament". The lawyer's exposition of this charge was nearly identical to that he had made in the case of the *National*. The charge of "hatred and contempt" was largely based on the *Globe's* advocacy of the Breton Association and upon Levavasseur's premise, that the phrase "government of the King" meant the ministers, as well as the Monarch. He also cited these words from the *Globe*: "Of all the crises we have passed since 1814, the present crisis is doubtless the most decisive for the house of Bourbon".

Dubois' fourth indictment of provocation to change the order of dynastic succession, was a relatively mild Orleanist suggestion, written by Dubois himself:

When the 8th of August Ministry appeared ... one felt monarchy compromised and attacked, the words of 1688 and the Stuarts returned; and since the 8th of August, royalist or liberal, the polemic has been only this great idea; once again the question of the dynasty has been posed.[28]

The prosecutor then read another passage from the editorial "France and the Bourbons", in which Dubois had recalled the murder of the present King's son and the reactionary crisis of 1820. The *Globe* had remarked that constitutionalist demands "gave access to royalist intrigues. Thus the reaction began by the dagger thrust of a fanatic who wished to stop the headlong plunge". Levavasseur, after completing this very prejudicial reference, assured the court that he was not accusing Dubois of wishing to murder the royal family, but demanded the full penalty of the law on each of the four charges.

At the next session of the *Globe's* trial, the Polignac Cabinet was castigated by Dubois' lawyer, Renouard: "The crisis which troubles us all, which the press has denounced since August 8 was the invasion of power by an antiparliamentary minority". Renouard defended, as an obvious fact, the *Globe's* incriminating remark, "When the Charter is in peril, there is peril for the dynasty and for monarchy", and then praised his client:

Never was a soul so generous allied with a stronger spirit. Never has a word of hate or envy smirched any of the many articles which came from his pen. Never has

[28] *Globe*, 15 March, 1830.

the desire for popularity held any more dominion over him than have the seductions and caresses of power... Religion, philosophy, history, politics, literature, he has dealt with them all; supporting them with his high reason, his imagination of an artist, and his fiery passion, the purest of them all, his passion for the law. Impartial, because he is sincere, he has extended the aid of his powerful logic to the Jesuits: Not, of course, out of any love for them, but from devotion to liberty... Such is M. Dubois: There is in him a sympathy for all that is generous; his heart is warm and just. ... He affirms that goodwill is the foundation of his soul and that no hatred against the dynasty or against monarchy has dictated his words.[29]

After this tribute, the lawyer offered his own views on political reaction, stating that, "Old abuse... which believes itself reborn with restored monarchies, has several times, history tells us, assisted in the inevitable collapse of monarchies blind enough to identify themselves with it". Renouard also cited recent unpunished inflammatory writings of Ultras. From Cottu's pamhlet advocating dictatorship, he then quoted a passage wherein the author had expressed fear that a *coup* might *not* take place and the Monarch would not even be able "to fall in glory". "How insolent"! shouted Renouard, slapping a copy of Cottu's pamphlet on the defense table, "*They* can suggest ... the fall of the Monarchy – but *we* are prosecuted for saying that if the Charter is in danger, so is the King"! He also read the insult to royalty which had been recently published without penalty in the *Drapeau Blanc*;[30] the article in which Martainville termed France a "republic" which the King must destroy; which had reduced Charles X to a "supernumerary, an old *rentier*, for whom, for some reason, no one has filed bankruptcy". Renouard caused a commotion in the audience when he read Martainville's suggestion that the King might be "expelled like a Stuart".

In a bold maneuver, as if to test his thesis that "government of the King" did not include ministers, Renouard suddenly referred to the Polignac Cabinet as "hated and contemptible" – the very adjectives used in the indictment! At this, the judges whispered to each other. The lawyer asked if the President wished to speak; the magistrate responded, "No, M. Renouard, continue". After the session, the skillful young attorney received congratulations from a milling throng of spectators.[31] Whatever the verdict, the defense had scored a political triumph.

The final session of the trial of Paul-François Dubois was held on April 2.[32] The prosecutor, who seemed to be defensive in summing up, drew disapproving

[29] *Gazette des Tribunaux*, 27 March, 1830.
[30] *Drapeau Blanc*, 28 February, 1830.
[31] *Gazette des Tribunaux*, 27 March, 1830.
[32] *Ibid.*, 3 April, 1830.

murmurs from the audience, when he denied that Louis XVIII's return to France had been supported by any force of arms. On this day, Dubois spoke in his own behalf, eloquently and simply. He denied any wish to see a rupture of authority in France. That is what the *parti* is striving for, he said, to give them a pretext for a *coup d'état*. "Eight months ago", he said, "We were peaceful, today we are troubled, today the fear of revolution opens our hearts to every suspicion". The editor's summation was superb:

And now, gentlemen, all is said between us. I have disguised none of my views to you. If they were guilty, the crime should leave our discussion a thousand times clearer than it was before; if they were innocent, it seems to me that their innocence should strike the most accusing eyes... I have used my right as a citizen, as the Chamber of Deputies has used its constitutional right. I have spoken with the freedom of history, of times long behind us. I have spoken with the freedom of good faith, and of dangers which weigh heavily on all our lives today. It was a right, or better, it was a duty. I have fulfilled it. I regret nothing.[33]

On the next morning, judgments were given in the cases of the *Globe* and the *National*. Sautelet of the *National* was found guilty of two of the three counts. The charge, "attack on the King's hereditary right", was found not "sufficiently justified", but the court found a fourth conviction, one which had been later *added* to the indictment: "Excitation of citizens to arm against royal authority". This was based on a very recent article of March 25, in which the *National* reported that, immediately after the prorogation of the Chamber, the royal guards were issued extra cartridges, and were warned that refusal to march would be a felony. The *National* had also incriminated itself by declaring that the Cabinet, distrusting army units assigned to the King's troops, had augmented the Swiss and given them extra pay. Considering the gravity of the *National's* offenses, Sautelet's sentence seems relatively light. He was ordered to three months in jail and to pay a one thousand franc fine.

Verdict and sentence of Paul Dubois of the *Globe* followed: For attack on the Charter granting right of the King, not guilty; for provocation, without result, to excite citizens to arm, not guilty; for attack on the King's hereditary rights, not guilty, though the words were found "intemperate"; for attack on the constitutional authority of the King, not guilty, since the expressed theory, though "false and dangerous" was not far enough developed. Dubois was found guilty of "provocation to change the succession to the throne" by his reference to "1688" and the "Stuarts", as well as his assertions that the Charter had saved France from counterrevolution. The magistrates also

---

[33] *Ibid.*

found him guilty of "hatred and contempt of the King's government", by interpreting this phrase to include ministers, in the royalist sense. Dubois was sentenced to a prison term of four months and a fine of two housand francs. This, too, was a low price for the excellent publicity which the trials gave to the militant cause; a fact recognized by Dubois' colleagues.

The *Globe's* editorials spoke for both convicted newspapers. In an article titled, "Our Goal", appeared a remarkable literary defense of the cases.[34] The verdict, according to Rémusat and Cousin, was prejudged. "We can no longer believe that our audacity aggravated our position, nor our moderation passed for meekness... we profited from our freedom". The editorial concluded by declaring that the *Globe*, if necessary, would do it all again.

Dubois and Sautelet, however, had only begun their ordeals. For each of these man who had courageously accepted the responsibility of an entire journal and of a political ideal, there would be further penance.

At a secret hearing, arranged by Guernon and Montbel, the Council of the University ordered the name of Paul-François Dubois stricken from the permanent faculty roster – the maximum possible censure for a professor convicted of a serious crime. When Dubois protested the high-handed action of the Minister of Public Instruction, on the ground that the accused must be faced by his accusers, he was told that the University Council was only a disciplinary court and therefore not subject to trial procedures,[35] a response with interesting parallels to modern university tenure appeals.

The fate of Sautelet came as an unexpected tragedy. While free on appeal, he became suddenly unbalanced by the prospect of his prison sentence. Alone and disturbed in his personal life, yet bearing a false front of optimism before his colleagues, Sautelet did not wait for the freedom that a revolution might soon bring. Five weeks after he was convicted, he killed himself with a pistol. His friend Carrel wrote a touching obituary in the *Revue de Paris*,[36] which not only reflected the loyalty of the militants to their colleagues, but demonstrated the psychological compassion of Carrel as he exposed the cruelty of society's attitude to suicide and the need for human understanding.

Yet, for all the price in punishment and personal grief, such trials could

[34] *Globe*, 4, 5 April, 1830.

[35] *National*, 5 May, 1830; *Temps*, 21 April, 1830. In the *Temps*, Guizot assailed the University Council: "Reckless fools! Do you know what you have done? You have launched the University into an unknown future: Its legal titles, its legislation, the structure of its organization will be explored, taken to pieces: What will be the amazement of the public to see an organization founded by imperial despotism, and exploited by *Congrégationist* influence? Guizot promised that "weapons would not be lacking" to Dubois in his new academic fight.

[36] Armand Carrel, "Un mort volontaire", *Revue de Paris*, Vol. VIII (June, 1830).

only strengthen the opposition. Publicity of its ideas was again magnified by the newspaper's free use of their right to print the often explosive oratory of the courtroom. Press trials were becoming even more political than the editorials which caused them. Perhaps Dubois and Chatelain, as they reflected in their cells at Sainte-Pélagie, consoled themselves by contemplating the uses of adversity.

CHAPTER XII

"THE KING WILL NOT YIELD"

Throughout the spring, Ultra political strategy pressed the Left toward a still more unified position. The government was scarcely able to conceal its designs, due to the unguarded clamor of journals in its own political camp. Ultraroyalist papers continued to be divided among themselves and immersed in stubborn feuds which reflected the very real dissensions in the Ministry itself. By the journalism of both extreme factions, the government was placed under a reading lens at a time when it most desired silence and secrecy. The Ministry was rebuilt that spring in a more absolutist fashion, it is true, but not until after the comte de Villèle had made an appearance. Like a visit from Lucifer, his arrival generated fears which further exposed the Ministry's motives to public inspection. The Cabinet's secret sessions amplified the growing rumor of a dissolution and, after this rumor was converted to fact on May 16, the predictions of both sides became more ominous.

Spring added heat to public emotions. Not since the barricades of November, 1827, which had marked the defeat of Villèle, had any clear manifestations of mass unrest occurred. In April, however, a frenzy of arsonist terror swept the Norman departments of Calvados and La Manche. These nocturnal burnings reached such alarming proportions that thousands of regular troops were dispatched to the area. This phenomenon was probably the result of epidemic hysteria and hard times rather than politics, but editors in Paris discovered something in it to serve their political cause. A more disturbing mob demonstration occurred at the Palais Royal, during a great ball attended by the King and the highest dignitaries of France. Such disorders at least indicate a growing sense of public tension that was not confined to the deputies or the journalists. Further evidence of the widening breach between parties during these months was a rise in anticlericalism and clerical reaction focusing on the Ministry.

While the press was still considering the consequences of the address of the

"221", Villèle arrived in the capital. Ostensibly, he had come to visit Mme. de Neuville, his eldest daughter, who was momentarily expected to bring forth his grandchild. Only such a paternal motive could have brought him to Paris, he asserted, and added he had even thought of turning back when, en route, he had heard of the prorogation![1] Nearly everyone, however, preferred to see politics, instead of parental devotion, as the reason for his return. Montbel in the Cabinet, and Genoude in the pages of the *Gazette*, had urged his political resurrection.

In the first week of April, Villèle was approached by two deputies, one of the center-Right and one of the center-Left, who implored him to prevent Polignac from throwing France "into a revolution". Though he rejected this offer to attempt a moderate coalition,[2] the press was aroused by his presence. Laurentie of the *Quotidienne*, who, like his predecessor Michaud, disliked Villèle, became an even more fervent disciple of Polignac, and, without naming Villèle, wrote: "It is M. de Polignac who produces good results, and he alone can perpetuate them".[3] The *Quotidienne*, lacking Michaud's restraint, also prayerfully awaited the assumption of power by Peyronnet, the intransigent Ultra whom liberal editors had predicted would break through Polignac's hesitancy. To the *Quotidienne*, with its crystalline opinions, the nomination of a sharper like Villèle was unthinkable, but Genoude's *Gazette*, on the other hand, was still trying to promote Villèle's cause. It answered the *Quotidienne* with a veiled slur against Polignac's capabilities: "We do not forget that before the year's end, there will be an electoral battle to win, a strong opposition, parliamentary debates, and a budget to put over".[4] This debate reopened a wound in the royalist side, amused the Left, and probably gratified Villèle himself.[5]

François Mignet wrote two articles in the *National*, dealing with the significance of Villèle's defeat in 1827, while the *Temps* declared one could no longer speak of the "Polignac Ministry", it was simply the *parti;* the conflict being, said the *Temps*, between "moderate men who have some recognition of the country and affairs, and those who have in mind only ideas of civil war and foreign intervention, becomes deeper every day and is now ready to burst open".[6] The *Temps*, whose analysis of the Cabinet was realistic, labeled Chabrol as an unwilling but fence-straddling Finance Minister, and Courvoisier, as a more legalistic person and certain to resign from his

[1] Villèle, *Mémoires*, V, 413-14.
[2] *Ibid.*, pp. 418-19.
[3] *Quotidienne*, 25 March, 1830.
[4] *Gazette*, 26 March, 1830.
[5] Villèle, *Mémoires*, V, 418.
[6] *Temps*, 27 March, 1830.

Justice portfolio. Like all the opposition journals, it also predicted the imminent acceptance of Peyronnet who had "no limit to his hopes". In another state-ment, this paper correctly predicted that naming Peyronnet would exclude Villèle, whom Polignac's faction considered "short-sighted" and only good for "small decisions". The *Temps* continued that Villèle, for his part, felt Polignac was "risking the Monarchy", and added, "In order not to compromise himself among such idiots, he will go far away and wait in reserve for the day when they will be useless".[7] The *Globe* believed Villèle's chances were fair and said that there were in France two classes of Ultras: "Those who are bankrupt and those who are capitalists. The first, having nothing to lose, want Polignac left alone; the second want the return of Villèle".[8] "We side with the latter", added the *Globe*, "M. de Villèle would hinder M. de Polignac; M. de Polignac would restrain M. de Villèle. Both would be mutually compromised". The following day it was reported that Villèle's latest kite had crashed to earth and the *Globe* taunted the ex-Minister with his own dictum: "No one can govern France without a majority!" On April 13, Villèle left for his native Toulouse in a mail coach. This public conveyance was chosen, gossiped an opposition editor, not for economy, but to avoid attention, and the coachman was reportedly tipped to inform the curious that his passenger was one of the "221" who voted the address![9] The opposition always paid Villèle the compliment of taking whatever he did seriously; while an air of incredulity touched with derision appeared in much of its discussion of Polignac.

The political heat was now being generated by the press, as the Chambers were prorogued and inarticulate. Without exception, the newspapers predicted a dissolution of the Chamber of Deputies. The *Temps* forecast the event for the first week of May, with elections to be held in June.[10] The *Quotidienne* and *Drapeau Blanc* urged no delay in dissolving the "revolutionaries"; but the *Gazette* expressed the hope that the royalists unite before the edict appeared. More important to all parties than the dissolution itself, which was assured, was the outcome of the elections constitutionally scheduled to follow. Would the "221" who defied the King be reelected? Was it legal for them to enter the electoral race? And, if they were reelected; what would be the consequence? These questions, each more serious in turn, were discussed and examined by the editors of both sides.

Opposition deputies held several *réunions*, disguised as public banquets,

---

[7] *Ibid.*
[8] *Globe*, 5 April, 1830.
[9] *Temps*, 14 April, 1830.
[10] *Ibid.*, 16 April, 1830.

which were denounced by the Right as revolutionary and conspiratorial, although as "social" assemblies, they did not need police permission. Organization of these *réunions* came from the active *Aide-toi* society and the largest was held on April 1 in the terrace of the *Vendanges de Bourgogne*, a restaurant on the Champs-Elysées. Attended by over seven hundred persons including Lafayette, Casimir Périer, and dozens of deputies, it revealed a growing solidarity among the various factions on the Left. Odilon Barrot, gave a speech in which he termed the current crisis a "battle between progressive and retrograde civilizations".[11] Another large *Aide-toi* banquet was held at the Tivoli garden in May. Here, Lafayette and Constant spoke on "electoral responsibility" and Paul-François Dubois was honored in toasts, partly for his recent trial performance and partly because he had recently made peace with *Aide-toi* after two years of separation. The *Drapeau* had termed the organization a "state within a state... a frightening power which tends to dominate all others".[12] The *Courrier* (April 19) promptly denied this: "No one in France is stupid enough to believe in these phantoms".

To counterattack, the *Temps* had already circulated reports of a more sinister *réunion*,[13] an alleged meeting at the home of Polignac of the Ministers Guernon-Ranville and Bourmont, and the Ambassadors of England, Austria, and Holland. From this, Guizot developed the plot – when the *coup* against the electoral laws and the newspapers was struck, the government was planning to request foreign military intervention to suppress a popular insurrection! The *Temps* hastily labeled its projections as mere speculation, but as proof that no one regarded Polignac's "innocent protestations", as anything but hypocrisy. As for the reelection of the "221", Guizot stated that Polignac feared the outcome because of discouraging reports from his prefects. He hoped, said the *Temps* editor, to first discover the military result in Algiers, before making final plans. The *Globe* felt certain that voters would return another liberal majority, and that Polignac was "feeble-minded" if he expected to find more support from electors in 1830 than in 1827. On the Right *or* on the Left, wrote the *Globe's* Rémusat, "where is the man with any common sense who thinks a ministerial majority is possible"?[14]

---

[11] Gerbod, *Dubois*, p. 91; see also, Viel-Castel, *Histoire*, XX, 331-33; and Pouthas, *Guizot*, pp. 423-24. Among the many healths proposed was the customary toast to the King. When Guizot and his friends offered this formality, the **Tribune** and **Jeune France** republicans refused to drink. Godefroy Cavaignac, speaking for this faction, declared hotly, "No never! If we are not released from such infamy we resolve to rise and break our glasses as a mark of protest"! Odilon Barrot healed the breach, but the "Fabrists" and the republican factions remained dedicated to their program.

[12] *Drapeau Blanc*, 16 April, 1830.

[13] *Temps*, 27 March, 1830.

[14] *Globe*, 20 April, 1830.

On April 13, the *Courrier Français* performed its customary service for the *Aide-toi* society by publishing a complete list of the "221" and urging their reelection. It also published the names of the 181 deputies who had voted against the address. In the latter group, only one-ninth of the names were without a non-Imperial title or rank. Of the "221", a scant fifteen were so titled. This is much more an indication of recent favors bestowed for loyalty than of a division among social classes. Opposition journals, including the *Débats* cooperated to advertise the names of the "221" and give them support.

The *Globe*, from its highbrow perch, attempted to conduct a learned forum on the crisis by addressing questions to the monarchic press.[15] The first group of propositions sought a definition of the King's powers vis-a-vis the Chambers. The second group concerned the eligibility of the "221". All of them, said the *Globe*, could be condensed into one: "Do we live, according to the Ministry, under a limited monarchy, or under an absolute monarchy"? In rather Villèlist fashion, the *Gazette* evaded the argument, and retorted that the *Globe's* questions could be condensed to this: "Is a faction that usurps the rights of a king within its constitutional rights"? Five days before, the *Gazette* had declared that the "221" "forfeited" their right to be elected when they refused their accord and the *Globe* had snorted in reply: "It is hard to believe, after fifteen years of representative government, that anyone could write such stuff"! Characteristically, the *Quotidienne* attempted a serious reply to the *Globe*. It answered "yes" to the question whether a minister's power was superior to law, because this power was in the name of the King. To questions about the origin of the royal power, the *Quotidienne* responded in two words, "from God". "Can the Chambers ever refuse any bill"? asked the *Globe*. The answer: It can refuse no bills. "Is the King sole arbiter, in case of a conflict between powers"? Answer: "Yes". The *Globe* seemed pleased with the frank declarations it had wrung from Laurentie.

The republican journalists, whose editors were at that time more influential in *Aide-toi* and student clubs than in their papers, were in general political agreement with their liberal cousins, but balked at the idea of reelecting all of the "221".[16] Many of these deputies, acceptable to the Constants or the Broglies, appeared as weaklings to the radical generation. The staffers of the *Nouveau Journal de Paris*,[17] the *Tribune*, and *Jeune France* urged the reelection of only those well to the Left. Their collective voice was modest, however,

---

[15] *Ibid.*, 23, 24 April, 1830.
[16] De Hauranne, *Histoire*, X, 495.
[17] Baron de Schonen's paper had achieved a circulation of 1330 by this time.

and the larger propaganda organs played a much louder tune. The republicans shrewdly realized that, in case of revolution, their only chance for a republic would lie in the degree of radicalism of the deputies they hoped to back them. Events were soon to justify their viewpoint.

The vendetta between the Ultra and the opposition editors as they both argued for a *coup*, as well as the hostility among the several monarchic papers, finally brought a rebuke from the embarrassed ministers. In the official *Moniteur*,[18] editor Sauvo attacked both extremes of the press impartially. His article stressed the unofficial nature of those royalist papers calling for a *coup* and admitted they furnished "a cheap means of resistance to the press of the Left". He defended the Cabinet for its secret sessions with the remark: "An indiscreet government is not a government", and called for more "elevated discussions" from the press. Then, the government's journal announced that it was below its dignity to take part in quarrels of "private egos" and that it refused to become an instrument in the hands of "rhetoricians and demagogues". But the ministerial rebuke, clearly aimed at the Right, had no effect on either warring faction.

The Cabinet's true feeling toward the press was secretly expressed a few days later. According to a document found at the palace during the Revolution of 1830, Polignac had given the King a confidential report on the periodical press.[19] This report alleged that all of the articulate opposition, all of the agitation of *Aide-toi*, all opinion critical of the government was but an exaggerated image projected by the "malevolent" liberal press! Polignac informed the King that the press caused "nearly all the agitation of spirits". After thus reducing the entire opposition of France to a few newspaper editors, Polignac offered the King his repeated assurances that public liberties were being respected and denied that any assault on these liberties was being considered, except of course, by the liberal press, which, he maintained, sought to "weaken the government". This extraordinary thesis ended with a guarded suggestion that Charles X take drastic measures.

However the Cabinet feigned innocence of motives, the Left received its cues from actual events. There was no apparent justification for an Ultra and clerical Cabinet unless an attack on the Charter was being considered. There was no reason for a threatening royal speech unless the Crown wanted to serve notice to the opposition.

[18] *Le Moniteur*, 11 April, 1830.
[19] Vaulabelle, *Histoire*, VII, 233-35. The document was apparently authentic since it was accepted as defense evidence at the later trials of the August 8 ministers. The protestations of innocence in the memoir, however, have led to the suspicion that it was "planted" during the July Days to help exonerate both Polignac and the King from the charge of conspiracy.

Guizot recognized this logic when he published, as a popular report in his new *Revue Française* for April, the following consensus:

> We are on the eve of a revolution. The existence of representative government, the existence of the reigning house, are at stake. The evils which threaten us are those which can only bring remedies, nearly as formidable.
>
> ... I take then the most delicate question, the most dangerous, the question of persons, or as they say, of the dynasty.

After this glaring Orleanist statement, Guizot asserted that, although this was a popular idea, *he* did not consider the "evil so far advanced" as to warrant its validity. The lines between government and opposition, he admitted, were clearly drawn, but there was no present danger:

> [The Ministry] came in in a detestable manner, in a way which could lead to anything; but its positive position has since not been affected. One sees plenty of evil which could start the danger, not the danger itself... But we are nowhere near a revolution.[20]

In both factions of the press, the anticipated *coup* was expected to include a blow at the press: An edict of severe censorship. Not dissuaded by the *Moniteur's* propitiatory language, opposition writers continued to build up defenses for journalism. They had seen the Ultra monarchists acquitted too often by the courts for the same offenses which would send them to prison, and the Ultra editors gloated over their impunity. The *Drapeau Blanc's* fire-eating editor condemned the criticism of the ministers. "If these journals", he said, "were edited by men of perfection and genius, it might be excusable for them to enter the sanctuary of royalty".[21] Alphonse de Martainville was also a self-anointed Royal Prosecutor in cases where he felt the government moved too slowly. Jacques Bavoux, one of the founders of the *Nouveau Journal de Paris*, had written an article for that republican paper which included a cautious encouragement to the French nation to "triumph" over the government. Martainville immediately demanded action against Bavoux. These two newspapers, at opposite political poles, had recently become intimate enemies.[22] Martainville had denounced the unlimited liberty of the press in a series of articles in February, but he staunchly advocated some sort of limited freedom. "What greater despotism is there", he asked, than to

---

[20] *Revue Française*, April, 1830.

[21] *Drapeau Blanc*, 14, 16, April, 1830. Nevertheless, he devoted a full page (January 24), to personal attacks on Thiers, Mignet, and Carrel.

[22] Their feud began in January, when the *Drapeau* remarked: "*Journal de Paris* writes of two poodles who can do arithmetic and translate six languages. We suggest they be employed to properly edit an article for the *Journal de Paris*".

"insult with impunity"?[23] "Insult" was a favorite word of the *Drapeau*; Martainville's politics were highly personal and all debate an affair of honor.

The *Temps* dismissed the *Drapeau Blanc* by labeling it the "Hébert of the *Parti*", a cruel brand, but not exclusively applied to the *Drapeau* faction by the Left. Villèle himself had once called La Bourdonnaye an *enragé*, the term applied during the Revolution to men like Hébert![24] The antipress diatribes of other royalist papers, such as one printed in the *Gazette* of April 4, were regarded more seriously. In a *Temps* editorial, "The Ministry without newspapers",[25] Guizot reprimanded Polignac for his disapproval of all newspapers, even including some belonging to the royalists. This, to Guizot, revealed the Minister's monumental contempt for public opinion and he added that no one before Polignac had so hastened the spirit of constitutionalism in France! Maintaining that "babbling" subservient papers were of less actual value to the Ministry than those which criticized, he referred to the *Moniteur*, which had recently editorialized on the press, as the "first eunuch of the Ministry". Guizot's talent for phrase making had again struck its mark squarely.

In the courts, new prosecutions of opposition journalists continued to attract crowds and receive publicity. Soon after the *causes célèbres* of the *Globe* and the *National*, the popular poet Béranger was sentenced to the maximum term of *six years* at forced labor, for his recent songs "Monseigneur", and an Ode to the Duchess of Berry, more personal and salacious than any of his earlier offenses to the Crown.[26] The lyricist had already spent much of his life in jail, but still he persisted in his art. Like Fontan, he became a martyr in the press because of the rigorous punishment his pen and wit had brought, and because he was a part owner of the *Constitutionnel* and a contributor to several papers. Had he been an ordinary poet-satirist, the penalty might have been lighter, but Béranger's seditious songs were memorized and sung by thousands throughout France.

In May, the trial of the *Gazette Constitutionnel des Cultes*, became a battleground between the anticlerical liberals and the allegedly *Congrégation*-inspired Ministry. The editor of the *Gazette des Cultes*, Brissaud, forty-two, was charged with "outrage to the religion of state" and "outrage to the Archbishop of Paris" as a result of several articles.[27] One of these, supposedly an unedited letter of the late free thinker Paul-Louis Courier, was called "On

---

[23] *Drapeau Blanc*, 7 February, 1830.

[24] *Temps*, 7 April, 1830; see also, Thureau-Dangin, *Royalistes*, p. 163.

[25] *Temps*, 14 April, 1830.

[26] *Gazette des Tribunaux*, 27 April, 1830. Sentence was postponed due to the poet's illness.

[27] *Ibid.*, 20 May, 1830.

the Influence Acquired by Priests through the Confession". Brissaud blamed the abuse of the confessional for the Fronde, the Revocation of the Edict of Nantes and the Holy League. Claiming to have the "inside story", he cited an alleged opinion by a priest:

> It has no longer much effect on men, it is true,... but on women, and from them we have the key to all the affairs, we know all the secrets of the nuptial bed and often, as we regulate pleasures, their husbands detest us, but... their wives govern them, and by our inspiration they assist. By their intervention we know... the political and religious opinions of citizens, and we again find the way to mix in politics.

Another guilty article, also said to have been written by the late Courier, had appeared in the issue for April 18, and discussed the desirability of marriage for priests. This article told of a priest who had three children by his domestic: "Paquette had the night and Our Lord Jesus Christ had the day! There was time enough for everyone".

A third indictment had been for the *Gazette des Cultes'* report of a religious ceremony held in Paris. On April 25, the official translation of the relics of the great humanitarian, St. Vincent de Paul, was performed in the church of the Lazarists. Leading the procession had been the Ultra Prefect of Police, Mangin, and the Archbishop of Paris, Mgr. Quélen. The celebration had been medieval, pompous, and costly, and had been criticized by all of the liberal press, including the paper on trial.

One of the incriminating passages in the *Gazette des Cultes* of April 22 brought Brissaud under the accusation of "outrage to the Archbishop of Paris". This consisted of fictional dialogue between "an archbishop" and a merchant of sacred relics. In the story, the merchant knocks on an archbishop's door. A lackey answers and orders the merchant away, saying that a ragged woman had the effrontery, earlier in the day, to beg bread for her children. The merchant then protests that he is a representative of the Pope, whereupon he is cordially received by the prelate who offers profuse apologies. The seller of relics then displays his wares and he and the archbishop haggle over the price of the "femur of Saint Prudenziana"!

The Crown attorney, Levavasseur, denounced the defendant, Brissaud, as one of those, who, "without attaching themselves to any cult, work with inconceivable perseverance to destroy beliefs... without ever asking themselves what they would substitute for the wholesome education of the destroyed faith". He called Brissaud's paper "a powerful auxillary to the religion-hating press".

The defense lawyer, Guillaume Mermilliod, admitted the difficulty of defense, but courageously assailed the revival of antique Church traditions under the Restoration as "the triumph of a fanatical party, insane with revenge". He described the spread of Ultra-Catholic influence through the lay *Congrégation*, the missions, the Jesuits, and the recent increases in church revenue. He defended his client's analysis of the Vincent de Paul ceremonies, remarking that many poor people had to sacrifice to pay for the lavish display, and added that the use of the "indulgence" system in regard to the relics was a "revival of the abuse of the sixteenth century". The lawyer expressed his own admiration of the kindly Saint Vincent, but pointedly recalled that the good man's canonization had been delayed by a century of contention. He stated that the Gallican clergy had then assumed an anti-Jesuit position. For a grand total of eleven editorials in the *Gazette des Cultes*, Brissaud drew a sentence of six months and a fine of one thousand francs.[28]

In July, the case was appealed to the high court of baron Séguier, the Royal Court of Paris, and, once again, the shade of Vincent de Paul stood before the bar. The defense lawyer recalled that this saint was not recognized as holy by some orders and was therefore called simply "Monsieur Vincent", and added that there was also good evidence that he had died adhering to the unitarian heresy of Socinianism. The defense also contended that the Concordat forbade religious processions in any urban area where more than one cult was represented. "We were never enemies of the clergy", the defense declared, "we have proclaimed their virtues, courage, and their charity; but we have not wished to tolerate intolerance". The court, after some deliberation, decided that the punishment which had been meted out at Brissaud's first trial was, nevertheless, justified.[29]

In the provinces, anticlericalism caused the convictions of two other newspapers. The editor of the *Courrier de la Moselle*, Harmand, and his printer, Lamort, were tried in Metz for the crime of "outrage to the state religion" and "hatred and contempt for the government" by virtue of an article which denounced Polignac as an instrument of the Duke of Wellington.[30] A third article, which merely quoted from the comte de Montlosier's latest anti-Jesuit pamphlet, led to the accusation of "outrage to a class of citizens" – priests – against Harmand. The incriminating quotation used to convict the editor was: "Under the Revolution, without priests, there was religion; with priests, such as they are now, there is even less of it. If this goes on, soon there will be no more".

---

[28] *Ibid.*
[29] *Ibid.*, 16 July, 1830.
[30] *Ibid.*, 2 June, 1830. For an earlier trial of this provincial paper, see chapter viii.

In its anti-Polignac editorial, the *Courrier de la Moselle* had remembered that Minister's youthful connection with Georges Cadoual's bomb conspiracy by referring to Polignac as the "hero of the infernal machine". For this and other phrases, the editor was found guilty of attacking the King's government. The charge of "outrage to religion" grew out of an editorial of April 15, in which the Lorraine paper had advocated the "necessity of a *Gazette des Cultes*". This Paris newspaper, Harmand had written, "having for its purpose to uncover Ultramontane maneuvers, is surely an urgent necessity at the present time". For the three articles, two of which were anticlerical, Harmand was given the heavy sentence of a year and a day in prison and a fine of one thousand francs. The printer, who had merely praticed his craft, was ordered to go to jail for three months and to pay six hundred francs. Polignac's campaign to break the provincial press was in full cry.

In Besançon, the editor of the *Impartial*, a weekly paper serving all of Franche-Comté, was prosecuted for "exciting hatred of the clergy" and "outrage to ministers of the state religion". [31] Before the trial began, several members of the bar association of the court deposed that they found nothing guilty in the May 9 article in question.

The defendant, Just-Muiron, was totally deaf and all conference with him was laboriously held in writing. "The most pronounced auxiliaries of the *Parti*", he had written in his journal, "are the members of the clergy; not these experienced ecclesiastics who have weathered the storms of revolution and judged sanely the political situation born of our new social state". Not these, said the editor, but rather priests devoted to Ultramontane doctrines, among whom "no one sees the world except as a seminary, who ignore almost entirely what interests hold the diverse classes of society". The editor of the *Impartial* had also reported a conversation with a local priest in which the latter had announced that "All those of his parish who would not vote for religion, that is for the Ministry, would be deprived of absolution".

The prosecutor asked the court why clergymen should not be counter-revolutionaries since they were the bulwark against anarchy, and attempted to weaken the editor's defense which was based on a distinction between two kinds of priests. The judge reprimanded Just-Muiron for having posed a choice "between the Bourbons or anarchy" in his article and found him guilty of outraging the priesthood as a class of citizens, for which he received a sentence of one month in prison and a fine. The editor was acquitted, however, of "hatred and contempt of the King's government", a charge made as a result of certain passages in the same editorial which imputed ulterior

---

[31] *Ibid.*, 3 June, 1830.

motives to the prosecution of the Algiers campaign. The opposition's policy toward the Algiers expedition was more topical than its traditional anti-Jesuit stand; the *Impartial* had said:

One wishes to punish the Dey of Algiers, in order to create prestige and glory for himself, regain the army's devotion, so it can show bayonets to people who dare to reason and admit to no other duty than obedience to laws.

This provincial newspaper of Besançon was not the only journal which touted the Algiers campaign as a step to facilitate a *coup d'état*. The liberal press was very careful not to insult the soldiers and sailors who were about to invade the African beaches, but concentrated their attacks on the motives of the Cabinet. Here, to change the picture, the liberals had a political disadvantage. To crititicize their own flag in battle, even though it bore a *fleur-de-lys*, might expose them to the odium of being bad Frenchmen. Although opposition writers tried to prevent glorification of the government through the African war, the royalist press found in this issue a natural propaganda weapon which they frequently swung at the Left. The *Moniteur* printed another official protest by the administration and referred to critics of Polignac's African policy as "disloyal", "unpatriotic", and even "enemies of the Christian name".[32]

The Dauphin, who had made himself nominal commander of the expedition, left for Toulon during the last week of April to supervise the staging of the army. The great fleet of 103 ships, bearing 70,000 soldiers and sailors, was expected to sail at the end of the first week of May, but did not raise anchor until the last days of that month. Delays, so annoying to the Cabinet's plans, were extended when foul weather forced the fleet to take refuge at Palma de Mallorca.[33] The actual assault on the Moslem kingdom did not start until mid-June, and the postponement allowed time for the opposition to preach away whatever "glory" the war might have held for the King and his Ministry.

The *Globe* asserted that Polignac, "to stimulate the imagination of the electors, had surrounded himself with a halo of glory, because he invented the Algerian war".[34] The *Temps* predicted the dissolution would occur soon after the Dauphin returned from his inspection of the fleet[35] and that Algiers would be sacked and destroyed because of the heavy artillery being taken by the French.[36] On April 26, the *Courrier Français* published a thorough

---

[32] *Le Moniteur*, 26 March, 1830.
[33] Viel-Castel, *Histoire*, XX, 396-412.
[34] *Globe*, 1 May, 1830.
[35] *Temps*, 3 May, 1830.
[36] *Ibid.*, 15 May, 1830.

editorial criticism of the Algerian campaign, opposing every aspect of the conquest. Thier's *National* sought to destroy the Minister's hope of winning the loyalty of the troops, and reported that sailors were being forcibly impressed in Languedoc.[37] The *National* also warned the Cabinet that simply because the citizens of Toulon received the troops enthusiastically, this did not indicate the war itself was popular.[38]

Not all the Left could so easily reject the campaign, and one of the editors of the *National* was forced to perform his soul-searching in public. This was Armand Carrel, who, although an intellectual liberal, had always remained a dashing captain of the line. In 1830, he saw his own country at war, and though he understood the government's selfish motives, he also knew that soon the sands of African beaches would drink the blood of French soldiers. To resolve his clash of sentiments, Carrel wrote an article, in which he tried to distinguish between liberal patriotism and blind loyalty:

A great nation is never alienated from that which concerns its wealth, its blood, and the prestige of its name. Success, if it avails, can be its work only, and on it also falls the shame of reverses in the eyes of rival nations... A bad general, a bad minister, fall in disgrace and contempt, the country which has supported them is left, when they are gone, alone and blamed with their dishonor. Thus today, it is no longer a matter of the personal lustre that the deserter of Waterloo could hope to recover in a distant and hazardous expedition. It is a matter of that still virgin honor of the young army, which discipline, instruction, and patriotism has reflowered in the shade of our institutions. It is especially a matter of the reputation, once so bright... of our navy, newly reborn.

We do not wish the honors of victory, either for the man who commands this expedition against the will of all France, or for the reprobate faction of which he has the pretension to be the weapon; but sure as we are that the success of this too great and too costly campaign should not be turned against us, we have nothing more for it henceforth than the ardent wishes of men impassioned for national glory.[39]

There were other events besides the Algerian war to excite public opinion and deepen the political crisis. Throughout spring, incendiarism continued to plague portions of Normandy. Between February 18 and July 7, 178 cases of arson were reported in this region.[40] This bizarre activity, although probably largely a matter of aimless protest and psychological contagion,[41] bore a political aspect because much of the fire-destroyed property belonged to liberals. The liberal press reported these crimes, but did not openly accuse the

[37] *National*, 25 March, 1830.
[38] *Ibid.*, 5 May, 1830.
[39] *Ibid.*, 18 May, 1830.
[40] Lucas-Dubreton, *Restauration*, p. 141.
[41] *Ibid.*; see also, Viel-Castel, *Historie*, XX, 372-74.

government of using so absurd a method to attack the opposition. In Falaise, most suspects who were questioned by police turned out to be domestic servants and poor feebleminded young men and women, with no organization of any kind.[42] The government, however, must have felt the necessity of reassuring the people. Troops were begged from Polignac, and several units marched into Normandy to restore order, as well as "confidence" in the government. It was perhaps only a coincidence that the elections soon to be held in Normandy were considered critical by the Ministry. The Prefect of Calvados, the comte de Montalivet, issued a proclamation (May 25) announcing the dispatch of soldiers to the province and urging citizens to rid themselves of the "false" notion that the government had any "interest" in the fires, except to capture the "cowards" who set them.[43] Such a purely defensive proclamation indicates a state of tension in the North.

Prince Polignac surely had more important plans for the liberals than the kindling of their barns and haystacks. Since mid-April, when Villèle had withdrawn his dark shadow from Paris, the Cabinet and its royal master had been refining their plans for a *coup*. They also ordered dismissal for many lesser government officials whose political views were "royalist", but not sufficiently Ultra.

On April 21, the Council of State met to discuss the possible reelection of another liberal majority to replace the "221", after the dissolution of the Chamber. The King and Polignac believed that if a liberal majority were returned, that would be the moment to strike with Article 14. Several ministers objected to this proposal,[44] the "loyal opposition" being led by the comte de Guernon-Ranville. As early as December, he had warned the King that such use of Article 14 would be a "violation of sworn faith", and that the bourgeoisie, far from isolated, as Polignac had maintained, were in daily contact with the masses.[45] The Minister of Justice, Courvoisier, seeking a pretext to resign, sided with Guernon-Ranville.

But the stubborn King was deferring more and more to Polignac, whose last modest resources of political sense were now deserting him. The President of the royal Cabinet was reported by colleagues to have claimed several miraculous visions, and to have told the King he had discussed the *coup* with the Mother of God and had been assured of success. The "mysticism" of the Prince de Polignac, exaggerated by spite, grew into an undeserved caricature, but the editor of the *Gazette* reliably quoted Lord Stuart, the British Ambassa-

---

[42] *National*, 5 June, 1830.
[43] *Le Moniteur*, 2 June, 1830.
[44] De Hauranne, *Histoire*, X, 488-90.
[45] Viel-Castel, *Histoire*, XX, 95-96.

dor, as having said: "Every time I visit the Council of State, I feel I have entered the Fool's Paradise of Milton".[46] Villèle could smugly reflect on his own failure to enter the Cabinet, as he confided to his wife: "These men, who ought to destroy the Revolution, are much more capable ... of demolishing what remains of the monarchy".[47] Ultra newspapers intensified their provocation of the King and chorused a new slogan: "No more concessions"! Polignac again assured his master, as he had done in his report on the press, that the bourgeoisie were too satisfied, too nonpolitical, and too property conscious, to tolerate a public uprising in Paris.

But Charles X wanted assurances of unity from his ministers before he would consider invoking the emergency powers of the Charter. The King also placed great stress on the success of the Algerian expedition and sincerely believed that, if his army won a decisive victory abroad, he would become invincible. Reasonable and scrupulous ministers, such as Guernon-Ranville, urged a policy of bluff-calling, which, according to modern legitimist sympathizers,[48] might have been wiser than the direct *coup* and might have succeeded. This plan was for the Ministry to present an early budget bill to the Chamber. If the deputies meekly passed it, the address of the "221" and the exhortations of the liberal press would be reduced to bombast. If the deputies rejected the bill, then they would be confronted by thousands of officials without salary, by soldiers and veterans without pay, and by bourgeois investors with no interest on their *rentes*.

The opposition was alert to the meaning of the frequent Cabinet sessions. An editorial titled "Evident Fact", written by Thiers or Carrel, appeared in the *National* on May 5. It was another disavowal of revolutionary aims on the part of the Left, yet it included an unmistakable threat or resistance in the case of a *coup d'état*, as it addressed Polignac:

If you remake the law by virtue of Article 14, you will be resisted, not with violence, oh no, but with still more legality. The continuation of your revolt would lead you to unsheathe your sword. But the gospel has told you what happens to one who lives by the sword.

The editor further contested the King's right to use the emergency provisions of Article 14, granting Charles X the "legal *coup d'état* of dissolution", but adding that, "if the pretended enemy is found again in the electoral colleges, then it is no longer an enemy; it is the nation itself, and the conspirator is you, who give to France the odious reputation that you alone merit". This

---

[46] Villèle, *Mémoires*, 2 July, 1830, Genoude to Villèle, V, 456.
[47] Villèle, *Mémoires*, 4 May, 1830, to Madame de Villèle, V, 430.
[48] Hudson, *Ultra-Royalism*, p. 161; see also, Roux, *La Restauration*, pp. 314-15.

malediction was applied to Polignac, but a reader might substitute for a subject the old Monarch. Few sons of St. Louis had been addressed in such a style!

But the cry "no more concessions"! rang in the royal ear. The plan of Guernon-Ranville required a series of steps and was not vigorous enough. On May 16, after warning only some of his ministers, the King dissolved the Chamber of Deputies. This same edict ordered the electoral colleges of the urban *arrondissements* and the less populous departments convoked on June 23, those of the larger departments for July 3, and those of the department of Corsica for July 20. The new Chamber was to open on August 3, 1830.[49] The two constitutional royalists in the Ministry, the comte de Chabrol and baron Courvoisier, immediately resigned, leaving the Justice and Finance posts vacant.

The press had perfectly divined the next day's events. The King and his "dear Jules" were now free of those temporizers, Chabrol and Courvoisier, and could at last "reinforce" the Ministry. Three new ministers, all Ultras, were brought into the Cabinet.[50]

Foremost among these "reinforcements", was the comte de Peyronnet, who was given the portfolio of the Interior, replacing Guy de Montbel, the Villèle partisan who was demoted to the now-vacant Finance department. Villèle's influence had clearly vanished. The nettlesome Peyronnet was, to the opposition, an even more hated figure than La Bourdonnaye and both men shared the quality of being offensive to enemies, as well as colleagues. Though once a member of Villèle's council, Peyronnet's relations with Villèle were far from cordial. He was a clerical Ultra, which made him valuable to Polignac, although the Prince was much closer to the King. Peyronnet's greatest parliamentary achievement up to this moment had been the sponsorship of the infamous "Law of Justice and Love" in 1827, which, had it not been killed by the Chambers, would have rendered the press helpless, servile, and possibly bankrupt. Newspaper editors of the Left had particular reasons for their fierce attacks on the new Minister.

The other additions to the Cabinet were comte Jean-Victor de Chantelauze at the department of Justice, baron Capelle at the Ministry of Public Works (a new office created on the same day as his appointment), and Count Ferdinand de Bertier to the secondary Ministry of Forests. Chantelauze had been the chief magistrate of the high court of Grenoble and had proved his Ultra faith by editing a recent brochure favoring a royalist *coup*. Capelle was

---

[49] *Le Moniteur*, 17 May, 1830.
[50] *Ibid.*, 20 May, 1830.

a nonentity whose servile royalism was considered dependable. The new director of Forests, de Bertier, was a founder of the *Congrégation*. Not a single member of this new "May 19 Ministry" was tainted with a compromising constitutionalism. Even Guernon-Ranville, although he opposed a royal dictatorship, was "Ultra" in his final loyalty to throne and altar. His hostile attitude toward the press was well known, as a result of his November speech before the Royal Court of Lyons.[51]

But the element of surprise, as useful to Restoration politicians as to those of today, was nearly absent. Dissolution and the shift toward the ultimate Right in the Cabinet had been forecast for several weeks by the press. Nevertheless, the maneuvers of that third week of May were necessary to set the stage of a *coup d'état*. With no representative body, journalists now, more than ever, were the paladins of constitutional liberty.

The *Gazette* accepted the final disgrace of its hero Villèle with petulance: "We leave one system for another and lose the advantages and gain all the inconveniences of both".[52] Peyronnet was far from pleasing in the eyes of the marquis de Genoude. The *Quotidienne* was naturally satisfied that the council had been thus rounded out and its editor, Laurentie, handed down the decision that anyone who voted for a member of the "221", would be guilty of a felony![53] This had been the earlier opinion of the nearly apoplectic Martainville in the *Drapeau Blanc*. Like a caged bear, he swallowed such morsels as the dissolution so quickly that they only stirred his appetite for more. Unless the King struck the full blow instantly, he cried, it would be too late![54]

To all of the opposition: Republicans, liberals, and disillusioned royalists, the comte de Peyronnet was the August 8 triumvirate reedited in one volume. He had the reputation of La Bourdonnaye for violence, Polignac for *Congré-gationisme*, and Bourmont for dishonor. Though the act of dissolution had been fully expected, it was generally treated as a political landmark.[55]

The *Courrier Français* (May 19) called the dissolution a "most serious circumstance" and urged the electoral colleges to vote, not only for themselves, but as representatives of national public opinion. The daily *Globe* published a set of electoral instructions with facsimiles of nomination blanks, the prototype of today's "sample" ballot. Pleading for the reelection of the "221",

---

[51] See *supra*, chapter vii. Guernon-Ranville was not informed in advance of the Peyronnet nomination.

[52] *Gazette de France*, 25 May, 1830.

[53] *Quotidienne*, 22 May, 1830.

[54] *Drapeau Blanc*, 21 May, 1830.

[55] *Globe*, 18 May, 1830.

the *Globe* declared: "The Ministry has sounded the tocsin of its fate. The counterrevolution is on the march; it is up to the electors to save France".

The defeat of Villèlism by the reckless Peyronnet wing was the key to the Ministry. The *Globe* predicted that the Cabinet's chief Villèlist, Montbel, would join "poor" Chabrol and "isolated" Courvoisier who had just resigned an incompatible Ministry.[56] The *Globe*, however, had misjudged the self-effacing Montbel. More loyal to his master than to his own ambitions, Montbel remained not only to cast his lot with the Polignac adventurers, but to accompany the King through his exile. He still hoped his presence in the Council would keep the door ajar for Villèle – in the event that Polignac should fail to kill, and only wound, the revolutionary beast.

To promote interest in the scheduled elections, the *Globe's* Rémusat especially urged the reelection of four of the "221": Professor Villemain of the Sorbonne, Dunoyer, the economist, Mérilhou, lawyer, orator, and a director of the *Courrier Français*, and Louis Bernard, the Breton politician who defended liberal causes. Rémusat urged his voting readers to show as much courage at the ballot box as these gentlemen had shown in the Assembly.

The staffers of the *Temps* believed that the purge of Villèlism was the most important result of the shift:

> M. de Polignac wins today; M. de Villèle is beaten. His interpreter to the world, the *Gazette*, opposed any change before the elections; yet the change is made. His domestic representative, M. de Montbel, loses the Ministry of the Interior.[57]

The *Temps* identified Peyronnet as one who had "alienated the courts" and against whom the whole Center-Right had voted in the Chamber. "The daredevil of the Villèle Ministry", said the paper, "will be the real manipulator of the Polignac Ministry". The *Temps* also claimed that the latest Cabinet changes would make a liberal election victory more certain than ever, and, of course, implying that the *coup* would be the royal response to that victory.[58]

As the new chief of the Interior post, Peyronnet sent a circular to all of his prefects in the departments. Except for an official demand for obedience, the tone of the letter was very mild,[59] and therefore disappointing to the

---

[56] *Ibid.*, 27 May, 1830.
[57] *Temps*, 21 May, 1830.
[58] *Ibid.*, 24 May, 1830.
[59] The full text of the Peyronnet circular to prefects (May 20) is as follows:

> The King has deigned to confide to me the direction of the Department of he Interior.

> I know the difficulties of that important administration; but the experience of the magistrates who belong to it gives me hope to surmount them.

Left. Other ministers sent out circulars. Polignac, as acting War Minister, sent a letter to each of the foremost military commanders; more political than that of Peyronnet and carrying this warning: "One cannot serve the government of the King and the opposition at the same time; loyalty and duty require a choice". Armand Carrel, speaking through the *National*, declared the latter circular "not only in bad taste, but illegal". As a former officer, Carrel wrote, scornfully, "And M. de Polignac pretends that because one is in the opposition, that is to say, because one would regard him as a detestable Minister, one would no longer defend France along the Rhine"![60] The young writer noted that in England, ministerial assistants were not threatened with a choice of "conformity" or "dismissal". The *Temps*, though unable to find a dark design against either the press or the Charter in the Peyronnet circular, called it an attempt to disavow the "sinister mission" felt by public opinion and "a protestation of his notoriety".[61]

The regime had for years depended on the provinces, where Villèle's legion of prefectural appointees and mayors could influence and even deceive electors. Now, thanks to the Ultra "defection", as well as the opposition press and *Aide-toi*, liberal ideas, and even republican ideas, were permeating the columns of stalwarts like the *Courrier de la Moselle* and the Lyons *Précurseur*. The links of these editors with such groups as *Aide-toi* and the "Friends of the Freedom of the Press", combined with their new influence, made their ordeal by trial under Polignac inevitable.

François Mignet, who was deeply concerned over the Ministry's persecution of the newspapers in the provinces, used the pages of the *National* to broadcast a message of hope to harried editors in the departments.[62] "It is against the

> I ask of them only the execution of the laws; I ask for it to be prompt, exact, complete, and loyal: Always do that which the law commands, work with the opportunity that it allows, never that which it forbids, such is in my eyes the duty of a wise and able administrator.
>
> There will be another aspect to it for me, it will by my duty to second them, as they should second me, and to see that full and good justice be given to their loyalty and zeal.
>
> I will tirelessly apply myself to this and I flatter myself that none of them would doubt that I will be faithful to this promise.
>
>   - Peyronnet -

[60] *National*, 5 June, 1830.
[61] *Temps*, 24 May, 1830.
[62] *National*, 5 June, 1830; see also, Collins, *Newspaper Press*, pp. 55, 58.

press", he wrote, "that the activities of the counterrevolutionary party have been constantly directed. The men of this faction felt that here was their real enemy, and that in *attacking* it; they were striking at all other institutions". Mignet praised several provincial newspapers for their resistance to this Ultra pressure: The *France Meridionale*, the *Precurseur de Lyon*, the *Sentinelle* of Niort, the *Messager de Marseille*, and several others, including the *Courrier de la Moselle*. The latter, he declared, had "so good an influence in its department, that our adversaries, previously victorious... in the elections, have lost their superiority". The Ministry had sought to discourage the departmental press, he declared, and vowed that these attacks will be as vain against it as they had been for fifteen years against the press of Paris. Mignet appealed to the provincial prejudice against the ruling metropolis, painting a glorified picture of a decentralized nation with political power vested in the provinces and won for them by provincial editors. Here the *National* used the same appeal as the republican *Tribune* and the *Aide-toi* society. Nevertheless, deputies were still filing for candidacy in departments to which they were strangers. On the subject of the coming elections, Mignet proclaimed:

The decisive moment approaches. It is up to the journals of the departments to concur in the defeat of the common enemy by their useful influence on the electors, by their active surveillance of authority, and by the denunciation of maneuvers which would be contrary to law.[63]

On the evening of May 31, at a ball given in honor of Neapolitan royalty, another "incident" occurred, which, like the burnings in Normandy, served, in these tense weeks, to illuminate the state of political emotions. The Bourbon King and Queen of Naples had recently arrived in Paris as guests of their royal cousins. They had come from Madrid, where they had given their daughter Cristina in marriage to the widower King of Spain. In addition to this connection, the King of Naples' sister, Marie-Amélie, was the wife of Louis-Philippe, and another of his daughters was the famous, or infamous, duchesse de Berri. A luxurious and expensive "family reunion" was held at the Palais Royal, the taxpayer-maintained home of the Orleans family. Over eighteen hundred guests sat down to dinner and remained for dancing.[64] The lavish party, which lasted until six in the morning, teemed with political significance. Such assemblies of royalty were rare. Although a mere three hundred yards separated their palaces, the ruling branch had few social contacts with the family of Louis-Philippe. This was due to the Duke's

---

[63] *Ibid.*
[64] *Le Moniteur*, 2 June, 1830.

politically calculated aloofness, not the King's attitude, which was always generous and cordial to the members of the cadet branch. These costly entertainments were nearly impossible at the Tuileries, since the King, who had lost much of his old revenue to revolution and was limited by a yearly civil list, was actually quite poor by the standards of Louis-Philippe!

The Queen of Naples was very fat and had a scandalous reputation. But when baron d'Haussez, the Navy Minister, suggested to the King of France that such a woman did not increase the Bourbons' prestige, the King replied with a good humor that such gossip was favorable since it showed that the people had no serious grievances to discuss.[65] Later that evening, however, a crowd of people – workers, idlers, and celebrating youths – swarmed into the shop-lined arcades of the palace and began to behave like a mob. Louis-Philippe, as his demagogue father before him, seldom closed the palace yard to the public and the gates had been left open that evening, according to Pasquier, to satisfy the Duke's "taste for publicity".[66] The unruly mob tore up flowers and shrubs, smashing windows and garden chairs. Inside the palace, the jewel bedecked revelers heard drunken shouts of "Down with the aristocrats"! To many of them, it was a ghost returning after forty years. Police and some of the palace guard succeeded in quieting the crowds without gunfire, but several youths were arrested. The comte de Salvandy joked to his host, "My lord, you are giving a truly Neapolitan party. We are dancing on a volcano"![67]

In the Paris of 1830, such news spread like a flame and editors of the opposition kept it burning for several days. The *National* referred to the incident as a "tumult" and cited the police charges against those who had been arrested: "Nocturnal and injurious disturbances, rebellion against public authority, and degradation or destruction of private property". Rémusat of the *Globe* was certain that Louis-Philippe had "calculated" the demonstrations in his gardens and said that everyone was comparing this incident to those of 1789.[68] In spite of all the gossip, the *Moniteur* could blithely announce that "the most perfect order was maintained among the multitude"![69]

The "volcano" caused a new tremor a few days after the Orleans *fête*. The little *Universel*, private newspaper of Polignac, had, in the first months of its slavery, denied the notion of a *coup d'état*. After February, however, the true voice of the First Minister began to speak from its pages. On June 1,

[65] Viel-Castel, *Histoire*, XX, 379.

[66] Pasquier, *Histoire*, VI, 227.

[67] Lucas-Dubreton, *Restauration*, p. 141.

[68] *National*, 5 June, 1830; Barante, *Souvenirs*, III, 548.

[69] *Le Moniteur*, 2 June, 1830.

it offered a long discourse entitled, "Can the King yield; Will the King yield"? It was reproduced the next day in the official *Moniteur*, as well as the *Quotidienne*. The Ministry's article began as a Socratic exposition of both sides of the "royal prerogative" question, but then developed into a declaration of war on the opposition. The only moderate element in this polemic was the statement that both liberals and royalists had been equally guilty of dogmatic generalizations on the subject of the King's rights. Admitting that circumstances are possible wherein the King's power is limited, Polignac's journal declared that, in the present crisis, the "King will not yield". To yield, said the *Universel*, would be to efface a formal provision of the Charter and to transfer "unconstitutionally" an essential part of the executive power to the legislature. This manifesto, issued directly by the order of the Prince de Polignac, concluded: "The King understands his dignity, our interests, and his oaths; the King, then will yield nothing... That is the King, strong and jealous".[70] Here was precisely what Adolphe Thiers had been waiting for. The *National's* editor could now write that Polignac himself, not one of his overzealous admirers, had threatened a *coup d'état* and had publicly tried to "intimidate the electors". Thiers tried to demonstrate the logic of his claim:

This declaration seems as inappropriate as a thing could be under the present circumstances. What could be signified by that expression, *The King Will Not Yield*!? It was conceived the day after the address, after the prorogation; because then there remained the dissolution, the legal means which the King had to resist the Chamber. But today, since the dissolution has been pronounced and this means used up, what could be meant by the phrase, *The King Will Not Yield*!?[71]

Thiers stated that the King was threatening the electors: "If you do not do as I wish, I will violate the laws". The King, he then explained, would not yield in his plan to exercise the national security provision of the Charter and this, wrote Thiers, would be regarded as a *coup d'état*. The prophet of the Orleanists was able to advance his policy a bit farther, and went on to urge the voters to "dare" the Ministry to violate the Charter. Like many on the Left, Thiers was growing impatient for the hour when Article 14 would test the fibre of French resistance and of his own political program.

The *Temps* seconded Thiers' editorial and called Polignac's manifesto an official threat.[72] The older newspapers of the opposition, including the *Débats*, solemnly agreed. The *Quotidienne* led the Ultra camp, incessantly and jubilantly parroting back the words: "The King will not yield"!

[70] *Ibid.*, 3 June, 1830.
[71] *National*, 5 June, 1830.
[72] *Temps*, 5 June, 1830.

CHAPTER XIII

"IT IS LIFE OR DEATH"

As the time drew near for the elections, journalistic propaganda became more polarized than ever. The Left could speak of little else but the "responsibility" of the voters to stand firmly against the threatened *coup*, while ministerial spokesmen hurled abuse at the "221" and denied their eligibility for reelection.

The Algerian expedition continued to be important in discussions, but only the Ultra papers gave it the brilliance that the King wanted for it. Liberal writers continued to treat the invasion of Algeria as a political trick, except on the few occasions when they praised the soldier's bravery in order to prove their own patriotism. The Mediterranean climate had been partisan to the liberals, by destroying all hope of a complete conquest of Algiers before the elections. The delay of the fleet in the Bay of Palma until the second week of June caused great concern at the summer palace in Saint Cloud; although there the King could more conveniently pursue his favorite sport, a political crisis notwithstanding.

The high clergy entered the electoral campaign with all the might of its sacerdotal power. Since its reproof at the hands of Martignac in 1828, it had become more factious. The bishops recognized their new champion in that zealous member of the *Congrégation*, Polignac. Episcopal letters and sermons denounced the "impious" press and the liberal candidates as foes of religion, while opposition papers advantageously played on this intervention. The *Globe* reproduced, for "the pleasure of readers", the words of Archbishop de Quélen, spoken from the pulpit of Notre Dame:

> The lily banner, inseparable from the cross, will once more leave the field victorious... if we never neglect *any* [italicized by the *Globe*] of the means which orders our duty to obtain monarchical and religious elections. We have reason to be interested in a cause so legitimate to the God of Clotilde and Saint Louis.[1]

---

[1] *Constitutionnel*, 3 June, 1830; *Globe*, 3 June, 1830.

Liberals were as confident of the reelection of a Left majority as they were that the King would promptly declare war upon it. Guizot wrote to a friend that the Left would succeed in the colleges, adding that the newspapers with "direction" (Orleanist) were doing well, but that this was in spite of the nonsense of "two or three subalterns" (the republican journals).[2] Back home in Nîmes, and no longer a "Norman", Guizot campaigned for his second election that year as a deputy, while his *Temps* fought for him in Paris. The *Aide-toi* society, in which he had remained, despite an influx of "subalterns", was active in the electoral campaign, and functioned in harmony with the press. Once, when the *Quotidienne* had again referred to the leadership of the society as a *comité directeur*, the *Temps* editors responded by warmly defending *Aide-toi*, [3] and the *Globe* promoted these electoral activities as a "healthy state of constitutional progress".[4]

The *Temps* pointed to the paradox implied in recent political events, blaming the Ministry for preparing to attack a new Chamber on the basis of its antecedents, while having crushed the old Chamber for judging a new Ministry on the basis of *its* antecedents! The *Temps* asked, with the customary slash at Marshal Bourmont, "Is the antecedent of the address equal to the antecedent of Waterloo, costing France 40,000 lives"?[5] Not only was this figure an exaggeration, but the *Temps* had apparently advanced Bourmont's crime from mere desertion to culpability for the entire disaster of 1815! The *Globe* reviewed reactionary legislation of the past and bade the electors to recall that the law of sacrilege had been made for the *Congrégation* and the law of the 3 percents for the *émigrés*. Hopeful of victory, the *Globe* nevertheless warned against electoral frauds. In the Paris area where 9755 of the nation's 90,000 electors were now eligible to vote, the prefect was accused of impeding the right of citizens to verify electoral lists.[6] In the *National*, Thiers expounded his doctrine of popular sovereignty to the electors and alluded to "1688", while Mignet exploited the spreading gulf between the royalist papers, especially the *Gazette* and the *Quotidienne*.[7]

On June 13, the "sacred person" of the King entered the political stage. In a proclamation to the electors, reprinted in the *Moniteur* and all the journals, the King called upon the voters as a "father and King" to frustrate the designs of "those who propagate fears" and "insidious language". Charles

---

[2] Barante, *Souvenirs*, Guizot to Barante, 18 May, 1830, III, 549.
[3] *Temps*, 19 June, 1830.
[4] *Globe*, 1 June, 1830.
[5] *Temps*, 5 June, 1830.
[6] *Globe*, 5, 6 June, 1830. For other government interventions, see Beach, *Charles X*, pp. 334-39.
[7] *National*, 5, 12, 14 June, 1830.

threatened with the words, "my immovable resolution" and distinctly urged his subjects to reject the "221". The *Quotidienne* rejoiced at this show of "prerogative",[8] but the opposition papers were faced with the onus of directly criticizing the King, a task which brought them the expected charge of "treason" from the *Drapeau Blanc*.[9]

Fortunately for the Left, Polignac, as customary, had countersigned the proclamation, so each of its devastating polemics against the royal appeal was prefaced by an assurance that the King's name was being basely used by the First Minister. The proclamation was thoroughly anatomized by the *Globe*[10] which shredded it into defenseless phrases, and the *National*, which refused to be "duped" into admitting that the King wrote it,[11] and in the legitimist *Débats*, which cleverly transformed it into an insult to the Crown by the Ministry. Bertin asked who could fail to see the hands of Polignac and Peyronnet in the proclamation and castigated them for doubting that the King would violate his coronation oath taken in 1824. The *Débats* asked how royalty could have possibly been offended by the address of the "221" which was an expression of "love", and asserted that the nation had the right to inform the King if harmony was lacking between people and Ministry. The royalist *Débats* then advanced one bold, heretical step to declare "sadly and with respect", that even kings were fallible! "Whatever the purity of their intentions", stated the *Débats*, "they can deceive themselves and be deceived! Only God's resolutions are immovable".[12] There was nothing here that even Bossuet would have opposed, but Bertin had issued a warning to the King. The *Temps* (June 19) addressed the nation's small electorate in phrases the *Débats* would have avoided: "Like Bonaparte to the Directory, France itself, citing the guilty in the tribunal, asks them to account for their incapacity and perverse designs".

Pious, honorable, and dutiful, but lacking political wisdom, the last King of France and Navarre persevered with a blind faith in the Algiers campaign as an event to magnify royal prestige. On June 13, the French armada at last descended on the Algerian fortress of Sidi-Ferruch, to establish a beachhead. Encouraged by the news, Charles took the unusual step of postponing the date of the elections in some twenty departments and the large *arrondissements* of Paris, constituencies of the Left. He also discharged, along with several minor officials, a member of the Council of State, Saint-Cricq, who

[8] *Quotidienne*, 14 June, 1830.
[9] *Drapeau Blanc*, 5 June, 1830.
[10] *Globe*, 14 June, 1830.
[11] *National*, 15 June, 1830.
[12] *Journal des Débats*, 15 June, 1830.

had been an active Minister under Martignac.[13] The crime of this royalist moderate official had been to send a circular to the electors in his native department, in which he had denounced the Polignac regime. The opposition press assailed the first of these maneuvers as evidence of fear on the part of the Cabinet and the second as blatant political intimidation of officials. Another factor that made the King bolder, was the April report by his "dear" Jules, in which the Ultra Minister had expounded his belief that the press had exaggerated the picture of opposition and that the "miser bourgeoisie" would be without the support of the masses in case of an uprising.[14]

The only serious dissent in the council now came from Guernon-Ranville who had legalistically combatted the plan for a surprise *coup* ever since his elevation to the Cabinet. When the King personally entered the electoral contest, Guernon asked to resign and was joined in this by the discredited Villèlist, Montbel. Guernon considered himself in a class with Chabrol and Courvoisier, who had recently quit their positions in disgust, although ideologically, he was to their Right. King Charles, however, managed to persuade both dissidents to return to their monarchic "duty" and so they remained to the fatal end.[15] At the time of the "221" address Guernon had shocked the council by informimg the King that he was not loved by the people; that he was even "unpopular"! Such was the only independent character in the Cabinet, a strange fusion of royalist, reactionary, upright lawyer, and provincial newspaperman.[16] At his trial, he would reiterate his feeling that, although the press was "everywhere calling the people to insurrection" against an "imaginary" *coup*, the emergency was not nearly sufficient to justify edicts under Article 14, and he so wrote to Polignac in December.[17] The Left knew, or made, little of Guernon's opposition, having previously branded him an Ultra in its journals because of his November speech against the press. The comte de Montbel, on the other hand, still received slight tokens of appreciation from liberal papers. Montbel's partial state of grace was because of a moderate speech he had made in 1828 about the press.[18] The Cabinet, though still harboring one nonconformist in the front rank, was falling increasingly under the spell of the Polignac-Peyronnet clique when the first elections were held.

---

[13] Viel-Castel, *Histoire*, XX, 441-45.

[14] Lucas-Dubreton, *Restauration*, p. 141.

[15] Comte de Guernon-Ranville, "Les mémoires de Guernon-Ranville", *La Revue Bleue*, No. 33 (14 February, 1874), pp. 793-94. (Hereafter cited as Guernon-Ranville, "Mémoires"). Afterwards the King thanked the Minister for his frankness.

[16] *Ibid.*; see also, Henri Prentout, "Caen en 1830", *Revue d'Histoire Moderne*, VI (March, 1931), 112. Guernon had once edited the *Observateur Neustrien* of Caen.

[17] *Procès des ministres*, I, 78-81, 90, 255-56.

[18] Fernand Giraudeau, *La presse périodique de 1789 à 1867* (Paris, 1867), pp. 55-56.

The republican *Tribune* (July 10) advised that the legitimist lawyer Berryer would replace Guernon-Ranville as head of the University, since Guernon, according to the satirical paper, was "far too liberal for such high responsibilities". Republicans were optimistic about the elections, although quite contemptuous of the "weaker" members of the "221", whom they wished to see defeated, and thus be done with "temporizing". "For the first time in fifteen years", wrote August Fabre, all thirty-two million Frenchmen would stand beside the voters.

Except for the twenty voting colleges whose meetings were arbitrarily postponed, the electors voted on June 23 and 24. The results, to paraphrase the words of the *Globe*, surpassed the liberals "wildest dreams".[19] Only seven of the candidates of the "221" failed, while thirty-eight of the former Ultra deputies were beaten. Of a total of 195 contested seats, 140 went to the opposition![20] And this was the result in the regions where the government had *expected* support; the more urban colleges, whose meetings had been postponed, could only be worse for the Ministry. Even Algiers could not reverse such a trend. The editor of the *Drapeau Blanc* sadly announced the return of 1793. Piqued because of the King's failure to heed his advice and crush the "revolution" months before, Martainville wrote, "Charles X is on the road that his unfortunate brother was forced to follow and at whose end was the scaffold. The electors have voted for the guillotine".[21] Polignac's *l'Universel* feigned nonchalance, and voiced the forlorn hope that the new Chamber would not refuse its accord as had the previous one.[22] The *Gazette de France*, whose godfather, Villèle, may have been secretly gratified by the Polignac rebuff, accurately summarized the futile triumph of the day: "Our troops are victorious in Africa and the royalists go down to defeat in the electoral battle".[23] But the old King was elated by the news from Algiers. On June 19, in a massacre of the Dey's antiquated army, the last troops to ever fight in a foreign land under the *fleur-de-lys* made possible the conquest of Algeria,[24] a legacy to modern Frenchmen of high profits and vast tragedy.

The capture of the *kasba* and the city of Algiers would now be assured. But this great milestone in empire-building was nearly ignored by the opposition. They were too well indoctrinated with the *Temps'* and *National's* false picture of the campaign as a "Wellington" scheme and with the *Globe's* more

---

[19] *Globe*, 25 June, 1830.
[20] Viel-Castel, *Histoire*, XX, 468.
[21] *Drapeau Blanc*, 25 June, 1830.
[22] *l'Universel*, 25 June, 1830.
[23] *Gazette de France*, 26 June, 1830.
[24] Viel-Castel, *Histoire*, XX, 446-50.

valid catechism that it was a bid for prestige by the Cabinet. For evidence of this, it was pointed out that baron d'Haussez, Minister of the Navy and chief planner of the whole combined land and sea operation, was defeated in each of the eight colleges in which he was filed as a candidate for deputy![25] The *Quotidienne*, on July 10, attacked the *National* for its criticism of Bourmont's strategy, and defended the hated general from what it called the "tacticians of the general headquarters" of the *National*.

The electoral victory made a *coup* more imminent. Said the *Temps*:

M. de Polignac, abandoned by everyone, seeks a means of recovery. Everyone cries out against him. "*Be silent!*", he will tell us, in the name of Article 14. This is no fiction: He dreams of censorship. That is a delirium of the disease.[26]

The *Globe's* Rémusat, substituting for Dubois, was another who projected a *coup* against the press. In an article, "Past and Present Hostilities against the Freedom of the Press", he wrote that Polignac could, if he dared, kill the press by ordering his magistrates to suppress "three or four" of the key newspapers of Paris.[27] The "dare", in this case, was on the part of Rémusat.

What was the state of the political press at this late hour in the Restoration? Opposition subscription figures were higher than ever: Over 50,000 if we include the 3000 or more republican issues; while the Ultras, even encompassing eighty purists who bought the *Apostolique*, had less than 20,000 paid circulation. A few papers were not true to these trends: The *National* had not met its costs with only 1590, while *Le Temps* claimed a healthy 4000, but admitted that seven hundred of these were sold on street corners or traded by mail for provincial papers.

The "1688" idea of switching dynasties was certainly established in most papers, excluding the *Débats* and the republican journals. Legal resistance or the Breton Association program was also uniformly praised by liberal editors. The Ultra press, on the other hand, was so split that Polignac had been obliged to purchase a journal to express his opinions, and even in this he appeared defensive. And there was always Villèle to worry about. Genoude and the *Gazette* made a last heroic attempt to induce Villèle to come to Paris. In what the *Temps* called "adventurous negotiations" between Paris and Toulouse,[28] the ex-Minister was urged to save the Monarchy by creating a moderate Cabinet. The interest in this possibility reached as far to the left as the *Débats*; Genoude reporting that Chateaubriand and Louis Bertin

---

[25] *Ibid.*, p. 520.

[26] *Temps*, 3 July, 1830.

[27] *Globe*, 23 June, 1830.

[28] *Temps*, 3 July, 1830. Circulation statistics for May, 1830, are in *Temps*, 28 May, 1830.

had offered a journalistic truce with the *Gazette de France*. Villèle rejected these pleas. With no desire to risk his head, he had shrewdly begun to ingratiate himself with the Duchess of Orleans![29]

But liberal editors were not without problems. One of the most respected, Dubois, was vegetating at Sainte-Pélagie; the humdrum of his easy prison life broken by numerous visits. At one time, there was a *salon* behind bars when Chateaubriand and Mme. Récamier called upon him.[30] Guizot was too occupied with his electoral campaign to devote himself to the *Temps*, but his reelection, this time from Nîmes, was described in triumph on the first page of his paper. Thiers was busy with the *National*, but contrary to early expectations, now heavily in debt. What he had not invested in the newspaper he had loaned to friends with no hope of repayment. In addition, he was plagued by the solicitations of his father, an idler whom he despised.[31]

The courts continued to prosecute press offenses by the Left and to exonerate those by the Right. On July 9, the comte de Madrolle was acquitted on appeal from an earlier conviction for his Ultra brochure, because he "disavowed any intention of guilt"! Brissaud of the *Gazette des Cultes*, however, was returned to prison for his criticism of the Church.[32] The liberal newspapers of Lille and Boulogne were convicted on the old charge of publicizing the Breton Association, but *not* for having suggested refusal of the budget. The new republican *Journal de Paris* was prosecuted for a revolutionary suggestion, and one of its youthful editors, Léon Pillet, was fined two hundred francs.[33] In another trial, whose publicity embarrassed the Ministry, the editor of a journal of caricatures was convicted. One Bellet, publisher of the *Silhouette* was ordered to pay 1000 francs and spend six months in jail for having caricatured Charles X as a Jesuit. In less anxious days, the King, like his late brother, had allowed himself to be caricatured unmercifully.[34] Yet, under the nominally "free" press of the July Monarchy, such penalties were to become commonplace.

The elections did not occur without trouble for the "constitutional"

[29] Villèle, *Mémoires*, to Mme. de Villèle, 5 June, 1830, V, 445 and Genoude to Villèle, 2 July, 1830, V, 456. Chateaubriand's paper had shown no restraint in attacking either Villèle or Polignac since the nomination of Peyronnet. His ambition never faltered, but it is very unlikely he would have served *under* Polignac or in any but a completely reshuffled Cabinet.

[30] Lair, "Le *Globe*", p. 289.

[31] F. Benoît, "M. Thiers a la conquête de Paris, documents inédites 1821-1833", letter of Thiers to Severin Benoît, 10 June, 1830 and to his father, 14 July, 1832, *Le Correspondant*, CCLXXXVII (June, 1922) 813-15. Only five months earlier, Thiers had been quite optimistic over the *National's* finances. Marquant, *Thiers et Cotta*, p. 33.

[32] *Gazette des Tribunaux*, 10, 14 July, 1830.

[33] *Ibid.*, 9 July, 1830.

[34] *Ibid.*, 26 June, 1830.

candidates. In addition to the customary questions of fraud raised by *Aide-toi*, there were cases of violence and slander. The *Universel* charged that the liberal candidate for the Pas-de-Calais was a relative of the late Maximilian Robespierre,[35] a remark passionately denied by the papers which were supporting the "221". Liberal editors were sensitive to this type of criticism, which linked their cause with the radical phase of the Revolution. Constantly seeking to dissociate themselves from the stigma of 1793, they were easily forced to defend themselves from such guilt-by-association charges.

In royalist Montauban, the victorious "221" candidate, baron Preissac, happened to be a Huguenot! The nonvoting populace, goaded by the local clergy, stoned both Preissac and a group of the electors who had seconded him. Polignac's own paper, the *Universel*, made heroes of the mob and declared that Preissac was fortunate to have escaped whole. The townspeop!-, who shouted "Death to Preissac!", said the increasingly reckless *Universel*, represented the true French opinion, not that of the "revolutionary" electors![36] The editor of the *Tribune des Départemens* (July 10) wrote of the *Universel's* reflections on the Preissac affair: "They confuse the people with the assassins of the Midi and the vile mercenaries of the *Congrégation*". Another election incident which horrified the liberal press occurred in Angers, where soldiers prevented two constitutionalist deputies, newly reelected, from participating in a victory parade through the town. The troops also roughed up some of the cheering citizens.[37]

On July 9, the Court received news of the formal surrender of the Dey of Algiers. Royalist editors glorified Charles X and made much of the discovery by the French of the Dey's treasury, sufficient, according to the Ministry, to defray all costs of the war! The price in human life had also been low for the French. About one thousand men were killed, half by disease and half by the Moslems. Ironically, one of the dead was captain Amedée Bourmont, son of the hated Marshal. Here was expiation of a sort, but not enough to repeal the crime of the father![38] Opposition papers still denounced the planners of the war, while cheering the success of the troops. The *Globe's* comment (July 13) typified the Left. It rejoiced in the military victory while pointing to the danger of the domestic crisis. Reporting that houses were illuminated and that children were playing with wooden swords in the streets, the Globists then observed: "Though the police do not oppose

---

[35] *l'Universel*, 4 June, 1830.

[36] *Ibid.*, 2 July, 1830.

[37] De Hauranne, *Histoire*, X, 511.

[38] Viel-Castel, *Histoire*, XX, 492; Bertier de Sauvigny, *Restoration*, p. 439, cites the political advantage of the seizure of the Dey's treasure, worth forty-eight million francs.

these natural displays of joy, it is very unlikely that they would be so tolerant if the election results cause similar demonstrations".

Undoubtedly, the King was encouraged in his domestic plans by these tidings from Africa. Further encouragement came on the following day when a deputation of coal-deliverymen called to congratulate the King, and their leader declared: "Sire, the coal dealer is master in his own house, may you be master in your kingdom". Thiers answered in the *National* (July 11) with a rebuke to the working class in which he denounced the seeming association with reactionary forces. Alienated as the bourgeoisie may have been from the workers; when the revolution came, there was no cause for alarm, except, perhaps, that the workers were *too* revolutionary! *Te Deums* in honor of the Algiers victory were celebrated in all churches. The Archbishop of Paris, whose tact approached that of the *Drapeau Blanc*, urged God to bring quickly to the King "other victories no less sweet".[39] Charles and his associates, however, had begun to crystallize their schemes several days before the victory report reached Paris.

Chantelauze, on June 29, submitted a general plan for a *coup*, employing Article 14 of the Charter. The scheme was similar to that which was later adopted, but had the added precaution of first placing Paris, Lyon, Rouen, and Bordeaux in a state of seige. Guernon-Ranville, the "legal mind", blocked approval and told the King that royal prerogative did not extend to such emergency actions simply because the electors had voted unfavorably.[40] Then, Polignac and Peyronnet, a week later, suggested this compromise: To call a corporative assembly of notables including peers, deputies, magistrates, and ministers, to explain the problems of the Crown. Guernon-Ranville again killed the proposal by arguing that such an unconstitutional body would be far less representative of the nation than the legal Chamber. With naive persistence, Guernon again proposed his own scheme: Wait one year, then call the enemy's bluff by presenting the budget. The Dauphin, a conscientious man, and just perceptive enough to realize that it was really *his* future being risked, took the part of Guernon, and backed his plan as the most legal method of attack.[41]

On the day the news arrived from Algiers, Peyronnet presented the definitive proposal. It consisted of twenty-two articles which would decree the use of Article 14 to abolish the liberty of the press and the electoral law and the nomination of several Ultras to official posts. It also included an odd provision

[39] De Hauranne, *Histoire*, X, 518.

[40] Guernon-Ranville, "Mémoires", pp. 794-95.

[41] *Ibid.* See also, Guernon's testimony at his later trial in December. *Procès des ministres*, I, 78-81, 150-52.

to dissolve the new Chamber of Deputies, which, of course, had yet to be convoked! With very little discussion, all but Guernon assented; even the Dauphin agreeing with some reluctance. Chantelauze was then commissioned to draft a report for the King, to convince him of the necessity to issue the decrees.

Guernon was thus outvoted, but rather than resign, he proposed a novel alternative. His new plan was to enfranchise so many electors as to render France democratic and therefore, he believed, royalist, since the "conservative" peasant and villager would then be able to influence policy. Given a chance, this somewhat tardy suggestion could have made a popular ruler of Charles X, but the Cabinet rejected it as absurd. Guernon-Ranville then quit his role of honest independent and surrendered to the majority will, wryly asking Peyronnet why he did not "replace the twenty-two articles in the edict by a single one like this: 'The deputies of each department will be named by the prefect'".[42] The *coup* was at last on paper.

Late elections, those of Paris and the twenty departments which had been postponed, were held on July 12 and 19. In Paris, the ratio of constitutionalist to Ultra voters was five-to-one. In the total balloting, only 143 Ultras had been elected, and instead of the "221" constitutionalists of the last session, there were now 274 in the opposition.

This liberal avalanche was seriously regarded in Vienna, Brussels, and St. Petersburg, as a major French crisis. Monarchs who had once been so pleased with Charles X for his apostleship of the Congress system, now began to fear his imprudence. The King's Ambassador to Russia, the duc de Mortemart, showed him a letter from Countess Nesselrode, wife of the able Russian diplomat. This lady reported a conversation with Tsar Nicholas in which that Emperor had declared that Charles X would stand alone if he violated the Charter. Charles quickly reassured the Countess that he would not attack the Charter. Prince Metternich, speaking for his Sovereign, issued a similar warning.[43] Were the floundering "Concert of Europe" and the ideal of "legitimacy" to be dashed by the stupidity of one old man and his purblind advisers? The talented architects of 1815 had to admit that possibility, and one of them was even willing to clear the path for such an eventuality. The prince de Talleyrand, who, at this time, was betting on Orleans, wrote to a friend: "We are heading toward an unknown world without a pilot and

---

[42] Guernon-Ranville, "Mémoires", p. 796.

[43] Vaulabelle, *Histoire*, VII, 287. Russia had previously rejected any serious consideration of Polignac's hare-brained diplomatic proposal to restructure Europe. He was being "written off" by European powers. Bertier de Sauvigny, *Restoration*, p. 432.

without a compass: There is but one thing certain, that is that all this will end in a shipwreck".[44]

The captain and his crew could not see the rocks and were deaf to the roar of the coming storm. They sailed blissfully on toward disaster. Equally blind were the editors of some Ultra papers. In their pleadings and their impolitic zeal, they had scarcely reckoned with the possibility of their own annihilation. The volatile editor of the *Drapeau Blanc* argued that the King had a legal right to leave the Chamber in abeyance and simply neglect to call it. This – at a time when liberal journalists were recalling Charles I! For several days before publication of the fateful edicts, Martainville called out for press censorship and urged a new electoral law. The present electoral law, he said, being the source of all schisms in France.[45] On the day before the edicts appeared, Genoude wrote in favor of a new electoral law and a new law of the press to "reestablish royal prerogative".[46] Genoude, at last, realizing the impossibility of a Villèle Ministry, had rallied to the banner of Polignac, as a loyal soldier, but not confident of victory. In May, Joseph Michaud, late of the *Quotidienne*, had left for extended travels in Egypt and the Holy Land. A man of sound historical sense, he remained abroad until well after the July Revolution.[47]

Opposition journalists, after long months of prophecy and propaganda, now saw that the time for decision was at hand. The *Globe* (July 21) used the word "revolt" in describing the electoral victory of the opposition and left no doubt that a further revolt would meet the expected *coup d'état*. Thiers, whose guiding star was still the ambitious Duke of Orleans, wrote in the *National*:

> They say that the press first warned against this encroachment of absolute power. This does not surprise us, because in the movement that has just occurred in France [elections], the press has the honor of ... being the most guilty party. But it will resist; it will, if need be, cause itself to be condemned and will protest with all its resources against a violation of the laws. It has no gendarmes, but it has courage, and it is a force not oppressed with impunity.[48]

So saying, Thiers predicted with reasonable accuracy that the "violation of the laws" would occur within the month.

On Sunday, the twenty-fifth of July, after the King had returned from mass, he summoned the Council of State. Polignac presented a manuscript of the

---

[44] Barante, *Souvenirs*, III, Talleyrand to Barante, 14 June, 1830.

[45] *Drapeau Blanc*, 22, 23, 24 July, 1830.

[46] *Gazette de France*, 26 July, 1830.

[47] Charles A. Sainte-Beuve, *Causeries du lundi* (15 vols.; Paris, 1857-1862), VII, 38.

[48] *National*, 21 July, 1830.

definitive edicts in the form proposed by Peyronnet. Chantelauze then read his "Report to the King", which was intended as justification for those edicts. After long discussions which lasted into the evening, the moment came for the final approval and the signatures. The King dipped his quill, gazed down at the decrees before him and signed his name. Then the sheets were passed around the table and each minister signed in his turn. Charles X looked up gravely and said to his Cabinet: "I am counting on you, gentlemen; you may count on me. Our cause is common. Between us, it is life or death".[49]

That evening François Sauvo, editor of the *Moniteur*, received a request to appear at the home of the Keeper of the Seals at eleven o'clock. Sauvo found Montbel with Chantelauze who handed the *Moniteur's* editor a copy of the decrees for publication in the official journal. Sauvo glanced at the manuscript briefly, gasped, and remarked: "May God save the King! May God save France"! Almost in unison, the two Ministers replied: "We certainly hope so"![50]

[49] Lucas-Dubreton, *Restauration*, p. 142.
[50] *Procès des ministres*, I, 216. This was Sauvo's direct testimony at the trial of the ministers.

CHAPTER XIV

THE JOURNALISTS IN THE *TROIS GLORIEUSES*

The next morning, July 26, the *Moniteur* appeared a bit later than usual. It contained the final decrees of the last King of France and Navarre. The "Report to the King", signed by the ministers, served as a preface. The edicts called for the dissolution of the new Chamber, which was not yet in session; the suppression of the freedom of the periodical press; a radical alteration of the electoral law in behalf of rural landowners; and the appointment of several Ultras to secondary positions and prefectures in the administration.

Each of the edicts was unprecedented in its stringency. The press edict, while leaving books free, applied censorship to pamphlets and booklets. Periodicals and newspapers were not to be censored; their fate was something far less hopeful. All newspapers must henceforth request a preliminary authorization to publish, valid for only three months and always revocable by the government! The press decree could thus effectively destroy the liberal papers while not inconveniencing those of the royalists with such trifles as mere censorship.

The electoral decree was more intricate than the press edict, but its intent seemed similarly destructive, as it could have led to a true provincial oligarchy of the royalist electorate. The generally liberal colleges of the city *arrondissements* were curtailed and their function reduced to the mere nomination of primary candidates, whom the departmental electors were required to use for only one-half of their final slate of candidates. Although the proportion of voters disenfranchised was not great, the arbitrary method implied in the edict seemed to herald the doom of parliamentary government.

It may appear strange that Polignac and Peyronnet hoped to dominate the Chamber by swinging influence to rural constituencies. Although cities were preponderantly liberal, there was no reason to believe that the "conservative" provinces were slightly Ultra, or that they would remain so, especially in view of the successes of provincial opposition newspapers. The Ministry's real power would lie in an even more authoritarian clause, which suppressed the rule making electoral lists inviolable. It also rendered electoral committees such as chapters of *Aide-toi*, illegal. Thus, quietly and behind a facade of representative aristocracy, the King's ministers could prevent any political activity but sheepish submission. The edict called for a new and smaller Chamber, elected under the new law, to meet in the following September. Its purpose would be to rivet the sanction of permanent law onto the July decrees. Such, briefly, was the Council's program for a utopia of Ultras. Even from the perspective of nearly one-and-a-half centuries, the edicts still seem to be what the liberals called them: A revocation of the Charter.

It is not surprising that one of the two pillars of this *coup d'état* was a decree against opposition journalists. Most of the ministers firmly believed that free expression and the printing press were the parents of "atheism" and "democracy". Polignac, the gloomy-visaged dreamer, nevertheless held that the masses would never rise and that the bourgeois class was so engulfed in materialism that political questions bored it.

The "Report to the King" which defended the necessity of the edicts, was chiefly concerned with the free press. This proclamation was edited by Chantelauze and signed by each of the seven ministers.[1] Chantelauze, however, did not attempt to minimize the depth of the opposition as Polignac had done, declaring that it was born *of* the press, and of the electors influenced *by* the press. In unequivocal language, the ministers called the King's notice to the "dangers of the periodical press":

At no period during the past fifteen years had this situation been present under a more grave or unpleasant aspect. Despite a material prosperity which has never been equalled in our annals, the signs of disorganization and symptoms of anarchy are manifested in nearly every part of the kingdom.

This anarchy, the report continued, is caused by "dangerous and subversive doctrines openly expressed". Contradicting Polignac's naive advice, it warned that political passions had "begun to penetrate the foundations of society and to stir the popular masses". Criticizing Anglophiles, the ministers said that certain educated men of good faith, "fascinated by the poorly understood example of a neighboring people", have been able to believe that the advantages of the press would balance the "inequities"; but added, "It has not been thus". Admitting previous censorship laws as failures, Chantelauze said that nothing could resist a "solvent as vigorous as the press".

---

[1] *Le Moniteur*, 26 July, 1830. The report, used later as trial evidence, also appears in *Procès des ministres*, II, 592-97. Bourmont was in Africa with the army, thus avoiding responsibility for the *coup*.

In other portions of the report, the ministers claimed that "agitations" were "almost exclusively produced and excited by the liberty of the press". Although they admitted the Martignac era election law to be "no less pregnant with discord", the statement accused the newspapers as the "principal source of the disease". Another example of the importance of journalism in provoking the edicts was the generalization that at *all* times, the press has been by nature, "only an instrument of disorder and sedition". And again: "The press tends to subjugate sovereignty and usurp the power of the state. Pretended organ of public opinion, it aspires to direct the debates of the two Chambers". This "tyranny", the ministers noted had been especially oppressive during the past two or three years.

Nothing illustrates the enormity of the psychological gulf dividing the Ultras from the Left in 1830 more than the candid and unquestionably sincere ideas voiced in this denunciation of public opinion; for that is what it was in its essential meaning. And yet, it reveals a reactionary mentality far different from that of the modern totalitarian bigot or megalomaniac who simply despises independent ideas. The ministers who signed the report (Polignac gladly and Guernon sadly) seemed always to be pleading for some ideal of free expression, according to old rules that were now being violated by newspapers:

[The journalists'] art consists, not in substituting for a weak submissive spirit a wise freedom of inquiry, but to reduce to questions the most positive truths; not to provoke fresh and useful controversy over political questions, but to present them under a false light and to resolve them by sophisms.

The press has thus thrown disorder into the soundest intelligences, inflamed the firmest convictions, and produced amid society a confusion of principles... It is by anarchy in doctrines that we reach anarchy in the state.

The minister's report attacked the press for its attitudes on the Algiers campaign, for having given secret debarkation information, for "discouraging" the soldiers, and for "causing hatred" toward their general. After appealing to outraged patriotism, the declaration struck at recent judicial decisions by which a few editors had been acquitted. Insinuating broadly that the courts were partial to the Left, the report observed that judges "tired" easily, while the "seditious press is never weary". In addition to the failings of the courts as agents of repression, the ministers reminded the King that, before the prosecutor can indict an editor, the damage has been done, and the "punishment only adds to it by the scandal of debate". At this late hour, the ministers recognized that their zeal to prosecute journalists had become a boomerang.

The official document even rejected the accepted interpretation of Article 8 of the Charter, which stated that "all Frenchmen have a right to write and publish their opinions". This provision, blandly declared the King's advisers, did not apply to newspapers or periodicals, which were simply "commercialized speculation" in opinions!

Near the end of the long bulletin, the King was urged to save the nation by resorting to Article 14 of the Charter. The *coup d'état* had been struck, and the same morning, "Robin Hood" left to chase his deer at Rambouillet, as if nothing of importance was expected to happen.

As crowds gathered about the arcades of the Palais Royal, in the reading halls, and in the cafés to read the *Moniteur*, excitement swept across the great city of nearly a million inhabitants. For several days, Paris had been suffering in intolerable heat,[2] but the natural lethargy created by such weather now gave way quickly to bristling activity. So much activity indeed, during those "Three Glorious Days" of July 27, 28, and 29, that volumes have been filled with eyewitness descriptions and memoirs of the events. Except for the needs of narrative, we detail what is related to the press: The journalists, the journals, and their journalism, in the July Days. This role was a dual one: Propaganda, in their newspapers and broadsides; and participation, in the streets and around conference tables.

Les Trois Glorieuses refer to the three days of revolution starting with Tuesday, July 27, yet the decrees appeared before noon on Monday. One cause for the delay in the outbreak of open resistance is clear. From the Prince de Talleyrand down to the humblest worker, no one could believe that such a bludgeoning of public liberties would be considered unless the King had taken every possible military and police precaution against an uprising. For this reason, on the twenty-sixth, one heard much talk of legal resistance and whether the people should refuse to pay taxes. Liberals of the middle classes were naturally reticent to face muskets or risk their property, without first attempting peaceful methods. When they discovered with what monumental naiveté the government had failed to guard against resistance, their position grew bolder; but among many of this class, the idea persisted of avoiding revolution with a liberalized government under the Bourbons. It is perhaps only attributable to the ignorance of the leaders in the Cabinet and the blind devotion of the rest, that security measures were so uncertain. Guernon-Ranville had recently asked Mangin, Prefect of Police, if popular agitation might endanger the public peace and the policeman had answered: "I cannot understand the motive that causes your interest, but – whatever you

---

[2] During the July Days, the daytime temperature averaged about 90° F, or 32° C.

do, Paris will not rise. Go ahead, I will answer for Paris with my head"![3] The complacency of the military was equally astonishing. Marshal Marmont, commanding the Paris garrisons, assured Polignac that his present forces could meet any exigency.

Marmont may not have understood the nature of the exigency, as he was never privy to Cabinet decisions, but even Polignac must have realized the statistical weakness of his forces. The best part of the Army was still tidying up in Algeria. Training camps at Luneville and Saint-Omer, well over three days march from Paris, had been partly depleted by the dispatch of troops to the Belgian border as an independence revolt against the Dutch seemed imminent. Polignac understood the danger of revolution in Brussels far better than in his own city! At best, Marmont could count on barely 12,000 men in the whole of Seine and Seine-et-Oise departments, including regulars, Swiss, and gendarmes. In addition, several battalions had been sacrificed to police Normandy because of the recent arson in that region. To make the Minister's negligence even more complete, many key royalist officers were also electors who had not yet returned from their constituencies. The only precaution that the Council had taken, then, was in keeping the date and the precise nature of the edicts secret; but the journals had even guessed these with some accuracy.[4]

"Vive le roi! Vive le roi!" the *Drapeau Blanc* crowed in triumph as it reflected the premature joy of many of the Ultras. Martainville proudly signed an article in which he sounded like the archetype of the poor but aristocratic chevalier. Through the "anarchic imprudence" of the newspapers, he wrote, sovereignty had "escaped the hands of the Prince, to pass into the hands of thirty thousand shopkeepers". He denied any violation of the Charter and warned that resistance would be "crushed and punished on the spot". The edicts, he cried from his *Drapeau Blanc*, mark the "dawn of a new era for monarchy. All Europe will applaud this new restoration". As usual, Martainville's rhetoric overcame him. Without realizing the dismal curse in his analogy, he drew a parallel between the edicts and the resistance of Louis XVI to the Third Estate![5] The *Gazette* gamely called the decrees a *coup de Charte* to invest them with a trace of legality.[6] The third spokesman of the Ultras, the *Quotidienne*, was strangely mild and reflective. Laurentie, a man of honest, though reactionary, intelligence, called the *coup* a great political event" of the kind that "changes the situation of empires", but

---

[3] Viel-Castel, *Histoire*, XX, 537.
[4] Roux, *La Restauration*, p. 322, Pinkney, *French Revolution of 1830*, p. 102.
[5] *Drapeau Blanc*, July 27, 1830.
[6] *Gazette de France*, 27 July, 1830.

added grimly: "All that can be said today, is that whatever happens, the Revolution has done it".[7]

The opposition response was swift. For months they had speculated about this reality which was now before them. The deputies around Paris held excited meetings at which little was concluded. There was much talk of legal resistance by refusal of taxes, but still some timid legislators were afraid to even "play the role of Hampden". The press carried the immediate responsibility for action. The *Constitutionnel* spoke bitterly of the "zeal with which hireling writers, pious prelates, and grave counsellors encouraged the Ministry to overthrow the Charter".[8] This newspaper, because it was such a large financial enterprise, and the *Journal des Débats*, because it was both rich and legitimist, did not publish any issues for July 27. Not wishing to resist the decree requiring authorization, they simply failed to appear on the first of the *Trois Glorieuses*. It is perhaps not a great coincidence that these two bourgeois-oriented papers were the largest and most capitalized in France.

Radical elements, on the contrary, eager to coordinate revolutionary action with propaganda, found themselves confronted by a wall of frustration. Delaforest, printer of the republican *Tribune* refused his press except on the condition that Auguste Fabre post a bond of 200,000 francs! The printer did not fear arrest or indictment; under the edicts just announced, he feared the destruction of his costly machine by Mangin's police. Fabre and his friends hustled about the entire journalistic empire of the Right Bank, begging for the assistance of a printer. Hopes were dashed repeatedly: The publisher Jules Didot consented to print a broadside of the *Tribune* and then thought better of it after wasting the editor's precious time; Thiers offered a half-page in the *National*, only to renege later. Heartbroken that his gospel would be unread at the climactic moment, Fabre at last requested a court judgment against his printer in the Commercial Tribunal of de Belleyme, Martignac's former police chief, and Delaforest was ordered to print the newspaper. Two precious days had been wasted and a regular issue did not appear until Friday. The *Révolution* was even less fortunate, its appeals for a government worthy of those who fought for it did not appear until August 3, when an "inclusive" issue was finally printed. The delays were later to become part of the republicans' catalog of grievances against the liberals, whom they felt could have made a more sincere effort to remove these obstacles to free expression at that crucial hour. Their bitter resentment may have been justified,

---

[7] *Quotidienne*, 27 July, 1830.
[8] *Constitutionnel*, 26 July, 1830.

but radicals were not the only journalists who found difficulty in having their papers accepted by printers.[9]

The *Journal de Commerce* and the *Courrier Français* cited their printers for refusing their presses. In the case of the *Journal de Commerce*, Magistrate de Belleyme, judged that the press edict was not effective as it was not yet in the *Bulletin des lois*, but he did not deny its legality. This feeble essay at legal resistance through the courts had no real value; the revolution was nearly over when the decision was given. Magistrate A.-H. Ganneron's verdict for the *Courrier* was more significant, but it also came too late to be of more than academic value. Ganneron ruled the decrees were illegal since they were not for the welfare of the state.[10]

Orleanist militants were more successful with their printing presses. The *National*, the *Globe*, and the *Temps* appeared in defiance of the decrees. In the *Globe*, de Rémusat wrote:

> The crime is consummated. The ministers have advised the King to give the edicts of tyranny. The *Moniteur*, which we reprint here, will acquaint France with its misfortune and its duty ... We call the force of public hatred on Polignac, Peyronnet, Chantelauze, Capelle, Montbel, Guernon-Ranville, and d'Haussez ... We trust the legal defense of our liberty to the bravest nation in the universe. The hour of a new glory has come to France.[11]

This declaration was also printed as a broadside and placarded about the city.[12] The *Temps* intoned: "No more Charter, no more political society... Everyone is agitated, resistance has become the dominant principle, the duty of all citizens". The paper then announced a grave financial crisis and urged all groups of officials to protest at the foot of the throne. The *Temps*, owned largely by deputies, pleaded with the electors not to let themselves become a revolutionary assembly and, fearing mob violence, called upon the defunct National Guard to mobilize immediately.[13]

The first politically-directed resistance of the July Revolution, however, was a defiantly-worded protest by the opposition journalists of Paris. On the afternoon of Monday, the twenty-sixth, four dozen writers from thirteen papers gathered at the law office of the elder Dupin and asked this old dean of advocates and friend of Louis-Philippe what could be their maximum legal resistance. Dupin answered that they must resist all attempts to enforce the decrees, but to get out of *his* office before they signed anything!

---

[9] Fabre, *Révolution*, I, 122-26.
[10] *Gazette des Tribunaux*, 26-31 July, 1830 (inclusive issue).
[11] *Globe*, 27 July, 1830.
[12] Hatin, *Histoire de la presse*, VIII, 507.
[13] *Temps*, 28 July, 1830.

Adolpe Thiers took this opportunity to invite the entire gathering to his editorial office at No. 10, rue Neuve-Saint-Marc. There, assisted by Cauchois-Lemaire of the *Constitutionnel* and Chatelain of the *Courrier*, he composed a bold attack on the press edict and the *coup d'état*.[14] This manifesto employed the same arguments against the use of Article 14 which had been given before. At one point in the proclamation, the journalists announced: "Thus today the government has violated legality. We are called to obey. We are going to publish our papers without asking for the authorization which is imposed upon us". Here, at last, was a promise of physical defiance, something far more significant than criticism. The threat, however, was too strong for the representative of the *Débats* and a few writers from the *Constitutionnel*, who left the meeting. Some of the others suggested that the declaration be published without signatures, as a general protest of journalists. Thiers, backed by the republicans and his own Orleanist colleagues, argued successfully for individual signatures. Forty-four editors and managers signed, and listed the names of the papers they represented. It was, in one sense, an editorial of the *National*, but as other papers published it that next morning, and because so many had signed it, it became the first revolutionary resistance to the regime, to be known as the "Protest of the Forty-Four". It was entirely the work of journalists.

Jean Henri Mangin, Prefect of Police, promptly issued forty-four warrants of arrest. His files, strangely enough, had no record of the writers' home addresses and by Wednesday many of the forty-four, including Thiers, had gone into hiding! Not one of the protesting writers was arrested before the revolution had carried the day. Mangin failed to live up to his satanic reputation.

Mangin's order to enforce the press edict was issued at five o'clock on Monday, the twenty-sixth of July. The *cabinets de lecture* were ordered closed. These small reading rooms, where the *Moniteur* and other papers were usually posted, provided their patrons with coffee, tea, or brandy as they read the papers of watched the passing parade. On Monday evening,

---

[14] *National*, 27 July, 1830. The text of this manifesto may be found in Appendix B. The journalists who signed the protest were:

For the *National*: Gauja, Thiers, Mignet, Carrel, Chambolle, Peysse, Albert Stapfer, Dubochet, Rolle; for the *Globe*: Leroux, de Guizard, Dejean, Ch. de Rémusat; for the *Courrier des Electeurs*: Sarrans; for the *Courrier Français*: Chatelain, Lapelouze, Guyet, Mousset, Avenel, Alexis de Jussieu, J.F. Dupont; for the *Tribune des Départmens*: Auguste Fabre, Ader; for the *Constitutionnel*: Année, Cauchois-Lemaire; for the *Temps*: Coste, Senty, Haussman, Dussard, Buzoni, Barbaroux, Chalas, Billiard, J.-J. Baude; for *La Révolution*: Levasseur, Plagnol, Fazy; for the *Journal de Commerce*: Bert, Larréguy; for the *Figaro*: Bohain, Roqueplan; for the *Journal de Paris*: Léon Pillet; for the *Sylphe*: Vaillant; and independently signed: Évariste Dumoulin.

Mangin's police made their first assault, under the new decrees, on a *cabinet de lecture* in the Palais Royal. The owner, one who had refused to close his establishment, was an eccentric old Ultra, the marquis de Chabannes. He published the *Régénérateur*, a periodical of doggerel which few read and no one took seriously. The Ministry's recent rejection of his offered services had converted him into a bitter foe of the Polignac regime, and raised his establishment to a novel popularity. At the moment when the police made their descent, his room was filled with citizens engrossed in one of his impassioned philippics against Peyronnet. The police were refused entrance and when they resorted to force, the marquis de Chabannes rallied his customers for battle. Eyes ablaze, the nobleman led a counterattack which drove the police from the arcades under a shower of missles.[15] Although not the usual revolutionary type, the old man became a sort of folk-hero among the petty shopkeepers in the Palais Royal. One resident of that building was not present to witness the tumult: The Duke of Orleans had wisely left for his private house in the suburb of Neuilly, there quietly to await what he expected would be important overtures.

A more serious episode in the journalists' insurrection took place the next morning, Tuesday, July 27, in the nearby rue de Richelieu. At 11:30, agents of the regime arrived at the office of the *Temps*, which had defied the edicts by publishing without authorization. Armed and led by a man wearing a magistrate's scarf, they were met at the door by Coste, a wealthy manager of the newspaper and one of the editors, Jean-Jacques Baude.[16] Baude told the magistrate that he had to be an imposter, as a magistrate only acts within the law. Refusing to open the heavy lock on the door to the pressroom, Baude faced the agents in the street and recited from the penal code, a copy of which he held in his hand, warning the officers that they were about to commit a breaking-and-entering theft, punishable by a prison term at hard labor. A huge crowd gathered around him and people hurried from the nearby shops and bistros to discover the source of the commotion. They cheered the editors, armed only with the law, and hurled insults at the disconcerted official and his gendarmes.[17]

As the argument wore on, the editors took pity on the officers who had not eaten that day, and brought them some refreshment. This kindness, Baude later remarked, was because the gendarmes had remained quiet and dignified

---

[15] Alphonse Perrot, *Rélation historique des journées mémorables des 27, 28, 29, Juillet, 1830* (Paris, 1830), pp. 36-40. (Hereafter cited as Perrot, *Rélation*.) Also see, François Rossignol and Jehan Pharaon, *Histoire de la révolution de 1830 et des nouvelles barricades* (Paris, 1830), pp. 65-66. (Hereafter cited as Rossignol, *Histoire*).

[16] Viel-Castel, *Histoire*, XX, 573-74.

[17] Lamartine, *Restoration*, IV, 428-29.

during an unpleasant task. Baude described the rest of the affair for the next day's *Temps:*

> Seven hours were consumed by these agents of violence in trying all methods to penetrate our premises. How well had the working class learned to expect the magistrates to respect the law, One of them, M. Pein, master locksmith, having read the article in the code, refused to aid in the breaking in, which a man garbed in a magistrate's scarf ordered him to do ... A second, from the Godot workshop, but with the same courage ... legally resisted all kinds of attempts for two hours to seduce or intimidate him. At last they could not find a worker in the whole quarter who wanted to ... be accomplice to a crime.[18]

It was clear that the officers hoped to enforce the edicts with a minimum of destruction. Finally, that evening, police agents located someone who agreed to break the lock of the press door, but he turned out to be an employee of the police, whose job was to rivet the leg irons on convicts! This disadvantageous fact was immediately made known to the partisan audience in the rue de Richelieu and later to all the readers of opposition newspapers. Baude called the picklock a "worthy symbol of the treatment that the rebels of July 26 visit on citizens". The door was finally opened and part of the press was dismantled, but it was not smashed. The editors carefully took inventory of everything removed. Baude wrote. "We acted as if they were mere criminals robbing us".[19] Soon after Coste and Baude had formally escalated the July Revolution by opposing an illegal seizure, the *National* received callers. Thiers had fled to the home of a friend after the "Protest of the Forty-Four" had been signed, but Carrel, Mignet, and Gauja, the new director, were present when the police arrived. With the same tactics that were used by the *Temps*, the editors made the law their only weapon. Gendarmes broke down the door to the *National's* pressroom and removed a few parts from the machine.[20] But thanks to wise precautionary measures, both the *National* and the *Temps* had their presses turning a few hours after the police had left![21]

These disturbances had a decisive effect on public inertia. They dramatized the idea of resistance before a huge audience, and they packed the narrow streets with turbulent crowds of exited Parisians. From the Palais Royal to the *Opéra Comique*, and from the Vendôme to the Bibliothèque Royale, the old Jacobin heart of Paris was now swelling with all classes

---

[18] *Temps*, 28 Juiy, 1830. The best account of the entire incident.
[19] *Temps*, 28 July. 1830.
[20] Viel-Castel, *His.   .*, XX, 572.
[21] Vaulabelle, *Histoire*, VII, 326-27.

of people, certain workshops and factories having closed. On Monday evening, the great financiers who drank at fashionable Tortoni's on the Boulevard des Italiens, had discussed the sudden drop in the 3 percent bonds. With the Bourse quotations unfavorable, and the new electoral edict hostile to their class, these men of great wealth had become suddenly "patriotic" and agreed upon a device which had been used at the time of French intervention in Spain: To discharge their workers (this time with wages) and close down their factories, blaming the action on the danger from unstable government. On Tuesday, baron Ternaux, a great industrialist and a deputy, sent his army of textile workers into the streets with eight days advance in pay.[22] In regard to the millionaire Ternaux, it may be added that he was one of the "221", a philanthropist, and, unlike many of his ilk, an advocate of the new humanitarianism. The great book printers and many of the commercial publishing firms also laid off workers. This action was decided at a meeting of publishers at the café Rotonde, at which Felix Barthe presided.[23] The reason given, real or pretended, for this lockout with pay was that the edicts had destroyed the printing industry, which Lamartine had estimated employed over 30,000 men in Paris alone.[24] Baron Capelle, the new Minister of Public Works, argued in the Council for the employment of these workers by the Royal Press, but his plan was not accepted.[25]

Scattered through the crowds and fanning the coals of revolt were hundreds of students from the Sorbonne, the Polytechnique, and the Hôtel-Dieu. As in so many revolutions, youth joined in eagerly, partly as a result of education and idealism and partly from a love of daring and excitement. Guernon-Ranville, as Minister of Public Instruction and Administrator of the University, had placarded near the college, an old law forbidding students to participate in political demonstrations upon pain of expulsion. But the students, unheeding, crossed the Seine and lent their zeal to the crowds.

In the middle of that first afternoon, about thirty deputies who were aware of the growing popular enthusiasm and afraid of the direction it might take, convened at the home of Casimir Périer. For all his parliamentary bluster, the "Lion of the Tribune" turned out to be a mouse. Casimir Périer not only dreaded damage to his property from the crowd of shouting people

---

[22] David Turnbull, *The French Revolution of 1830* (London, 1830), p. 51. (Hereafter cited as Turnbull, *Revolution*).

[23] Roux, *Restauration*, p. 320.

[24] Lamartine, *Restoration*, IV, 423. According to Professor Pinkney, printers were the only skilled group directly injured by the edicts but they were active in propaganda among other workers in crafts. See David H. Pinkney, "The Crowd in the French Revolution of 1830", *American Historical Review*, LXX, No. 1 October 1964), 1-17, hereafter cited as Pinkney, *Crowd.* See also Pinkney, *The French Revolution of 1830* (Princeton, 1972), 259-261.

[25] Roux, *Restauration*, p. 321.

who gathered outside, but he was also agonizing over the ideology they espoused: Périer's company paid low wages and made high profits. Laffitte, who had urged only peaceful resistance, was still satisfied with the direction of events. He had spent all Monday afternoon in his magnificent palace at Maisons, convincing himself of the timeliness of the Orleans solution and reassuring himself that the Duke had always been a republican at heart.[26] The caucus at Périer's came to no conclusion except that all agreed they wanted to avoid a democratic mob in arms. It is worth noting that this same fear also motivated Polignac's demand to King Charles to place Paris under martial law!

Still another caucus, or parliamentary rump, met at Gassicourt's pharmacy that day, where the deputies resolved to implement the Breton Association tax refusal scheme at the *arrondissement* level and also to mobilize the National Guard under Lafayette without a royal order. By then, the latter suggestion was unnecessary as guards in uniform and with muskets were starting to appear in public and to muster themselves under officers. The Deputies were all running around in circles that Tuesday; a shooting war had not really begun; and the first, and least violent, of the Three Glorious Days belonged to the Journalists of Paris.

On this first day, the milling crowd of irregulars from across the river and the poor suburbs could not be called an insurrection. It was angry but not armed. The popular outpouring included a great proportion of craftsmen and skilled workers, who although employed, nursed old grievances against the Monarchy and feelings of republicanism dating back to 1789. Hundreds of students from all the faculties also took the streets along with young professional men, firemen, artists, and a large and most useful contingent of retired soldiers whose dream of past glory now contrasted with their reduced status and pension.[27]

Some of these partisans had long since received their orders and secret instructions for the tasks ahead by "Friends of Truth", the University-centered clandestine club, whose overt activity was republican journalism. For six months, Fabre, along with his colleagues Morhéry, Sempoil, and a clever organizer appropriately named Danton, had been sounding out opinion among all disaffected classes. In close association with the other republican factions

---

[26] Laffitte, *Mémoires*, pp. 146-49; see also, Vincent W. Beach, "The Fall of Charles X", *University of Colorado Studies* (November, 1961), p. 33.

[27] Pinkney's studies of records of those compensated for losses in combat in 1830 reveal a very high representation among skilled craftsmen such as joiners and cabinetmakers: Neither a very depressed nor an oppressed class, they nevertheless felt threatened and alienated by the Bourbons: (Pinkney, *Crowd*, p. 4). Pinkney, *French Revolution of 1830*, 269-271, discounts military claims of students as leaders and stresses the role of ex-soldiers. George Rudé, *The Crowd in History* (New York, 1964), p. 165 also testifies to this artisan preponderance.

under Cavaignac, Bastide, and Raspail, they even made tentative political programs. They also approached several sympathetic generals, who, according to Morhéry, merely offered the vaguest promises. Only Lafayette was steadfastly behind the Fabre group which flattered his vanity in exchange for the prestige of his moral support. Danton and his comrades not only succeeded in building secret cadres among artisan and student groups, but in providing many with weapons. Doubtless exaggerating the importance of his role, Danton boasted that 30,000 of these citizens had been prepared for combat before July. Fabre's stated tactics seem startlingly "Maoist": To avoid the direct encounter with regular troops, but to employ his guerillas to disrupt and demoralize soldiers and urge them to defect to the revolution. His best marksmen, he assigned as snipers high above the narrow streets.

Tuesday was the last day for "legal" resistance. The following two days, in terms of sacrifice and courage, would belong to the common people of Paris. But all classes would at least contribute their energies and talents to what, for the moment, was the cause of all. We see a rather bourgeois version of this ideal of revolutionary unity in Delacroix's famous painting, but we do not see there that the reward for such heroics would soon be stolen by other men.

During the still predawn hours, organizers quietly went among the working-class streets of the Faubourg Saint-Marceau, where alone they claimed "five or six thousand" volunteers. Thousands of cobbles were pried up and piled in carts and baskets. By dawn, the motley force with its primitive arsenal had traversed the long narrow streets to reach the Seine and begun to throw up its barricades and place supplies of missles on the high rooftops. Some of these temporary fortresses were built around the University and the Quais, but most of them were concentrated in the short constricted alleys on the Right Bank; nearly fifty barricades in that densely-peopled quadrangle bordered by the Vendôme and the Palais Royal at the ends and the rue de Rivoli and the Petits-Champs along the sides. Parisians watched from their windows, but neither police nor soldiers intervened in the face of such a crowd. By clear day, the insurgents were in prepared positions on roofs and behind their little forts, their officers ready to give orders. Fabre claimed only to be the second in command; their general, he asserted, was Lafayette. But at that moment, the "Hero of Two Worlds" was not available to his army: He had discreetly left for the suburbs.[28]

Wednesday, the twenty-eighth of July, produced extremely hot weather. The crowds gathered quickly as merchants closed their grills and shutters.

---

[28] Fabre, *Révolution*, I, lxvii-lxviii, lxxxiv, 126-30.

Many shops which sold muskets, pistols, and fowling guns were forced open, their helpless owners resigned to the costly task of arming the citizenry on credit. Etienne Arago, republican journalist and theatre director, armed his group of actors. The Left deputy, Audry de Puyraveau, is said to have distributed hundreds of muskets which he had been hiding in his carriage depot.[29] Beyond the theft of some weapons, however, the Revolution of 1830 was remarkable for the absence of looting and for the self-discipline of the crowds. In the hot, early hours, a small organized band occupied the Hôtel de Ville and ran out the symbol which, after fifteen years, stirred Frenchmen's hearts: The tricolor! Later, as the great bells rang, other adventurers hoisted the national flag on the towers of Notre Dame.[30] The tricolor removed the monopoly of resistance from the hands of partisans and helped to nationalize the insurrection.

Out at Saint-Cloud, a complacent King was informed of these events when General Marmont, in words reminiscent of 1789, sent him this message: "This is no longer a disturbance, this is a revolution... It is urgent that your Majesty take means of pacification. The honor of the Crown can yet be saved, but perhaps tomorrow it will be too late".[31] Charles then consented to declare Paris in a state of siege, which meant that gendarmes or soldiers could shoot citizens who disobeyed orders.

Marmont decided to send four columns through the rectangular area of the barricades. This, he knew, was to be a "war of chamber pots", for the citizens on the rooftops over the narrow streets, were armed with all that was hard and deadly. Marmont deployed but a single battalion to the Panthéon, scene of student uprisings, and concentrated on the barricaded area of the Right Bank. One column was to retake the Hôtel de Ville. A second and third were to encircle the defended streets between the outer boulevards and the Seine. A fourth column was wasted in sniper skirmishes in the Champs Elysées and the rue Royale. Those remaining columns whose task was to tighten the ring on the insurgents received most of the chamber pots, as well as paving stones, and deadly bullets. In the infernal heat, the royal troops wore full packs, woolen tunics, and heavy shakos. To their added discomfort, Marmont had been unable to supply them with wine or bread! One of these columns was forced to flee across the Seine and then recross to seek refuge in the Tuileries. Another column fared as badly and was pinned down and isolated by the rebels. These troops were finally able to

---

[29] Perrot, *Rélation*, pp. 48-49.

[30] De Hauranne, *Histoire*, X, 561.

[31] This letter appeared as evidence at the later trial of the ministers. *Procès des ministres*, I, 172.

break out of their trap and, escorted by a detachment of Swiss, to struggle back to the safety of the Tuileries. The barricades had held. Royal guards and regulars, though in a strong position in the palaces and the Place Vendôme, were nearly prisoners in their own fortresses. To strengthen the defense of the Tuileries and the Louvre, the Hôtel de Ville had to be all but abandoned during the night.[32]

The deputies met three times that day. At Audry de Puyraveau's, Lafayette appeared for the first time since the edicts had been posted, and François Mauguin urged the establishment of a provisional government: A "municipal commission" for Paris, with no national jurisdiction, was all that was agreed upon, but even this suggestion horrified the now frightened Casimir Périer. At this noon meeting, Guizot, who had hurried back to Paris to shout about "legal resistance" and try to prevent a republic, helped to draft a protest to the King. Under a flag of truce, a delegation was to be sent over to the Tuileries to approach Marmont and the ministers who were there about a cease-fire. This delegation consisted of Périer, Laffitte, Lobau, Mauguin, and Gérard. Lafayette, too notoriously republican to go along, urged the committee to remind Polignac that they spoke for the "sovereign people" and to warn him of his peril. It was the only real act of daring for some of these gentlemen during the revolution; Périer was very afraid that they would be arrested or shot on the spot. But Jacques Laffitte later ridiculed his trembling colleagues, claiming that, as they had walked toward the palace, he could not hear the "whine of a single bullet", and Marmont, who relayed Polignac's responses back from the council chamber where the ministers were gathered, was very cordial. Polignac fielded the responsibility for decision to the King; only the King could agree to withdraw the edicts, only the King could order a truce. But Polignac was willing to forget his "duty" in at least one area: He had just received eight arrest warrants when the deputies arrived. These included two of the envoys, Laffitte and Mauguin, as well as Lafayette and Puyraveau. In a gesture which Laffitte recalls as the mark of a man, who, though a "fanatic", bore a spirit of "honor and delicacy", Polignac threw all eight of the warrants into the fireplace.

Marmont told the delegates how deeply he resented his present duty and promised to forward their protest to Saint-Cloud. But Marmont's messenger was delayed after he reached Saint-Cloud and his return message was merely an order for Marmont to continue fighting; in other words, a rejection.[33]

[32] Vaulabelle, *Histoire*, VII, 362.

[33] Laffitte, *Mémoires*, pp. 150-56; see also, *Procès des ministres*, I, 392-93; II, 107-8. Various testimonies at Polignac's trial confirmed his courtesy, as well as the breakdown in the chain of command from Saint-Cloud, to the Tuileries, to the military itself.

Without waiting for the royal response, fourteen deputies reconvened, and further escalated the revolution by reediting Guizot's protest to omit the formal pledge of loyalty to Charles X. These gentlemen, pushing now toward the Orleans solution, and having so far risked nothing themselves, at this moment began to "assume" the revolution already in progress.

At a later meeting, it was determined that negotiations were essential in the face of an obvious military stalemate.[34] Armand Carrel, as a soldier, had voiced this same opinion earlier in the day. The opposition felt gloomy and depressed; still dreading a radical direction and dismayed that so few regulars had yet come over to their side, rather than fire on the people. There were also vivid memories of fresh corpses from the barricades, that republicans had paraded about the streets. Even the fighting youths, who, for the first time in most of their lives, were engaged in a deadly war, were sobered and saddened by the sudden reality.

The second of the *Trois Glorieuses* had demanded a bloody payment, but it had given the insurgents the key to victory. The Hôtel de Ville was theirs for the taking; the royal army, though intact, was actually under siege; and, even more important, the masses had proved they would fight. No one heeded the Prefect of Police when he issued placards ordering citizens not to assemble in crowds, because of the presence of a "great number of brigands in the capital".[35] The royal artillery had also proved virtually useless. One of the exasperated officers asked Marmont, "What can cannon do against paving stones and furniture that fall on the heads of our soldiers from every window"?[36]

That same afternoon, a friend of Marmont, the scientist Dominique Arago went to the Tuileries under another flag of truce with an unsuccessful appeal for a cease-fire. He was amazed to find there several royalist editors, including nearly the entire staff of the *Quotidienne*.[37] These writers had seen the specter of defeat and the *Quotidienne* for the twenty-eighth reflected this feeling. On Tuesday it had said "The Revolution is beaten today". Now, on this Wednesday, the *Quotidienne* was simply amazed: "The Revolutionary party would raise the populace, arm citizens, and finally renew the saturnalia of '93". Perturbed over the "popular front" of their enemies, the editors wrote: "How astonishing! Wealthy men, bankers, industrialists, who, as politicians belong in their countinghouses, do not hesitate to play on popular passions". How wrong had been Polignac's assurances that the "miser"

[34] De Hauranne, *Histoire*, X, 579.
[35] Turnbull, *Revolution*, p. 111.
[36] Vaulabelle, *Histoire*, III, 365.
[37] *Ibid.*

bourgeoisie would never close ranks with the "people"! But the *Quotidienne* had seen the error too late.

The *Gazette* was extremely cautious.[38] Its editor took no note of the bloodshed of the day and undertook a legal defense of the July edicts. "In the circumstances in which we find ourselves", wrote Genoude, "the language of wisdom is necessary for organs of publicity, as soon as passions are excited the voice of calm reason must make itself heard". The *Gazette* even ventured so far toward moderation as to declare that the government would soon "rediscover" the "necessities of representative forms". Here, Genoude was either trimming or he was leaving a door through which Villèle might return to the rescue of Charles X and the dynasty.

The *Drapeau Blanc* published a night edition on Wednesday. Avoiding any mention of the day's street fighting, Martainville boasted about the King's action and blamed liberal editors for starting the revolution. He also gloated that the press edict would henceforth prevent the appearance of all the liberal papers, which he zealously enumerated, with the *National* at the top of the list.[39] This was the swan song of bellicose Alphonse de Martainville and his feverish *Drapeau Blanc*. A month later, in the agony of seeing the collapse of all he had lived for, the white haired Quixote of Ultra editors was felled by a stroke.[40] The *Drapeau Blanc* expired with him; partly from bankruptcy, partly from irrelevance, but mainly because it was so much his personal creation. He had been a plumed knight in an age when men wore trousers and waistcoats and even rode on steam-powered machines. He had been ridiculed for his fanatical royalism and baroque intemperance, but it is not likely that many of his fellow journalists despised him.

Opposition papers appeared in several editions. Such news as was being made would certainly heve staled in the twenty-four hours between ordinary issues. Editors played a role similar to that of modern on-the-scene reporters, wandering about the embattled areas of Paris and observing the details of the struggle. Darmaing, the lawyer who edited the *Gazette des Tribunaux*, gave a remarkable performance as a roving reporter, and many of the more credible "human interest" stories of the July Days come from his pen. He recounted the tale of a young butcher's apprentice who, upon seeing a young woman shot, angrily carried her body before the royal soldiery, shouting "This is the way you treat women"! Darmaing also praised the justice of certain journalists

---

[38] *Gazette de France*, 28 July, 1830.

[39] *Drapeau Blanc*, 28 July, 1830.

[40] Hatin, *Histoire de la presse*, VIII, 494. Hatin, however, errs on his death date, which was August 27.

who interceded on behalf of some royalists at the Bourse, sparing them from a possible lynching.[41]

The *Constitutionnel* delayed publication until the thirtieth and then hypocritically declared that only "physical force" had prevented an earlier issue. The *Globe*, *National*, and *Temps* appeared as frequently as possible, not always in a standard form. The republican side was denied a press until Friday and seethed in its growing bitterness and frustration. The *Globe* issue of midnight on the twenty-ninth was only a five inch handbill. The morning issue of the twenty-eighth spoke eloquently of the "corpses carried by the people" and called for a communal government "both energetic and moderate" to preserve order. The editors then reminded their readers of the difficulty in circulating the *Globe* and hoped that they all would severely judge the "odious acts" of the Ministry.[42]

In spite of the crackling gunfire, sections of Paris were undisturbed. The fighting was still confined largely to the Right Bank. Nearly all of the threatres closed, but a few spectators attended the Luxembourg theatre that evening, where the play was named "The Day of Events"! With the army confined around the Louvre and the Tuileries, some Parisians were able to sleep soundly, although people's guards were posted on the barricades.

Before daybreak on Thursday, the twenty-ninth of July, the barricades were again manned in full strength. One of the most gifted of the amateur engineers who arranged these walls of furniture and wagons was Théophile Feburier, a young writer for the *Temps*.[43] Under such inventive leaders, those ramparts previously breached were quickly repaired by lantern light. Another of the rebels' nocturnal actions had been the liberation of political prisoners. In their enthusiasm to reenact the storming of the Bastille, these patriots released a great number of convicts who perhaps scarcely deserved a pardon. A botanist named Plée escorted an escaped thief back to his quarters at Sainte-Pélagie and exchanged him for Magallon of the *Album*. Plée was praised in the bourgeois press as an example of the responsible revolutionary; proof positive that the horrors of 1792 were impossible in this more sophisticated year.[44] Paul Dubois of the *Globe* was also set free in time for him to witness the action of that final "Glorious Day". Out at Poissy, a band opened the prison without resistance and Fontan walked out into the new day. Unfortunately, we have no corroborating evidence that his hair had turned white from his months in jail.

---

[41] *Gazette des Tribunaux*, 26-31 July 1830.
[42] *Globe*, 27 July, "in the night", 1830.
[43] Rossignol, *Histoire*, p. 319.
[44] *Ibid.*, p. 292.

Not long after the blazing sun had risen, insurgents captured the Hôtel de Ville from the small holding force that Marmont had left behind. Royal regiments now controlled only the Louvre, the Tuileries, part of the Palais Royal, and the Place Vendôme on the Right Bank; and the Panthéon and the Caserne Babylone on the Left Bank. Only the rather unlikely arrival of fresh regulars could break this tense balance of forces. Marmont's strategy was easily discerned: He hoped to hold his positions until reinforcements marched from Luneville, Normandy, and the Belgian frontier, perhaps a matter of three days. The rebels' task was equally clear: To break these royal strong points and rout their garrisons as quickly as possible. Insurgent leaders, now nearly all republicans, including Fabre, Bastide, and Cavaignac, realized that the day's combat would be the most cruel, and yet the most decisive, of the revolution.

Marshal Marmont, hoping to stall the rebels and also, as a discredited apostate of 1814, to announce his distaste for the butchery that duty imposed upon him, had the *Moniteur* print a proclamation which soldiers with white flags managed to post on the walls:

"Parisians:
  Yesterday caused many tears to fall and even more blood to be spilled. In the name of humanity I consent to suspend hostilities in the hope that good citizens will retire to their homes and resume their business; I urge them to make haste.
                                    H.Q. of Paris, 29 July, 1830,
                                    Marshal, Duke of Ragusa".[45]

A day earlier, this could have made a critical difference. But now, as an answer to the offer of clemency, Parisians attacked the Tuileries in force. While marksmen covered the windows from the gardens, waves of insurgents rushed at the main entrances of the palace. It was a costly battle, reminiscent of that terrible August tenth, thirty-eight years before. Before the palace was entered, its gardens were littered with dead. Among those corpses was that of a doctor, Georges Farcy, who had been a rising young writer for the *Globe*. He died in the arms of another physician-journalist, Dr. Jules Loyson, who had helped to treat nearly three hundred wounded at the Hôtel de Ville and Palais Royal.[46] Dubois published his epitaph: "The *Globe* has just paid a debt to the nation in blood".[47] Another journalist who was distinguished in the assault on the Tuileries was Gauja, who had replaced Sautelet on the *National*. He was in the first group of fifty men to enter the Tuileries and

[45] Perrot, *Rélation*, p. 61.
[46] *Globe*, 31 July, 1830; Perrot, *Rélation*, p. 116.
[47] *Globe*, 31 July, 1830.

force the retreat of the garrison.[48] Some Orleanists and liberals fought as comrades with republicans on this final day of combat.

Soon after this victory, someone broke the lock on the iron grill which fenced the Tuileries gardens from the Louvre, but the battle for the Louvre was of short duration. Newspapers had printed a broadside addressed to the soldiers, in which they were called "heroes, not assassins" and were urged to desert the "criminal" Ministry which had ordered them to duty over the "corpses of their parents". Whether from such propaganda or from their growing hunger and thirst, the cohesion of the royal line regiments suddenly fell to pieces. The bulk of the troops at the Louvre and Tuileries refused to fire on their compatriots and deserted the lily banner for the tricolor. Very few officers had enough folly or courage to try to thwart such mutinies. Two entire line regiments, the fifty-third and the fifth, went over to the people. Several officers, royalist and titled, also surrendered. The attitude of many was contained in the resignation of comte Latour-du-Pin, who wrote to Polignac:

"My lord:
After a day of massacre and disaster, an enterprise against all divine and human laws, and in which I have not participated except by a human respect for which I reproach myself, my conscience strongly forbids me to serve a moment longer".[49]

Those defenders who did not defect, escaped by the quais and soon their entire force was in full retreat up the Champs Elysées. They made one holding stand at the Pont de Neuilly and then fled for Saint-Cloud where the Royal Family was trying to pretend that all was not lost. Back at the Louvre, crowds flooded the corridors in jubilation, embracing and giving wine to the soldiers who had joined their cause and yelling *Vive la Charte!* and *Mort au Polignac!* A few cries of *Vive l'empereur!* and *Vive Napoléon-deux!* were heard in the tumult, but there were many discontented old sergeants and half-pay majors in the throng and such cries were now merely a part of their tradi-tion.[50] Still, no one had mentioned the name of Louis-Philippe in shouted or printed proclamations.

Meanwhile, on the other side of the Seine, a group, including Polytechnic and medical students, some of whom worked for republican journals, seized the Panthéon artillery and captured the garrison established there.[51] Now, the only regulars who held part of Paris were the three hundred Swiss

[48] Rossignol, *Histoire*, p. 310.
[49] Perrot, *Rélation*, p. 80.
[50] Turnbull, *Revolution*, pp. 112-13.
[51] *Globe*, 29 July, midnight, 1830.

mercenaries at the Caserne Babylone. They resisted the revolution because it was their paid duty and their tradition. Stateless and unloved, as in 1792, they displayed such bravery that even their enemies paid them honor. In the next day's attack against the Swiss, led by Auguste Fabre's sickly brother, Victorin, some workers and students fell; among them a Fabrist writer named Ader whose brother was a co-editor of the *Tribune des Départemens* and one of the "Forty-Four".[52] The Babylone attack was a dubious strategy as the Swiss could perhaps have been pinned inside their own barracks without such a waste of lives. But the rebels, by mopping up the Left Bank, made their "victory" more thorough. Just before the assault, Victorin gave his troops the Rousseauian order of the day: "Be humane; that is your first duty"![53]

Some of the printing workers who had been locked out, were among the more active revolutionaries during the July Days. One, Feytaud, maimed several Swiss by dropping rocks from a high window. In another case, however, a gang of printers and typesetters supported the July Revolution while they opposed the Industrial Revolution. Only the quick thinking of a bystander prevented them from smashing the new English mechanical press at the firm of Duverger![54]

If English machines and Prime Ministers were suspect in France, English visitors certainly were not, at least during the July Days. The Whigs, the Tories, the *Times*, the new King "Billy", and even Wellington himself, all promptly agreed that Charles X was receiving his just desserts. Liberal newspapers heaped lavish praise on the large British colony of Paris, a few of whom fought with the people. British physicians tirelessly treated the wounded[55] and other Englishmen helped operate the ambulance service which had been established at the office of the *Journal du Commerce*. American tourists and students also participated generously in the revolution.[56]

The twenty-ninth of July was distinguished for the military victory of the united people of Paris, but it was also a day of political intrigues. The patriots in the streets were intent on revolution; few then asked themselves: "What next"?

While workers, students, shopkeepers, and even some journalists were risking their lives, politicians were mounting enough courage to usurp the city government. A large convention of deputies met at the town house of

[52] Rossignol, *Histoire*, p. 311.
[53] Fabre, *Révolution*, I, xi.
[54] Rossignol, *Histoire*, pp. 294, 323.
[55] *Constitutionnel, Globe*, 1 August, 1830.
[56] Rossignol, *Histoire*, p. 369.

Jacques Laffitte. Before their meeting began, soldiers from the fifty-third regiment entered the courtyard of Laffitte's residence and were given a huge ration of wine. At the sight of the bayonets, some of the deputies were seized with fright, but after two hours they were at last reassured that the fifty-third had joined the national cause.[57]

François Mauguin, to a chosen few in Laffitte's library, again proposed the municipal commission as a provisional regime to rule Paris and coordinate revolutionary activity. Now the idea was accepted. The first commission selected consisted of soldiers and millionaires: Laffitte, Périer, General Gérard, Odier, and Lobau. Gérard, who had also taken full command of the regular and irregular army in Paris after Marmont's retreat, was unable to serve. Odier also declined to serve on the Commission, though several documents were published in his name. The places of Gérard and Odier were then filled by two nominal republicans, baron de Schonen and Audry de Puyraveau. The president of the Commission was named by Puyraveau without his being informed of the honor – that old "monument going around looking for a pedestal" – Lafayette.[58] The Municipal Commission also issued a statement announcing that Lafayette had accepted the command of National Guard. That afternoon, Lafayette and Gérard appeared publicly in full uniform and General Lafayette issued a trite proclamation in which he innocently declared: "There is no need for me to make a profession of faith. My feelings are known. Liberty will triumph or we die together. *Vive la liberté, Vive la Patrie*"![59] Nothing in these words should have been particularly encouraging to the republicans.

That evening, the deputies met again at Laffitte's house. Two liberal royalists proposed that the assembly agree to accept the negotiations of the duc de Mortemart, Ambassador to Russia, to mediate a peace between Charles X and the "fired-upon people". Mortemart was to be accredited only if he brought a signed revocation of the edicts and a list of new ministers containing several leaders of the Left. Mortemart failed to arrive that evening and, as the *Globe* later remarked with a sigh of relief, "a shameful treaty was avoided".[60] At nine o'clock a mission arrived from Saint-Cloud,

[57] *Globe*, Special, 4 A.M., July 30, 1830. The *Globe's* factual report of the deputies' sessions and the Municipal Commission were written to show the contrast between the spirit of the revolutionaries and the timidity of the deputies. *Globists* showed more sympathy for the radicals than other Orleanist papers. See also, Laffitte, *Mémoires*, p. 165.

[58] Laffitte, *Mémoires*, p. 135. Laffitte had thus referred to the General in a conversation with Royer-Collard early in July. When the banker repeated the phrase to Lafayette, the old soldier laughingly agreed that it was an apt characterization.

[59] *Globe*, 30 July, 1830.

[60] *Ibid.*, 1 August, 1830.

and was not recognized by the deputies as it carried no credentials or anything signed by the King; although it delivered an unsigned note offering to fire the Polignac Cabinet and replace it with one led by Mortemart, Gérard, and Périer. The still timid and nonrevolutionary majority of the deputies voted to allow the Mortemart mission to attend a formal session of the deputies they had self-convoked for the next morning at the Palais Bourbon. In opposing the legitimist intrigue of their timid colleagues, the Orleanists and republicans were thrown together as allies of circumstance. Speaking for a coalition of these groups, Mauguin and Shonen stoutly protested against any dealings with the King and seemed to carry the day. Casimir Périer, who was watching his dream of glory fade away, appeared stupified by the objections from the Left. During this meeting only, the republican voice was heard. Lafayette was still nominally their chief and they were speaking with the sanction of their recent activities in the streets.[61] Crucial at this moment, however, was Lafayette's unpromising coyness. Aside from a few radical deputies, the republicans had few sympathizers and lacked a proclaimed titular leader at the moment of critical decision. The rump "Chamber", which actually had no more legality than the municipal Commission, was being polarized between those who envisioned a runaway republic in the hands of the fighting revolutionaries and those who dreamed of a parliamentary monarchy under, perhaps, a designated heir of Charles X. One group raised the specter of disorder and foreign intervention; the other, the possibility of betrayal and counterrevolution. Over at the Hôtel de Ville, there was also a doubtful pair of alternatives: The Republic, full of imagined dangers, or the Duke of Reichstadt, even more remote from realization.[62] Some sort of *deus ex machina* was needed to resolve these dilemmas, and it could be supplied.

Between the vertices, Republic, Empire, and Bourbons, there was a refuge, which according to some responsible citizens, was the *just milieu*. But no deputy, even Laffitte, had yet spoken openly about the Duke of Orleans. The real initiative for this compromise had begun several hours before the meeting at Laffitte's.

Adolphe Thiers and François Mignet left the *National* office that afternoon to witness the meeting at Laffitte's town house. As they walked down the rue de Richelieu, from which the barricades were now being removed, Thiers noticed a curious phenomenon. Merchants who had displayed "by appointment" crests to Charles X, had torn down these symbols, while those who

[61] Weill, *Parti républicain*, p. 24.
[62] *Ibid.*

indicated Louis Philippe as their patron had left the notices in view. Thiers recalled the sugar-coated manifesto of old Lafayette and the precise organizational ability of the young republicans across the Seine. Indicating the rows of bourgeois shops, he asked Mignet "Are they by chance thinking about the Duke of Orleans"? Once at Laffitte's house, Thiers conferred privately with Generals Sebastiani and Gérard, whose principles were known to be more republican than anything else. Point-blank, Thiers asked them if "Orleans could move them from their position". Certainly, they both answered, but what does M. de Orléans think of the idea? Encouraged, the prophet of a new "1688" replied: "What does that matter? Let us enlist him without consulting him".[63]

The royalist press was nearly defunct. Until late Thursday, Polignac's orders and Marmont's proclamations were under "censorship" as the rebels had seized the royal printing office.[64] The *Gazette* and the *Moniteur* agreed to print official proclamations and announcements. The *Drapeau Blanc* was dead. The *Quotidienne* did not appear until August 1, when a simple black bar replaced the royal crest on its masthead. Opposition papers which did appear were too concerned with the astonishing fact of their morning victory to discuss the confused tangle of political programs that demanded unraveling. Dubois and Rémusat described the day's triumph in their *Globe*.

This morning, Paris conquered, for France, the enemies of its institutions. They retreated stained by lies and the blood of a peaceful population. They will cry about the insurrection of 1830, as they branded that immortal rebellion begun on a 14 July, but now, as then, these sophisms... fall on deaf ears.[65]

Back in the *National's* office, Thiers and Mignet composed a manifesto in praise of the Duke of Orleans, which was fed into the press of the *National*. It was to appear early the following morning before the palace negotiators were expected to arrive at the Chamber. Their timing was perfect.

[63] Lacombe, "Conversations", p. 22.
[64] Beach, "Fall of Charles X", p. 36.
[65] *Globe*, 29 July, midnight, 1830.

CHAPTER XV

THE REVOLUTIONARY INFLUENCE OF JOURNALISM

In the early hours of Friday, the thirtieth of July, this placard, originating in the office of the *National*, was posted everywhere in the city:

Charles X can never return to Paris; he has shed the blood of the people.
The Republic would expose us to dangerous disunity; it would bring us into hostilities with Europe.
The Duke of Orleans is a prince devoted to the cause of the revolution.
The Duke of Orleans has never fought against us.
The Duke of Orleans is [sic!] a citizen-king.
The Duke of Orleans has borne the tricolor under enemy fire; only the Duke of Orleans can bear it again. We will have no other flag.
The Duke of Orleans does not commit himself.
He waits for the expression of our wishes.
Let us proclaim those wishes and he will accept the Charter as we have always understood it, and as we have always wanted it. It is from the French people that he will hold his crown. [1]

By this strategic stroke, Thiers started all Paris talking about the cadet prince before the deputies had finished their breakfasts. He had supplied the missing name.

The Orleans "manifesto" was particularly crippling to the republicans, whose work and sacrifice had barely begun to result in serious recognition. Two of the commissioners at the Hôtel de Ville were only sentimentally republican and all of them were conservative enough to be in some way haunted by the terrifying ghosts of an earlier radicalism. Then too, the commissioners had modestly declined their opportunity to claim more than a municipal police power – holding the elected, but still disorganized, deputies to be their legal representatives. In addition to a lack of overall unity, the republican spirit was everywhere permeated to some small degree with Bonapartism, a natural mating of the unfulfilled, which was to bear blighted issue in 1850.

---

[1] Placard, with *National*, 31 July, 1830.

These factors served only to dilute the nascent, though widespread, republicanism of 1830. On the other side, the legitimists, though discredited by the *coup d'état*, had not all vanished into the air during the July Days. Liberals of Périer's type had, even at this late hour, begun to see some uses for the old dynasty. Into this tempest Thiers had cast the magic phrase which itself offered the panacea: "Citizen-king".

The masses of the Parisian population expected either a republic or a leashed Charles X. The suggestion of a new sort of monarchy was a novelty they regarded with suspicion. The Ultras, quite naturally, were also opposed to the suggestion, but for different reasons. The first gentleman to the Dauphin spoke for his class when he wrote: "Thiers and Mignet, whose names written in letters of blood, would henceforth be the signal of all revolution,... judging their fruit was ripe, pronounced for the first time the name of M. le duc d'Orléans".[2]

To be sure, it was the first time since the inflammatory pamphlet of Cauchois-Lemaire, that the name of Orleans had been exploited politically. But for months, the press, especially the *National, Temps,* and *Globe,* had been painting the portrait and their readers had no difficulty in supplying the title.

Another caucus of deputies was held at Laffitte's house. The host, whose activities included the management of Louis-Philippe's great fortune, now frankly advocated a government of the Orleans prince.[3] When, at ten o'clock, the duc de Mortemart arrived at Laffitte's with a signed surrender from the King, Laffitte's colleagues were all but converted. After waiting nearly all night at Saint-Cloud for the Monarch to admit defeat, Mortemart had accomplished his mission. Charles X had agreed to revoke the edicts, to call the already elected Chamber for August 3, and to reestablish the National Guard. He had now officially dismissed the Ultra ministers and named a Cabinet of the Left and Center that included his courier, Mortemart. At Guernon-Ranville's insistence, the King refused to authorize the tricolor or to order a general amnesty. He wished to preserve a bit of royal "face" by making these decrees of his own will, so they would not seem to have been wrung from him by force.[4] Charles X had also requested a list of grievances from the people. However, Laffitte and the other deputies, claiming lack of jurisdiction, sent the impatient Ambassador away, asking him to attend the first plenary session of deputies at 11:30. The deputies were then joined by

[2] G. duc de Guiche], eyewitness, "Les Journées de Juillet 1830", ed. by duc de Lesparre, *Le Carnet,* II (Paris, 15 July, 1898), 461.

[3] *Globe,* 1 August, 1830.

[4] Roux, *Restauration,* p. 334.

an eminent Peer, the duc de Broglie, who spoke in favor of making Orleans the Lieutenant-General of the Kingdom, an ancient and variable monarchic title similar to a regency.[5]

At this "regular" session, in the rebuilt hall of the National Assembly, the deputies chose a committee to visit the Chamber of Peers at the Palais Luxembourg, and to gain the accord of the upper Chamber in negotiations with Saint-Cloud. Whether by purpose or accident, Hyde de Neuville, a member of the delegation, made the error of praising legitimacy, and, in the sharp debate which followed, the negotiator, Mortemart, was forgotten. The "legitimate" Prime Minister of France, he had despaired of the deputies and had made his own futile mission to the Luxembourg. In a last gesture, he sent an underling, de Sussy, over to the Palais Bourbon with the belated signed surrender decrees of Charles X. The deputies, the majority of whom had spent the morning praising the Orleanist movement, routed poor de Sussy to the *de facto* "government" at the Hôtel de Ville. There, the commissioners told him that he should deal only with the deputies! De Sussy tried next to have the decrees printed in the *Moniteur*, but deputies had already forbidden Sauvo to publish them.[6] During all this tragi-comic deceit, the Orleans cause was steadily growing, while "legitimacy" lost its last thin chance to survive.

Back at the Palais Bourbon, a proclamation was passed for signatures. It began with the words: "Charles X has ceased to reign". The declaration recalled that the "heroic" people had a right to be governed with "no more fear for rights already acquired; no more barrier between us and the rights we still lack". The declaration then offered the Duke of Orleans, not as King, but as "Lieutenant-General", the honor of establishing a new government. It stated that the Duke wished jury trials in press cases, a long sought goal of Constant and other liberals. Orleans was also quoted as saying "A Charter will henceforth be a reality".[7] The commissioners in the Hôtel de Ville, however, issued a statement which denied the throne to Charles X, but did not mention Orleans.[8] Ninety deputies signed the Chamber's appeal for Orleans. They included many factions: Nominal republicans like Puyraveau, Laborde, and General Sebastiani; liberal royalists like de Hauranne, Dupin, Villemain, and Vatimesnil, and, of course, Laffitte and Benjamin Constant, whose *Courrier* had helped the Orleans cause. Casimir Périer refused to sign the appeal and later went to the *Moniteur* office to insure that

[5] *Globe*, "Récit de M. Armand Marrast", 1 August, 1830.
[6] Beach, "Charles X", pp. 50-52.
[7] *Le Moniteur*, 1 August, 1830.
[8] *Ibid.*

his name was not being used. He was correctly suspected of treating with the King through Charles's grand huntsman, the comte de Girardin. The deputies Armand Marrast, Guizot, Villemain, Benjamin Constant, and Bérard formed a committee to draft separate proposals and conditions to be presented to the Duke of Orleans and to define the powers of the Lieutenancy-General of the realm.[9] Now to find Louis-Philippe and hitch him to their wagon!

The Duke, who had left the Palais Royal for a summer house in Neuilly as soon as the decrees were issued, was now, as Thiers remarked, "playing dead".[10] Talleyrand and Laffitte each sent a messenger to Neuilly. Laffitte's courier, who arrived first, was Adolphe Thiers, chosen for his political daring and his sense of timing, though Thiers had never had a political conversation with the Duke of Orleans.[11] Unlike the hapless duc de Mortemart, Thiers made the most of his sudden opportunity for political greatness. Laffitte sent a companion with him, Ary Scheffer, the famous artist, who was tutor to Louis-Philippe's granddaughters and a confidant both of the Duchess and of the Duke's ambitious sister, Madame Adélaide.[12] Laffitte had been in communication with these ladies at Neuilly for two days,[13] apparently aware of the influence of Mme. Adélaide over her brother. Thiers and Sheffer received two horses from the Prince de la Moskowa (Laffitte's son-in-law) and left for Neuilly. The National Guard still controlled the avenues leading west toward Saint-Cloud, so the two riders avoided delays by taking the outer boulevards. Upon arrival at the Orleans villa, Sheffer performed his task, which was to introduce Thiers to the future Queen of the French. The cautious Duke, not wishing to appear ambitious, had left, like a fugitive, for another of his houses at Raincy, garbed as a simple bourgeois and wearing a tricolor cockade in his hat.[14] Thiers had to discuss the fate of France with a pair of ladies.

When Thiers consulted the Duchess, Marie-Amélie, about a Lieutenancy-General under her husband, the proposal horrified her. Her family had always been well treated by the reigning branch and she greatly feared the public attitude; "They would call him a usurper", she declared, "he, the most honest of men". Thiers reply, which he had already prepared, was:

If the Duke of Orleans refuses to yield to the wishes of the deputies, he delivers the nation to demagoguery; in which case the liberalism of his principles cannot save him

[9] *Globe*, "Récit de M. Armand Marrast", 1 August, 1830.
[10] Lacombe, "Conversations", pp. 23-24.
[11] *Ibid.*, p. 21.
[12] *Ibid.*, p. 23.
[13] *Globe*, 1 August, 1830.
[14] Jules Bertaut, *Le Roi Bourgeois* (Paris: Grasset, 1936), p. 75.

from blind furies; he must choose between the Crown and exile; between royalty and a passport.[15]

The future Queen still hesitated, but Adélaide's response was instantaneous. She hinted broadly that her brother had nursed legitimate ambitions for such a position as Thiers described; her only doubts were in the problem of international reactions. Thiers then preached to these ladies his doctrine of "1688", and of how well the Prince of Orange had been received. The princesses needed little else to convince them; Madame Adélaide even threatened to come to Paris herself if her brother could not be persuaded at Raincy![16] Thiers, more than satisfied, set out for Raincy to find the Duke. Shortly afterwards, the messenger from Talleyrand arrived at Neuilly with a note to Mme. Adélaide, urging the necessity of a crown for her brother.[17]

Adolphe Thiers found a very frightened citizen-king at Raincy. The Duke's ambition, his years of trying to endear himself to the bourgeoisie, his cooly "correct" attitude around Charles X, had now found their reward; but Louis-Philippe was appalled. As Thiers said later, he had no scruples of *conscience* over accepting the Lieutenancy-General, but "he was very hesitant, shocked, and afraid of the difficulties of the task he assumed ... little convinced of success".[18]

' After summoning his last reserves of courage, Louis-Philippe returned to the Palais Royal, *incognito*. The next day, escorted by a great parade of deputies and dignitaries, he made his way to the Hôtel de Ville. The crowd did not applaud him. The people *did* cheer for Lafayette, however, and for the host of recent combat veterans, standing behind the old republican who was about to reject another republic. When the Duke alighted before the seat of provisional government, a deputy, Viennet, bluntly demanded of him the guarantees of freedom that the nation had earned by spilling its blood. The Duke, somewhat shaken, managed the reply: "I deplore, as a Frenchman, the crime done to the Nation and the blood which has been shed; as a prince, I am happy to contribute to the welfare of the Nation. Gentlemen, let us enter the Hôtel de Ville".[19]

Nominated as Lieutenant-General, the Duke then stepped to a balcony that faced the huge crowds and fluttered the tricolor bunting with his hand. Then Citizen Lafayette emerged to play his last, and certainly not his noblest,

---

[15] Théodore Juste, *La révolution de Juillet, 1830* (Brussels, 1893), pp. 46-47. (Hereafter cited as Juste, *Révolution.*).

[16] Allison, *Thiers*, pp. 119-20.

[17] Juste, *Révolution*, pp. 46-47.

[18] Lacombe, "Conversations", pp. 23-24.

[19] *Le Moniteur*, 1 August, 1830.

role as national patriarch. He put his arm about Louis-Philippe. They shook hands: A superficial bond of republic and monarchy! A huge cheer came up from the crowd below. Louis-Philippe addressed the waving masses, promising them real guarantees for their freedom. At this speech, Lafayette's countenance lightened and seemed suddenly more cheerful. Later, as if to convince himself that he had not forced a king on a republican nation, the old soldier reminded Louis-Philippe of his admiration for the American constitution. He called it the "best in the world". "I agree with you", responded the Duke of Orleans, "no one could spend two years there as I did and not be convinced of it". Lafayette was satisfied. Credulous and a trifle senile perhaps, but he had not actually deceived his republican supporters. As if in a half-realized apology, Lafayette issued a proclamation to the citizens, explaining that Orleans was chosen "in the urgency of the circumstances" and called him a "young patriot of '89".[20]

And yet, at this otherwise rapturous moment, the real betrayal of the militant republicans and the masses they believed in, was being enacted. For at this point, the Duke of Orleans was only the "Lieutenant-General of the Realm" – a trustee in crisis – not a monarch. At Saint-Cloud, the old King apparently believed that his cousin was indeed *his* loyal delegate; while the republicans, having secured a victory in the streets, desperately tried to forestall this "caretaker" government's easy slide into a new royal dynasty.

The new quasi royalty at the Palais Royal now set about helping Paris bandage its wounds and acting out its "citizen" image. The Orleans princesses visited the hospitals where about eight hundred persons, including royal troops, were still being treated for injuries suffered during the recent struggle. The ladies could have done nothing better to popularize themselves and the Duke than these errands of mercy.[21] Orleans donated, with attendant publicity, the sum of 100,000 francs to a widows' and orphans' fund, set up to care for victims of the July Days.[22]

One the night of August 30, the Royal Family, with a strong escort, left

---

[20] *Ibid.*, 2 August, 1830. But there had been one unpleasant confrontation between the old idol and his troops. On Saturday, a group of leaders of the Fabrist republican faction urged Lafayette, as commandant of the Guard, to escort Louis-Philippe and his entire family to temporary exile in Cherbourg, to facilitate a national referendum. This Lafayette refused to do. See, Laffitte, *Mémoires*, p. 190.

[21] *Ibid.*, 5 August, 1830.

[22] This fund was raised largely by the newspapers, particularly the *Constitutionnel*. In the first few days, its readers pledged over 63,000 francs. Baron Rothschild donated 15,000 francs, Talleyrand gave 500, and the American students in Paris, 2,000. The initial Public collection, which was managed by the Ministry of Finance, netted only 9,573 francs, but 1,000 francs of this was in sous, indicative of working class support. See, *Le Moniteur*, 4, 5, 6, 12 August, 1830. For the later growth of the fund, see Pinkney, p. 245-46.

for the Chateau of Rambouillet. They had been driven from Saint-Cloud by a calculated threat of "sixty thousand" citizens and National Guard who were reportedly marching toward the palace. Talleyrand's counsel had dissuaded most of the diplomatic corps from following the King, and only the Ambassadors of the Pope, Sweden, and Naples went with him.

On August 1, a Sunday, Charles X formally recognized the Lieutenancy-General of his cousin. He realized that defeat was merely a matter of time. The army, now under Gérard, gladly took up the tricolor as Louis-Philippe ordered. In Algeria, Bourmont chose exile for himself, but ordered the edicts of the new government enforced.[23] Algeria was Polignac's victory; but it became Louis-Philippe's coronation gift.

The next day, August 2, with units of the National Guard escorting a considerable mob toward Rambouillet, the King finally agreed to abdicate. Charles X and the Dauphin both renounced their rights to the throne in favor of the "miracle" son of the duchesse de Berri, who was to be called Henri V. The Duke of Orleans (as Lieutenant-General) was ordered to form a government to facilitate this change; in other words, to become regent.[24] By French custom, regency went to the Queen Mother, but even Charles X had no respect for the duchesse de Berri. At that moment, she was dressed in a man's suit, booted and armed with horse pistols, and talking wildly about raising a revolt in the Vendée.

Even the more timid deputies now realized that the armed revolutionaries would reject so poor a trophy as Henri V, so Bérard drafted an amendment to the Charter allowing an Orleans Monarchy. Without bothering to dissuade Charles from his regency plan, the Municipal Commission, having dispatched the National Guard to Rambouillet, now operated on the presumption of an Orleans Monarchy. Ferreted from his lair a second time, the former King and his party now began the dismal journey to Cherbourg and their last exile.[25]

The *Constitutionnel*, which, after the fighting ended, grew brave as a lion, offered its appraisal of the old man who had been King. Its editors regarded the abdication with "emotions between indignation and pity". "What!" they exclaimed, "Charles X has so much pain over the evils which affect and

---

[23] Roux, *Restauration*, pp. 339-40.

[24] *Le Moniteur*, 3 August, 1830.

[25] The old Monarch was returning to an even more inhospitable exile than he had known in his youth. He soon outlived his welcome in an unsympathetic Britain. Next, he sought repose in Vienna, but his presence there proved embarrassing to the Emperor, so he was given a castle near Prague. Saddened deeply by the Duchess of Berry's scandals, he retired to Gorizia, near Trieste, where, in 1836, he died of cholera. He was buried in a simple tomb by Franciscan monks.

could threaten HIS people!... HIS people! Thanks to God and their courage, the French people belong to no one".[26]

The cause of "legitimacy" under liberty had failed and the man whose polemic had been spent in that cause wept over the exile of Charles-Philippe de Bourbon. The vicomte de Chateaubriand had come to Paris during the July Days, calling for legitimacy, but praising the journalists' resistance. When he went to the Luxembourg, he was carried on the shoulders of the people who shouted "Long live the champion of the liberty of the press"! To his paramour, he wrote, "I will not betray the King any more than the Charter... thus I have nothing to say or do, but to wait and weep over my country".[27] After the Lieutenancy-General was established, he warned the deputies:

I understand that freedom is sought and especially freedom of the press, by which and for which the people have obtained a brilliant victory. ... The liberty of the press can only exist in security under a government whose roots are deeply set.[28]

Most of the liberal monarchists, whose views were reflected by the *Débats*, used this argument in favor of preserving the old dynasty. For them, Martignac, the man who had tried to unite legitimacy with liberty, became the resurrected hero of the Restoration. Saint-Marc Girardin, whose August editorial in the *Débats* helped to destroy the dynasty, was astonished when he later reread the editorials of 1829:

It seemed to me that we were not very convinced that the Ministry of M. de Martignac was the last chance of a liberal Restoration, and that after this Ministry, there was only revolution or counterrevolution, that is to say, two abysses.

Girardin also reflected that the *Débats* staff had preferred the "triumph of revolution to the triumph of *coup d'état*", but would have better preferred to "avoid this sad alternative".[29]

Louis-Philippe, who learned in 1848 that he pleased no one, attempted, in 1830, to at least mollify everyone. He expanded the Municipal Commission into a quasi ministry which included Admiral de Rigny, Broglie, Guizot, and baron Louis. The republicans Delaborde and Bavoux were made Prefect of Seine department and Prefect of Police, respectively, as rewards for their deserting their cause.[30] Later, under the Ministry of Laffitte, J.-J. Baude,

---

[26] *Constitutionnel*, 4 August, 1830.
[27] Rossignol, *Histoire*, p. 365; Récamier, *Souvenirs*, II, letter, 29 July, 1830, 389.
[28] Turnbull, *Revolution*, p. 409.
[29] Hatin, *Histoire de la Presse*, VIII, 440, 474-75.
[30] But Bavoux was replaced by a more Orleanist official two days later.

the defender of the *Temps*, was named Prefect of Police. Two lawyers, whose oratory had dramatized the struggle of the liberal press, were promoted. Felix Barthe became Prosecutor of the Lower Tribunal of the Seine and Joseph Mérilhou was made secretary to the Minister of Justice.[31] The Charter of 1814 was reedited. Article 8, which dealt with the press, was amended to forbid any use of censorship. Article 14, which Charles had used to justify his July decrees, was changed to prohibit the King from alterning the laws. The jury was later instituted for press trials.

On the ninth of August, the self-convoked Chambers concurring, Louis-Philippe d'Orléans was inaugurated as the first and only "King of the French". The new title for the King and the fact that he was not called "Philip VII" gave evidence that France had failed to copy England's example of 1688 in all details. The deputies had neither accepted a republic nor had they allowed any pretense of legitimacy. By this course, they had further exposed the Orleans Monarchy to the charge or "usurpation" from all factions. An Ultra pamphlet in 1833 termed the July Monarchy, "a Monarchy surrounded by republican institutions, a monstrous centaur".[32] But, by 1833, most republicans would have regarded the first part of this description as the bitterest irony.

While Chateaubriand and his kind lamented the fallen Monarchy, those republicans who sincerely wished a republic adopted a hostile, but not a vindictive, attitude.

The *Révolution, Journal des Intérêts Populaires*, in a special issue during the July Days, condemned the entire Orleanist program as another *coup* and an illegal usurpation. Its young editors rightly asserted that the Lieutenancy-General had been an "advantageous precedent in favor of this prince, to occupy the throne of France". "Louis-Philippe", they wrote angrily "can have no more real power than the assent of the people and nothing has been decided about the form of government that will be adopted". The *Révolution* went on to recall that the masses have a "repugnance" for Monarchy and would oppose the "efforts of those who would finagle a throne for their patron". Throwing the liberals' argument back in their faces, the paper warned that, "civil war and anarchy might result if the government were usurped". The *Révolution* called for a national constituent assembly, not a rump of the

---

[31] *Le Moniteur*, 1, 2, 3 August, 1830.

[32] E. Gigault, *Vie politique de M. le Marquis de Lafayette* (Paris, 1833), p. 37. The Duke was aware of his anomalous role from the start. As he was dressing for his balcony appearance with Lafayette at the Hôtel de Ville, he confided to Bérard, as the latter helped him into his coat; "Oh, M. Bérard! I am a republican and I have condemned a republic to death"! See, Laffitte, *Mémoires*, p. 193.

deputies, to decide the fate of France. On August 3, the paper spoke again in bitterness and heat about the Orleans *coup*, while avowing its editors' love for Lafayette.

On Friday, the *Tribune*, some of whose staffers had manned the barricades, announced that, "after forty years, the dawn of glory shone again for us". Pleading for a republic, though in milder terms than those of the *Révolution*, the *Tribune's* editors expressed the hope that the workers and youths who fought in July would have some voice in government, and that *subjects* would truly become *citizens*. Only the symbol of Lafayette, they declared, could give France the "real profits of its triumph". In spite of his rejection of radical demands to temporarily exile Louis-Philippe, Lafayette was still the republican's only visible chief and none of their public reproaches were aimed in his direction. The Fabrists attacked the Orleanist deputies for assuming the right to make a decision "that the people alone have the right to give".

Although Auguste Fabre, editor of the *Tribune*, at last tentatively accepted the Orleans settlement, his brother Victorin did not. Writing in the *Tribune*, Victorin Fabre observed that his journal was republican under Polignac and that it would continue with this attitude. "Our doctrines were opposed", he remarked accusingly, "by hypocrites who dragged the nation behind them like a troupe of marionettes".[33] Other republican papers were more self-effacing and denied any idea of raising a republic by violence. The Orleanists were relieved by this unexpected restraint on the part of these popular and deserving activists of the July Days. When Duvergier de Hauranne, the historian and *Globist*, expressed his gratitude to Godefroy Cavaignac, who had helped to organize students and workers for victory, Cavaignac answered: "You are wrong to thank us; we only yielded because we were not strong enough. It was too difficult to make people understand, who had fought at the cry 'Long Live the Charter'! Later, things will be different".[34]

The republicans were betrayed, whether by design or by their own idealism, it makes little difference. As the natural "opposition" to King Louis-Philippe, they would slowly push his government into the same kind of reactionary

---

[33] *Tribune des Départemens*, 31 July, 1830; Fabre, *Révolution*, I, xxiii.

[34] De Hauranne, *Histoire*, X, 651. A weaker faction that received little benefit from the settlement was that of the Bonapartists. Although they had no possibility of presenting their candidate, their dissatisfaction was not ignored. An interesting anonymous poem in pamphlet form appeared in August, *L'aigle d'Austerlitz et le coq Valois*, Ledru-Rollin Collection, University of California, Berkeley, 217:1. In this, the Orleans cock explains the anticlerical aspect of the July Revolution to the Napoleonic eagle. The eagle becomes convinced that the Duke of Reichstadt had lived too long among the Jesuits and finally agrees to the choice of Louis-Philippe!

reflex pattern that had been exhibited by the Bourbons. They remained in *Aide-toi le Ciel t'aidera* and assumed its leadership. By 1832, purely republican *Aide-toi* societies were flourishing in thirty-five departments. In 1833, fifty-three provincial newspapers were being operated by republicans.[35] Thus, within three years, Louis-Philippe was confronted by a mighty republican opposition which was one day to drive him down the road of ridicule to disaster.

By its almost complete disregard of the rights and aspirations of this more radical generation of the nineteenth century, the Orleanist party was to reap a whirlwind. Too concerned with its own prospects of survival, it forgot its liberal principles of 1830. In the case of the press alone, one may notice this cruel paradox. There was no censorship under the new Charter of 1830, but neither had there been total suppression under that of 1814. Louis-Philippe's ministers resorted to the judicial process, albeit with juries, to prosecute their critics. Polignac, because of the 1828 press law, had done the same, although without juries. While Polignac's government had indicted about fourscore newspapers during its year of conspiratorial rule, the court censorship of the Citizen-King prosecuted 400 press cases between July, 1830 and February, 1832![36] Legitimists who openly espoused the claim of "Henri V" were often acquitted, but the republicans, as a more real threat, were rigorously punished. During the first four years of the July Monarchy, the republican *Tribune des Départemens* underwent 114 political trials, of which it was acquitted in ninety-one. For the twenty-three condemnations it received, the owners of the paper paid 159,000 francs in fines,[37] or an average of nearly 7000 francs per fine. It may be recalled that one thousand francs was regarded as a severe penalty under Charles X. Special apartments were set aside in Sainte-Pélagie prison for the managers of the *Tribune* and the *National*, which under Carrel became republican. Prosecutions of legitimists along with republicans, created a sincere sympathy between these two opposite, but "betrayed", factions which was evident in their prison friendships.[38]

Here was a fundamental liberal goal, in which the Revolution of 1830 had failed, but it was not the only goal unfulfilled by the heroism of July. The gains of 1830 were in the legal and philosophic advances along the path of French democracy, and the maturity of a new political generation, rather than in the uninspiring and disillusioning eighteen years of Louis-Philippe's reign.

[35] Weill, *Parti Républicain*, pp. 56, 75, 77.
[36] Fernand Giraudeau, *La presse périodique de 1789 à 1867* (Paris, 1867), p. 38.
[37] *Ibid.*, p. 22.
[38] Burnand, *La Vie Quotidienne*, pp. 192-93.

What part, then, may we attribute to political journalism in the overthrow of the old regime and the establishment of the new? Was the revolution simply what the comte de Carné and thousands after him have suggested, "... machinated by a few Warwicks of the bank and the press to the profit of an ambition waiting at Neuilly"?[39] The trouble with such an oversimplification is that it holds enough truth to allow it to endure – it cannot apply fairly to the broad picture of the Revolution of 1830 or to the factors behind it. Although one is faced with the ancient dilemma of whether the press molds or reflects popular opinion, it is undeniable that the periodical press, especially after the fall of Villèle, developed into a political force, powerful of itself and, equally important, feared by a government which always managed to blunder on cue.

The understandable reference to Thiers and his companions as "Warwicks" may be justified if we only consider the rendezvous of time, place, and persons that was involved in the *démarche* to Louis-Philippe. For months, the militant press, led by Thiers' own *National* had suggested an Orleans dynasty in a dozen different ways. The historical analogies to England's "1688", backed by the scholarship of respected historians, such as Thiers, Mignet, Carrel, and Guizot, undoubtedly built a consciousness of, if not a sympathy for Orleans, among the literate classes who read the magazines and papers. But to suggest a candidate, to advertise a name; is this to *foment* a revolution, as some of the Ultras believed? To be sure, this helped to *refine* a revolutionary spirit, to guide its course, but this spirit was growing for several years; its components as diverse and complex as Restoration society itself.

Thiers, Mignet, Guizot, Chatelain, Carrel, Baude, Cauchois-Lemaire, and all the others who adopted the "1688" propaganda device had merely signed a name on the bottom of an open political contract. The "Warwicks of the bank", especially Jacques Laffitte, were less influential. Laffitte exercised his power in nearly every case as the rich liberal deputy, the parliamentarian, not as the financier. His social and economic position attracted the adherence of industrialists like Ternaux and members of the high bourgeoisie. But even the high bourgeoisie had a part in the revolution that transcended mere capitalist striving, and they naturally opposed the drain of wealth and favors benefitting the aristocrats. And what about the "ambition" that waited at Neuilly? Only a few, including Guizot, would deny that Louis-Philippe was ambitious.[40] Thiers recognized his ambition and made use of it.

[39] Carné, "Souvenirs", p. 608.
[40] Guizot, *Memoirs*, II, 11-12.

Years later, Prince Metternich asked Thiers whether the Duke of Orleans had "conspired" for the Revolution of 1830. Thiers made the concertmaster of Europe laugh by replying: "Louis-Philippe did not conspire; he aspired".[41] Insofar as the actual promotion of Orleans was successfully achieved, a great share of responsibility must go to Thiers and his friends, as well as to the Duke himself. But the candidacy and the title "King of the French" were not by themselves a revolution, though not so great a perversion of a revolution as most republicans believed.

The role of the press in the events which precipitated the July Days may be considered from several viewpoints. First, there is ample evidence that the Polignac Cabinet, and the Ultras in general, considered the press the greatest obstacle to their goals. Opinions expressed by Ultra deputies and peers during the 1828 debates over the new press law reveal clearly the depth of this fear. Polignac's April report, in which he declared the press to be the sole source of unrest in the nation, was of prime importance as it was an advice from a First Minister to the Sovereign who trusted him. The *rapport au roi*, edited by Chantelauze to justify the July decrees, was another exposure of the formidable enemy which the Ultras saw in a free opposition press. The Ultra press itself, represented either by unbridled demands for dictatorship of the *Drapeau Blanc* or *Quotidienne*, or the more subtle appeals of the *Gazette*, drove the Ministry into an accelerated program of repression which failed because it was so goaded by its zealots, and so poorly conceived by its directors.

The trial of the Polignac Ministry took place the following December. In nearly all the long impassioned speeches by the four accused ex-Ministers and their attorneys, the subject of journalism and its influence arose. They not only admitted to the effectiveness of newspapers in bringing about their overthrow, but went considerably beyond this. One of the defense advocates, Sauzet, said that journalists had made it impossible for the Restoration to maintain its credit with the nation. With increasing skill, he asserted, they condemned as alien and sinister all the historical and philosophical bases of the dynasty, and at last, made it unacceptable to France.[42]

The opposition press was politically powerful because it was free. A fascinating paradox – the press of France was less fettered under the "tyranny" of Polignac than at almost any other period in its history before 1873.

---

[41] Lacombe, "Conversations", p. 24.

[42] *Procès des ministres*, II, 506-8. The four former Ministers, Polignac, Guernon-Ranville, Peyronnet, and Chantelauze, were sentenced to life in prison at Ham, a castle sixty miles north of Paris. In the amnesty of 1836, their sentences were reduced to exile. Montbel, d'Haussez, and Capelle were sentenced in absentia; they had managed to escape from France.

Martignac's press law of 1828 had left the press strong enough to develop an almost unlimited journalism of opinion. Even the restriction of financing, which discouraged a more popular or radical voice, was somewhat eased by endowments from patrons and by the drastically reduced *cautionnment* of 1828. Despite his personal desires, Charles X was unable to crush newspapers by censorship. One by one, the liberal papers had denounced the symbols of reaction: The Jesuits, the *Congrégation*, the Ultras of the Chamber, the Ultras of the royalist press, the foreign policies of the government, and the origin of the Restoration itself. During the early period the ramparts were manned by such papers as the *Constitutionnel*; the upstart republicans and the *National* were not yet born. To have opposed censorship to this mounting opposition from the journals, Charles would have had to attempt a law through the Chambers; but, at every bye-election, the opposition majority was growing, making such a law less possible. The provincial press was growing, too, and in spite of judicial persecution, it radiated the ideas of the opposition and coordinated electoral strategy in all corners of France. To destroy the press by edict, the course eventually taken, might incur serious risks for the Monarchy. But, to let the monster live was to expose the Monarchy to a slower, but equally deadly peril. Chantelauze's report at last recognized the negative propaganda effect of the government prosecution of journalists in public trials.

With the advent of Thiers and the new "1688" concept in political journalism the royal problem was magnified, although there had been some bold editorial analogies to 1688 before the *National* appeared. The "1688" propaganda was an escalation beyond criticism, and bore the obvious implications of revolt. Still the King faced the necessity of yielding to this force that he believed was destroying him, while the journalists of his own camp advertised his dilemma by urging him not to yield. Instead of ignoring the threat of "1688", the government augmented its own jeopardy through publicized press trials and those irresponsible journals on its own side, which daily shouted for blood. Talleyrand, who was not a journalist, but a keen enough political spectator, sympathized with the royal perplexity:

And it was by no means one of the least foolish acts of this imbecile Ministry to have thus influenced public opinion. There was no lack of warning in this respect, but there was a decided want of that courageous loyalty and fairness, which might have arrested a feeble and credulous prince on the downward path. And that was a crime, it can be called by no other name, for it was the cause of the Revolution of July, 1830.[43]

---

[43] Talleyrand, *Memoirs*, IV, 226.

It became obvious to King and ministers that removal of the liberal electorate required the strangulation of the liberal press, and that this, in turn, demanded the subservience of the deputies who were, in the first place, elected by the press-influenced electors. The King's problem was thus an endless chain; all links had to be broken at once if any were to be broken. And this was the *coup d'état*, the July decrees. Of the links in that chain, the opposition press was the most formidable in the ministers' eyes. To their *émigré* minds, the "license" of journalism was the most shocking and obvious manifestation of a power opposing them – a power they could neither control nor understand. They feared the "revolutionary" press, but when they tormented it they only roused its fury and nourished its strength.

After 1828, the periodical press was continually "in session", an active forum when the deputies were sitting, as well as during the long months of adjournment or prorogation. Journalism, for all its limitations, reflected a greater variety and range of political opinion then than now. The day of the penny-press and the industrially-owned paper was yet to come and, although wealth backed some newspapers and ignored others, there was no monopoly on ideas in the press. Fabre and his fellows were heard and their ideas evaluated. Orleanism was by no means the "consensus" of that period, drummed into the public mind by an appeal to conformity, as ideas are so often accepted in more recent times – "1688" was simply the most expedient philosophy for the most pragmatic politicans and journalists; it allayed the fears of the propertied class, while it made vague promises to the masses.

If we grant the press of the Left its measure of credit for the revolution, must we not also award credit to the Right? The fanaticism of some clergymen, for an example, increased with the exposure of the little seminaries and benefitted the opposition when this was reflected in the Polignac Ministry; the *Gazette's* constant support of Villèle created a broad crack in the armor of the Right, and so on. The free press was the most obvious incongruity of the Restoration, a period when elements of the antique and the modern were already in sharp contrast.

Charles X was confronted with the legality of the Charter of 1814, granted by his own brother. To violate this Charter, by whatever pretext, was to break the law. And here the origins of the 1830 Revolution draw us back through the years. For that Charter of 1814 was his family's sullen surrender to living spirits of the past: The nationalism of the red, white, and blue Empire; the ideological storms of the Revolution; and even perhaps of the *cahiers* of the Third Estate, Voltaire's barbed pen, and Rousseau's radical vision. Charles X and his advisers were unable to kill the revolution because of the evolution, during four decades, of the French political mentality, a mentality which was nourished by and found its ideal expression in, the political press.

Little has been said in these pages about the social pressures of the Restoration era and their impact on the revolutionary spirit. Studies of revolutionists in 1789-1795 indicate the effects of economic frustration as being more potent than the effects of outright deprivation or misery in driving men to the barricades. Even if Charles X had been more judicious or aware, the general economic conditions would probably have alienated large parts of the nation to the breaking point within a few years. Still, one must consider two relevant facts. Masses of workers, chiefly artisans and craftsmen, took the streets in the July Days, while Polignac's dream of a provincial *Chouannerie* went up in smoke. Those workingmen behind the barricades were distrustful of the regime so isolated from their interests and they had at last found sympathetic spokesmen in the camp of some newspapers, especially those of the republican Left, whose propaganda they believed. Journalists had guided many members of this stratum of society to regard the King as their enemy and the clergy as their exploiter.[44]

In exile in Bohemia, Charles X once asked a traveler to seek out Thiers and ask him how he had been able to make the revolution "succeed so well". In his reply to the former King, Thiers denied personal responsibility, saying with an uncharacteristic modesty that the revolution had been merely the result of "the march of events".[45] Was Thiers right? Was the die already cast and, as Beach and others believe, the result unavoidable in view of the militant Left's refusal to consider a regency? Could Charles himself have saved the day, as Bertier holds, by rescinding the edicts and naming a liberal Cabinet before the military phase was too far advanced? Or, would the threat of revolution never have come at all, if, as Girardin reflected, the moderate Left had supported Martignac's earnest efforts rather than subverted them?

But only one course became the reality of history, and, as at no other time in France, this course was largely directed by journalists during the last years of the Bourbon Restoration. Out of a fusion of all the cross-currents of ideals and prejudices, the final course was set; its destination, for better or worse, a new epoch in the history of France and Europe.

---

[44] See chapter I for a brief discussion of economic conditions. See Pinkney, *French Revolution of 1830*, 57-72 and George Rudé, *The Crowd in the French Revolution* (New York, 1959).

[45] Lacombe, "Conversations", p. 24.

THE JULY REVOLUTION AND THE
PROVINCIAL PRESS

Although its indirect influences reached as far as Poland and Russia, the Revolution of 1830 has been aptly called "The Paris Revolution". Three days of combat and three more of political maneuvering in Paris had established the new regime as an accomplished fact before any major counterrevolution could have flared up in the provinces. It is of some importance, however, to record the reactions of smaller cities to the news of events in the capital, especially in those areas where political journalism had been active.

In most of the provincial capitals, as well as in lesser towns, the National Guard was a more decisive agency of both revolution and order than it had been in Paris. Liberal newspaper editors in the provinces, victims of Polignac's judicial assaults, opposed the press edict in several cases by physical resistance. Some commanders in garrisoned towns were torn between their oaths to the King and the opposition of townspeople and even their own troops. A few prefects tried to assume dictatorial powers and drew the open hostility of citizens.

News of the decrees and the Revolution arrived almost simultaneously within three days of the events in most parts of the nation. Reports came by private letters from Paris, as well as from daily dispatch riders who rode a general circuit of France; couriers visiting the same points on successive days. The *télégraphe*, or hill-to-hill semaphore system, was also employed.

In the north and the regions surrounding Paris, the reception of the edicts caused wild disturbances and excitement, but little shedding of blood. In Rambouillet, of course, all was serene. The forest and the Chateau were held by the Royal Guard and the *fleur-de-lys* waved overhead.

At Versailles, the citizens rose, crowds filled the streets, and the local garrison troops retired peacefully to their barracks.[1] Meudon was placed under the National Guard, whose commandant sent to Lafayette for instruc-

---

[1] *Journal du Commerce*, 30 July, 1830.

tions.[2] Tours experienced no great unrest. Royal troops stationed there adopted the tricolor on August 1,[3] while in Chartres, the National Guard assumed the direction of affairs.[4] Le Havre responded to the emergency with tremendous enthusiasm. The National Guard seized jurisdiction of the seaport and organized for a march into Paris. A great number of residents, joined by a crowd of celebrating American sailors on liberty, swelled the exodus to the capital. An atmosphere of great levity, probably with delays for refreshment, accompanied the journey of this delegation.[5] The populace of Rouen remained calm, but the *Journal*, the liberal newspaper, pledged Paris the aid of the city's 40,000 able-bodied men. The royalist city council voted to retain the Bourbon flag, but many citizens flew the tricolor. When the news of the Paris victory reached them, the council members agreed to hoist the national flag, but they draped the royal flag in mourning.[6]

The textile city of Lille was closer to the Brussels revolution of 1830 than to that of Paris. When the decrees arrived, the two royal prosecutors of the city resigned rather than pursue indictments of editors who published in contravention of the press decree. Garrison troops fraternized with the people and there was little violence, although a colonel of Curassiers, who threatened to charge into a crowd of civilians, was nearly stoned to death.[7] In Calais, offices and workshops closed. The local general, commanding the port, polled his aides on the question of loyalty – they voted unanimously to join the revolution.[8]

Normandy had been one of the most politically disturbed regions of France under Charles X. In Caen, the editor of the *Pilote de Calvados* watched the reports from Paris with pleasure. Since 1824, this paper had been especially friendly to the Duke of Orleans, because he had employed, as librarian of the Palais Royal, a local citizen who had been disgraced by Louis XVIII. The *Pilote's* motto: "Steer your boat with prudence", was taken from an opera about the revolt of Naples in 1647. During the recent elections, Caen had been under heavy royalist pressure, but had voted Left, in tune with the editorials of the *Pilote*. Two regiments had been dispatched to the city by Polignac, ostensibly to prevent arson activity, but the Minister Guernon-Ranville, a citizen of Caen, had in this case, protested the use of troops. On July 28, the *Pilote* printed the edicts without comment, and was

[2] *Ibid.*
[3] *Le Moniteur*, 2 August, 1830.
[4] *Ibid.*, 4 August, 1830.
[5] *Ibid.*, 5 August, 1830.
[6] *Ibid.*; *Journal du Commerce*, 30 July, 1830.
[7] *Le Moniteur*, 2, 3 August, 1830.
[8] *Ibid.*, 4 August, 1830.

not suppressed for publishing without authorization. On the thirtieth, a crowd of several hundred gathered in the Place Royale shouting, *A bas Charles X!* Some one daubed the following words on the statue of the Sun-King, Louis XIV: *L'état, c'est moi! Révocation de l'édit de Nantes! Les Dragonnades!*[9]

In the west, the proud cities of Nantes and Angers faced the July Revolution in different ways. In Nantes, the Prefect was baron de Vaussay, an extreme Ultra, while the Mayor was an honest, though reactionary, royalist, and the city council was composed of Ultras. Military headquarters of the western division was located in Nantes under comte Despinois, another Ultra. The local opposition journal was the *Ami de la Charte*, whose editor had received a six month jail term and a 2000 franc fine only a few days before the July decrees were issued. His crime had been to print a republican testimonial and an anticlerical editorial. Public sentiment was not with the government because of this conviction and because of economic depression. In this city, the unemployment rate was 17 percent and the average laborer earned two francs for a twelve to fifteen hour working day,[10] comparable to the worst wages in Paris.

The edicts were first announced to a theatre audience in Nantes on the evening of July 28. An uprising spread from the theatre to the town and soon, sixteen persons had been arrested and several gendarmes wounded. On the thirtieth, the Mayor ordered all cafés and shops closed in the evening. A mob stole six hundred inferior muskets from an armorer and patrolled menacingly in the central district. One group of 150 men attacked the barracks of the Visitation and were surprised by 120 troops of the line. A terrible fight ensued: Of the demonstrators, ten were killed and thirty-nine wounded, while the army, in this sudden fight, lost six dead and thirteen injured. The city, which always had more than its share of slaughter, was frozen with horror. The heartbroken Prefect released all his prisoners and General Despinois left on a futile mission of Ultra honor to raise the peasants in the Vendée.[11] The Nantais martyrs were given an impressive funeral: Their revolution had been "won", but by a tragic blunder. It was revealed that the royal soldiers only fired on the insurgents because the commandant had assured them reinforcements were being sent from Rennes.[12]

Nearby Angers, also a royalist stronghold, lived through the July Days in

---

[9] Henri Prentout, "Caen en 1830", *Revue d'Histoire Moderne*, VI (1931), 114.

[10] Giraud-Mangin, "Nantes in 1830 et les journées de Juillet", *Revue d'Histoire Moderne*, VI (1931), 459.

[11] *Ibid.*

[12] *Le Moniteur*, 4 August, 1830.

near-tranquillity, as contrasted with the bloody day of fighting in Nantes. When the edicts were read in Angers on the afternoon of Wednesday, the twenty-eighth, the Prefect immediately closed the office and press of the *Journal de Maine et Loire*, for its adherence to constitutional principles. For two days the restless people lived on sporadic rumors from Paris. On August 1, the Mayor allowed the formation of the National Guard. The Ultra gendarme commander was seized by the mob but the order-conscious Guard took him into protective custoday. The Prefect at last fled and the Mayor set up a provisional government, while the nearby castle of Saumur was stocked with 1500 guns as a precaution against a new *Chouannerie*.[13] It was clear that, all over France, both the Ultras and Left had overestimated the possibility of peasant risings.

The south and south-central regions received the revolution as a *fait accompli* since the July edicts were not disseminated there until several days after their issuance. There were, however, a few revolutionary episodes. Throughout Saturday, the great industrial and republican center of Lyon was under a revolutionary anarchy. The previous day, manufacturers had ordered a general lockout, following the example of nearby Grenoble. The National Guard of Lyon organized a force of 8000 armed men in a remarkably short time and the line troops and *chasseurs*, sent by the Prefect to quell the demonstrations, wisely surrendered to the Guard.[14] In France's second city, the National Guard successfully prevented violence from both Left and Right.

The cities of Clérmont-Ferrand, Toulouse, Limoges, and Avignon, were shaken only slightly by the eruption at Paris. In Limoges, the two largest porcelain manufacturers proclaimed the lockout and royal prosecutors refused to enforce the decrees against the press.[15] In Toulouse and Clérmont, the National Guard moved so swiftly that the soldiers of the King were completely surprised and adopted the tricolor of their compatriots.[16] The Avignonese had suffered greatly in the "White Terror" of 1815, but their actions in 1830 bore no spirit of vengeance. The National Guard assumed control of the town on August 4. The opposition paper of Avignon, the *Franc-Parleur*, had been prosecuted on July 17 and public opinion was roused in sympathy for its editor.[17] As in Nantes and elsewhere, Polignac's provincial press policy was counterproductive.

---

[13] "La Révolution de 1830 et les Angevins", *l'Anjou Historique*, XXI (1921), 55-58.
[14] *Le Moniteur*, 2, 4 August, 1830.
[15] *Ibid.*, 2 August, 1830.
[16] *Ibid.*, 4, 5 August, 1830.
[17] Fernand de Mély, "Un Souvenir de 1830", letter of F. de Mély, dated Avignon, 5 August, 1830. *Le Carnet*, II (1900), 379-81.

Bordeaux's Catholic-royalist newspaper *Mémorial Bordelais* greeted the edicts in the hope that the ministers would observe the Charter, but added gloomily, that they had "already compromised the future of France". On this same day, Wednesday, the presses of the *Indicateur* were seized and locked by the police. The next day, a gang of youths retaliated by smashing the press of a small royalist weekly, the *Defenseur de la Monarchie*. At this, the Ultra Prefect, de Curzay, flew into a blind rage and rushed from his office into the street, swinging a sabre. Before he could be stopped, he had killed one man and wounded another. He was only saved from a lynching by Maître Gallot, a leading Bordelais deputy.[18]

Burgundy, Franche-Comté, and Alsace-Lorraine were strongly in favor of the revolutionary cause. A republican-tinged press had fought a winning battle. Thanks to the National Guard, the Revolution passed quietly in Mâcon, Auxerre, Joigny, and Strasbourg, but it was far from accepted as a *fait accompli* in several other cities.

Dijon was nearly free of soldiers since the entire local garrison had been ordered to Algeria. The Duchess of Angoulême – the Dauphine – arrived in Dijon two days after the edicts had been posted there and was greeted politely by civic leaders. That evening at the theatre, however, she heard shouts of *Napoléon II* and *République*, as well as the more personal *A bas la garce*! As late as February, 1831, the city still had not "accepted" the July Monarchy; republicanism had become well entrenched in the Côte-d'Or.[19]

In Franche-Comté, the *Impartial* of Besançon was powerful and popular. Aside from his usual attacks on the Polignac regime, editor Just-Muiron had a local score to settle with the Ultra Prime Minister.

The famous scholar, Amedée Thierry, had been fired from his faculty position in the college of Besançon as a result of Polignac's political pressure, and had since become impoverished. The *Impartial* maintained such a withering barrage against the government for this dismissal, that the professor was finally restored to his chair. When the edicts were known, placards appeared, declaring: "Frenchmen, to arms! Down with the Tyrant"! The city split in two. The Mayor and some army officers took the lily banner, the liberals, republicans, and retired Bonapartists the tricolor. There was no serious fighting and all hostilities ceased when the new Mayor, appointed by Louis-Philippe, arrived. Amedée Thierry, Besançon's hero of academic liberty, became the new Prefect of the Department.[20]

[18] *Le Moniteur*, 2, 4 Agust, 1830.
[19] R. Durand, "La Révolution de 1830 en Côte-d'Or", *Revue d'Histoire Moderne*, VI (1931), 170.
[20] *Ibid.*

Violence gripped the town of Chalôns-sur-Marne, east of Paris. Everywhere, the insignia of the *fleur-de-lys* was smashed. Anticlerical demonstrations got out of hand and resulted in the destruction and pillage of a Jesuit seminary.[21] The fortress city of Metz, however, had a rather peaceful revolution of its own, nearly independent of that of Paris. During the Paris barricades of November, 1827, Metz had been placarded with provocations to smash the Cathedral, hang the Mayor, and burn the priests. In 1830, a similar disregard for the order of things returned to the city.

The *Courrier de la Moselle* of Metz had fóught a vigorous battle against Polignac and had taken its punishment in the courts. On June 1, 1830, this sole opposition paper was suppressed by a court order. The edicts were posted on July 28. That evening, a placard appeared on the city hall telling the citizens not to pay taxes to the King who had broken his oath. The Mayor, sensing trouble, allowed the National Guard to form a provisional government and the tricolor was hoisted on the tower of the city hall. But Metz was a powder keg. In its great fortresses were 10,000 royal troops of the line![22] Polignac, who planned for the frontiers, if not for Paris, had concentrated forces there out of a fear of Prussian intervention in the nearby Belgian revolt.[23] The general of the garrison, having received no communications from Paris, refused to allow his men to wear the national cockade. The citizens, however, were able to dissuade the troops from obeying this order and they adopted the tricolor. Even after the abdication of Charles X was known in Metz, National Guards and soldiers were forced to occupy the palace of the uncooperative Bishop.[24] Metz, like several other cities, had been guided only indirectly by events in Paris. The town did not accept a tailor-made revolution from the capital.[25]

---

[21] *Le Moniteur*, 4 August, 1830.

[22] Henri Contamine, "La Révolution de 1830 à Metz", *Revue d'Histoire Moderne*, VI (1931), 116.

[23] *Le Moniteur*, 2 August, 1830.

[24] Contamine, "La Révolution de 1830 à Metz", pp. 118-22.

[25] Pinkney, *French Revolution of 1830*, Ch. VI, gives a thorough account of the July Days in the provinces.

THE MANIFESTO OF THE FORTY-FOUR JOURNALISTS
(FROM *NATIONAL*, 27 JULY, 1830)

It has been said for the last six months that the laws would be violated, that a *coup d'état* would be struck. Sound public opinion refused to believe it. The Ministry rejected this suspicion as a calumny. However, the *Moniteur* has at last published these memorable edicts, which are a most flagrant violation of the laws. The rule of law is thus broken; that of force has begun.

In the situation in which we are placed, obedience ceases to be a duty. The citizens first called upon to obey are writers of the newspapers; they should set the first example of resistance to authority which has divested itself of the character of law.

The reasons on which they stand are such that it is enough to announce them.

The matters ordered by the edicts today are those that royal authority cannot, according to the Charter, pronounce unilaterally. The Charter (Article 8) states that the French, in matters of the press, will be held to conform *to the laws*; it does not say to edicts. The Charter (Article 35) says that the organization of the electoral colleges will be regulated by the laws; it does not say by edicts.

The Crown has itself, until now, recognized these articles; it has not even dreamed of fighting against them, either by a pretended constitutional power or by power falsely attributed to Article 14.

Each time, in fact, that circumstances, allegedly serious, appeared to them to require modification, in either the regulation of the press or in electoral regulation, they have had recourse to the two Chambers. When it was necessary to modify the Charter to establish the septennial law and the integral renewal, it had recourse, not to itself as author of the Charter, but to the Chambers.

Royalty has thus recognized and itself practiced these Articles 8 and 35, and arrogated to itself, in their case, neither a constitutional nor a dictatorial power that did not exist.

The courts, which have the right of interpretation, have solemnly recognized the same principles. The Royal Court of Paris and several others have condemned the publishers of the Breton Association, as authors of an outrage against the government. It has considered as an outrage the supposition that the government would use the authority of edicts where the authority of the law alone could be accepted.

Thus, the formal text of the Charter, the practice followed until now by the Crown, the decisions of the courts, all establish that in matters of the press and electoral organization; the laws, that is, the King with the Chambers, only could prevail.

... Thus, today the government has violated legality. We are called to obey. We are going to publish our newspapers, without asking for the authorization which is imposed upon us. We bend our efforts so that today, at least, they can reach all of France.

Here is what our duty as citizens imposes upon us, and we are fulfilling it.

We do not have to point out its duties to the illegally dissolved Chamber. But we can ask it, in the name of France, to seize its obvious right, and to resist, so far as it can, the violation of the laws. The right is equally as sure as that to which we cling. The Charter states in Article 50 that the King can dissolve the Chamber of Deputies; but for this it is necessary that it had been convoked, constituted as a Chamber, and finally supported a program capable of provoking its dissolution. But, before the meeting, and the constituting of the Chamber, only the elections had been held. Now, no part of the Charter says that the King can annul elections. The edicts published today have annulled the elections; they are therefore illegal, because they are a thing which the Charter did not authorize.

The elected deputies, convoked for the third of August, are thus well and duly elected and convoked. Their right is the same today as yesterday. France implores them not to forget this. All that they can do to make the law prevail, they ought to do.

The government has lost today the character of legality which commands obedience. We resist it for that which concerns us; it is up to France to judge to what point she should extend her own resistance.

(Followed by signatures.

See note no. 14, chapter xiv).

PRINCIPAL SOURCES CONSULTED IN
PREPARING THIS BOOK

For the background of the press, the author has relied chiefly on published laws, memoirs, and secondary works. My primary sources have been the Restoration journals themselves, for their opinions and political strategies. The *Gazette des Tribunaux* provided the most reliable and definitive *procès-verbal* for the press trials.

I. GENERAL WORKS ON THE RESTORATION AND
THE REIGN OF CHARLES X

Artz, Frederick B., *France under the Bourbon Restoration*. Cambridge, Mass., 1931. This work opened a new period of interest in the Restoration as a distinctive era.
—, *Reaction and Revolution, 1814-1832*. New York: Harper and Brothers, 1934.
Bertier de Sauvigny, Guillaume de, *The Bourbon Restoration*. Translated by Lynn M. Case. Philadelphia: University of Pennsylvania Press. 1966. A superior and balanced synthesis including much recent sholarship about the period. A legitimist sympathy never intrudes upon the author's careful handling of subject matter.
Capefigue, J.-B., *Histoire de la Restauration et des causes qui ont améné la chute de la branche ainée des Bourbons*. 4 vols. Paris, 1842. Contains first hand knowledge; some legitimist bias.
Charléty, Sebastien, *La Restauration*. Vol. IV: *Histoire de la France contemporaine*. Edited by Lavisse. Paris, 1920-22.
Duvergier de Hauranne, Prosper L., *Histoire du government parlementaire en France, 1814-1848*. 10 vols. Paris, 1871. The author uses first hand knowledge and, except for a current of liberal bias, is usually objective.
Gorce, Pierre de la. *Charles X*. Vol. II: *La Restauration*. Paris, 1928. Royalist and clericalist, but more of the latter.
Lamartine, Alphonse de, *The History of the Restoration of the Monarchy in France*. 4 vols. London, 1854. Useful for personalities and literary figures.
Lucas-Dubreton, Jean, *La Restauration et la monarchie de juillet*. Paris, 1937.
Nettement, Alfred, *Histoire de la Restauration*. 8 vols. Paris, 1872. Shows a slight legitimist bias, but useful for political insights.
Pinkney, David H., *The French Revolution of 1830*. Princeton, 1972. Balanced and thorough, the result of great archival labors. New interpretations, especially of economic factors.
Roux, Marquis de, *La Restauration*. Paris, 1930. Interesting royalist interpretation in terms of time of writing. More literate than scholarly.

Thureau-Dangin, Paul, *Le parti libéral sous la Restauration*. Paris, 1876. Benevolently conservative, the author offers personal insights into the various figures of the period and discusses their motives.

—, *Royalistes et républicains*. Paris, 1874. Disconnected essays, consciously written with an eye to the contemporary scene: The infant Third Republic.

Vaulabelle, Achille de, *Histoire des deux Restaurations jusqu' à la chute de Charles X*. 7 vols. Paris, 1854. The earliest attempt at a complete history. The author had access to sources now unavailable. Liberal bias results in some weakness and omissions.

Viel-Castel, Louis de, *Histoire de la Restauration*. 20 vols. Paris, 1878. For all its bulk and detail, of somewhat less historical value than De Hauranne or even Vaulabelle; best for foreign relations.

Weill, Georges, *Histoire du parti républicain en France, 1814-1870*. Paris, 1928. A useful and scholarly work, but only a fraction is devoted to the Restoration.

II. Works dealing with Specialized Subjects

A. The press:

Avenel, Henri, *Histoire de la presse française*. Paris, 1900.

Boivin, Émile, *Histoire du journalisme*. Que sais-je No. 368. Paris, 1949.

Bruly, Léon, *Régime préventif des journaux et des brochures sous la Restauration*. Paris: Faculty of Law, 1907. Legalistic study of Restoration censorship.

Collins, Irene, *The Government and the Newspaper Press in France, 1814-1881*. London: Oxford University Press, 1959. Excellent analysis of the relation between the censoring authority and the press, treated as an evolutionary process.

Germain, Alfred, *Martyrologie de la presse, 1789-1861*. Paris, 1861. Contains a good (brief) account of Restoration censorship.

Hatin, Eugène, *Histoire politique et littéraire de la presse en France*. 8 vols. Paris, 1891. Because of unaccountable omissions and errors of fact and chronology, this huge labor of love falls short of being "definitive". The last volume deals with the Restoration: An extremely valuable source if used with caution.

Ledré, Charles, *La presse à l'assaut de la monarchie, 1815-1848*. Paris, 1961.

Mazédier, René, *Histoire de la presse parisienne de Théophraste Rénaudot à la IVᵉ République, 1631-1945*. Paris, 1945.

Merson, Ernest, *La liberté de la presse sous les divers régimes*. Paris, 1874. An Ultra polemic during the Third Republic.

Nettement, Alfred, *Histoire de la Gazette de France*. Paris, 1846. Very little of this work relates to the Restoration *Gazette*.

Ségu, Frederic, *Le premier Figaro, 1826-1833*. Paris, 1932. A useful brief study of this and other satirical journals.

Weill, Georges, *Le journal, origines, évolution, et rôle de la presse périodique*. Paris, 1934. A scholarly survey which regards the Restoration as an important era in journalism.

B. The Clergy:

Dansette, Adrien, *Histoire réligieuse de la France contemporaine de la révolution à la IIIᵉ Republique*. Paris, 1948. Contains bias, but useful. Lacks notes and bibliography.

Debidour, Antonin, *Histoire des rapports de l'église et de l'état en France de 1789 à 1870*. Paris, 1911. Won the crown of the Academy in 1912, when anticlericalism was more appreciated. Good details and documentation.

Garnier, Adrien. *Frayssinous, son rôle dans la Université sous la Restauration (1822-1828)*. Imprimatur. Paris, 1925. A clericalist apology, but reveals much of problems of moderate Gallicanism in the Restoration.

C. Social and political life:

Bagge, Doménique. *Les idées politiques en France sous la Restauration*. Paris, 1952.

Baudouin, Alexandre, *Anecdotes historiques du temps de la Restauration*. Paris, 1853.

Burnand, Robert, *La vie quotidienne en France en 1830*. Paris, 1943.

Hudson, Nora E., *Ultra Royalism and the French Restoration*. Cambridge, England, 1936. One of the first modern "revisions" of the liberal shool of Restoration history.

Jacomet, Pierre, *Le palais sous la Restauration*. Paris, 1922.

D. The July Days:

Fabre, Auguste, *La Révolution de 1830 et le véritable parti républicain*. 2 vols. in one. Paris, 1833. Essential for establishing the activities of the hard-core republican movement of 1830, as opposed to more temporizing republican groups.

Juste, Théodore, *La Révolution de juillet, 1830*. Brussels, 1893.

Perrot, Alphonse, *Rélation historique des journées mémorables des 27, 28, 29 juillet, 1830*. Paris, 1830.

Rossignol, François, and Pharaon, Jehan, *Histoire de la Révolution de 1830 et des nouvelles barricades*. Paris, 1830. As eyewitness accounts go, somewhat more reliable than Perrot, above.

Turnbull, David, *The French Revolution of 1830*. London, 1830. Shows serious and detached observational quality by a foreign eyewitness. A simplistic radical bias only makes it more interesting.

E. Biographical studies:

Allison, John M.S., *Thiers and the French Monarchy*. Boston and New York, 1926. Excellent study, but lacks investigation of baron Cotta.

Beach, Vincent, *Charles X of France: His Life and Times*. Boulder, Colorado, 1971. A definitive biography based on much archival material and correspondence.

Beau de Lomenie, Emmanuel, *La carrière politique de Chateaubriand*. 2 vols. Paris, 1929.

Daudet, Ernest, *Le ministère de M. de Martignac, sa vie politique et les dernières années de la Restauration*. Paris, 1875. Although pro-Martignac, it is very scholarly and useful.

Fourcassié, Jean, *Villèle*. Paris, 1954. Shows Villèle as a skillful politician rather than a sinister reactionary.

Gerbod, Paul, *Paul-François Dubois, universitaire, journaliste et homme politique, 1793-1874*. Paris, 1967.

Institut de France, *Discours de M. Charles Levêque et M. Bersot, prononcé aux funerailles de M. Dubois le 17 juin, 1874*. Paris, 1874.

Lucas-Dubreton, Jean, *Le comte d'Artois, Charles X, le prince, l'émigré, le roi*. Paris, 1927.

Marquant, Robert, *Thiers et le baron Cotta*. Travaux et mémoirs des instituts Français en Allemagne, No. 7, Paris, 1959. A mine of information on patrons and literary patronage.

Nobécourt, René G., *Armand Carrel, journaliste*. Rouen, 1935.

Petit, Edouard, *François Mignet*. Paris, 1889.

Pouthas, Charles H., *Guizot pendant la Restauration*. Paris, 1923. Excellent study; opens many approaches to entire Restoration.

Vivent, Jacques, *Charles X, dernier roi de France et Navarre*. Paris, 1958.

III. PUBLISHED MEMOIRS, CORRESPONDENCE,
AND DOCUMENT COLLECTIONS

Année, A., ed., *Le livre noir des messieurs Delavau et Franchet ou repertoire alphabétique de la police politique sous la ministère déplorable*. 4 vols. Paris, 1829. Together with the memoirs of Col. Vidocq, chief of detectives, this pirated collection is revealing for the Villèle period.

Barante, Claude de, *Souvenirs de baron de Barante*. 4 vols. Paris, 1894. A liberal peer, Barante wrote for Guizot's *Revue* – reliable.

Bourgin, Georges, and Bourgin, Hubert, *Les patrons, les ouvriers, et l'état sous la Restauration, documents inédites*. Vol. III of *Le regime de l'industrie en France, 1824-1830*. Paris, 1941.

Broglie, Charles Victor de, *Personal Recollections of the Late Duke de Broglie, 1785-1870*. 2 vols. London, 1887. Objective and nonapologetic memoir of the liberal-royalist persuasion.

Chambre des Pairs de France, session de 1828. 5 vols. Paris, 1828. The only *procès-verbal* of the peers as the press was only allowed to summarize the debates of the upper Chamber.

Chateaubriand, René, vicomte de, *Mémoires d'outre tombe*. 5 vols. Paris, 1948.

Duvergier, Jean-Baptiste, ed. *Collection complet des lois, décrets, ordonnances, régelements, et avis du conseil d'état*. 30 vols. 1st series. Paris, 1824-1830.

Faure, Gabriel, *Chateaubriand, Dubois, et le Globe, 12 lettres inédites de Chateaubriand*. Grenoble and Paris, 1944.

Flandin, Jean-Baptiste, *Révelations sur la fin du ministère de M. le cte. de Villèle*. Paris, 1829.

Guernon-Ranville, Martial Magloire Annibal-Marie, comte de, *Journal d'un ministre*. Edited by J. Travers. Caen, 1873.

Guizot, François, *Memoirs to Illustrate the History of My Time*. 3 vols. London, 1858. Written after the author became an unshakeable conservative, but still revealing for the 1820's.

d'Herbelot, Alphonse, *Lettres d'Alphonse d'Herbelot à Charles de Montalembert et à Léon Cornudet*. Paris, 1908.

Laffitte, Jacques. *Mémoires de Laffitte (1767-1844)*. Paris: Firmin-Didot, 1932. Along with considerable self-promotion, the author provided valuable details of political factions and personalities.

Pasquier, Étienne d'Audiffret, *Histoire de mon temps*, mémoires de chancelier Pasquier. 8 vols. Paris, 1895. Balanced perspective by an old peer whose career spanned an entire age.

Procès des derniers ministres de Charles X, MM. de Polignac, de Peyronnet, Chantelauze, Guernon-Ranville, Montbel, d'Haussez, et Capelle. 2 vols. Paris: au bureau des editeurs [1831].

Récamier, Jeanne Françoise de, *Souvenirs et correspondance tirés des papiers de Mme. Récamier.* 4 vols. Paris, 1853-1860. These are most applicable as they relate to Chateaubriand.

Sainte-Beuve, Charles-Augustin, *Causeries du lundi.* 28 vols. Paris, 1851-1870. Biographical sketches of literary personalities – artistically written with psychological understanding.

Salaberry, Charles, comte de, *Souvenirs politiques du comte de Salaberry sur la Restauration, 1827-1830.* 2 vols. Paris, 1900. An old Ultra gives his candid views of events and men.

Véron, Louis, *Mémoires d'un bourgeois de Paris.* 6 vols. Paris, 1853. This *Figaro* editor's sketches of social and political trivia help explain Paris in the Restoration.

Villèle, Jean-Baptiste Séraphim Joseph, comte de, *Mémoires et correspondance du comte de Villèle.* 5 vols. Paris, 1890. Along with the usual self-vindication, this political memoir reveals an intelligent, hardheaded, and capable statesman.

IV. ARTICLES IN PERIODICALS

Artz, Frederick B., "The Electoral System in France during the Bourbon Restoration". *Journal of Modern History*, I (June, 1929), 205-18.

Beach, Vincent W., "The Fall of Charles X of France: A Case Study of Revolution". *University of Colorado Studies.* No. 2 (Boulder, November, 1961), 21-60.

—, "The Polignac Ministry: A Re-Evaluation". *University of Colorado Studies.* No. 3 (Boulder, January, 1964), 87-146.

Benoit, Fernand, "Monsieur Thiers à la conquête de Paris". *Le Correspondant*, CCLXXXVII (10 June, 1922).

Beslay, Maurice, "Souvenirs d'un vièux républicain". *La Nouvelle Revue*, VI (1913).

Carné, comte de, "Souvenirs de ma jeunesse au temps de la Restauration". *Le Correspondant*, L (1872).

Daudet, Ernest, "La police politique sous la Restauration". *Revue des Deux Mondes* (1 December, 1909), 596-628; (1 January, 1910), 186-215.

Garson, Jules, "L'évolution Napoleonienne de Victor Hugo". *Le Carnet*, II (1900), 28-46.

"Les Mémoires de Guernon-Ranville". *Revue Bleue*, XIII (14 February, 1874). An unsigned review of *Journal d'un ministre*, J. Travers, ed. (Caen, 1873).

"G" [de Guiche, comte]. "Les journées de juillet, 1830". Edited by duc de Lesparre. *Le Carnet*, II (1898).

Janet, Paul, "Le *Globe* de la Restauration et Paul-François Dubois". *Revue des Deux Mondes*, XXXIV (1879).

Lacombe, Bernard de, "Conversations avec M. Thiers". *Le Correspondant*, CCLXXXIX (1922).

Lair, Adolphe, "La *Globe*, sa fondation, sa rédaction, son influence, souvenirs inédites de M. Dubois". *La Quinzaine*, LVI (1904).

—, "Paul-François Dubois". *Revue Bleue*, No. 12, VIII (1907).

Mazade, Charles de, "Un royaliste parlementaire, Berryer". *Revue des Deux Mondes*, XXXIV (1879).

Orlik, O., "La Révolution française de 1830 dans la presse russe". *Revue d'Histoire Moderne et contemporaine*, XVI (July-September, 1969), 401-13.

Pinkney, David H., "A New Look at the Revolution of 1830". *Review of Politics*, XXIII (South Bend, Indiana: University of Notre Dame Press, 1961), 490-501.

—, "The Crowd in the Revolution of 1830". *American Historical Review*, LXX (October, 1964), 1-17.

Thureau-Dangin, Paul, "Les libéraux et le liberté sous la Restauration". *Le Correspondant*, CIII (1876), 761-90.

V. NEWSPAPERS, MONTHLY PERIODICALS, AND PAMPHLETS: PRIMARY SOURCES

A. Pamphlets:

Cauchois-Lemaire, Louis-François, "Sur la crise actuelle, lettre à S.A.R. le duc d'Orléans". Paris, December, 1827. Ledru-Rollin Collection, University of California, Berkeley, 217:10.

Chabrol de Solihac, "Opinion de M. Chabrol de Solihac". Paris, February, 1827. Ledru-Rollin Collection, University of California, Berkeley, 172:17.

"Histoire scandaleuse, politique, et bigote de Charles X". Paris, 1831. Typical of the scandalous sort of anonymous *exposés*, many of which concerned the Duchess of Berry.

La Boëssière, marquis de, "Discours prononcé par M. le general marquis de la Boëssière". Paris, February, 1827. Ledru-Rollin Collection, University of California, Berkeley, 175:15.

—, "Developmens de la proposition ..." Paris, 15 March, 1827. Ledru-Rollin Collection, University of California, Berkeley, 175:17.

B. Monthly or Quarterly Periodicals:

l'Ancien Album. Paris, 1828-1829.
Revue de Paris. VII, 2nd ed. Brussels, 1829.
Revue Française. Paris, 1828-1829.

C. Newspapers, all published in Paris; various dates of issue given in chapter notes:

Le Constitutionnel. 1827-1830.
Le Courrier Français. 1827-1830.
Le Drapeau Blanc. 1827-1828; 1829-1830.
Le Figaro. 1829-1830.
La Gazette de France. 1827-1830.
Gazette des Tribunaux. 1827-1830.
Le Globe. 1827-1830.
La Jeune France. 1829-1830.
Le Journal du Commerce. 1828-1830.
Le Journal des Débats. 1827-1830.
Messager des Chambres. 1828-1829.

Le Moniteur Universel. 1827-1830.
Le National. 1830.
Le Nouveau Journal de Paris. 1828-1830.
Patriote. 1830.
La Quotidienne. 1827-1830.
La Révolution, Journal des Intérêts populaires. 1830.
Le Temps. 1829-1830.
Tribune des Départemens. 1829-1830.
L'Universel. 1830.

INDEX